Matthew J. McCarthy

black & white
Business Computing

Fourth Edition

Cover photograph courtesy of iStockPhoto.

Copyright © 2011, 2010, 2009, 2008 by Pearson Learning Solutions
All rights reserved.

This copyright covers material written expressly for this volume by the editor/s as well as the compilation itself. It does not cover the individual selections herein that first appeared elsewhere. Permission to reprint these has been obtained by Pearson Learning Solutions for this edition only. Further reproduction by any means, electronic or mechanical, including photocopying and recording, or by any information storage or retrieval system, must be arranged with the individual copyright holders noted.

All trademarks, service marks, registered trademarks, and registered service marks are the property of their respective owners and are used herein for identification purposes only.

Pearson Learning Solutions, 501 Boylston Street, Suite 900, Boston, MA 02116
A Pearson Education Company
www.pearsoned.com

Printed in the United States of America

1 2 3 4 5 6 7 8 9 10   V011   16 15 14 13 12 11

0002000102706652325

NM/LP

ISBN 10: 1-256-05169-1
ISBN 13: 978-1-256-05169-5

This edition is dedicated to

Al Seaquist †

Loving Husband & Father, Engineer, World Traveler
...never pass up the opportunity to listen...

Everything is the way it is because it can be.
Nothing changes unless it is economically advantageous to a majority.
Everything that happens no matter how good or bad, benefits someone.

Thank you to all of my family and friends for their unending encouragement and help writing this book. Very special thanks to Gretchen Anderson, Emily Locknick, and Linda Prince.

About the Author

Matt McCarthy is full-time faculty at Arizona State University's W. P. Carey School of Business in the Department of Information Systems. He is actively involved in many student groups like the Department of Information Systems Club and the Black Business Students Association to name a few. Matt has taught a wide array of computing courses at the undergraduate level, from advanced database theory to business programming languages to core business computing, which is the inspiration of the **Black & White Business Computing** series. Matt has designed and taught the required core business information technology computing course at ASU to thousands of students over the past many years. In his spare time, he and his wife Theresa play tennis, travel, windsurf, kite surf, ski, cycle, and take photographs of the outdoors.

Preface

In my experience teaching core information technology classes to thousands of university business students at the undergraduate level, I am often posed with the same question; why do I have to know this? Why does an accounting major need to know the difference between a motherboard and a keyboard? **Black and White Business Computing** answers this question in every chapter as well as other questions like; what's important to know, and how does it relate to business?

It goes without saying that information technology (IT) courses through our daily lives and is an essential part of business. In fact, IT is so incredibly broad, that it becomes extremely difficult to know what's worth knowing, and what's not, especially in a business environment. A university student in a business school might legitimately ask why anyone needs to know the differences between a Windows and Mac operating system. When that same business student eventually becomes the director of a large marketing department and is faced with the prospect of buying two thousand new computers for business applications and graphics, choosing the right operating system becomes critical. This is not to say that **Black and White Business Computing** will make that student an expert at all facets of computing, but will certainly make them an intelligent part of the conversation and begin to prepare them for business decisions relating to computing.

Once the first question is answered, the next question is obvious; given the fact that IT is so broad, what should a business student know? The answer starts with the introduction of important baseline concepts of information technology and business, and demonstrates their interrelated dependency on one another. **Black and White Business Computing** defines these dependencies, and then expands them with real-world examples and applications. This book introduces computing concepts, defines those concepts, and then relates them to business. **Black and White Business Computing** is specifically designed to be **repetitive** in nature. Many baseline concepts like networking, storage and connectivity are not limited to a single chapter. This book introduces and defines hundreds of concepts throughout the book and is able analogize them in many different contexts and examples. Students will be able to grasp information and evolve their understanding of how information technology and business are interrelated to prepare them for successful academic careers in a business school setting.

Personal Experience

Authors typically recognize their inspirations and the countless people who helped them with their book, typically in a dedication page, but these people deserve more.

When I first started writing textbooks, I thought it was going to be purely writing and research. I soon found out that there was way more to it then I had imagined and I would have to depend on many people. It was dumb luck that I ran into **Jill Promesso** who introduced me to **Mark Gafney** a few days later. Without their help I would never have started the *Black & White Business Computing* series. They were able to help me make profound changes in my classes at Arizona State University that allowed me to focus on education in ways I did not think possible. I must thank them for their professionalism, tireless efforts, and eventual friendship.

Jill and Mark eventually introduced me to **Gretchen Anderson**, one of the most energetic, thoughtful, and professional people I have ever met. She's also really nice and I am lucky to count her as a friend. There is only one person I call more than my wife, and that is Gretchen. Over the last many years she has solved so many critical problems for me that I have lost count. She has also been a source of inspirations and ideas for this book. Thank you to Gretchen, for everything.

2012 Table of Contents

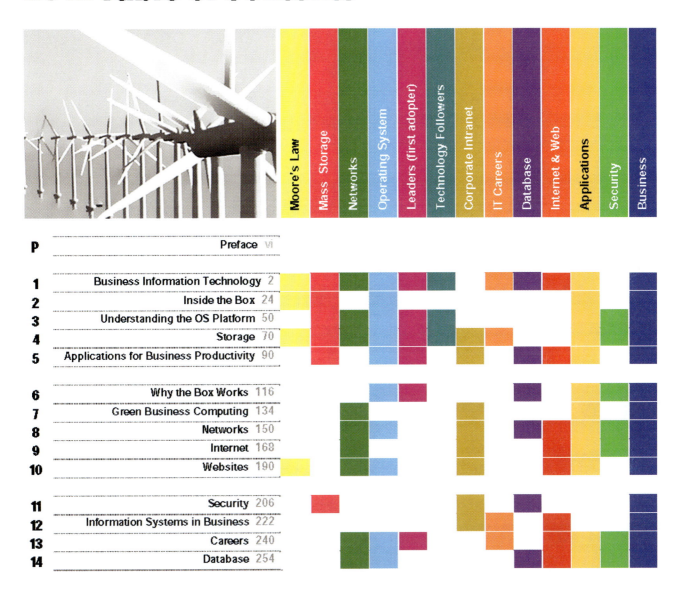

#	Title	Page	Moore's Law	Mass Storage	Networks	Operating System	Leaders (first adopter)	Technology Followers	Corporate Intranet	IT Careers	Database	Internet & Web	Applications	Security	Business
P	Preface	vi													
1	Business Information Technology	2	■	■	■	■	■			■	■	■	■		■
2	Inside the Box	24		■		■						■			■
3	Understanding the OS Platform	50			■	■		■					■	■	■
4	Storage	70	■		■			■	■	■			■	■	■
5	Applications for Business Productivity	90		■		■	■		■		■	■	■		■
6	Why the Box Works	116				■	■				■		■	■	■
7	Green Business Computing	134			■				■			■	■	■	■
8	Networks	150			■	■			■			■	■	■	■
9	Internet	168			■	■						■	■	■	■
10	Websites	190	■		■	■						■	■	■	■
11	Security	206		■					■		■	■	■	■	■
12	Information Systems in Business	222							■	■		■	■	■	■
13	Careers	240			■	■	■		■	■		■	■	■	■
14	Database	254									■				

Black & White Business Computing is exceedingly repetitive by design. Repetition is the *key* to learning. Essential vocabulary like 'business' and 'operating systems' appear in chapter after chapter to reinforce some of the most important terminology in information technology.

Contents

one | business information technology   2

    Paradigm & Critical Business Decisions   3
    Business Information Technology   4
    Business Computing Hardware   8
    System Software   9
    Operating Systems   10
    Application Software   11
    Business Computing Software   12
    Fundamental Business Application Software   13
        Word Processing Software   13
        Spreadsheet Software   14
        Database Software   15
        Presentation Software   16
    Specific-use Business Application Software   17
    Browser Software   17
    Networks   17
    Summary   19
    Matching   20
    Multiple Choice   21
    Blanks   22
    Short Questions   23

two | inside the box   24

    Inside the Box   25
    The System Unit   26
    Microcomputer Configurations   27
    Expansion Slots & Cards   33
    Input & Output Devices   37
    Output Devices   43
    Summary   45
    Matching   46
    Multiple Choice   47
    Blanks   48
    Short Questions   49

three | understanding the OS platform   50

    Revolutionaries in Business   51
    Understanding Operating Systems   52
    Processes / Multitasking   52
    Memory Management and Storage   55
    Disk Management   55
    File Management   56
    Networking   58
    Device Drivers   58
    Graphical User Interface   59
    Embedded Operating Systems   59
    Microsoft Windows® versus Mac OS®   59

Major Operating Systems   60
Open Source Operating Systems   63
Summary   65
Matching   66
Multiple Choice   67
Blanks   68
Short Questions   69

four | storage   70

Business Network Options   71
Data Storage   74
Ones and Zeros   76
Physical Storage Characteristics   78
Characteristics of Storage Media   79
Business Storage Strategies   81
Data Archiving and Backup Strategies   83
Summary   86
Matching   87
Multiple Choice   88
Blanks   89
Short Questions   89

five | applications for business productivity   90

Application Software   91
Business Application Software Suites   92
Word Processing Software   93
Spreadsheets   94
Databases   95
Presentation Software   96
Sharing Information   98
Best Practice   99
Applying Application Software to Best Practice   99
Case Study Problem   100
Case Study Solution   101
Improving Best Practice and Business Repercussions   102
Specialized Application Software   103
Web Authoring Application Software   104
Other Business Application Software   107
Collaborative Application Software   110
Summary   111
Matching   112
Multiple Choice   113
Blanks   114
Short Questions   115

six | why the box works   116

System Software   117
Starting the Computer   118
Administering Application Software   120
Memory Management   120
Device Drivers   121
Interfacing and Utilities   121
File Management Systems   124

System Software Utilities 127
Backup Utilities 127
Antivirus Utilities 128
System Updates 129
Summary 129
Matching 130
Multiple Choice 131
Blanks 132
Short Questions 133

seven | green business computing 134

Green Business Computing 135
Information Technology Challenges and Opportunities 137
EPEAT - Electronic Product Environmental Assessment Tool 138
EPEAT Criteria 138
Energy Star® Specifications 142
The Green PC 142
Green Computing Business Plan 143
Telecommuting 145
Summary 146
Matching 147
Multiple Choice 148
Blanks 149
Short Questions 149

eight | networks 150

Networks 151
Building a Computer Network 155
Network Operating Systems 157
Network Topology 157
Types of Computer Networks 160
Network Security 160
Summary 163
Matching 164
Multiple Choice 165
Blanks 166
Short Questions 167

nine | internet 168

Internet History 169
Internet and World Wide Web Structure 170
Internet Address 171
Websites 172
Browsers 172
Browser Features 175
Internet Service Providers (ISP) 176
Search Engines 176
E-commerce 178
Security 181
E-mail 182
Voice over Internet Protocol (VoIP) 183
Intranet 183
Summary 185

Matching   186
Multiple Choice   187
Blanks   188
Short Questions   189

ten | websites   190

Business Website Alternatives   191
Early Website Technology   192
Hypertext Markup Language   194
Website Styles & Categories   196
Types of Websites   197
Website Online Software   199
Online Advertising   200
Summary   202
Matching   203
Multiple Choice   204
Blanks   205
Short Questions   205

eleven | security   206

System Security & Computer Privacy   207
Business System Threats   207
Firewalls   208
Malware Threats   209
Malware Solutions   212
Passwords   213
Internet Fraud   213
Computer Privacy   215
Identity Theft   217
Summary   218
Matching   219
Multiple Choice   220
Blanks   221
Short Questions   221

twelve | information systems in business   222

Business Functions   223
Information Systems Role in Business Departments   223
The Accounting Department   224
The Human Resources Department   225
The Marketing Department   226
The Research and Development (R&D) Department   226
The Production Department   227
Information Systems Collaboration   228
Business System Reporting   231
Summary   236
Matching   237
Multiple Choice   238
Blanks   239
Short Questions   239

thirteen | careers 240

Information Technology Careers 241
Business Information Technology Perception 242
Information Technology Jobs 243
Knowing the Business 245
Enterprise Resource Planning Solutions 246
ERP Advantages 247
ERP Disadvantages 247
Unified Modeling Language 247
System Development Methodologies 248
Summary 249
Matching 250
Multiple Choice 251
Blanks 252
Short Questions 253

fourteen | database 254

Database Definition 255
Database Structure 256
Business Database Advantages 260
Structured Query Language 261
Business Database Scenario and Implications 261
Business Database Scenario Advantages 265
Business Database Scenario Disadvantages 266
Summary 268
Matching 269
Multiple Choice 270
Blanks 271
Short Questions 272

Glossary 273
Index 295

one | business information technology

- Business Information Technology
- Business Computing Hardware
- System Software
- Operating Systems
- Application Software
- Business Computing Software
- Word Processing Software
- Spreadsheet Software
- Database Software
- Presentation Software
- Other Application Software
- Browser Software

Paradigm & Critical Business Decisions

On December 17th, 1903, Wilbur Wright successfully flew the world's first airplane for less than a minute, and *everything* changed. Just 66 years later, Neil Armstrong walked on the moon. In 1953, James Watson, Maurice Wilkins, and Francis Crick won the Nobel Prize in part by exploiting Rosalind Franklin's work for co-discovering the double helix structure of DNA, and *everything* changed. Because of this discovery, medicine has changed so drastically that some diseases have been eradicated altogether. On October 4th, 2004, SpaceShipOne, a non-governmental organization of private citizens successfully flew into outer space, and *everything* changed. What's next, an elevator into space? Maybe people will be able to just take a ride up a rope into outer space. If that happens, (which it will), *everything* will change, again. It's called the space elevator, look it up.

BLACK & WHITE
Information technology (IT) is the study, design, development, implementation, support, and management of computer-based information systems, particularly software and hardware.

GRAY MATTER
Will Goggle Earth become Goggle Live? Will we be able to go on the Internet and see the Earth live instead of a few blurry neighborhoods? The answer is yes, and *everything* will change.

Brilliant men like Sir Richard Branson and Burt Rutan make space flight into a viable business

Courtesy of Robert Galbraith/Associated Press.

Will Google Earth become Google Live? Will we be able to go on the Internet and see the Earth live instead of a few blurry neighborhoods? The answer is yes, and *everything* will change. Satellites clicking a few indistinct images from space will be replaced by live cameras fed directly to Google. Will parents be able to locate their children with Google? Will the police be able to track criminal activity on Google Live? Will something like Google Live affect privacy in the most profound ways? Will traffic cameras be a thing of the past if law enforcement can see you speeding from cameras from outer space? The answer to all these questions is 'yes'. The next obvious question; when does this all come to fruition? The answer is way, way sooner than you think.

Technology, inventions, concepts, and knowledge are advancing so fast that it is simply an indistinguishable blur. How fast? No one really knows for sure, but the consequences of not knowing are dire, especially in business. Paradigm's shift so fast that it's difficult to decide what technological concepts are real, what will last, and what will happen next.

Information technology is firmly based in business. Consider business retailers selling the first MP3 digital music player in 1999 that held 10 songs and cost $450. Today, MP3 players hold tens of thousands of songs. As a matter of fact, an MP3 player is redundant and doesn't need to be purchased anymore with the dawn of the Smartphone and Apps like Pandora Radio. As a retailer, were you ready for that paradigm shift? Did it occur to you that MP3 players would lose ground or do you have a glut of MP3 inventory in your back room that you're forced to put on sale and lose money on a daily basis?

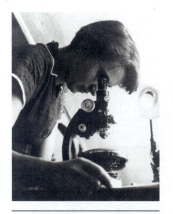

Rosalind Franklin never received the Nobel Prize although her work was the lynchpin in the discovery of the double helix structure of DNA

Courtesy of Science Source/Photo Researchers, Inc.

Now start to consider one of the primary business tools, the personal computer (PC). In 1988, a single state-of-the-art PC costs $14,000. Today, $14,000 can buy twenty business-ready personal computers that are exponentially faster and more powerful. Will PC prices and power change as radically in the future? The answer is a resounding 'yes'. Making decisions on an ever-moving and speedy technology starts to seem unfeasible.

Time to make a critical business decision: which is the correct Smartphone for your employees? You're the Chief Financial Offi-

BLACK & WHITE

Without people, a computer is just a plastic box of microchips and wires. People are smart, a computer is not. People use computers and are called the end-user. It's very important to make that distinction to understand that smart people make computers smart.

GRAY MATTER

Business is *not* an endeavor where everyone gets a hug and a ribbon for doing their best. Doing your best in business is an assumption, doing it right is an expectation.

File managers help organize computer files

WHITE BOARD

How fast is technology advancing?
Why is it important to understand that technology changes constantly?
Discuss possible changes that might occur in society as technology advances.
Doing your best in business is a(n) _____, doing it right is a(n) _____.

Information technology is firmly based in _____.

cer (CFO) for a medium sized pharmaceutical company. You need to purchase 250 of the right Smartphones, today, right now for your representatives in the field. By the way, if you choose incorrectly, you're fired. If you choose incorrectly, and your competitor chooses appropriately, they win, and you lose. Business is *not* an endeavor where everyone gets a hug and a ribbon for doing their best. Doing your best in business is an assumption, doing it right is an expectation. Business decisions are critical and incredibly difficult when it comes to technology given the incredible speed of its advancement. This is a decision you cannot afford to get wrong. The good news is that there is a way to make sound tactical and strategic decisions regarding technology.

Business Information Technology

Information technology (IT) is the study, design, development, implementation, support, and management of computer-based information systems, particularly software and hardware.

Early in the 21st century, a prestigious academic publication suggested that information technology (IT) didn't matter. The publication concluded that IT was simply a plentiful commodity that could be easily acquired by anyone. If you were to only look at IT as computer hardware and software, these conclusions would probably be true. The issue was hotly debated in the media, but what was ignored in the publication was people's role in IT. Without **people**, a computer is just a plastic box of microchips and wires. People are smart, a computer is not. People use computers and are called the **end-user**. It's very important to make that distinction to understand that smart people make computers smart. Smarter people will have a decided advantage over those who mistakenly assume a computer is already smart, especially in business. Conversely, the not-so-smart will be poor computer users, and do poorly in business. This suggests that people are the most important and integral part of an information system. The prestigious academic publication; they were dead wrong. Information technology matters, everywhere.

Every computer ever made was developed by many people to do exactly as it was intended, and many times, more than the user ever imagined. This holds true whether its personal computer, a Mac, an

Information technology courses through every aspect of life
Courtesy of Roger Ressmeyer/Corbis Images.

CHAPTER 1 | Business Information Technology

Attitude towards information technology plays a pivotal role towards gaining computer competency.
Courtesy of Prentice-Hall, Inc.

iPod, or the computer programming that runs a microwave oven and makes popcorn with the touch of a button.

Information technology courses through every aspect of life, and business is no exception. Too many times businesses have treated information technology as if it were a commodity, and have paid dearly for this arrogant thinking. It is not uncommon for an organization to supply their employees with many thousands of devices that rely on IT, like laptops, Smartphones, personal computers, and at the same time, do not bother to gain the proper competency to achieve the ability to use these devices in a way that could leverage them into a competitive business advantage. This isn't to say that the business man or woman needs to be an expert in every aspect of IT; it is simply to understand that information technology can be leveraged into a competitive advantage only by the people who operate their systems better than their competitors. Information Technology is a **core competency** in business.

Gaining **computer competency** in business is paramount to success. **Competency** is the knowledge that enables a person to understand something, in this case, a computing system and its relationship to business. How does one gain this competency, or even know what computing aspects one needs to know? This book is designed to answer these questions and prepare you to make sound business decisions regarding information technology and computing in general.

Attitude towards information technology plays a pivotal role towards gaining computer competency. A computer should never be thought of as a mysterious box with a mind of its own, it is plainly a tool whose boundaries are only limited by the **imagination** and **ingenuity** of its user. Can a computer accomplish your business application; the answer is always yes, but only in the hands of a competent and smart end-user. Computers are astounding devices in the hands of the person or people whose attitude towards computing is fearless, but not reckless. Your learning process will be fraught with mistakes, as with any learning process. It is your attitude towards these mistakes that will determine your success. Starting a business is fraught with failure; learn to embrace it, to learn from it. You can choose to look at a mistake as a roadblock and become **frustrated**, or simply choose to understand that it an integral part of any learning and decision making process.

Critically thinking people have the **humility** to understand a task can always be done better and more efficiently, and this same thinking can be applied to business computing as well. **Critical thinking** is a way of thinking that involves analysis and evaluation and includes considering all possible outcomes in order to form a solid decision. It's this type of thinking and attitude that should course through business computing applications, not just to complete a task, but to complete it better and more efficiently than your competitors to gain a competitive advantage.

One of the first things to understand is that learning to use a computer can seem like an overwhelming undertaking, especially in business, where stakes are high. The best way to embark on your learning experience is to start small and keep

BLACK & WHITE

In business, best practice is a management process, technique, or method that is most effective at arriving at a desired outcome, or best outcome than any other process, technique, or method.

GRAY MATTER

Critical thinking, humility, and ingenuity are terms that should be attached to any endeavor worth learning or doing, including information technology and business.

A computer should never be thought of as a mysterious box with a mind of its own. It is plainly a tool whose boundaries are only limited by the **imagination** and **ingenuity** of its user.
Courtesy of Jose Luis Peleaz/Corbis Images.

> **BLACK & WHITE**
>
> People are by far the best resources when learning a computing system.

> **GRAY MATTER**
>
> Gordon Moore is right, maybe to a frightening extent, and he will continue to be right well into the 21st century. Is there another industry where paradigm happens on such a regular basis?
>
> As computing and information technology hurdles forward, critical strategic and tactical business decisions have to be evaluated and re-evaluated on a regular basis to keep up.

it simple. Try to learn one thing at a time, and learn that one thing well, and learn why it worked. When you've completed the task, understand that there is probably a better way to do it. This is not to say that "good is not good enough", just to understand that computing systems and applications can always do better. Don't get discouraged by overused acronyms and over-baked terminologies that IT professionals are so fond of.

In business, **best practice** is a management process, technique, or method that is most effective at arriving at a desired outcome, or best outcome than any other process, technique, or method. Simply stated, it's the best way to do something and remember how to do it for future reference. Best practices strives to find the most efficient and effective way to achieve a business goal, store these practices so they can be used in the future, and arrive at the best results with the least amount of effort. Business computing also has best practices, which tries to find the best way to do something, and start to understand beyond "good is good enough" and insure the right way to repeatedly attain a desired business computing outcome.

It may not be in your best interest to try to learn a computing system or application by rote, which means simply memorizing keystrokes to accomplish a task. If a computing system accomplishes your given task, try to understand why it worked. The same holds true if your results do not meet your expectations. A person that simply memorizes keystrokes to accomplish a task will not be prepared to assess why they got an unexpected outcome, whereas the person that understands what the keystrokes do and why has a far greater chance of overcoming a problem and learning from the process.

Enhancing computer competency is greatly facilitated by having a specific application. An **application** in computing is something with a practical use and expected outcome. Always question what you want to get accomplished with a computer. Find a reason to use a computer like creating a simple budget with a spreadsheet. Simply doing a tutorial can become too mechanical and the user might to lose sight of the lesson being taught. Remembering keystrokes to accomplish a task can be counterproductive to the learning process. Tutorials are excellent for practice, but need

Critical thinking is a way of thinking that involves analysis and evaluation and includes considering all possible outcomes in order to form a solid decision.

Courtesy of Prentice-Hall, Inc.

CHAPTER 1 | Business Information Technology

People are by far the best resources when learning a computing system
Courtesy of Joe Madere/Corbis Images.

to be complimented with relevant applications. Even when you accomplish a task, question it, stay open-minded. What am I trying to accomplish? What was my expected outcome? What did I learn? What else can be accomplished? Are you using the right software and hardware? Talk to other users about how they might carry out your task. People are by far the best resources when learning a computing system.

In business computing, as with business itself, the learning process never ends. New business concepts and laws like the Sarbanes-Oxley Act of 2002 that attempts to protect investors from accounting and reporting fraud rocked the business world and created an entirely new industry of jobs and computing applications. Business and technological advances go hand in hand and hurdle forward at a startling rate, and it is up to the user to keep pace, or to be left behind.

Gordon Moore, one of the founding fathers of Intel made the astounding observation in 1965 called **Moore's Law** that computing power doubles every eighteen months, and that prediction still holds true today, and is most likely to continue well into the century. This essentially means that if a business purchases a microcomputer today, in eighteen months, there is a microcomputer available that is twice as good. Imagine buying any other product and knowing it is almost obsolete in less than two years. This points out how very important IT knowledge is from a purchasing standpoint alone. Some organizations buy new technology as it comes to market in the hopes it will afford them a competitive advantage. These businesses are called **leaders**. Another term for a leader is a **first adopter**. Some organizations hold off buying new technology and wait for it to improve from its original version and also deciding there is no competitive advantage to be gained. These businesses are called **followers**.

For instance, should the large pharmaceutical company buy its representatives the first version of a Smartphone to replace their cell phones, and therefore be a technological leader? The answer is yes if the pharmaceutical business has decided that a Smartphone will give them a **competitive advantage**, and no if they won't.

How does the pharmaceutical company know if they will get a competitive advantage? The answer is that they need to **stay current** in information technology news. An investment company certainly is expected to stay current with stock markets worldwide the same way all businesses are

BLACK & WHITE

A computer is made up of hardware and uses system software to make it work. Hardware is the physical part of the computer and software is collection of computer programs that accomplish a specific task.

GRAY MATTER

Although this book is primarily about **microcomputers,** mainframe and midrange computers play a very important role in business. For instance, millions of people use credit cards daily and the transactions that have to be stored and processed would bring a microcomputer to its knees.

How does a business know if they will get a competitive advantage from technology? The answer is that they need to **stay current** in information technology news. An investment company certainly is expected to stay current with stock markets worldwide the same way all businesses are expected to stay current with technology.

Any time you are involved with business information technology, especially decision making, it is imperative that you think of the future
Courtesy of Susan Van Etten/PhotoEdit.

expected to stay current with technology. There are thousands of technology news outlets on the Internet, and many in print. A business doesn't need to be reading up-to-the-second technology news, rather keep apprised and in its business' 'consciousness'. Websites like Gizmoto.com, ZDNet.com, and Wired are all excellent resources to stay current.

Any time you are involved with business information technology, especially decision making, it is imperative that you think of the future. Today's astounding technology with promises of competitive advantages can be tomorrow's mistakes. Staying current simply involves paying attention, keeping an open mind, and considering your business and technologies future. To prepare for a career in business, it becomes important to understand information technology and its long term implications. It's a misnomer to think you need to know everything about IT, instead, focus first on a baseline understanding of hardware, software, and networks, and what they can do.

> **WHITE BOARD**
>
> Why do people play such an important role in information technology?
> What are different attributes that make up a good end-user?
> Who was Gordon Moore and what did he do?
> Why are some business organizations leaders and some followers?
> What is another name for a 'leader"?

Business Computing Hardware

Business computer hardware is the tangible or physical aspects of a computer, like circuit boards, chipsets, and keyboards. Hardware rarely changes during the life of a computer, but certain components can be added on to enhance its power and usability.

Much of this book is concerned with computing devices, specifically microcomputers that can be leveraged in business for a competitive advantage. Consider hardware from the standpoint of purchasing and deployment at a large scale. Businesses buy tens of billions of dollars of computer hardware, and with any purchase need to make sure their decisions of what hardware they invest in

CHAPTER 1 | Business Information Technology

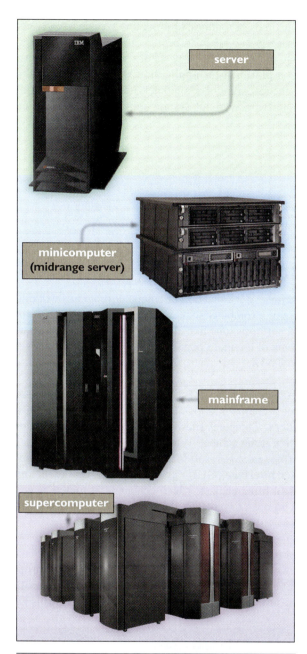

Business computers come in many configurations
Courtesy of IBM Corporation; courtesy of Hewlett-Packard; and courtesy of Cray, Inc.

will pay off. There are many types of computers that participate in the business arena starting with mainframes.

Mainframe computers are massive room-sized computers that process and store enormous amounts of bulk data and information, and are typically used by very large organizations like credit card processors that employ them for transaction processing and vital applications. Mainframes require a huge amount of physical space and have special requirements like specialized air conditioning units and fire protection systems. For instance, American Express needs mainframe computers because it has millions of cardholders making millions of transactions every day. The amount of data and memory to track all of this information is mind boggling.

Midrange computers (sometimes called **minicomputers**) are less powerful and smaller in physical size than mainframe computers, but do many of the same things, simply on a smaller scale. Small to medium-sized businesses who either cannot afford or even need mainframes can leverage midrange computers in the exact same way large organizations leverage mainframes.

Microcomputers are smaller than mainframes and midrange computers, and are so common that they are most commonly referred to as simply computers, and sometimes just referred to as a **box**. They are the least powerful computer in terms of processing and come in three typical configurations; A **desktop**, **laptop**, and **handheld**. A desktop computer is made to reside on a desk and is not portable whereas a laptop has the same basic components and is designed specifically for portability. In the past, a laptop computer was more expensive than a desktop, and a less powerful, but with advances, that gap has narrowed, so the biggest difference is physical size and portability. Handheld computers often referred to as Personal Digital Assistants or PDAs are compact, but far less powerful than desktops or laptops. They have embedded operating systems and are suited best for a business environment, and typically organize information.

BLACK & WHITE

Mainframe computers are massive room-sized computers that process and store enormous amounts of bulk data and information, and are typically used by very large organizations like credit card processors that employ them for transaction processing and vital applications.

GRAY MATTER

A computer is made up of **hardware** and uses system **software** to make it work. Hardware is the physical part of the computer and **software** is collection of computer programs that accomplish a specific task. When a computer is turned on, hundreds of routines, or programs execute to carry out technical details that make a computer run properly and begin to become useful to the end-user, and typically, with **no human interaction**.

System Software

A computer is made up of **hardware** and uses **system software** to make it work. Hardware is the physical part of the computer and **software** is collection of computer programs that accomplish a

> **BLACK & WHITE**
>
> Application software is designed to serve the user and carry out whatever task they can imagine, like create a document or a spreadsheet.

> **GRAY MATTER**
>
> Application software can perform any business task that one can imagine, but it's important to understand that choosing the appropriate application software is critical.
>
> A resume or large relational database can be created with spreadsheet software, but it is clearly the wrong tool for the job. Be careful to understand what application software does, and which is best for your business application.

specific task. When a computer is turned on, hundreds of routines, or programs execute to carry out technical details that make a computer run properly and begin to become useful to the end-user, and typically, with **no human interaction**. The most important aspects of system software is that an **operating system** is enabled and becomes a **platform** for **application software** to work. An operating system is the software that manages the resources of a computer, like memory and application programs. Application software does not work without system software or an operating system.

> **WHITE BOARD**
>
> Define business hardware.
> Name three types of computers and what they do.
> What is system software?

Operating Systems

An **operating system (OS)**, often called a **platform** is a collection of computer programs working together that manage the hardware and software of a computer so they work properly. The platform is the groundwork for all system software and performs jobs like allocating memory, administrating input and output, and file management. Some of the more popular platforms in today's market are **Microsoft Windows**, **Mac OS**, **Linux**, and **UNIX**.

File management – One of the most important jobs of an OS is file management; a way to store and organize computer files to the memory of a computer. Operating systems are made up of a hierarchy of **directories**, typically called **folders**. Computer files are the modern counterpart of printed documents of the past that were kept in a filing cabinet. Hundreds of different file formats exist representing programs, system software files, etc. Microsoft Windows represents its file management system visually with a **graphical user interface (GUI)** environment. It's best to simply think of this as the inner workings of a physical filing cabinet, which contains file folders which house paper files. A **file manager** is a part of an operating system that a computer uses to display the filing system.

Multitasking – In the past, switching from one application software to another was a difficult and time-consuming task for a computer as it would only allow a user to use single applications at a time. If the user wanted to use a spreadsheet but was already using a word processor, they would have to save their work in the word processor, turn in off, and then start the spreadsheet. This all changed with **multitasking**. Any task a computer performs is called a **process**. When a computer can run more than one process at a time it is referred to as multitasking. Modern operating systems feature multitasking which allows a user for example to run application software like Excel, Photoshop, and Word all at the same time.

Memory management - Operating systems coordinate a computer's memory, which includes **cache**, **random access memory (RAM)**, **registers**, and **virtual memory**. Simply put, memory holds data and information in an assortment of ways. Some of the types of memory include **Random Access Memory (RAM)** which is primary storage. RAM is a type of mem-

Operating systems are the most important system software
Courtesy of Prentice-Hall, Inc.

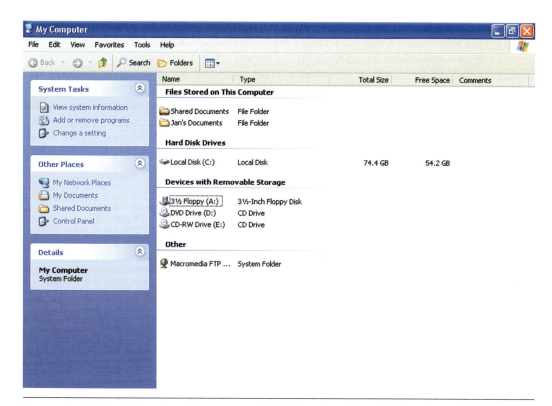

File managers help organize computer files.
Courtesy of Microsoft Corporation.

ory that allows data to be accessed in any order without physical movement of the silicone media. **Virtual memory** is memory the operating system uses to coordinate, track, and efficiently allocate the use of CPU cache, registers, RAM, and disk storage.

Disk management – An OS is in charge of reading and writing data and information to a disk, typically a hard drive. **Disk storage** is non-volatile, secondary storage that is recorded to a physical device, like a hard drive or optical disk with a read/write apparatus. The OS needs to be able to save information to a disk in the most efficient manner possible so it can be read files efficiently and therefore quickly. A general way to do this is (with a Microsoft platform) to create a sort of table of contents for the disk called a **file allocation table**, or **FAT**. The FAT directs the read/write arm of the hard drive to where data exists and accesses it upon the user's request.

WHITE BOARD

Define an operating system and describe what it does.
List some of the specific tasks an operating system performs.
What is FAT and what does it do?
Why is virtual memory different from other memories?
Describe multitasking and its advantages.

Application Software

Application software performs particular tasks people need, like creating a budget for accounting or supply chain, creating a resume, or making a professional presentation for a business proposal. Application software is extremely powerful, and often underestimated by most computer users. Commercial application software has been developed by hundreds, even thousands of people and is

> **BLACK & WHITE**
>
> Cutting and pasting allows the user to select an area in one application, copy the information into memory, switch to a different application, and then paste it in the desired area. Cutting and pasting is the most straightforward method of data sharing, the copied information is static.

> **GRAY MATTER**
>
> Sharing data between applications is one of the most powerful and useful concepts of a software suite.
>
> Before sharing data like text and pictures between application software, consider whether to need the data to "always match", and reconcile. Cutting and Pasting will only match in both applications until one of them is edited whereas Object Linking guarantees matching.
>
> In business, it can be critical that information in a document file reconciles perfectly with an attached spreadsheet file.

constantly evolving to meet the infinite needs of the end-user, so the chances of application software not fulfilling a user's needs are remote. On the other hand, choosing the wrong application software can seriously affect a business' ability to compete effectively.

The most commonly used application software in business is are **email**, **word processors**, **spreadsheets**, **databases**, **presentation software**, and **project management software**. Other common application software in business is a **browser** to access the Internet, and **networking operating systems**, all of which are described in further detail later in the chapter. These are the application software a business **must** embrace to be successful.

Business Computing Software

Software is the programs that enable a computer to work. There are two basic categories of software; **application software** and **system software**. The main difference is that system software requires very little, if any user intervention. Application software is designed to serve the user and carry out whatever task they can imagine, like create a document or a spreadsheet.

Business computing software is concern with four basic applications; spreadsheets, word processors, databases, and presentation software, many times sold as a software suite, or application suite. A **software suite**, often called a **productivity suite** is a collection of computer application programs of associated functionality that share a common graphical user interface (GUI) and the capacity to smoothly exchange data with each other. Software suite manufacturers like Microsoft who makes Office 2010 know it can be more economical to buy suites as one large package than to buy software individually.

Attitude towards application software is as important as is it when learning a computing system. Commercial application software on today's market are simply astounding tools, often grossly underestimated by most users. Consider word processing software that has been available for purchase for twenty years. Thousands of imaginative people have contributed to its development and evolution throughout those twenty years. Simply concluding that word processing software only creates, edits, and updates documents like resumes and contracts would be closed-minded and ultimately a mistake.

An important and very powerful characteristic of a productivity suite is the capability to share data and information between application software. Spreadsheet analysis can be combined with a word processing document, or database results can be added to a presentation.

Productivity suites offer three ways of sharing data and information. The most basic is **"Cut and Paste"**. Cutting and pasting allows the user to select an area in one application (**source data**), **copy** the information into memory, switch to a different application, and then **paste** it in the desired area (**destination**). Cutting and pasting is the most straightforward method of data sharing, the copied information is static.

The second and third method of sharing information and data is called **Object Linking and Embedding (OLE)**. **Object embedding** allows a user to select an entire area from one application and make it part of another. A budget spreadsheet (**source file**) can be embedded in the proposal document (**destination file**). Object embedding is static, and only takes a snapshot. When the proposal document is reopened, it can be edited, but the budget spreadsheet source file cannot. The budget spreadsheet is only as current as the last time it was embedded.

Object linking is similar to object embedding, but differs in one very important way. Object linking is dynamic. When the source file is linked into the destination file, both files stay up to date. Unlike object embedding which simply takes a picture, object linking is a dynamic link where both files are current, and both files are editable.

> **WHITE BOARD**
>
> Define application software and what differentiates it from system software.
> What are some of the advantages of a productivity suite?
> List three ways to share data between application software and how they work.
> What's the point of making different software have the same familiar look?
> Why does attitude play such an important part of learning application software?

Fundamental Business Application Software

Word Processing Software

A **word processor** like **Microsoft Word 2010**® is an application software used to create, compose, edit, format and print documents. Basically, word processors started as electronic typewriters except they are exponentially more powerful. Businesses can use word processors to create memos, legal documents, or any other document application. Word processors are often underestimated in their ability to create almost any format of document, from a letter to an entire manuscript, including automatically formatted indexes and table of contents. Documents typically contain text but can also include images and much more. This book was created with word processing application software.

Adobe Acrobat® is another very powerful word processor that allows a user to create, edit, format and print **portable document files** (PDF) and has enormous business implications. PDFs can be accessed on virtually any platform (operating system). For instance, an organization may have printed a contract that is hundreds of pages long and used FedEx to ship it across the country to their legal department for collaboration and approval. The legal department might make several changes and FedEx the printed document back, repeating this costly process several times. With a PDF, the same organization can collaborate with their legal department on the required changes by making the contract available electronically on a network that both parties can access without having to worry that either party can open the document because of its portability. It doesn't matter if one office is using Microsoft Windows and the other is using Mac, both are able to open the document.

> **BLACK & WHITE**
>
> A spreadsheet is an electronic grid of columns and rows often used to create, model, and manipulate numerical and often financial information.
>
> Database software or a database management system (DBMS) software is a collection of related files called tables that consist of records (rows) of data separated by fields (columns) that can be queried to produce subsets of information.

> **GRAY MATTER**
>
> Spreadsheets help you predict the future, or at least see what a possible future would be like by providing "what-if" analysis.
>
> What if your business was heading towards increasing costs and economic predictions called for rising inflation? Spreadsheets have the ability to quickly model data based on these variables, and help you make intelligent business decisions and forecasts.

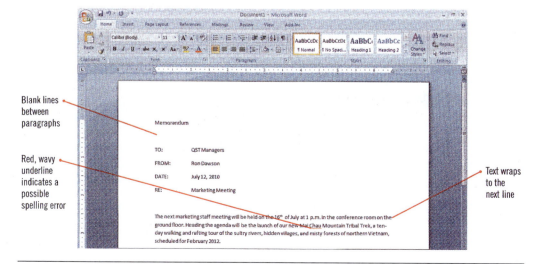

Blank lines between paragraphs

Red, wavy underline indicates a possible spelling error

Text wraps to the next line

Courtesy of Cengage Learning.

BLACK & WHITE

Presentation software is used to present information in a slide show format. Presentations are usually displayed on-screen, and often are projected for an audience.

GRAY MATTER

Presentation software can be an extremely powerful tool to convey ideas and concepts in business. A good presentation slide show is **not** meant to be read to an audience, it compliments a business presentation.

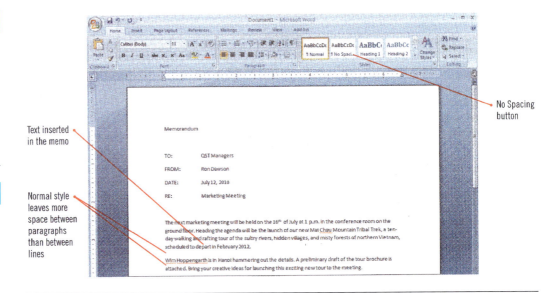

Courtesy of Cengage Learning.

Spreadsheet Software

A **spreadsheet** like **Microsoft Excel 2010®** is an electronic grid of columns and rows often used to create, model, and manipulate numerical and often financial information. Columns are labeled with letters and rows are labeled with numbers. When a column and row intersect, they form a cell. Spreadsheets have thousands of cells that make up a rectangular grid that was originally used for accounting and bookkeeping ledgers. Each cell can calculate hundreds of mathematical functions and combined to summarize financial information. Spreadsheets allow a user to type in their own formulas or take advantage of hundreds of pre-built functions.

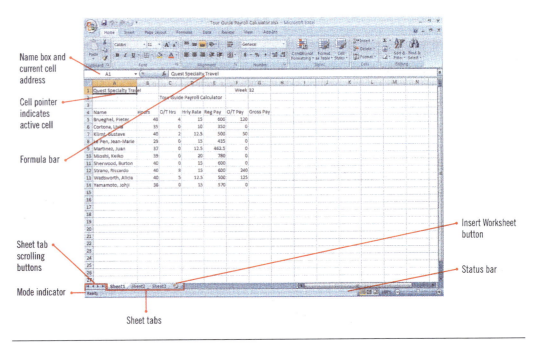

Courtesy of Cengage Learning.

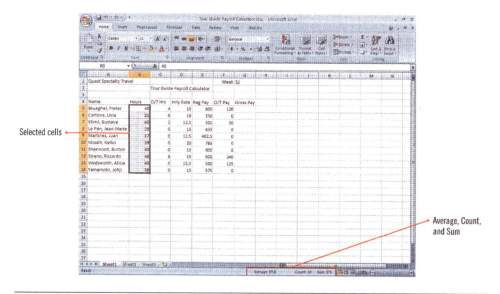

Courtesy of Cengage Learning.

BLACK & WHITE
Information Technology requires thoughtfulness and imagination to truly leverage its vast potential, and in the business environment where stakes are high, the smartest and brightest typically win. IT can be considered as a way to extend our talents and resources.

GRAY MATTER
Understanding information technology means understanding what happens and why it happens.

Many businesses would argue that spreadsheets are the most powerful and useful business application software because of its ability to model financial information and perform **"what-if"** analysis. For instance, a business can create a sales forecast on a spreadsheet to project future earnings for the next three years. Knowing that inflationary rates can affect their forecast, the business is able to apply variable inflation rates to their forecast by changing just one cell that allows them to ask "what if inflation goes up, down, or stays the same over the next three years?" and then make decisions based on this information.

Database Software

Database software or a **database management system** (DBMS) software is a collection of related files called tables that consist of records (rows) of data separated by fields (columns) that can be queried to produce subsets of information. The information retrieved by these queries becomes information that can be used to make business decisions.

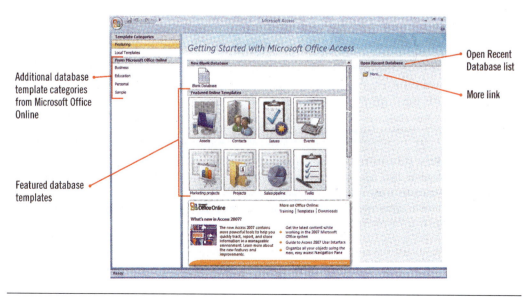

Courtesy of Cengage Learning.

Databases can consist of hundreds of related tables so they are referred to as **relational**. One table called CUSTOMERS can contain thousands of rows of customer information, with each row divided by columns that contain an individual customer's identification number, customer's name, address, city, state, and so forth. The CUSTOMER table can have a related table called TRANSACTIONS can be linked to the CUSTOMER table by including a customer's identification number, but have multiple rows of transactions for one customer. Transaction data might include the date of a purchase, product purchased and so on.

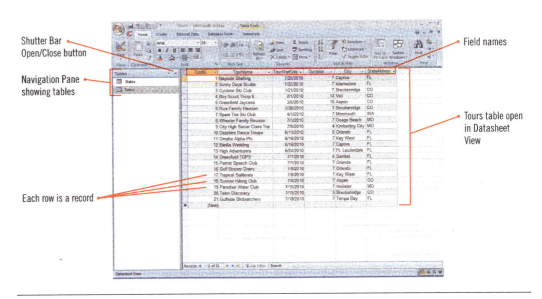

Courtesy of Cengage Learning.

Once the CUSTOMER and TRANSACTION tables are linked, the DBMS can display the information on a monitor with a **form**, which is database file that allows a user to view one customer at a time and include their transaction data. The database can then be **queried** to include only specific customers and their transactions. When the **data** is processed with a query and becomes useful, it is then considered **information**.

Presentation Software

Presentation software is used to present information in a slide show format. Presentations are usually displayed on-screen, and often are projected for an audience. Slide presentations are made with a presentation software editor that lets a user insert and format text, graphics, video, and many other display elements.

Businesses rely heavily on presentation software to visually communicate and collaborate in strategic and tactical meetings. For instance, a slideshow presentation can compliment an oral business presentation to a board of directors for a much more impactful and effective presentation. Presentation software also allows the user to distribute printed copies of a slide show to further enhance a presentation. Since presentation software slide shows are electronic, they can be distributed via the Internet meaning presentations can be made for an audience across the country or across the world.

> **WHITE BOARD**
>
> What is the main purpose of a word processing software?
> Why is a PDF file so valuable in business?
> Which application software features a "what-if" analysis?
> How is a DBMS different from spreadsheet software?
> Why do businesses rely so heavily on presentation software?

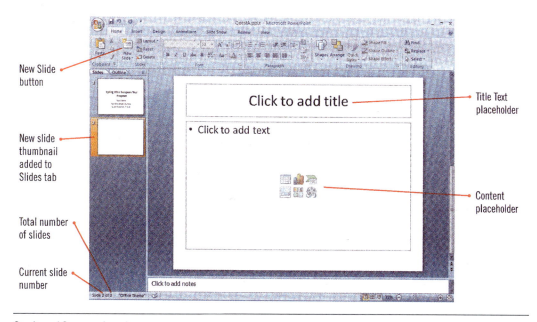

Courtesy of Cengage Learning.

Specific-use Business Application Software

Business application software is not just the domain of software suites. Two applications software not typically included in software suites but just as important to business are browser software and network software. Browsers are software that allows a user to view the Internet and the World Wide Web. Network software allows computers to communicate with each other.

Browser Software

A **browser** or **web browser** is user interface software that lets a user to display web pages on the World Wide Web. Browsers can display text, pictures, video, and much more. Browsers also include hyperlinks, which is a clickable navigation element that lets the user navigate from one web page to another.

Networks

A **computer network** is simply two or more computers connected together for resource sharing and communication. Resources refer to computer files, folders, software, and also peripheral hardware like printers, scanners, webcams, etc. The advantages of a computer network over a stand-alone system are so significant that businesses cannot compete effectively in the marketplace without a network of some kind, even if the business is a sole proprietorship.

18 CHAPTER 1 | Business Information Technology

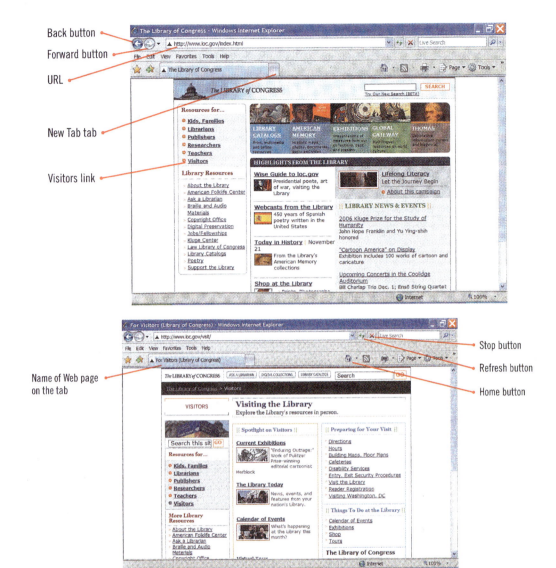

Courtesy of Cengage Learning.

Summary

Consider just a few of the thousands of inventions that have changed business over the last hundred years. The telephone expanded the reach of businesses that previously depended on mail for communications. Copy machines eliminated the jobs of thousands of people working in typing pools. Airline travel allowed businesses to expand all over the world. But all these inventions have one thing in common: it doesn't take an expert to use them. Anyone can use a telephone or copy machine and it doesn't take an expert to board an airliner. Information technology along with its hardware and software is different. It requires **thoughtfulness** and **imagination** to truly leverage its vast potential, and in the business environment where stakes are high, the smartest and brightest typically win. IT can be considered as a way to extend our talents and resources.

Information technology is moving forward at such an alarming rate that in business, it requires our constant attention and the ability to predict the future or at least be able to make intelligent decisions regarding it. Consider when the Internet started in 1969, did anyone really understand the enormity of its impact on business? So-called experts predicted that printed newspapers would have no chance of surviving the up-to-the-second news and awesome distribution the Internet affords, yet newspapers still flourish. Postal mail has been affected, but not to the extent predicted when email became commonplace.

Many so-called experts predicted mass hysteria if the "Year 2000" (Y2K) bug wasn't fixed, and many said it couldn't be done. The hottest computing devices have come and gone just within the 21st century. What did happen with the Internet is that Information technology afforded businesses to truly operate on a global scale. Employees can easily and inexpensively communicate with one another even if they are scattered all over the world. Computers have transformed business functions like accounting, production, human resources, research, and marketing almost overnight many, many times, and will continue to do so as information technology evolves. The point is to simply pay attention to technology.

The question arises as to where and what information technology a business should pay attention, especially given that most people involved in business are not IT professionals? One of the best resources is the **media**, like National Public Radio or the Wall Street Journal that regularly feature technology and their relationship to business. An obvious resource is the **Internet** which has endless amounts of information on technology and its future implications on business. The best resource however is **people**, specifically people in business that have experience with information technology. The question still remains: Does Information Technology matter? The answer is a resounding yes. Do people matter? They are by far the most valuable resource any business has with information technology infinitely extending their ability to create new paradigms.

Matching

Match each key term in the left column with the most accurate definition in the right column.

C	1. Best Practice	A.	The study, design, development, implementation, support, and management of computer-based information systems, particularly software and hardware.
E	2. Computer Hardware	B.	Plays a pivotal role towards gaining computer competency.
A	3. Information technology	C.	Management process, technique, or method that is most effective at arriving at a desired outcome, or best outcome than any other process, technique, or method.
I	4. Operating System	D.	Computing power doubles every eighteen months
G	5. Midrange Computers	E.	Tangible or physical aspects of a computer, like circuit boards, chipsets, and keyboards.
L	6. Software Suite	F.	Process and store enormous amounts of bulk data and information
N	7. Spreadsheet	G.	Less powerful and smaller in physical size than mainframe computers, but do many of the same things, simply on a smaller scale.
O	8. Presentation Software	H.	Smaller than mainframes and minicomputers, and are so common that they are most commonly referred to as computers.
B	9. Attitude	I.	The most important aspects of system software.
H	10. Microcomputers	J.	Does not work without system software or an operating system.
F	11. Mainframe Computers	K.	Programs that enable a computer to work.
J	12. Mainframe Computers	L.	A collection of computer application programs of associated functionality that share a common graphical user interface.
M	13. Word Processor	M.	An application software used to create, compose, edit, format and print documents.
K	14. Application Software	N.	An electronic grid of columns and rows often used to create, model, and manipulate financial information.
D	15. Moore's Law	O.	Presentation software is used to present information in a slide show format.

Multiple Choice

1. Information Technology is a _____ in business.
   a. Know how
   b. Choice
   c. Hub
   d. Core competency

2. _____ towards information technology plays a pivotal role towards gaining computer competency.
   a. Frustration
   b. Attitude
   c. Aggravation
   d. Approach

3. A _____ is an electronic grid of columns and rows often used to create, model, and manipulate financial information.
   a. Word processor
   b. Database
   c. Spreadsheet
   d. Presentation software

4. PDF stands for _____.
   a. Portable document file
   b. Portable data file
   c. Passable document file
   d. Passable data file

5. Databases can consist of hundreds of related tables so they are referred to as _____.
   a. Realistic
   b. Relative
   c. Relatable
   d. Relational

6. _____ is the most basic way to share information.
   a. Cutting and pasting
   b. Object Linking
   c. Object embedding
   d. None of the above

7. There are two basic categories of software; application software and _____ software.
   a. Function
   b. Assembly
   c. Production
   d. System

8. _____ Software performs particular tasks people need.
   a. Firm
   b. Suite
   c. Application
   d. Business

9. When a computer can run more than one process at a time it is referred to as _____.
   a. Caching
   b. Processing
   c. Multitasking
   d. All of the above

10. Operating systems are made up of a hierarchy of directories, typically called _____.
    a. Folders
    b. Trees
    c. Ladders
    d. Chains

Blanks

_____ is the study, design, development, implementation, support, and management of computer-based information systems, particularly software and hardware.

Without _____, a computer is just a plastic box of microchips and wires.

_____ is the knowledge that enables a person to understand something.

_____ is a management process, technique, or method that is most effective at arriving at a desired outcome, or best outcome than any other process, technique, or method.

_____ are smaller than mainframes and minicomputers, and are so common that they are most commonly referred to as simply computers, and sometimes just referred to as a _____.

A _____, often called a _____ is a collection of computer programs working together that manage the hardware and software of a computer so they work properly.

When a computer can run more than one process at a time it is referred to as _____.

_____ towards application software is as important as is it when learning a computing system.

_____ software or _____ software is a collection of related files called tables that consist of records (rows) of data separated by fields (columns) that can be queried to produce subsets of information.

A _____ is simply two or more computers connected together for resource sharing and communication.

Short Questions

What is the most basic way to share data and information between applications?

What are the most commonly used application softwares in business?

What is it called when a computer can run more than one process at a time?

What are the three configurations of a microcomputer?

Who claimed processing power doubles every eighteen months?

What is the term for people that use computers?

two | inside the box

The System Unit
Microcomputer Configurations
Expansion Slots & Cards
Input & Output Devices
Output Devices

Inside the Box

When you buy a car, you can afford to be unaware of how it specifically works. To a certain extent, if your car starts every time, sounds good rolling down the road and the gauges aren't showing any problems, your only problem is keeping it washed and waxed. Does it really matter how an alternator, sparkplug, or wheel bearing operates? When you bought the car, maybe you did your homework and based the purchase on solid research of automobile manufacturers, model comparisons, and your own personal wants and needs. Even if there is a problem with the car, there's always someone who can fix it. By the way, do you know the guy that fixed it? Is there a guarantee? Did you just trust him and pony up the money for a repair the he said was necessary? Did you even have a clue what was really wrong with your car? Maybe it's under warranty and you don't care.

BLACK & WHITE
A motherboard is the primary circuit board, which is a complex array of electronics that connect and help different parts of the computer communicate with one another.

GRAY MATTER
The system unit is an unimportant as the engine in a car, until it breaks and you're required to speak intelligently about it with a mechanic.
  Understanding how a system unit works can lead to informed business decisions when purchasing or upgrading a computing system.

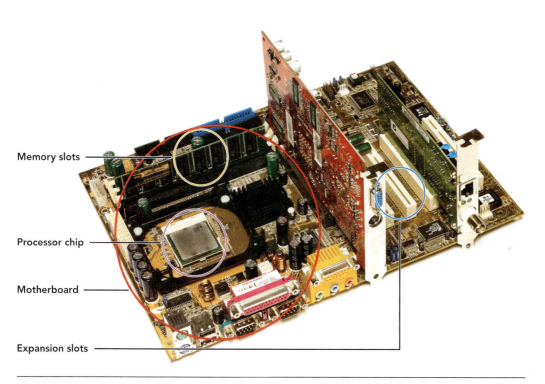

A typical PC motherboard
Courtesy of Antony Nettle.

  Business isn't forgiving, especially when everyone is watching. You may find it vitally important to know some of the "inner workings" of a car if you were asked to buy a fleet of two hundred vehicles for a delivery business. Miles per gallon, leasing options, maintenance, environmental impact, fleet discounts, service, reliability, budgeting, tax credits, and a host of other criteria become exponentially more important with so much at stake. Learning about wheel bearings starts to look like a pretty good idea if a particular model has a history of wheel bearing failure.

  In business, it may seem inconsequential to know the physical inner workings of a microcomputer's system unit until you're called upon to purchase hundreds of computers to replace hundreds of old computers, which is not unusual. Will these hundreds of computers be obsolete in eighteen months? Do they have proprietary parts that can only be serviced by one company? Do they have the electronic components allowing them to be networked together easily? Will newer computers work with the older computers an organization intends to keep, and can they be upgraded? When the computers in question were assembled, do they have a state-of-the-art superfast microchip attached to an inferior motherboard with subpar bus lines?

BLACK & WHITE

On the inside of a microcomputer, the core component is the system board commonly referred to as the motherboard.

GRAY MATTER

A microprocessor, sometimes referred to as simply the "chip" is the brains of a computer.

Understanding the system unit as a whole and the role of the microprocessor can lead to a better understanding of processing speed and efficiency of the overall computing system and the business decisions they affect.

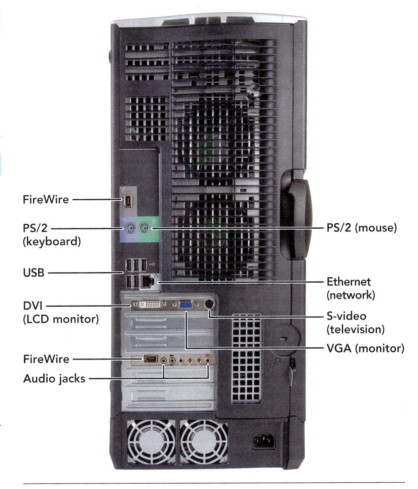

The connectors on the outside of a system unit enable you to connect peripherals such as keyboards, printers, and a mouse.
Courtesy of iStockphoto.com.

Remember, you don't have to be an expert at system units, just an intelligent part of the conversation when they relate to business; or you can always just trust the information systems geek that just told you that you're going to have to spend three million dollars above and beyond you budget on motherboards.

The System Unit

The **system unit** is the main body of a computer, containing a **motherboard**. Assorted computer components like power supplies, cooling fans, disk drives, primary memory, secondary memory, expansion cards, and much more are plugged into the motherboard. The system unit is the inner workings or insides of a computer, essentially everything inside the box.

From a business standpoint, does it really matter how the box works, or is it enough to know how to use it? Remember, countless people drive cars successfully and are completely unaware how an engine or suspension works. Most people that use computers successfully are completely unaware how the system unit works, so why bother to find out?

A firm understanding of the system unit's inner workings and technology can enhance the ability of a business to assess whether buying new computers is even necessary. Typically, micro-

There are many types of system units
Courtesy of iStockphoto.com

processor chip speed and storage space have historically been a main concern that many times drives computer purchasing decisions. **Gordon Moore**, co-founder of Intel rightly predicted that computing power doubles about every eighteen months, which means after eighteen months, computers are available on the market that are twice as fast. This is referred to as **Moore's Law**. It is not an unusual accounting practice to depreciate a computer's value to zero dollars after just three years.

It is true that computers and computing power doubles about every eighteen months, and will continue to do so for many years to come, so it is simply assumed that new computers or upgrades are always in order, or are they? Do you even need new computers? Thousands of computers cost millions of dollars in hardware, software, and time. Purchasing ten computers for the same purpose can still be a daunting decision, so a misinformed choice can be devastating to a business. These are just a few of hundreds of questions that make it worthwhile to start to take in interest in how a system unit works inside of a microcomputer.

Microcomputer Configurations

To understand a microcomputer's physical architecture, it's best to start externally, the actual box that encases the system unit's components. It has become common practice to refer to a microcomputer as a

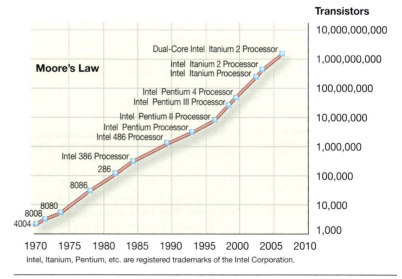

Moore's Law
Courtesy of Intel Corporation.

28 CHAPTER 2 | Inside the Box

BLACK & WHITE
Bus lines are the pathways that transfer data and power between components inside of a computer, and sometimes between computers.

GRAY MATTER
Binary numbers can be represented by any sequence of bits which can be represented by any apparatus able of being in two mutually exclusive states. (On/Off, True/False, Yes/No)

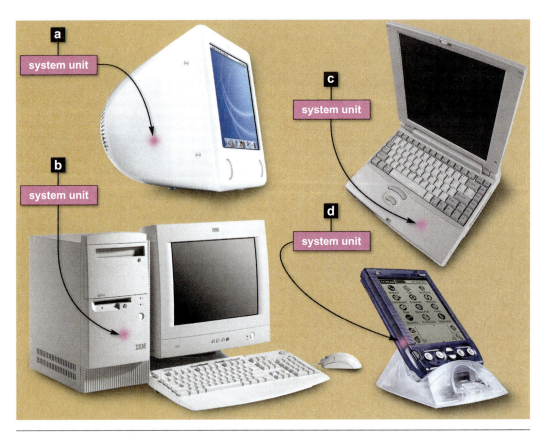

Courtesy of IBM Corporation.

box. The box itself is called a **case**, or **chassis** which encloses the main components of the computer. Cases come in a variety of sizes and configurations which are typically determined by the size and shape of the motherboard.

On the inside of a microcomputer, the core component is the **system board** commonly referred to as the **motherboard** (Apple computers refer to motherboards as **logic boards**). A motherboard is the primary circuit board, which is a complex array of electronics that connects and helps different components of the computer communicate with one another. A **circuit board**, sometimes called a **printed circuit board** (PCB), is a logical and economical way to replace what would be loose wiring by applying copper wires directly to a sheet of non conductive plastic.

A motherboard is analogous to the land that buildings, storm drains, roads, telephone lines and any other infrastructure reside on. Keep in mind that the land itself connects the entire infrastructure. A **microprocessor**, sometimes called a microprocessor chip is plugged directly into a slot on the motherboard and serves as the brains for the microcomputer. Contained within the microprocessor is the **central processing unit (CPU)**. The CPU interprets program instructions and processes data by performing arithmetic and logical operations. The CPU is what gives a microcomputer to ability to be programmed.

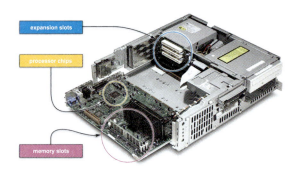

A PC motherboard inside a system frame.
Courtesy of IBM Corporation.

Modern microprocessors.
Courtesy of Intel Corporation.

Microcomputers are often discussed relative to speed, or how fast they can perform an operation, and speed is directly, but not solely related to the CPU. A microcomputer's speed is measured by **clock rate** which is the cycles per second that a computer can perform its most basic tasks, measured in **gigahertz**. Keep in mind a CPU is only ever dealing with bits, represented electronically by either a positive or negative charge. Any input into the computer has already been translated into bits by an input device like a keyboard because bits are all that a CPU can understand. Output devices like screens will translate the bits back into something a person can understand. The time it takes a CPU to process the bits that represent instructions is a large part of what determines its speed for a microcomputer.

Microprocessors have different algorithms to process bits efficiently. The first truly useful personal computers processed 8 bits at a time, eventually doubling to 16 bits, then 32 bits, and then to 64 bit. Microprocessor manufacturers are constantly trying to improve processing speed, and one novel way is through the development of **multicore** chips, which are simply many chips encased on one chip package working together. **RISC** (Reduced Instruction Set Computer) architecture chips are designed for efficiency, and were the first 64 bit processors.

If the motherboard is the land that infrastructure sits on, then the main building on the land is the microprocessor chip (CPU) that serves as a super-efficient distribution warehouse distributing bits and bytes. Imagine that inside this distribution center are state-of-the-art robotics, ultra-efficient conveyor belts, and any other highly technical machinery. But what about the roads that leads to and from the distribution center? If there are only a few two-lane roads going in and out, it doesn't really matter how efficient the distribution center is. The same holds true with a motherboard-microprocessor chip relationship. A microprocessor can be the newest, best, fastest technology, but if its roads, called bus lines on a motherboard are deficient, it renders the microprocessor less effective.

Bus lines are the pathways (or roads in our analogy) that transfer data and power between components inside of a computer, and sometimes between computers. Bus lines are controlled by software that enables them to connect peripheral devices like computer cards and printers. The relationship between the components and the bus lines are of great importance. If a bus is only a two-lane road, its ability to handle traffic is greatly reduced. Adding lanes or widening the "roads" leads to more efficient the bus lines able to handle larger volumes of traffic. This is why bus lines are measured in **bus width**. Another useful description is to think of the bus line a pipe, or straw. The greater the straw's width, the more can flow through it.

WHITE BOARD

Name several components of a system unit.
Why is a good understanding of a system unit essential in business?
What are bus lines and what do they do?
Why is Moore's Law significant when it comes to the system unit?

> **BLACK & WHITE**
>
> Most microcomputers use the American Standard Code for Information Interchange (ASCII) coding scheme.

> **GRAY MATTER**
>
> 01010111 01001000
> 01001111 01001001
> 01010011 01001010
> 01001111 01001000
> 01001110 01000111
> 01000001 01001100
> 01010100

It is possible that a computer manufacturer might have the fastest microprocessor chips available in the boxes they sell, but might also have buses with low width on their motherboards. If a business purchases five hundred computers based on the microprocessor chip alone which is often the case, they might be sorely disappointed if they didn't do their homework regarding bus width. Below is a list of bus types:

PCI	Peripheral component interconnect
AGP	Accelerated graphics port
USB	Universal serial bus
Firewire	High performance serial bus

What is it that travels through bus lines and the motherboard? Essentially, electricity is the traffic that travels throughout the motherboard and in a computer. Computers are electronic devices and electricity has only two states; on or off. A two state system on a computer is called **binary system**. Binary means something is made up of two parts, and in this case, either a "1" or a "0". When a user inputs data or information into a computer system, regardless of content, it is always converted into ones and zeros so the computer can work with it. The ones and zeros are referred to as **bits**. When eight bits are combined, they become a **byte**.

Term	Size	Roughly...
Byte	8 bits	Typically represents one character.
Kilobyte	1,024 bytes	One thousand bytes
Megabyte	1,024 kilobytes	One thousand kilobytes
Gigabyte	1,024 megabytes	One thousand megabytes
Terabyte	1,024 gigabytes	One thousand gigabytes
Petabyte	1,024 terabytes	One thousand terabytes
Exabyte	1,024 petabytes	One thousand petabytes
Zettabyte	1,024 exabytes	One thousand exabytes
Yottabyte	1,024 zettabytes	One thousand zettabytes

Bytes can then be used to represent characters like the alphabet or numbers. It is these ones and zeros that are stored in secondary storage. Most microcomputers use the **American Standard Code for Information Interchange (ASCII)** coding scheme to represent bytes listed on the following page.

System units need power, and in the case of a computer, electricity. Once again, if the motherboard is the land, then the power supply is power plant that supports the entire infrastructure. A computer **power supply unit** (PSU) is the part that supplies electricity. A PSU is typically converts 100-120 volt or 220-240 volt **alternating current** (AC) to a lower voltage **direct current** (DC) that can be used by the internal components of the system unit. 100-120 AC current is used in North America and Japan whereas 220-240 AC current is used in Europe, Australia, and parts of Asia. Some PSUs have ability sense a wide range of AC current and convert it to usable DC current automatically. Obviously, a global business, or any business for that matter would have to be cognizant of PSU specifications when purchasing any computer.

American Standard Code for Information Interchange (ASCII) coding scheme							
01000001	A	01001110	N	01100001	a	01101110	n
01000010	B	01001111	O	01100010	b	01101111	o
01000011	C	01010000	P	01100011	c	01110000	p
01000100	D	01010001	Q	01100100	d	01110001	q
01000101	E	01010010	R	01100101	e	01110010	r
01000110	F	01010011	S	01100110	f	01110011	s
01000111	G	01010100	T	01100111	g	01110100	t
01001000	H	01010101	U	01101000	h	01110101	u
01001001	I	01010110	V	01101001	i	01110110	v
01001010	J	01010111	W	1101010	j	01110111	w
01001011	K	01011000	X	01101011	k	01111000	x
01001100	L	01011001	Y	01101100	l	01111001	y
01001101	M	01011010	Z	01101101	m	01111010	z

System units also need to store, retain, and process memory. There are two types of memory; **primary storage** (volatile) and **secondary storage** (non-volatile). Memory holds information electronically stored on a computer like data files, programming, and software. In a computing system, primary storage can be analogized as what a user is currently working on and secondary storage is where the user stores their work when they are finished. Data and information pre-loaded on a computer that requires no user interaction is stored in secondary storage.

WHITE BOARD

Why is primary storage volatile and secondary storage non-volatile?
How does the power supply work in the system unit?
Describe a binary system outside of a system unit.
Why does a computer have to be binary?

In the "motherboard as land" analogy, primary and secondary storage are like inventory processing and storage warehouses. Primary storage can be analogized as a place inventory (memory) is processed before it is put away and secondary storage is where inventory (memory) is stored after processing.

In the system unit, primary storage is random access memory (RAM) in the form of **RAM chipsets** that are mounted on the motherboard. RAM allows data and information to be accessed in any order; hence the word "random", without physical movement of the RAM chipset, as opposed to a secondary storage device that typically spins and requires a moving read / write head. Types of RAM chips are listed on the following page.

Because RAM has no moving parts and can be accessed in any order, it is extremely fast. Many times a computer's performance can be increased dramatically by unplugging lower capacity memory storage RAM chipsets from the motherboard and replacing them with higher capacity memory

DRAM	Dynamic random access memory
SDRAM	Synchronous dynamic random access memory
DDR	Double data rate synchronous dynamic RAM
Direct RDRAM	Dynamic random access memory

RAM chipsets and their slots on the motherboard.
Courtesy of Intel Corporation.

storage RAM chipsets. However, RAM is volatile memory, which means it does not retain its data and information after the computer is turned off. All data and information in RAM must be saved to secondary storage, like a hard disk if it to be retained. Businesses can potentially avoid replacing older computers by increasing their performance with RAM alone.

When a computer is started, it requires the same critical programming information every time the computer is turned on. Computers need to know how much RAM is plugged into the motherboard, what sort of disk drives are on board, and much more crucial information for the system to work properly. The programming information to perform this startup task resides in a chip called a **complimentary metal-oxide semiconductor**, or **CMOS** chip. CMOS does not lose its contents and is therefore non-volatile memory.

Motherboards have other forms of memory plugged into them in the form of ROM chips (Read-only memory). **ROM chips** are preprogrammed and require no user intervention and serve to perform specialized internal tasks like starting the computer. Since the programming on ROM chips is unchangeable, they are sometimes called **firmware**.

Secondary storage is installed onto a motherboard typically as a hard disk device. The hard disk represents the neatly stacked and well-recorded inventory which of course is in the form of data files in reference to a system unit. Secondary storage is **non-volatile** which means it retains its data and information even when the system unit loses power, and is somewhat slower than primary storage as it does not have a direct connection to the microprocessor. Data and information in primary storage is temporary until it is saved, or stored in secondary storage.

There are several different types of secondary storage devices starting with a hard disk drive which is a storage device that stores data on quickly spinning magnetic platters. Hard disks are considered internal hard disks when they are inside the box and generally can't be removed easily. Conversely, external hard drives reside outside the box.

In business, it's unusual that a computer is stand-alone, that it wouldn't be connected to a network that allows it to share other resources like printers and data files, and specifically, mass storage devices. As a matter of fact, it is impractical for a computer to be stand-alone in business. If a computer is connected to a network that allows it to store and save most of its data and information to secondary external mass storage, then how important is its internal hard disk? A home computer may need as much internal hard disk storage as it can get to perhaps store large video and music files, software, and a large array of other data and information because it is not part of a network. Business computers attached to a network may not need large internal hard disks as many of its

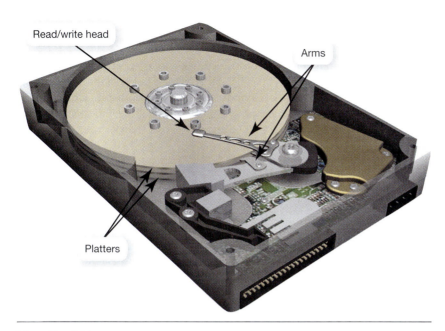

Internal hard drive
Courtesy of Pearson Education.

> **BLACK & WHITE**
>
> In the system unit, primary storage is random access memory (RAM) in the form of RAM chipsets that are mounted on the motherboard.

> **GRAY MATTER**
>
> One of the most effective ways to increase the speed of a computer is to increase its random access memory.
> From a business standpoint, making a decision to increase RAM can be far less expensive than replacing an entire computer.

> **WHITE BOARD**
>
> Why are some ROM chips called firmware?
> What does the programming do on a CMOS chip?
> Why can it be advantageous to use an external hard drive?
> Describe what "volatile" and "non-volatile" mean when referring to memory.

data files and software often reside somewhere else on a network. This can be a legitimate consideration when deciding to purchase computers for any sized business organization.

An **external hard drive** is like outsourcing your inventory. External hard disks or external optical disks are secondary storage and outside the box or chassis and many times connected via USB cables, are very reliable, and have reasonable file access speed that are often comparable to internal hard disks. Although spinning internal hard disks are very popular and inexpensive to use as internal secondary storage onboard a motherboard, inexpensive external solid state secondary storage prices are dropping dramatically. Once again, this may point out that **internal hard drive** storage capacity for a business computer may not be as important purchasing criteria as it once was.

Expansion Slots & Cards

Motherboards have **expansion slots** to receive **expansion cards**. An expansion card is a specialized circuit board plugged into a motherboard's expansion slot that adds further functionality to a computer, like networking and connectivity. Some expansion cards allow a computer to serve as a television while others can enhance a computer's audio ability. Business computers come with a modem and networking card which eliminates the need for expansion. Video gamers now use two expansion slots to take advantage of a dual video card setup.

In the system unit, a **port** is a specific outlet that serves as a connection, or interfaces between a computer and other devices like digital cameras, keyboards or printers and provides signal transfer,

CHAPTER 2 | Inside the Box

BLACK & WHITE

Motherboards have expansion slots to receive expansion cards. An expansion card is a specialized circuit board plugged into a motherboard's expansion slot that adds further functionality to a computer, like networking and connectivity.

GRAY MATTER

Many times it is far less expensive in the long run to purchase a computer with network, modem, and sound cards already on-board.

or communication between the computer and the device. A port is like an electrical outlet that a device's cable can be plugged in to.

Hardware ports are divided by two groups based on the way they transfer information from the system unit and the specific device; serial ports and parallel ports. These types of ports are becoming obsolete as USB and Firewire gain acceptance. Serial ports send and receive information from the device to the system unit one bit at a time and parallel ports send multiple bits at a time. Parallel ports require the device and system unit to communicate first to "agree" on data transfer rate, information

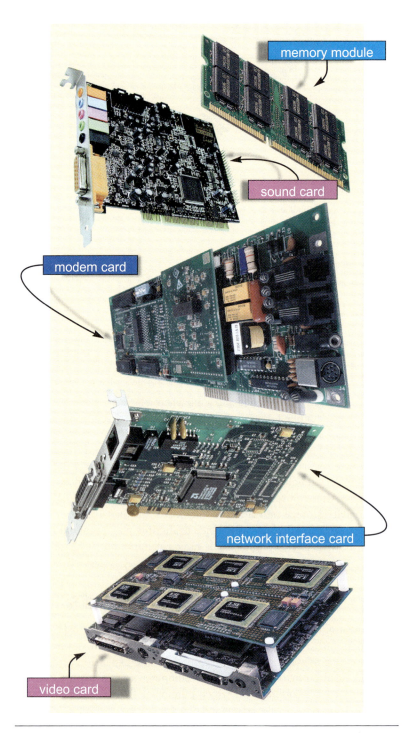

Expansion cards allow you to improve your computer
Courtesy of Prentice-Hall, Inc.

CHAPTER 2 | Inside the Box

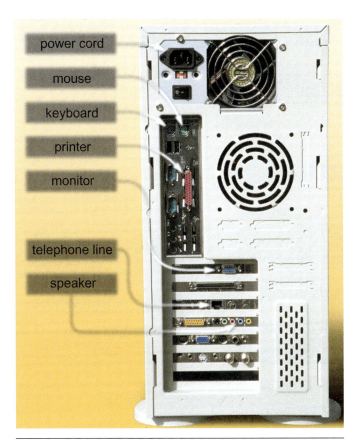

Ports allow you to connect peripheral devices like printers to the system unit
Courtesy of IBM Corporation.

to be transferred, and other necessary information before an actual connection is made.

Although a port may seem like an insignificant component, in business, it can become very important aspect when choosing hardware to work with a system unit, and can play a vital role in purchasing decisions for external devices. Ports use a system called **"Plug and Play"** which are designed so a device automatically works when it is plugged in to a system unit, which has not always been the case. In the past, if a device was plugged in, a user had to typically install specialized software to enable the device to work properly. Today's operating systems have preloaded software so users simply plug in a device and it starts working immediately.

The two most popular ports which are "Plug and Play" are **FireWire** and **Universal Serial Bus (USB)**. FireWire ports were started by Apple and are typically used with video equipment and digital cameras whereas USB ports are designed to provide a standard to most other devices. USB were originally designed for personal computers and are intended to facilitate the retirement of older non-standard serial and parallel ports.

BLACK & WHITE

ROM chips are pre-programmed and require no user intervention and serve to perform specialized internal tasks like starting the computer. Since the programming on ROM chips is unchangeable, they are sometimes called firmware.

GRAY MATTER

An external hard drive is like outsourcing your inventory. External hard disks or external optical disks are secondary storage and outside the box or chassis and many times connected via USB cables, are very reliable, and have reasonable file access speed that are often comparable to internal hard disks.

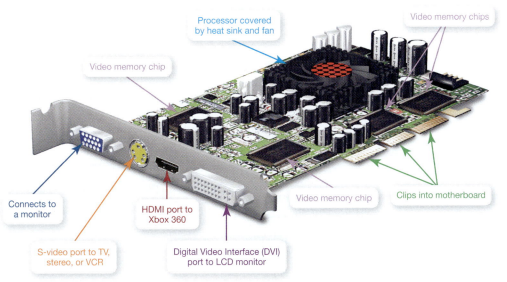

Video cards have grown in popularity with gaming
Courtesy of Pearson Education.

> **BLACK & WHITE**
>
> Devices that plug into computer systems units can be categorized as either an input device, or an output device, and are often called peripheral devices.

> **GRAY MATTER**
>
> Standardization of ports has allowed peripheral device manufacturers to reach larger markets because they know more and more computing systems will accept USB and Firewire.

Connector	Use
DB-25, 25-pin female	parallel port for printer
DB-25, 25-pin male	serial port for printers, modems, or scanners
DIN, 6-pin female	mouse or keyboard
DB-15, 15-pin female	VGA video (monitor)
RJ-11	phone line
RJ-45	network
stereo miniplug female	microphone, speakers, or headphones
USB	port for many devices on PCs and Macintoshes
FireWire	port for cameras and portable storage

Courtesy of Prentice-Hall, Inc.

Input & Output Devices

Devices that plug into computer systems units can be categorized as either an **input** device, or an **output** device, and are often called **peripheral devices**. Sometimes it is hard to remember that a system unit is an electrical machine that only understands bits, bytes and electrical pulses and requires a way to translate data and information input from a human so the system can use it, and has to translate data and information output so a human can understand it.

A computer understands only one real language called **machine code** or **machine language**. Machine language is a binary system of ones and zeros representing patterns of bits that representing instructions that a computer's **central processing unit (CPU)** can understand. Different series of bit patterns represent different instructions. Humans on the other hand understand images like photographs and languages like German or English. This means that for a human to **input** instructions into a computer, the system must first translate the human language into machine language. The same is true when the computer **outputs** information to a human; it must translate machine language into a human language, or at least something a human can understand.

> **BLACK & WHITE**
> A computer keyboard is a basically modeled after the typewriter keyboard and is designed mainly for the input of text and characters.

> **GRAY MATTER**
> The QWERTY keyboard has been around since 1874, and will probably be around well into the 21st century as one of the main input devices for a computing system.

Courtesy of Intel Corporation.

Input is data and information that enters a computer system and **translated** for processing. The data or information can be as simple as typing a résumé with a keyboard or scanning a photograph with a flatbed scanning device. **Output** is data and information that exits a computer system and **translated** for a human to comprehend. Output's data and information has many forms, like a printed document, an image on a screen, or music playing from speakers. Keep in mind that input and output are directional, input enters a computer system while output exits, and both require translation. Both Input and output can be words, pictures, sounds, and any other medium a human understands into a format a system unit can process.

An input device is computer hardware apparatus that translates data and information that a person understands into the machine language that a Central Processing Unit (CPU) can understand and process. This data and information can be typed characters from a keyboard like words or numbers, but often includes sounds, pictures, and motions. Most of the time, an input device is directed by the end-user.

The first and most obvious input device of a microcomputer is the **keyboard**. A computer keyboard is a basically modeled after the typewriter keyboard and is designed mainly for the input of

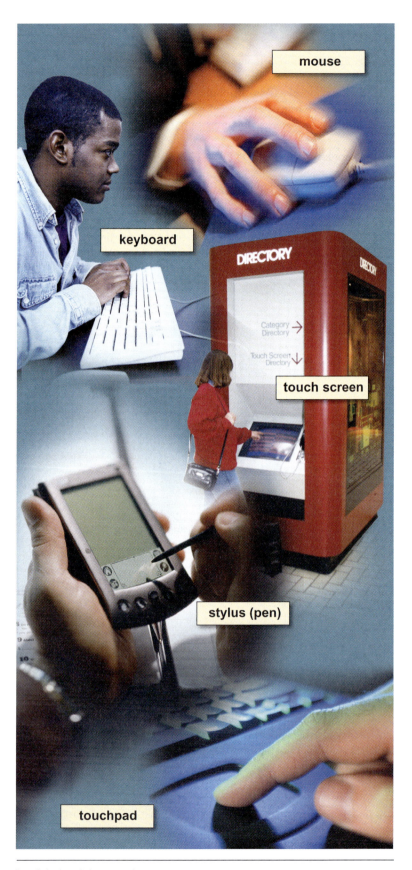

Input devices take many forms
Courtesy of William Whitehurst/Corbis Images.

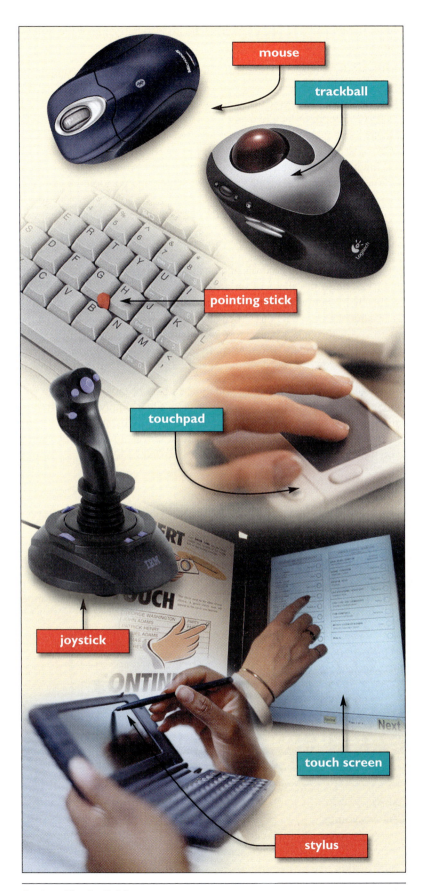

Courtesy of Prentice-Hall, Inc.

BLACK & WHITE

Input is data and information that enters a computer system and translated for processing. Output is data and information that exits a computer system and translated for a human to comprehend.

GRAY MATTER

Computers only understand binary information. Any input or output device is required to translate from or to the computer so a human can interact with it.

text and characters. Along with traditional keys, a computer keyboard also has some of the following additional keys and features:

- **Escape:** The "Escape" (Esc) key is used to effectively discontinue or cancels a computer's operation, and typically means "stop".
- **Return:** The "Return" key, or "Enter" key typically finishes and keyboard entry.
- **Function:** Function keys serve specific tasks like using "F1" for help and are used as shortcuts. Many times function keys are used in combination with other keys to extend their usefulness.
- **Alternate:** The "Alternate" (Alt) key and "Control" (Ctrl) key are used in combination with other keys to modify their input and extend the usefulness of the entire keyboard.
- **Arrow:** The "Arrow" keys allow a user to navigate around the screen and position the cursor in a specific direction.
- **Keypad:** A Numeric keypad serves as a "ten key" keypad to enter numbers for convenient calculations, arithmetic operations, and cursor control.

A **mouse** functions as a pointing device that controls and positions the screen's cursor. Depending on the context, the cursor can be in the shape of an arrow or an insertion line. Most "mice" have a **"left click"** and **"right click"** button to perform several shortcut functions like launching computer applications or accessing alternative menus. Mice also have a **wheel button** between the right and left click buttons to scroll through a page more efficiently. Like many input devices, mice, and other pointing devices come in many different configurations, many of which are listed below:

- **Mechanical mouse:** A mechanical mouse is the most widely used type of mouse that has a ball on the bottom that rolls along a desk surface or mouse pad. A mouse pad simply consistent provides traction for the ball. Mechanical mice are attached to the system unit by an electrical cord. When the user pushes the mouse forward, the cursor on the screen moves up. When the mouse is backward, the mouse on the screen moves down and so forth.

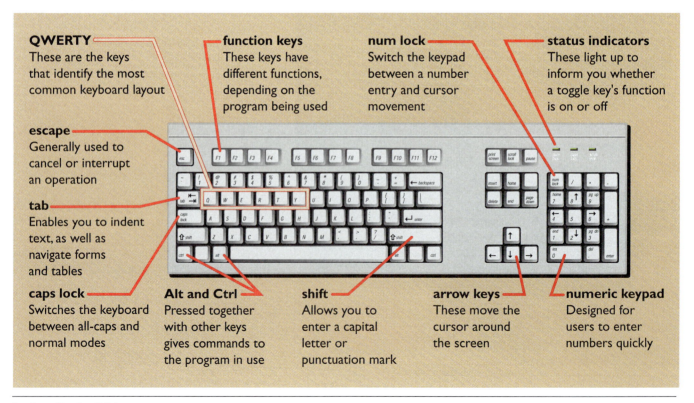

Courtesy of Prentice-Hall, Inc.

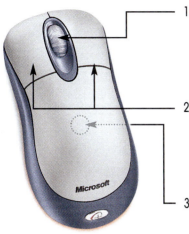

1. The wheel button enables you to scroll more quickly because you don't need to use the on-screen scroll bars.
2. Customizable buttons enable you to use the buttons to perform different commands in different programs.
3. An optical sensor enables you to use the mouse without a mouse pad.

A mouse with a wheel
Courtesy of Microsoft Corporation.

Courtesy of Microsoft Corporation.

WHITE BOARD

Why are most keyboards referred to as QWERTY?
List different keys besides the alphabet on a keyboard and their functions.
List some pointing devices and how they work.
When will keyboards be obsolete and what will replace them?
When will a mouse be obsolete and what will replace it?

- **Optical mouse:** Instead of using a mechanical mouse with ball, an optical mouse emits a beam of light to the surface of the desk and then recaptures the light's reflection to sense its direction to control the movement of the cursor on the screen. Many optical mice are cordless and popular with laptop users.
- **Touch pad:** Many microcomputers provide a surface a user can slide their finger over to control the movement of a cursor and can eliminate the need for a mouse. Touch pads provide left and right buttons like a mouse.
- **Stylus:** Some laptops, called tablet computers or graphic tablets provide their users a pen-like device called a stylus that allows them to simulate writing directly on the computer's screen, although there is no ink involved. The screen recognizes the movement of the stylus by sensing pressure on the screen and in turn controls the cursor. A stylus can also provide a way for the user to input information into their computer with their own handwriting. The tablet computer can learn its user's style of handwriting and allows them to write notes, documents, and any other written input.

Many other peripheral devices serve as input devices, and all have the same thing in common; they provide data and information to the system unit and are required to translate it into a form the system unit can understand and process, some of which are listed below.

> **BLACK & WHITE**
>
> An RFID is an input device that can be applied to a product for identification and transmits the product's information through radio waves.

> **GRAY MATTER**
>
> The implications of a radio frequency identification tag is far reaching, whether it is replacing the need for an employee to count inventory, or its ability to affect a business's supply chain policies and procedures.

Microphone: A microphone is a sound-sensing device that allows users to record sound and instructions that can be translated and stored digitally to a computer. Many microphones have the ability to direct the operation of a computer through **speech recognition software**. Speech recognition is the process of converting speech to digital data and information.

Digital cameras: A digital camera is an electronic input device that records and stores single photographs digitally to a computer. **Video cameras** are input devices similar to digital cameras but capture motion pictures. Both types of cameras can store and translate their photographs or movies to a system unit where they are often manipulated and enhanced by specialized application software.

Speech recognition is used in many businesses
Courtesy of Associated Press.

Image scanners: Image scanners, often called optical scanners are devices that analyze, convert, and translate images, printed text, or handwriting to a digital format a system unit can recognize and store. Some scanners are configured like printers and are called **flatbed scanners**, while others are handheld.

Image scanners can save businesses enormous amounts of time by converting printed text, called **hard copy**, into digital text with a technology called **Optical Character Recognition** (OCR). If a law firm had a printed contract that was 400 pages, they might choose to have someone retype it into Microsoft Word so it could be modified easily at a later date. Obviously, this would be a long and arduous process, fraught with potential inaccuracies. A flatbed scanner with OCR on the other had would be able to essentially copy each page of the contract, translate each character, or word, and convert them to a digital format like Microsoft Word.

Digital cameras have revolutionized photography
Courtesy of Fujifilm U.S.A., Inc.

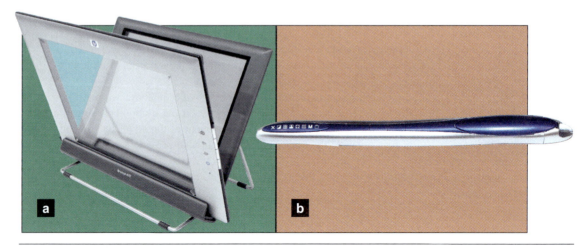
A. Flatbed scanner. B. Handheld scanner
Courtesy of Hewlett-Packard.

Webcams: A webcam, short for **web camera** is a real-time, typically low resolution video camera attached to the computer whose video images can be translated to a system unit. Webcams are typically used for real-time conversations on the World Wide Web in concert with instant messaging, and many times in business for global collaborative work.

Barcode readers: A barcode reader is an input device for reading barcodes printed on various surfaces. A **barcode** is a machine-readable depiction of information using dark ink on a light background to create high and low reflectance which is translated by a system unit and converted to 1s and 0s. Barcode systems are extremely inexpensive which makes them very desirable in business.

Radio Frequency Identification (RFID): An RFID or RFID tag is an input device that can be applied to a product for identification and transmits the product's information through radio waves. Some tags can be read from several meters away and beyond the line of sight of the reader.

Consider the use of an RFID in business. Imagine a wheelbarrow sitting at Home Depot with an RFID transmitting it's information to the store's computer, like what brand it is, its price, color, size, etc. In fact every wheelbarrow in the store is transmitting everything there is to know about these wheelbarrows, and every product in the store is doing the same. Now ask the question: Will Home Depot ever manually count inventory again? The answer is no, the RFIDs are doing inventory constantly, storing it on the store's computer. The store's computer can transmit its inventory information to their distribution center's computer and always be assured that their store will be efficiently restocked.

> **BLACK & WHITE**
> Resolution is then defined by the amount of pixels inside a defined dimension on a monitor, commonly referred to as dots per inch (dpi).

> **GRAY MATTER**
> "Dots per inch" or dpi is mainly concerned with printing images or documents. Computer monitors on the other hand typically have low dpi relative to printers.

Output Devices

When a computer provides data and information to an end-user, it is called **output**. Output can take many forms like text, images, and sounds and can be provided by a large array of peripheral output devices. Computer output does not necessarily have to be for an end-user, it can be for another computer's processing. Output devices do the opposite of input devices, translating machine code than a computer can process into a form a human can understand. For instance, when a photograph appears on a computer screen, the user sees the image although the computer is presenting it in the background with a series of 1s and 0s, or bits and bytes. The screen is defined as an output device because of its ability to translate these bit and bytes into a format the user can understand. A **computer display screen**, referred to as a monitor is the most common output device and one of many ways a system outputs its data and information. The following is a list of monitors and their features.

- **Cathode Ray Tube:** Because of their reliability and low cost, CRTs used to be the most common computer monitor. CRTs work like a television, which accelerates and deflects electrons onto the back of a fluorescent screen to provide its user with images and text.
- **Flat Panel Monitors:** A flat panel monitor is much less bulky than a CRT but more expensive. Most flat panel monitors use **Liquid Crystal Displays (LCD)** which use a then transistor, or series of transistors to display images and text on its screen. Flat panel monitors also use a lot less energy than a typical CRT. As prices for LCDs drop they are quickly replacing CRTs. Consumers are also becoming aware that CRTs are much more environmentally problematic than LCD as they use more electricity and are more difficult to dispose of.

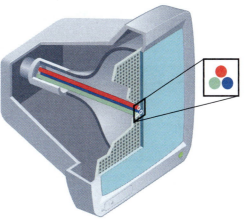

Cathode Ray Tube
Courtesy of Prentice-Hall, Inc.

17 inch monitor and flat-screen monitor.
Courtesy of IBM Corporation.

Whether a computer screen is a CRT or flat panel, they all share the same aspects which determine the quality of the image projected, or output. The most important feature is **resolution**. Computer monitors are made up of small dots called **pixels**, which is a single dot on a graphic or text image. Resolution is then defined by the amount of pixels inside a defined dimension on a monitor, commonly referred to as **dots per inch (dpi)**. For instance, the more pixels a monitor has per square inch, or higher its dpi, the better resolution in can present to the end-user, and vice versa.

Printers are another common output device, translating data a computer can process, into data and information a human or another computer can understand. In the case of a printer, output is delivered in the form of a printed document, photograph, bar code or many other tangible formats. Printers are also measured in dpi. The higher the dpi, the higher quality the image or text printed. This means that an image with 1,200 dpi should be crisper and sharper on the page than the same image at 300 dpi. Some of the more common printers are listed below:

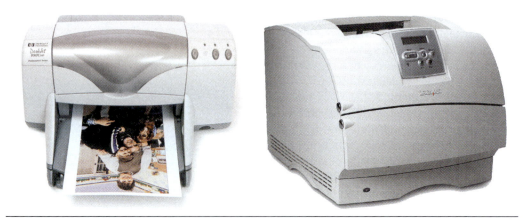

Inkjet and Laser printers.
Courtesy of Prentice-Hall, Inc.

- **Laser Printer:** A laser printer is a common type of printer that produces high quality text and graphics by using a laser to basically "burn" text on plain paper, much like a photocopier. Laser printers produce high-quality text and can print at very high dpi rates.
- **Ink-jet Printers:** These printers are designed to spray ink dots on paper coated with special light-sensitive chemicals and have extremely high dpi capability to produce ultra-clear photographs. Ink jet printers have become so good and reliable that they provide photo-quality output.
- **Plotters:** A plotter is sometimes referred to as a vector graphics printing device used to print complex line art like architectural drawings.

Sound can be output from a computer meaning than **speakers** and **headphones** attached to the system unit are output devices. Both devices are connected to a sound card than in turn is plugged into the motherboard.

Table 2.1 Common PC Monitor Resolutions

640 x 480	VGA	Video Graphics Array
800 x 600	XGA	eXtended Graphics Array
1,024 x 768	SVGA	Super Video Graphics Array
1,280 x 1,024	SXGA	Super eXtended Graphics Array
1,600 x 1,200	UXGA	Ultra eXtended Graphics Array

Courtesy of Prentice-Hall, Inc.

Summary

The analogy of a system unit as a small city can be helpful understanding how the box works, and more importantly, what to look for when making business decisions regarding computer purchase, replacement, deployment and upgrades. One of the most striking aspects of understanding the system unit in relationship to a city is the effect of storage and memory.

Secondary storage (hard drives, etc.) was referred to as "where inventory is kept" in the system unit city. Nowadays, secondary storage devices are extremely inexpensive and might not be as important an aspect as in the past. Further, system units can offload their "inventory" (data and information) easily and safely to other "cities" (network hard drives). What becomes apparent at least from a system unit performance standpoint is that processing the "inventory" (data and information) quickly and efficiently happens in random access memory (RAM). RAM is the people and machines in the city processing inventory, therefore, the more people and machines; the faster the system unit will perform.

Keep in mind that secondary storage and its relationship to memory is just one of many important aspects regarding the system unit and points out the necessity that a sound understanding of a system unit cannot be understated, especially in business. Computers permeate the landscape of all successful businesses, and understanding the system unit can lead sound business decisions and a competitive advantage.

Matching

Match each key term in the left column with the most accurate definition in the right column.

___	1. Gordon Moore	A.	The main body of a computer, containing a motherboard.
___	2. Motherboard	B.	Co-founder of Intel rightly predicted that computing power doubles about every eighteen months, which means after eighteen months.
___	3. Keyboard	C.	On the inside of a microcomputer, the core component.
___	4. Output	D.	The logical and economical way to replace what would be loose wiring by applying copper wires directly to a sheet of non conductive plastic.
___	5. Input	E.	Interprets program instructions and processes data by performing arithmetic and logical operations.
___	6. Circuit board	F.	Cycles per second that a computer can perform its most basic tasks, measured in gigahertz.
___	7. System Unit	G.	Pathways (or roads in our analogy) that transfer data and power between components inside of a computer, and sometimes between computers.
___	8. ROM Chips	H.	Something that is made up of two parts.
___	9. Byte	I.	When eight bits are combined.
___	10. Binary System	J.	Preprogrammed and require no user intervention and serve to perform specialized internal tasks like starting the computer.
___	11. CPU	K.	Specific outlet that serves as a connection, or interfaces between a computer and other devices like digital cameras.
___	12. Bus Lines	L.	Designed so a device automatically works when it is plugged in to a system unit.
___	13. Plug and Play	M.	Data and information that enters a computer system.
___	14. Port	N.	Data and information that exits a computer system.
___	15. Clock Rate	O.	The first and most obvious input device of a microcomputer.

Multiple Choice

1. The _____ is the main body of a computer, containing a motherboard.
   a. System Unit
   b. Chassis
   c. Case
   d. Circuit Board

2. The _____ interprets program instructions and processes data by performing arithmetic and logical operations.
   a. Motherboard
   b. CPU
   c. RAM
   d. Memory

3. A microcomputer's speed is measured by _____ which is the cycles per second that a computer can perform its most basic tasks.
   a. Megahertz
   b. Clock Rate
   c. Storage capacity
   d. Amount of RAM

4. _____ are the pathways (or roads in our analogy) that transfer data and power between components inside of a computer, and sometimes between computers.
   a. Multi paths
   b. Wires
   c. Bus lines
   d. Streams

5. A two state system on a computer is called a _____ system.
   a. Two-way
   b. Digital
   c. Binary
   d. Two fold

6. _____ chips are preprogrammed and require no user intervention and serve to perform specialized internal tasks.
   a. ROM
   b. RAM
   c. CMOS
   d. Intel

7. Secondary storage is _____ which means it retains its data and information even when the system unit loses power.
   a. Stable
   b. Unstable
   c. Volatile
   d. Non-volatile

8. Motherboards have expansion _____ to receive expansion cards.
   a. Slots
   b. Plugs
   c. Ports
   d. Holes

9. _____ is data and information that enters a computer system and translated for processing.
   a. Electricity
   b. Keyboarding
   c. Output
   d. Input

10. A _____ functions as a pointing device that controls and positions the screen's cursor.
    a. Mouse
    b. Keyboard
    c. Keypad
    d. All of the above

1.01000001 | 2.01000010 | 3.01000010 | 4.01000011 | 5.01000011 | 6.01000001 | 7.01000100 | 8.01000001 . 9.0100010010.01000001

Blanks

The _____ is the inner workings or insides of a computer, essentially everything inside the box.

It has become common practice to refer to a microcomputer as a _____.

On the inside of a microcomputer, the core component is the system board commonly referred to as the _____.

The _____ interprets program instructions and processes data by performing arithmetic and logical operations.

_____ Architecture chips are designed for efficiency, and were the first 64 bit processors.

_____ are the pathways (or roads in our analogy) that transfer data and power between components inside of a computer, and sometimes between computers.

The ones and zeros are referred to as _____. When eight bits are combined, they become a _____.

A PSU is typically converts 100-120 volt or 220-240 volt _____ to a lower voltage _____.

In the system unit, primary storage is random access memory (RAM) in the form of _____.

_____ Chips are preprogrammed and require no user intervention and serve to perform specialized internal tasks like starting the computer.

Short Questions

What system do computers use so a device automatically works when it is plugged in to a system unit?

Devices that plug into computer systems units can be categorized as either an input device, or an output device, and are often called what?

What is the most common input device?

Why are cathode ray tubes still the most common computer monitor?

To covert printed text to digital text, businesses use a technology called what?

Name three input devices and three output devices?

three | understanding the os platform

- Operating Systems
- Processes / Multitasking
- Memory Management and Storage
- Disk Management
- File Management
- Networking
- Device Drivers
- Graphical User Interface
- Embedded Operating Systems
- Microsoft Windows® versus Mac OS®
- Major Operating Systems
- Open Source Operating Systems

Revolutionaries in Business

iPad's roots
Courtesy of National Museum of American History.

Name any product that dominates its industry on a global scale like **Microsoft Windows**. How about DeBeers, Nestlé, Toyota, maybe Monsanto? Nope, not like Microsoft's dominant operating system (OS). Windows is the operating system software (sometimes called a 'platform') that allows almost any application software to run on a personal computer. It's not like this just happened either, Windows has been the dominant platform for years. This begs the question; how did it happen?

It would be tempting to answer the question by saying Windows is the superior product relative to other operating systems, and that would be debatable. All major personal computer platforms are incredible products. The question still remains; why Microsoft Windows? The answer is that **business circumstances** determined that Windows would become the world-wide leader as a personal computer platform.

In 1980, Bill Gates and Paul Allen sold IBM a PC operating system called MS-DOS (Microsoft Disk Operating System 'MS-DOS', the precursor to Windows) for a one-time fee of $50,000. IBM in turn distributed their MS-DOS PCs worldwide. Gates kept the copyright on MS-DOS because he believed other computer companies would want MS-DOS as well. He was right; it was a brilliant decision. From then on through every evolution of Windows, Microsoft started their march as the dominant player in the OS market, and has never looked back.

The lesson is that information technology is deeply embedded in business. Business determines what happens in IT, not necessarily possessing a superior product. Having a superior product on the market is simply an expectation if it's likely to survive in business. Some would argue that Mac's operating system (Mac OS) is far superior to Windows, yet it only commands a small market segment. If one argues successfully that Mac OS is far superior, then why doesn't it command the market? Once again, business circumstances determined the outcome. Steve Jobs and Steve Wozniak pursued different business marketing plans and made far different strategic decisions then Gates and Allen. All of these men are brilliant, truly revolutionaries, and some of the most philanthropic people of all time.

Gates and Allen
Courtesy of Doug Wilson/Corbis Images.

BLACK & WHITE

A job or task a computer performs is called a process. When a computer can run more than one process at a time it is referred to as multi-tasking.

GRAY MATTER

Choosing an operating system is perhaps the single most important software choice an individual or business can make with far reaching implications.

Since an operating system is system software, it plays a large part in determining what sort of application software it will support and run.

BLACK & WHITE

Aside from multitasking, operating systems also coordinate and arrange the computer's memory, which includes cache, random access memory (RAM), registers, and virtual memory.

GRAY MATTER

Memory management can be analogized as a large business office full of employees that commit their work to paper.

At the end of the day, the paper needs to be stored in filing cabinets, and easily retrieved the next day. The filing cabinets need a system like alphabetical order for retrieval and enough space to hold the paper.

Understanding Operating Systems

When a computer is powered up, hundreds of system software programs automatically run to configure the computer so it operates as it was intended. One of the main tasks of these system programs is to load the **operating system (OS)**. An operating system is a collection of computer programs that administer the hardware and software of a computer so they work properly. The OS is the groundwork for all system software and performs important tasks like controlling and allocating memory, administrating input and output, and managing the filing system. Many times operating systems are referred to as **platforms**. Some of the most widely-used platforms are **Microsoft Windows, UNIX, Linux**, and **Mac OS**. Most operating system functions run with little or no user interaction.

Once an OS (system software) is up and running, the computer user can use application software like Microsoft Excel and Adobe Photoshop. Application softwares cannot run or even be installed without an operating system.

An operating system (system software) can be likened to freeways, roads, traffic lights, and parking structures in a very large city, whereas the traffic and people that use these resources would be considered the application software. Operating systems make sure that computer resources are used correctly and softwares do not conflict with each other, the same way a traffic light insures that cars don't collide. One basic task of an operating system is to store data and information, like document files and spreadsheets on a computer in the most efficient manner possible, similar to the way a modern parking garage allocates spaces for cars.

Processes / Multitasking

In the early days of computing, computers could only do one thing at a time. If a user wanted to print a spreadsheet and was already using a word processor, they would have to save their word

Courtesy of Getty Images; and courtesy of Roger Ressmeyer/Corbis Images.

CHAPTER 3 | Understanding the OS Platform

BLACK & WHITE

Files are displayed in a hierarchy, in a computer system, sometimes called a tree. A hierarchy is a way to rank and organize files. For example, a Word document would be in a folder, and the folder would be contained by the hard drive.

GRAY MATTER

Defragmentation is a program that reorganizes the hard disk. Files and folders still reside in the same place, but with the "clutter" removed, and therefore, the disk can perform more efficiently. Defragmentation also moves data to the inside concentric tracks of a hard drive so the read/write arm a moves a shorter distance and is therefore more economical.

Which one is right?
Courtesy of ShutterStock.

Courtesy of Cengage Learning.

> **BLACK & WHITE**
>
> Operating systems are in charge of device drivers that are computer programs that allow peripheral hardware devices like printers or scanners to interface with a computer system and work properly.

> **GRAY MATTER**
>
> "Plug and Play" drivers or programs that allow peripheral devices like printers and scanners to work are provided by the peripheral manufacturer to the operating system manufacturers so the user has a seamless and easy way to install their new device.

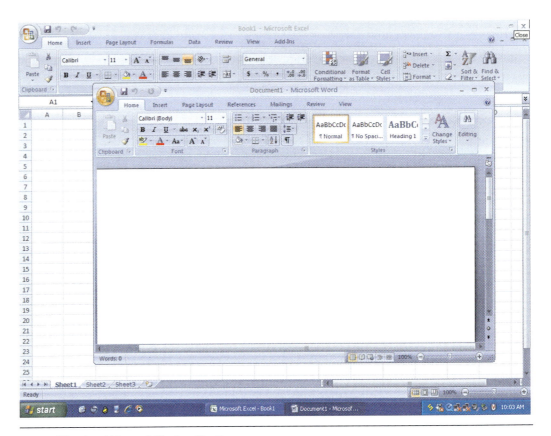

Microsoft Excel and Microsoft Word multitasking

document, shut down the word processing software, open the spreadsheet software, load the spreadsheet, print the spreadsheet, shut down the spreadsheet software, and return to the word processor. Switching from one application software to another was an arduous and time-consuming task. In the early 1990s, all of this changed with **multitasking**.

A job or task a computer performs is called a **process**. When a computer can run more than one process at a time it is referred to as multitasking. Modern operating systems feature multitasking which allows a user for example to run application software like Excel, Photoshop, and Word all at the same time. (Picture)

Although a modern computer user may take multitasking for granted, without it, computing would be difficult at best. Creating a strategic spreadsheet that reports on comparing different industries without the ability to run a browser to research information on the Internet would be completely impractical. Sharing data from one application software to another without both running at the same time is technically feasible, but certainly inefficient.

> **WHITE BOARD**
>
> Name the most widely used operating system.
> Name the four main operating systems in business.
> What determines if an operating system dominates the market?
> What did Bill Gates and Paul Allen do to make Windows number one?
> What did Jobs and Wozniak do differently that Gates and Allen?
> What is a process?
> What is multitasking and why is it important?
> Another name for an operating system (OS) is a _____.

Memory Management and Storage

Aside from multitasking, operating systems also coordinate and arrange the computer's memory, which includes **cache**, **random access memory (RAM)**, **registers**, and **virtual memory**. The operating system also facilitates **disk storage**. Simply put, memory retains digital data and information in a variety of ways. Below is a list of some of the types of memory and storage an operating system manages:

CPU Cache (CPU – central processing unit) is small, very quick memory because it stores copies of information and data from the most regularly used parts main memory. CPU cache helps decrease the time it takes to access memory. For instance, if your computer notices that you are a frequent Adobe Photoshop user, it starts to store common parts of Photoshop in CPU cache so it loads faster when it's turned on.

Random Access Memory (RAM) is primary storage. RAM is a type of storage that allows stored data to be accessed in any (random) order without physical movement of the storage media. RAM is considered **volatile** memory because its contents is lost if it is not saved to a **non-volatile** device like a hard drive. For instance, if an end-user creates a spreadsheet to do a what-if analysis but fails to save it when they are done, all of the work will be lost as if it never happened. Further, an end-user might open an existing spreadsheet and make changes. The changes are essentially held in RAM and need to be saved to a non-volatile device for the changes to be saved.

Registers are extremely fast very small amounts of memory used to quicken the implementation of computer programs by providing access to commonly used calculated values.

Virtual memory is memory the operating system uses to coordinate, track, and efficiently allocate the use of CPU cache, registers, RAM, and disk storage. Virtual memory is actually a technique that lets application programs like a spreadsheet use fragmented pieces of memory and makes it easier for large applications to use physical memory.

Disk storage is non-volatile, secondary storage that is recorded to a physical device, like a hard drive or optical disk with a read/write apparatus. For example, information is physically written to a disk storage device like a hard drive that has a spinning platter. The device records a positive or negative charge on the platter to represent a one or a zero, the only two possible choices on a computer's binary system.

> **BLACK & WHITE**
> Embedded operating systems are extremely reliable and since manufacturers know they will have little or no end user modification, they can be more meticulously tested for better reliability, which in turn leads to better cost control.

> **GRAY MATTER**
> To think of one operating system being better than another is wrong. It is more appropriate to think of one operating system being better for a particular job or application than another, which can be a critical business decision.

Courtesy of Prentice-Hall, Inc.

Disk Management

Operating systems are responsible for reading and writing data and information onto a disk, typically a hard drive, optical device, or a solid state storage device. The OS needs to be able to save, or write information to a disk in the most efficient manner possible so it can be read files efficiently and therefore quickly. A general way to do this is (with a Microsoft platform) to create a sort of

BLACK & WHITE
Open source software is when software's source code or programming is open to anyone who cares to access and perhaps even modify it.

GRAY MATTER
As with any aspect in business, open source software will either flourish or fade based primarily on economic reasons.

table of contents for the disk called a **file allocation table**, or **FAT**. The FAT directs the read/write arm of the hard drive to where data exists and accesses it upon the user's request.

The drawback of FAT is that when data and information, or files are deleted on the hard disk, and new information is added, the disk ends up with fragments of information scattered all over. The answer to this is **defragmentation**, which is a program that reorganizes the hard disk. Files and folders still reside in the same place, but with the "clutter" removed, and therefore, the disk can perform more efficiently. Defragmentation also moves data to the inside concentric tracks of a hard drive so the read/write arm a moves a shorter distance and is therefore more economical. Unfortunately, defragmentation is a lengthy process and needs to be performed on a regular basis to keep the FAT well-organized.

Maybe a better way to think of defragmentation is to consider laundry. Imagine taking all of your laundry out of the dryer and simply throwing it all over your bedroom. The advantage is that you save a lot of time putting your clothing away, the disadvantage is that it takes time to find what you want to wear. Essentially the operating system throws information all over the hard drive like throwing laundry in your room; granted it's fast, but becomes disorganized after a while and the hard drive struggles to find information after a while. That's where defragmentation comes in, organizing all the 'laundry' on the hard drive.

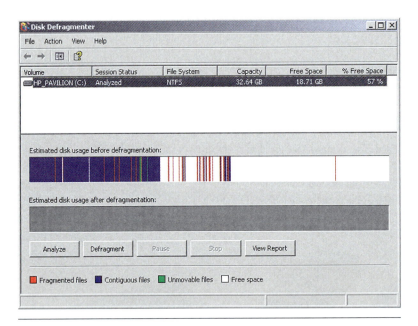

Defragmentation should be done on a regular basis

File Management

All operating systems feature file management; a way to store and organize a user's work represented by computer files to the memory of a computer. Operating systems are made up of a hierarchy of directories, (more commonly called "folders"). Computer files can be considered as the modern counterpart of the files of printed papers that conventionally exist in business offices. A user for example might create their résumé in Microsoft Word 2007 and its file name would be resume.docx. Hundreds of different file formats exist representing programs, system software files, etc.

Microsoft Windows® represents its file management system visually with a **graphical user interface (GUI)** environment. (Picture) It's best to simply think of this as the inner workings of a physical filing cabinet, which contains file folders which house paper files. A **file manager** is a computer program that displays a user interface to work with file systems.

Generally, file managers can create, search, open, view, print, rename, copy, delete, and move files. File managers also allow a user to change properties and attributes of files, and even set security permissions. Files are displayed in a **hierarchy**, in a computer system, sometimes called a **tree**. A hierarchy is a way to rank and organize files. For example, a Word document would be in a folder, and the folder would be contained by the hard drive. Modern file managers have started to take on the look of web browsers, with forward and back navigation buttons for a more universal feel throughout the computing system.

BLACK & WHITE
Once a product or software is accepted by the market, it is called diffusion.

GRAY MATTER
Diffusion is not limited to a business environment alone, it can also be seen in social mores.

WHITE BOARD
Name different types of memory an operating system coordinates and their functions.
Describe defragmentation and why it is used.
What is FAT?
Why is defrag' like laundry?

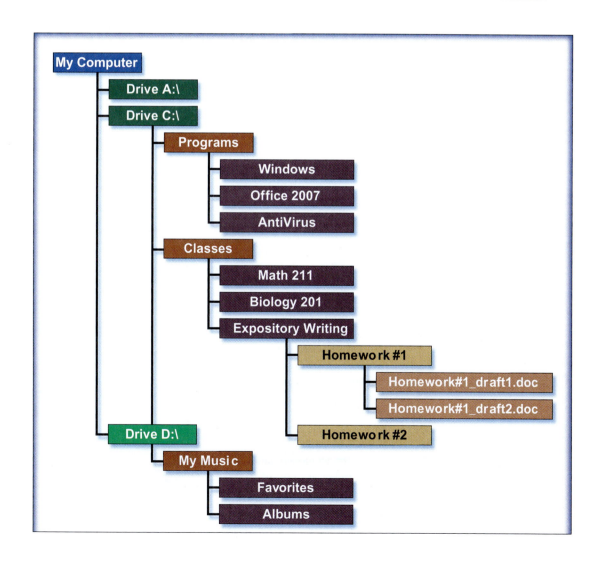

> **BLACK & WHITE**
>
> Leading and following are considered business strategies, and one is not better than the other, although each has its advantages and disadvantages.

> **GRAY MATTER**
>
> Leading and following play a part in both strategic and tactical business decision making.

Networking

Computers that are not connected to any other computer are referred to as **stand-alone**. Simply stated, when a computer is connected to one or more computers it is called a network. A network of just two computers is exponentially more powerful than a stand-alone system because of its ability to share resources, like software, storage and hardware.

Consider four stand-alone computers that need to have the capability to print and scan documents. Essentially, that means all four computers need to have their own printers and scanners (four printers and four scanners). On the other hand, a network would connect all four boxes to a centralized computer called a server. Once the server is up and running, you only need one printer and one scanner attached to the server that all four computers can access. Also, computer files reside on the server that the other four computers can access and facilitate collaboration.

Operating systems need to be able to offer networking, and do so through a set of rules called **transmission control protocol** and **Internet protocol (TCP/IP)**. TCP/IP is simply a set of rules for transferring information from one computer to another, not unlike traffic lights that insure safety on city streets. A traffic light is timed and lets a specific amount of traffic pass through an intersection; TCP/IP does the same electronically by breaking up files into **packets** and passing them from one computer to another. When the packets arrive at a networked or receiving computer, TCP/IP ensures that the files are intact and usable by rebuilding the packets into the original file. The Internet is the world's largest network and uses TCP/IP to transfer and receive files.

Operating systems many times refer to stand-alone computers, but it is important to note that networks are run by network operating systems (NOS) which are a type of system software that controls an entire network of computers which is accessed by many users.

Device Drivers

Operating systems are in charge of **device drivers** that are computer programs that allow peripheral hardware devices like printers or scanners to interface with a computer system and work properly. The device driver or driver for short allows the OS to communicate with peripheral hardware. For instance, when a document is printed, data is sent to the printer from the operating system by employing a specific driver.

In the past, when a new peripheral device was plugged into a computer (like a printer), it required the user to manually install drivers from a disk supplied by manufacturers that would essentially reconfigure parts of an operating system to insure proper operation. A modern OS has **Plug-and-Play**, which is preloaded and configured drivers that peripheral manufacturers have previously supplied to the operating system manufacturer, so when a new device is detected, no driver installation is necessary, because it is already loaded on the operating system.

In business, when a peripheral manufacturer makes printers, external hard drives, or any other device, it is in their best interest to use standard drivers. In 1996, **Universal Serial Bus (USB)** ports were developed and gained traction with Microsoft and today are considered a standard, and essentially use the same drivers that many other manufacturers employ. Peripheral consumers now consider USB as part of their purchasing criteria so they are insured smooth operation and seamless integration and installation.

USB drive
Courtesy of Wolverine, Inc.

Graphical User Interface

Obviously, operating systems do an enormous amount of processing, organization, and administering in the background without user interaction, but still needs to provide a way for a user to interact with the computer. The answer is to provide a **graphical user interface**, or **GUI**. A GUI is a presentation on a computer monitor that allows a user to interact with a computer and the devices connected to it. Many GUIs have **ic**ons, and other visual indicators like menus that launch programs like PowerPoint, documents, and many other requests from a user without having to issue programming commands with the click of a pointing device, like a mouse. GUIs can be configured and personalized to suit a user's needs in an infinite variety of ways. (Picture)

Embedded Operating Systems

It is easy to forget that not all operating systems are made for personal computers. Many devices and appliances that rely on computing need **embedded operating systems**, like cash registers, automatic teller machines (ATMs), microwave ovens, and specialized handheld devices to name a few. **Embedded computing** refers to a computing system or device that performs a dedicated function. In most cases, these systems cannot be modified by the end user. Embedded operating systems are very compact and efficient, and typically do not have as many functions that non-embedded OS have because they do not need them.

Embedded operating systems are highly modified, basically stripped down version of larger operating systems that manufacturers produce for specific tasks and devices, like a Blackberry®, Android®, or an iPhone. Typically, embedded operating systems are extremely reliable and since manufacturers know they will have little or no end user modification, they can be more meticulously tested for better reliability, which in turn leads to better cost control.

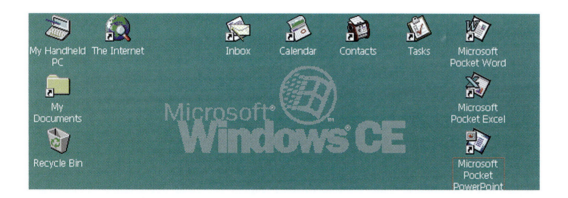

Microsoft Windows® versus Mac OS®

Choosing the right operating system whether personally or in business can be difficult. Two major players in operating systems are Microsoft, which dominates the market with its Windows platforms, and Mac. Many experts will argue vehemently against one or the other, while sometimes ignoring core issues. It is certainly true that both operating systems can claim a clear advantage over the other, for instance; Mac platforms are far better for graphics than Microsoft, yet Microsoft has a deep-rooted advantage in the business applications market. Mac might boast of a superior architecture and ease-of-use, while Microsoft boasts of better support and innovation. The core questions an end-user should be asking is what type of platform they are most likely to use, especially in business and which one will give them a clear competitive advantage.

Courtesy of LWA-JDC/Corbis Images; and courtesy of Jose Louis Peleaz/Corbis Images.

A college graduate from a business school might find out that the accounting firm where they are hired uses Microsoft exclusively, where a student from a graphic design college finds out their future firm uses Mac exclusively. The fact is, both platforms are excellent products and well-established in the marketplace. Regardless of your preference, it is well worth noting what platform you are most often and likely to use. Arguing which platform is better is a valueless pursuit. Arguing which platform is a better fit for a particular application should be the end-user's focus.

The fact is, according to MarketShare.com, Microsoft Windows products dominate the microcomputer operating system market with over 90%, followed by Mac OS with over 7%, and then by Linux with just under 2%.

Microsoft Windows	90%
Mac OS	7%
Linux	2%

Major Operating Systems

Windows is a proprietary graphical user interface-based (GUI) operating system developed by Microsoft Corporation and has dominated the personal computer operating system market. Microsoft was founded by **Bill Gates** and **Paul Allen** in 1975. The name Windows refers to a family of operating system versions from Microsoft's whose current version is called **Windows 7**.

The first version of Windows (1.0) was released in 1985 to compete with Apple's GUI operating system and was deficient in functionality and did not initially gain market acceptance. Microsoft's previous operating system (non-GUI) was called Disk Operating System (DOS) and Windows simply extended DOS functionality with a GUI interface. Throughout the years, Windows has been upgraded and has enjoyed worldwide acceptance.

Mac OS is a proprietary graphical user interface-based (GUI) operating system developed by Apple Inc., formerly Apple Computer, Inc. in 1984. Originally, Apple, which was started by **Steve Jobs** and **Steve Wozniak**, downplayed their operating system to make their computers seem more user-friendly and avoid comparisons with Microsoft's existing operating system. (At the time call Disk Operating System (DOS)). Apple eventually named their operating system Mac Operating System, or Mac OS for short. Mac's current operating system is called **Snow Leopard**.

CHAPTER 3 | Understanding the OS Platform

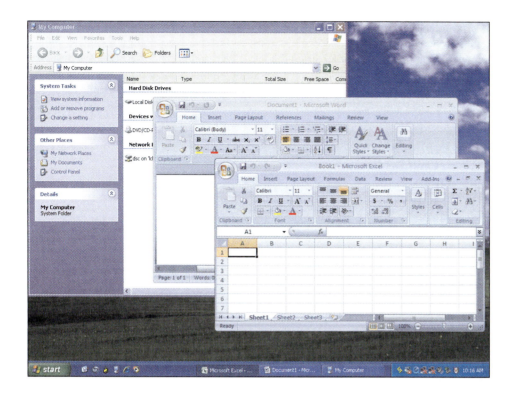

Mac OS was a paradigm in operating systems at the time of its introduction as it required almost no intervention from its user and was the first OS to be completely GUI based. Because of its architecture, use of memory, and clever interface, Mac has evolved into a very powerful operating system that excels in graphics, audio, video, and any other memory based application software.

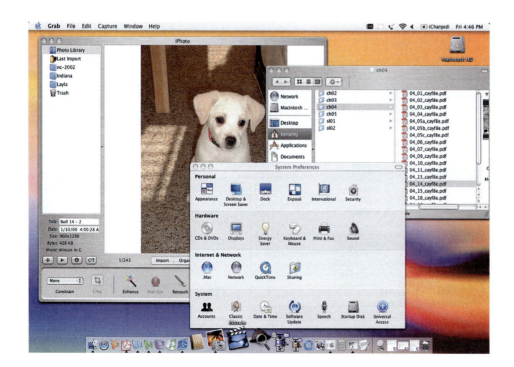

UNIX is a proprietary operating system developed in the 1960s and 1970s Bell Labs. Today's UNIX operating systems are split into various versions, developed over time by AT&T as well as various commercial computing vendors. During the late 1970s and early 1980s, UNIX's influence in academic circles led to large-scale adoption of UNIX by commercial startups, the most notable of which is Sun Microsystems. UNIX platforms are popular for large processing applications like credit card transaction and approval.

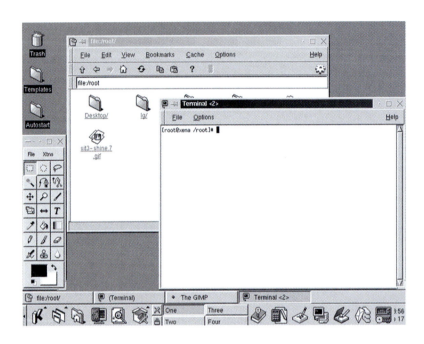

Although a company called the SCO Group owns the UNIX System V Code (UNIX programming language), it does not own the UNIX trademark. It is being contested in court who owns the rights to UNIX and what they are allowed to do with it. SCO claims IBM unlawfully donated part of UNIX to develop Linux to bolster their own Linux-based business. Because of this dispute, it can have a large repercussions industry wide when deciding which platform is right for your business.

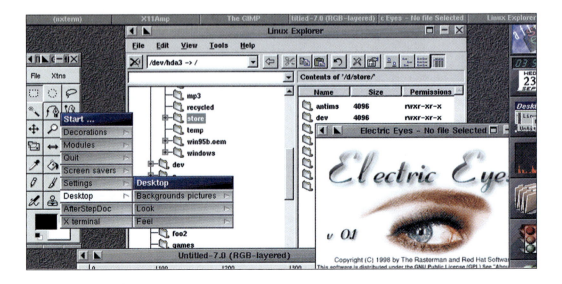

Linux was originally started by **Linus Torvalds** and is a non-proprietary UNIX-like computer operating system. Linux is one of the most prominent examples of free software and open source development. Linux source code, the programming that makes it run can be modified, used, and redistributed by anyone, freely. Largely known for its use in servers, Linux has found support of corporations like IBM, Sun Microsystems, and Hewlett-Packard, and is used as the OS for a wide array of computers, including desktops, supercomputers, and mobile phones.

> **WHITE BOARD**
>
> Name the four major operating systems.
> Which operating system is most widely used in business?
> Which operating system is best?
> Is Windows better than the Mac OS?
> Why is UNIX so different from Mac OS and Windows?
> What are the advantages of the Mac OS?
> What are the advantages of Windows?
> What are the advantages of Linux?

Open Source Operating Systems

Open source software is when software's source code or programming is open to anyone who cares to access and perhaps even modify it. For example, the programming that makes up Microsoft Windows 7® is closed, and cannot be modified, or even accessed by an end user. Microsoft Windows 7® is considered **proprietary** software. The programming that makes up the Linux platform is open source, and can be modified, changed, and possibly improved by whoever has the skill and inclination. Further, once the open source code is modified, it can usually be distributed free of charge, and even changed and improved again. Linux is considered **non-proprietary** software.

Business implications of open source software are far reaching; for instance, compare Microsoft Windows 7® and Linux. Both are both very good operating platforms, both will run essentially any kind of application software. Microsoft Windows 7® is closed source, proprietary, and costs hundreds of dollars while Linux is open source, non-proprietary, and essentially free. The obvious question is why does the Microsoft Windows family of operating systems dominate the operating system market share?

Consider open source software from an economic standpoint. For example, a software developer creates proprietary software that is not open source and sells it in the business marketplace and the new software flourishes. The software developer's main asset is her **intellectual property**, essentially her innate ability to create business solution software that is better than anyone else can produce, or at least good enough to be very profitable. She recognizes the **demand** for her software is high and understands that the **supply** of people that can do what she does is very low, which means she can sell her product at a higher **clearing** price.

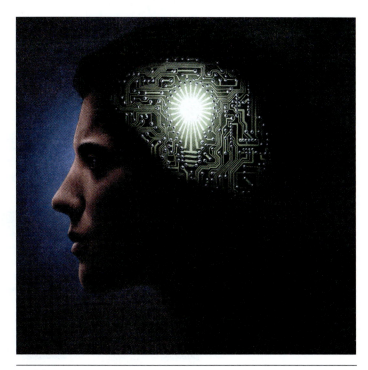

Courtesy of Prentice-Hall, Inc.

Now consider the same scenario in the example above, but make the same software non-proprietary. Once the software becomes non-proprietary, anyone can copy it and market it themselves with no fear of copyright infringement. In effect, what the developer has done by making her software open source is increase the supply of people that can do what she does, and given the same high demand, actually lowered the clearing price and became less profitable. This is not to say anything good or bad occurred, they are simply the factual realities of economic principals.

Think about a developing country that employs tens of thousands of computers to support its nation's infrastructure, like health care, traffic systems, and tax collection. Each of these computers requires an operating system, and proprietary operating systems cost money. Multiply the cost of one proprietary operating system times the tens of thousands of computers and you have a very significant dollar amount. Multiply the cost again every time the operating system releases a newer version. What if that same country wanted to eliminate these costs by using a non-proprietary, open source operating system like Linux? Operating platform costs for that country would plummet.

Why is it that all countries don't adopt non-proprietary operating systems if cost reduction is so dramatic? One of the things that can happen in open source software is the loss of standardization. Good or bad, proprietary operating systems have a built-in guarantee that it will work consistently, at least within its own version. Although this may seem rigid, many user and software developers depend on operating systems to remain consistent so they can rest assured that their application software will be supported. Open source operating systems on the other hand suffer from having so many modifications made from so many different sources that some systems can support certain software and others cannot. One version of Linux might not support particular application software whereas another version of Linux might support the exact same application software.

As technology hurdles forward, businesses have to make critical decisions whether to adopt new technologies like an upgraded operating system. Once a product or software for instance is

Courtesy of Clark Quin Photography.

accepted by the market, it is called **diffusion**. In the case of an operating system like Microsoft Windows 7®, diffusion does not happen overnight. Some computing products achieve diffusion only to lose it as other products and software take its place. For instance, versions of Windows reached diffusion only to be replaced by new versions of Windows as the product evolved. Diffusion doesn't happen overnight, it depends on businesses to become **early adopters**. An early adopter in business feels like the first version of a product will give them a decided advantage over their competitors. Many businesses are early adopters, often called **technology leaders**, and many prefer to **technology followers**. A business that leads is one that might choose to upgrade computer system hardware and software the day a new product becomes available. For instance, leaders might upgrade their operating platforms from Windows XP to Windows 7® the first day Windows 7® is available. A leader may also be the first to change platforms from Windows to Linux.

Business followers are a bit more cautious, preferring to hold off on technology decisions until they can gather more information. They might contend that brand new products have not been tested rigorously enough in the business environment, and therefore are more comfortable waiting for the product to improve and sometimes wait for years.

Leading and following are considered **business strategies**, and one is not better than the other, although each has its advantages and disadvantages. What if a new operating system truly does give the early adopter an advantage? The business follower will fall behind. What if the early adopter finds there was no advantage, especially when time and cost are factored in? The follower, by essentially doing nothing will have the decided advantage.

Summary

A platform can run more than one process at a time which is referred to a multitasking and allows a microcomputer to run multiple application programs at once, like Microsoft Word and Adobe Photoshop. Platforms typically use a graphical user interface and are in charge of memory management, storage, disk management, and file management.

An **operating system** or **platform** is the most important system software, without which application software cannot exist. Different platforms offer different features and it's not unusual for midsize to large businesses to use multiple platforms. From a microcomputer standpoint, operating systems have the same criteria for selection as any other information technology; is it the right tool and does it afford a competitive advantage?

Matching

Match each key term in the left column with the most accurate definition in the right column.

B	1. CPU Cache	A.	A job or task a computer performs.
A	2. Process	B.	Small, very quick memory that stores copies of information and data from the most regularly used parts main memory.
M	3. Windows	C.	Type of storage that allows stored data to be accessed in any order.
N	4. Mac OS	D.	Extremely fast very small amounts of memory used to quicken the implementation of computer programs.
O	5. UNIX	E.	Non-volatile, secondary storage that is recorded to a physical device.
L	6. Embedded Computing	F.	Memory the operating system uses to coordinate, track, and efficiently allocate the use of CPU cache.
D	7. Registers	G.	Way to store and organize a user's work represented by computer files to the memory of a computer.
E	8. Disk Storage	H.	Responsible for reading and writing data and information onto a disk, typically a hard drive or a solid state storage device.
F	9. Virtual Memory	I.	Computers that are not connected to any other computer.
C	10. RAM	J.	Type of system software that controls an entire network of computers which is accessed by many users.
G	11. File Management	K.	Computer programs that allow peripheral hardware devices like printers or scanners to interface with a computer.
H	12. Operating Systems	L.	Refers to a computing system or device that performs a dedicated function.
K	13. Device Drivers	M.	Proprietary graphical user interface-based (GUI) operating system developed by Microsoft Corporation.
J	14. NOS	N.	Proprietary graphical user interface-based (GUI) operating system developed by Apple Inc.
I	15. Stand alone	O.	Proprietary operating system developed in the 1960s and 1970s Bell Labs.

Multiple Choice

1. Many times operating systems are referred to as _____.
   a. Multi-software
   b. Applications
   c. Firewalls
   d. Platforms

2. A job or task a computer performs is called a _____.
   a. Software
   b. Process
   c. Multitask
   d. Thread

3. Files are displayed in a _____ in a computer system, sometimes called a tree.
   a. GUI
   b. Row
   c. Hierarchy
   d. All of the above

4. A _____ is a computer program that displays a user interface to work with file systems.
   a. File manager
   b. Application manager
   c. System manager
   d. Software manager

5. Computers that are not connected to any other computer are referred to as _____.
   a. Nonproprietary
   b. Connectionless
   c. Networked
   d. Stand-alone

6. Operating systems need to be able to offer networking, and do so through a set of rules called _____.
   a. TCP/IP
   b. Ruling behaviors
   c. RAM
   d. Computing policies

7. Which of the following is not computer memory?
   a. Cache
   b. Virtual
   c. Disk storage
   d. TCP/IP

8. A(n) _____ is a collection of computer programs that administer the hardware and software of a computer so they work properly.
   a. Suite
   b. Software suite
   c. Operating system
   d. Compilation

9. _____ is primary storage.
   a. Hard drive storage
   b. CMOS
   c. RAM
   d. Solid state

10. Once an OS is up and running, the computer user can use _____ software.
    a. Application
    b. Firmware
    c. CMOS
    d. All of the above

68 CHAPTER 3 | Understanding the OS Platform

Blanks

An operating system is a collection of computer programs that administer the _hardware_ and _software_ of a computer so they work properly.

Switching from one application software to another was an arduous and time-consuming task. In the early 1990s, all of this changed with _multitasking_.

A job or task a computer performs is called a _process_.

RAM is a type of storage that allows stored data to be accessed in any (random) order without physical movement of the storage media.

Registers are extremely fast very small amounts of memory used to quicken the implementation of computer programs by providing access to commonly used calculated values.

Virtual memory is actually a technique that lets application programs like a spreadsheet use fragmented pieces of memory and makes it easier for large applications to use physical memory.

The _FAT_ directs the read/write arm of the hard drive to where data exists and accesses it upon the user's request.

Microsoft Windows® represents its file management system visually with a _GUI_ environment.

Computers that are not connected to any other computer are referred to as _stand-alone_.

Embedded computing refers to a computing system or device that performs a dedicated function.

Short Questions

What is the most widely used operating system in the world?

Which operating system(s) is considered open source and non-proprietary?

What is it called when a product gains acceptance in a market?

What is the purpose of device drivers?

What program is used to reorganize a hard disk?

Why is Random Access Memory considered volatile?

four | storage

Data Storage
Ones and Zeros
Physical Storage Characteristics
Characteristics of Storage Media
Business Storage Strategies
Data Archiving and Backup Strategies

Business Network Options

Imagine a large financial services business (FSB) with 1,500 employees, each with a computer on their desk that is networked to a large bank of server computers. All of these employees use these on-site centralized servers to save their work like spreadsheets, databases, and documents, share resources like printers and scanners as well as collaborate on business projects. Now start thinking about what it costs for the servers. Servers are expensive, and the people to keep them running are even more expensive. Moore's Law indicates that the servers are depreciating in speed and space in a scant 18 months.

The question is; can FSB reduce the cost of the servers and avoid its depreciating assets? The answer is yes. Mass storage companies specialize in helping companies by providing off-site servers that the financial services business will lease instead of own. This method yields all kinds of advantages. One advantage is that FSB will no longer have to own a depreciating asset (the servers that previously served their network). That becomes the problem of the mass storage com-

> **BLACK & WHITE**
>
> There are two main types of storage; primary storage and secondary storage. Primary storage can be analogized as what a user is currently working on and secondary storage is where the user stores their work when they are finished.

> **GRAY MATTER**
>
> Computer storage is the variety of ways a computer system can store (save) data and information. Stored information includes spreadsheets, documents, graphics, software, drivers, or any of the hundreds of file types used by a computer. Computer storage is very similar to a filing cabinet. Filing cabinets contain file folders that hold paper while a computer has electronic folders that hold computer files.

The basic components of every computer system
Courtesy of Dell Computer Corporation.

pany. Another advantage is that FSB only leases as much memory as they need. For instance, when they owned their own servers, they may have purchased 25 terabytes for their 1,500 employees to share when in reality they found out that they only needed 14 terabytes. FSB can now lease exactly 14 terabytes from the mass storage company. When FSB had their servers 'in-house', they overspent for an additional 11 terabytes they never used. If FSB needs more space from the mass storage company, they simply buy as they go.

The mass storage company offers all the same network services FSB comes to expect, like backup, restoring files and anything else that good network administrator(s) provide. Using off-site mass storage begs a new question; can they provide the same services in a timely manner? What if an important spreadsheet file that contains budget information is accidently deleted by the user?

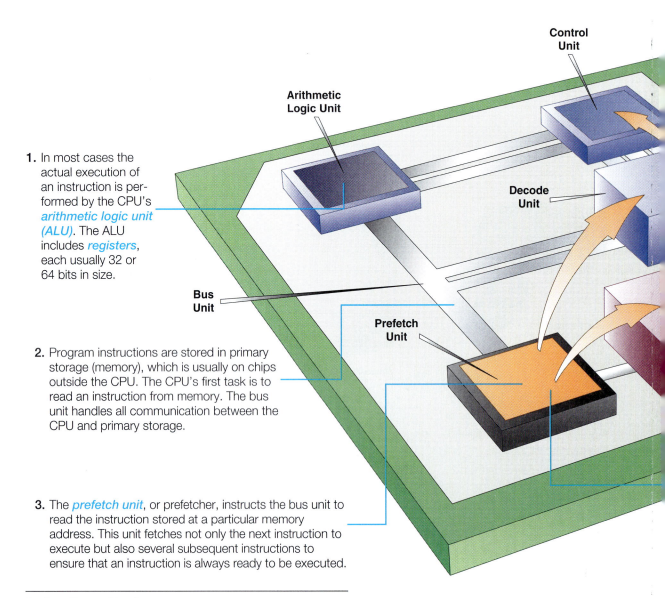

1. In most cases the actual execution of an instruction is performed by the CPU's *arithmetic logic unit (ALU)*. The ALU includes *registers*, each usually 32 or 64 bits in size.

2. Program instructions are stored in primary storage (memory), which is usually on chips outside the CPU. The CPU's first task is to read an instruction from memory. The bus unit handles all communication between the CPU and primary storage.

3. The *prefetch unit*, or prefetcher, instructs the bus unit to read the instruction stored at a particular memory address. This unit fetches not only the next instruction to execute but also several subsequent instructions to ensure that an instruction is always ready to be executed.

Courtesy of Pearson Education.

Can the mass storage company restore it in a timely manner? Now that all of FSB's data and information reside off-site, do they trust that their data and information is secure? These are all important questions to pose when making such a tactical and strategic decision.

There are many more important decisions to make when deciding to contract with a mass storage company, but one in particular; if FSB decides to use off-site mass storage for their networks, what happens to the **people** that administered the network previously? Technically, they are no longer needed, and as a matter of fact, if FSB lets them go, they have actually saved more money

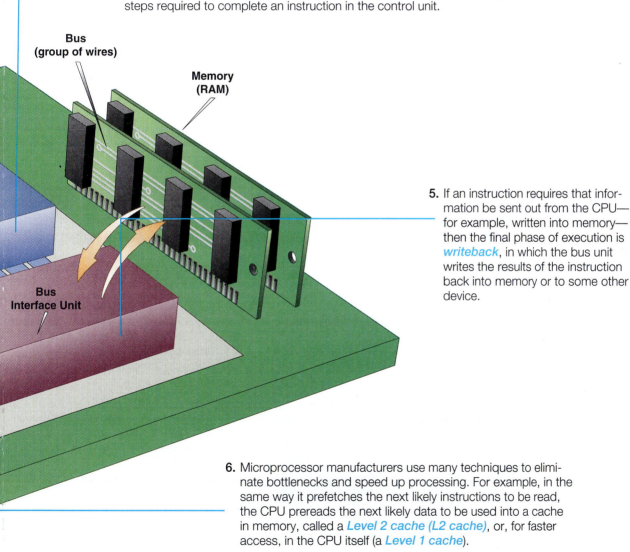

4. The *decode unit* takes the instruction read by the prefetcher and translates it into a form suitable for the CPU's internal processing. It does this by looking up the steps required to complete an instruction in the control unit.

5. If an instruction requires that information be sent out from the CPU—for example, written into memory—then the final phase of execution is *writeback*, in which the bus unit writes the results of the instruction back into memory or to some other device.

6. Microprocessor manufacturers use many techniques to eliminate bottlenecks and speed up processing. For example, in the same way it prefetches the next likely instructions to be read, the CPU prereads the next likely data to be used into a cache in memory, called a *Level 2 cache (L2 cache)*, or, for faster access, in the CPU itself (a *Level 1 cache*).

> **BLACK & WHITE**
>
> Random Access Memory (RAM) is primary storage that is temporary and volatile. RAM is a type of storage that allows stored data to be accessed in any order without physical movement of the storage media or device.

> **GRAY MATTER**
>
> The easiest way to make a computer faster is to add random access memory, where "work is done". Many times adding RAM is a less expensive alternative to replacing slow computers.

by choosing the mass storage option. Sometime using technology eliminates jobs. The question still remains; what happens to the people whose jobs have been lost?

Data Storage

Computer **storage** is the variety of ways a computer system can store (save) data and information. Stored information includes spreadsheets, documents, graphics, software, drivers, or any of the hundreds of file types used by a computer. Computer storage is very similar to a filing cabinet. Filing cabinets contain file folders that hold paper while a computer has electronic folders that hold computer files.

If you think about it, almost everything a business owns can be stored on a computer in one fashion or another. Businesses own **tangible property** and intellectual property. Tangible property includes things like desks, computers, tractors, and other physical items. **Intellectual property** is the legal claim a business has to names, inventions, and ideas.

Tangible property can be stored on a computer, or at least records of it, like maintenance records for a company car, a digital picture of real estate, programming that operates a physical assembly line, architectural plans of a business' building, and many, many others.

Intellectual property can include a boundless amount of ideas only limited by the **imagination.** Lyrics to music, legal contracts, corporate secrets, policies and procedures, instructions to build a certain type of car, programming for a microwave oven, gaming programs, employee profiles and work history, and anything else that makes up an organization.

In the past, companies kept their information on paper which was easily lost, like being consumed in a fire, or simply misplaced. The consequences were devastating, and often sounded the death knell of the organization. When information began to be stored digitally, many believed it was just as unsafe as paper, and maybe even more risky. At least paper is tangible and maybe stored in a fireproof safe. Digital storage meant risking company information on a storage device that was often untested, or worse, that the information itself could become corrupted, easily deleted, quickly stolen, and a host of other pitfalls.

As storage devices became more reliable, less expensive, and safer, organizations started to store all of their information digitally, both tangible and intellectual, but still realized without well thought out computer storage plans, its information could still be at risk. Building codes require structures to be built with emergency exits, fire abatement devices, and many other safety features to ensure the safety of the building's occupants. Like building codes, storage plans include when, where, and what should be digitally stored outlined by risk assessment to ensure the safety of an organizations data and information. Keep in mind that a business' existence is at stake should these critical computer storage strategies, policies, and procedures are ignored.

Courtesy of Bill Bachman/Photo Researchers, Inc.

There are two main types of storage; **primary storage** and **secondary storage**. Primary storage can be analogized as what a user is currently working on and secondary storage is where the user stores their work when they are finished.

Random Access Memory (RAM) is primary storage that is temporary and volatile. RAM is a type of storage that allows stored

Ram can increase performance
Courtesy of Terra Nova Design.

> **BLACK & WHITE**
>
> Microcomputer systems are binary. Binary means something is made up of two parts, and in this case, either a "1" or a "0". When a user inputs data or information into a computer system, regardless of content, it is always converted into ones and zeros so the computer can work with it.

data to be accessed in any order without physical movement of the storage media or device. RAM is like working at physical desk that has paper spread all around. The person at the desk can read, edit, or update any of the papers on the desk (primary storage), and when they are finished, return the paper into file folders and store them appropriately inside a filing cabinet (secondary storage).

Most RAM (**primary storage**) is **volatile**, which means it requires the computer to supply power for it to be used. If the computer loses power without the contents in RAM saved to secondary storage, all of its contents will be lost. If a user is in the process of developing a budget spreadsheet, which resides in RAM, and the computer unexpectedly loses power, all of the contents of the budget that have not previously been saved to secondary storage will be lost.

Secondary storage is **non-volatile** which means it retains its data and information even after the computer system is turned off. Secondary storage memory is not directly accessible to the central processing unit (CPU) of the computer so it needs to make use of input/output channels. Secondary storage is typically slower than primary storage but usually has higher storage capacity which makes it ideal for storing data and information.

> **GRAY MATTER**
>
> Secondary storage is non-volatile which means it retains its data and information even after the computer system is turned off. Secondary storage memory is not directly accessible to the central processing unit (CPU) of the computer so it needs to make use of input/output channels.

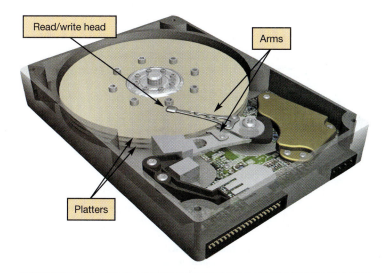

Typical hard drive
Courtesy of Prentice-Hall, Inc.

76   CHAPTER 4 | Storage

> **WHITE BOARD**
>
> Describe primary storage and its associated devices.
> Describe secondary storage and its associated devices.
> Describe the concept of intellectual and tangible property.
> What are some of the advantages to off-site networked mass storage?
> What would you do with the network administrators at FSB?

Ones and Zeros

Microcomputer systems are **binary**. Binary means something is made up of two parts, and in this case, either a "1" or a "0". When a user inputs data or information into a computer system, regardless of content, it is always converted into ones and zeros so the computer can work with it. The ones and zeros are referred to as **bits**. When eight bits are combined, they become a byte. Bytes can then be used to represent characters like the alphabet or numbers. It is these ones and zeros that are stored in secondary storage.

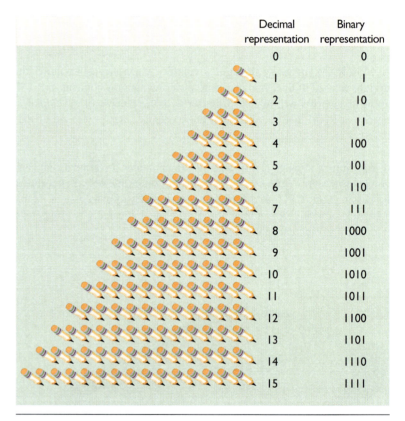

In a binary coding scheme, numbers are represented by unique patterns of 0s and 1s
Courtesy of Prentice-Hall, Inc.

Physical storage media represent ones and zeros with positive or negative electromagnetic charges. A negative charge represents a zero (bit), and a positive charge represents a one (bit). To save the ones and zeros, the system needs to be able to record, or **write** them on the appropriate media, which in turn needs to be accessed, or **read** for future use. The most common way to read and write to digital media is on to a spinning magnetic disk with a "read/write" device, so the bits and bytes will "stick to it".

Term	Size	Roughly...
Byte	8 bits	Typically represents one character.
Kilobyte	1,024 bytes	One thousand bytes
Megabyte	1,024 kilobytes	One thousand kilobytes
Gigabyte	1,024 megabytes	One thousand megabytes
Terabyte	1,024 gigabytes	One thousand gigabytes
Petabyte	1,024 terabytes	One thousand terabytes
Exabyte	1,024 petabytes	One thousand petabytes
Zettabyte	1,024 exabytes	One thousand exabytes
Yottabyte	1,024 zettabyte	One thousand zettabytes

BLACK & WHITE

Most microcomputers use the American Standard Code for Information Interchange (ASCII) coding scheme to represent bytes. In ASCII, there are 256 possible combinations of eight bits to a byte. Only 95 characters in the ASCII set are printable.

GRAY MATTER

A storage device needs a read/write head to scan across the surface of a spinning disk to record and/or access data and information. The read/write head looks similar to a record player's arm.

Most microcomputers use the **American Standard Code for Information Interchange (ASCII)** coding scheme to represent bytes. In ASCII, there are 256 possible combinations of eight bits to a byte. Only 95 characters in the ASCII set are printable. Not all computing systems use ASCII; larger computers like mainframes which are typically extremely large data processing systems use a coding scheme called **Extended Binary Coded Decimal Interchange Code (EBCDIC)**. Further, some computing systems are designed to support international languages like Chinese and Japanese which need to deal with special characters other than the English alphabet. These computers use a code scheme call **Unicode**.

American Standard Code for Information Interchange (ASCII) coding scheme							
01000001	A	01001110	N	01100001	a	01101110	n
01000010	B	01001111	O	01100010	b	01101111	o
01000011	C	01010000	P	01100011	c	01110000	p
01000100	D	01010001	Q	01100100	d	01110001	q
01000101	E	01010010	R	01100101	e	01110010	r
01000110	F	01010011	S	01100110	f	01110011	s
01000111	G	01010100	T	01100111	g	01110100	t
01001000	H	01010101	U	01101000	h	01110101	u
01001001	I	01010110	V	01101001	i	01110110	v
01001010	J	01010111	W	1101010	j	01110111	w
01001011	K	01011000	X	01101011	k	01111000	x
01001100	L	01011001	Y	01101100	l	01111001	y
01001101	M	01011010	Z	01101101	m	01111010	z

BLACK & WHITE

Storage capacity refers to the amount of data and information a storage device can hold.

Access time refers to the amount of time it takes to get data and information from a storage device to its user.

GRAY MATTER

Organizations that offer storage solutions make difficult decisions every day, weighing the dropping cost of storage against pricing their services.

Physical Storage Characteristics

A storage device needs a **read/write head** to scan across the surface of a spinning disk to record and/or access data and information. The read/write head looks similar to a record player's arm. Since the information is electronic, the read/write head is typically an electromagnet that reads or writes electromagnetic charges that make up the bits and bytes. Unlike a record player, the read/write head "flies" above the disk platter and reads the positive and negative charges on the disk without actually touching it.

Magnetic Disks

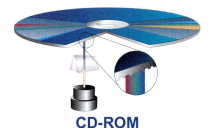
CD-ROM

DVD-ROM

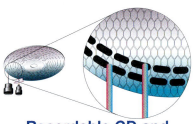
Recordable CD and DVD Drives

Courtesy of Prentice-Hall, Inc.

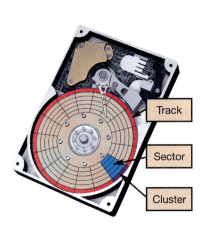
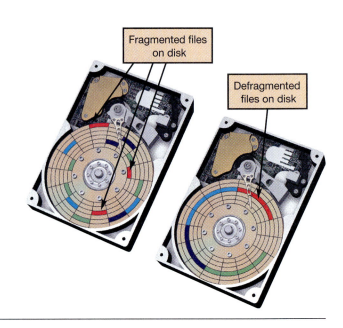

Tracks and sectors on a hard drive
Courtesy of Prentice-Hall, Inc.

Like a record, a **track** is a concentric circular band around the disk that is divided in to pie shaped wedges called **sectors**. More than one sector comprises a **cluster**. To keep track of the electromagnetic charges on the disk that make up computer files, the computer's operating system records a separate table. Microsoft Windows calls this table a **File Allocation Table (FAT)** that serves as a table of contents for the disk, so the read/write head knows where to store or access data and information, like a Microsoft Excel file. Microsoft Windows 7 uses a system similar to FAT call **New Technology File System (NTFS)** which is essentially an improved FAT.

Characteristics of Storage Media

In business, the most important aspects of data and information storage are **storage characteristics**. What sort of device(s) is appropriate, how much data can it hold, how long does it take to write to the device, and how long does it take to read the device? These questions become even more difficult when determining what is needed now and for the future, and how new storage technologies may play a part in the outcomes of your decision.

To begin to make a sound business decision, it is necessary to understand what sort of storage **media** is available and what it does. Some important considerations are the **capacity** of storage media, or simply stated, how much information it will hold. Another consideration is **access time**, or how long it takes to read and write to storage media. Listed below are different storage options.

Floppy Disk (non-volatile) - A floppy disk is a very thin flexible magnetic storage disk that rotates inside a square plastic shell. Floppy disks are read and written by a floppy disk drive. Although they are still in use today, their market share is waning. Most computer systems sold no longer accept floppy drives.
Capacity: 1.44 Mg.

Hard disk drive (non-volatile) - A **hard disk** is a storage device which stores data on rapidly rotating platters with magnetic surfaces. Many hard disks are **internal hard disks** within the computer's chassis and cannot be removed. **External hard disks** reside outside of the computer and are connected via USB or Firewire, and are a very viable alternative for backups and extra storage, and are also portable.
Capacity: 40 GB to 5 Terabytes

> **BLACK & WHITE**
>
> Magnetic tape is an old data storage media packaged on reel-to-reel cartridges like a cassette tape. Data and information are accessed sequentially giving magnetic tape very slow access.

> **GRAY MATTER**
>
> Just because a storage media is slow does not mean it is useless. Magnetic tape can be used to backup and archive information overnight and be very cost effective.

Courtesy of Western Digital; and courtesy of IBM Corporation.

Flash Memory / USB Flash Thumb Drive (non-volatile) - **Flash memory** is a technology that is primarily used in memory cards for digital cameras and thumb drives. Flash memory is solid state, (no moving parts) and is typically used for general storage that is connected to a computer system with USB. Because of its very small size and low cost, it is ideal for transferring or backing up small amounts of data.
Capacity: 256 MG – 500 Gigabytes

Courtesy of Victorinox Swiss Army.

CD, CD-R, CD-RW (non-volatile) - A **Compact Disc (CD)** is an optical disc used to store digital data. CDs remain the standard medium for commercial audio recordings. Standard CDs have a diameter of 120 mm and can hold about 80 minutes of audio. There are also 80 mm discs, sometimes used for CD singles, which hold around 20 minutes of audio. **CD-R** means the optical disks is recordable and typically only one time. **CD-RW** (meaning rewritable) can be written to and erased and can be used for data storage, but other storage alternatives like flash and hard disks make it untenable. Because of the nature of any CD, it does not hold electromagnetic charges; instead, a laser marks it with pits and lands to comply with a computer system's binary nature.
Capacity: 600 MB – 1 GB

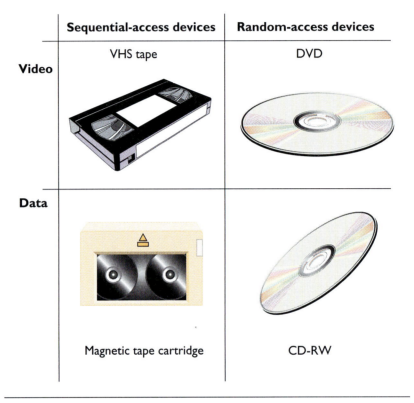

Courtesy of Prentice-Hall, Inc.

DVD (non-volatile) - **DVD** (Digital Versatile Disc)" is an optical disc like a CD that can be used for data storage, but more typically used to deliver high-definition movies and sound. DVDs resemble Compact Discs but they are encoded in a different format for higher density and are therefore more desirable for movie formats.
Capacity: 15 GB – 30 GB

Blu-Ray (non-volatile) - A **Blu-Ray Disc** (BD) is a high-density optical disc for storing digital media like high-definition videos. Blu-Ray is in direct competition with DVD. Although BD holds almost twice as much data as a DVD, but **HD-DVD (High Definition DVD)** has superior image quality. Eventually, the market will determine who will eventually prevail.
Capacity: 25 GB – 30 GB

Magnetic tape (non-volatile, sequential access) - Magnetic tape is an old data storage media packaged on reel-to-reel cartridges like a cassette tape. Data and information are accessed sequentially giving magnetic tape very slow access. Magnetic tape is still used extensively for mainframe computing and backing up large amounts of data.
Capacity: Unlimited

RAID (Redundant Array of Inexpensive Disks) – RAIDs are a series of stacked, spinning hard disk platters connected to one another that divide and replicate data and information to provide more reliable storage. A microcomputer or network works together with a RAID as if it were a singular hard disk, so it retains its fast access time which makes it an ideal choice for large organizations and Internet providers at a relatively inexpensive cost.
Capacity: Unlimited

Courtesy of IBM Corporation.

Internet Drive - An Internet Drive or **iDrive** is a storage service on the World Wide Web. Organizations can upload their computer files to hard drives that reside on the web for a fee. Internet Drives can be very convenient in that a user can access any of their files from the Internet, regardless of their location. Disadvantages include very slow access time, and security concerns.
Capacity: Unlimited

Mass Storage - In computing, **mass storage** refers to storage of large amounts of data and information. Media for mass storage include hard disks, flash memory, optical discs, magnetic tape, and many others. Companies like eBay and American Express rely heavily on mass storage to record their millions of daily transactions.
Capacity: Unlimited

BLACK & WHITE
Archiving is when data that is no longer used on a daily basis is stored electronically, but may need to be accessed at a future date.
Data backup refers to making copies of data, or computer files that can be restored in the event that the original files are lost.

GRAY MATTER
Typically, archived data takes longer to restore to a computer than backed up data.

WHITE BOARD
List some of the different storage media and their appropriate usage.
Describe Mass Storage and what sort of organizations would use it.

Business Storage Strategies

In 1987, random access memory was one of the most expensive components of a computer system. In the first Intel Pentium computers, it was not uncommon to have 8 megabytes of RAM. At the time, to upgrade to 16 megabytes of RAM, it cost about $80 per megabyte. In 2007, purchasing 2 gigabytes (2000 megabytes) of RAM cost about $49. The same amount of RAM in 1988 at $80 per megabyte would cost an astounding $160,000. This example illustrates the ever-changing nature of computer storage and the volatility of its associated costs.

In business, organizations need to carefully consider where and when to store their data and information. eBay needs to store, or **backup** their thousands of daily transactions so that they can access them if necessary at a later date. Typically, they store a terabyte of transaction data per day, and that figure is growing quickly. Because of this, eBay needs to carefully consider the following business storage aspects:

Capacity
Access time
Advances in technology
Security
Costs
Disaster Recovery

Capacity - Many business storage aspects are interlaced, like the example above that shows the relationship between costs and advances in technology, but it's best to address them individually. Capacity refers to the amount of data and information a storage device can hold. eBay needs to calculate the anticipated amount of data they will store plus their future storage needs, and have the necessary capacity ready.

Courtesy of Ivan Sekretarex/Associated Press.

Access Time - Access time refers to the amount of time it takes to get data and information from a storage device to its user. An internal hard drive in a typical personal computer has extremely fast access time. In the eBay example, the terabytes of daily transactions may be housed offsite in large computer storage facilities, but may not need to be accessed on a regular basis, so eBay needs to gauge how often this data needs to be accessed and determine the importance of access time.

All businesses need to backup information that has been created, updated, or deleted at least on a daily basis. If a business has a 1000 gigabyte network, they need at least 1000 gigabytes of backup computer storage space. Although they can store their information on a storage device with extremely fast access time, which is typically more expensive, they may want to consider a cheaper alternative like magnetic tape. Magnetic tapes have sequential access and have a relatively slow read / write capability, so a relatively slow access time. The business may be able to backup their information during off hours, so the storage device they choose may not need fast writing capabilities. The same business knows that they don't have to restore lost or deleted files very often, so may not put a premium on fast access time. Even though magnetic tape suffers from slow access time, it is still a sound alternative for mass computer storage.

Advances In Technology - Every business needs to pay attention to advances in technology, and data storage is no exception. Many mass storage devices rely on clusters of spinning hard drives with many moving parts. Should a business store their information on a safer but more expensive solid state device? On the other hand, solid state storage devices are growing exponentially in capacity and dropping as quickly in price as technology advances. Unfortunately, companies that manufacture solid state storage see their profits dwindling as the price for their product plummets.

Sometimes technology is developed that promises fast and reliable a storage like holographic storage. **Holographic storage** stores information in a three dimensional photopolymer. An optical disk like a DVD has on one surface to record information whereas holographic has many, and therefore can hold much more information. **Molecular storage** is obviously very small and relies on special chemicals to change the state of a singular molecule from a positive charge to negative charge. This technology could lead to incredibly small circuits, and is most likely years away.

> ### WHITE BOARD
> Describe "access time" and its implications in terms of data storage.
> Describe "capacity" and its implications in terms of data storage.
> Will data storage become more or less expensive in the future?

Data Archiving and Backup Strategies

How does a business decide on its data storage needs? Businesses cannot afford to lose critical data, like financial statements. Any number of factors can go into data loss, like computer **viruses**, **natural disasters**, and **human error**. Every business needs to employ archiving and backup strategies. **Archiving** is when data that is no longer used on a daily basis is stored electronically, but may need to be accessed at a future date. Data **backup** refers to making copies of data, or computer files that can be restored in the event that the original files are lost. Businesses must come up with archiving and backup plans, or strategies to avoid critical data loss. Several factors listed below must be considered when devising archiving and backup strategies:

Courtesy of Argonne Laboratory.

Cost: Cost is a major consideration when it comes to selecting a storage device and strategy. Many devices are inexpensive, but may be slow when it comes to data recovery, or simply not provide the amount of computer storage space required for a particular job. No storage device or strategy is works for all situations. Careful consideration must be adhered to when cost is involved. Businesses must resist the temptation to consider cost alone.

Location: It doesn't make a lot of sense to back up data and information of a computing system and then leave the backup device next to the very computer it just backed up. Location of a backup device is critical. If someone backs data and information to a flash drive, which can be a perfectly legitimate storage strategy and then leaves it next to the very computer it backed up, who's to say that the flash drive won't be lost in a disaster like a fire or flood. What if the flash drive is simply stolen which can put a business' intellectual property at risk? On the other hand, data and information that is kept off-site can increase the time it takes to restore critical data, even if the off-site device is accessed through the Internet. Part of a storage strategy always needs to consider location.

Type of Data - A business must indentify critical data, information that the business cannot function without. For instance, a company's human resources department may be able to do without policy and procedure documents posted on its intranet for a few days, but when a company selling MP3s online as its main source of income has lost their musical computer files, and consequently their profitably, they may see this as critical backup and attach a higher priority to backing up.

> ### BLACK & WHITE
> Disaster recovery is when a business suffers a disaster like Hurricane Katrina and needs to regain critical control of their company, much of which is to regain access to their critical data and information.

> ### GRAY MATTER
> Many global companies keep critical data in cities that have less natural disasters like hurricanes, earthquakes, and floods. Since it has very few natural disasters, Phoenix, Arizona is a city that has many data and call centers for businesses from around the world.

CHAPTER 4 | Storage

BLACK & WHITE

A backup storage plan can be implemented that includes regularly scheduled backups. The schedule can be set to carry out backups daily, weekly, monthly, or even continuously, and based on the nature of the storage media and data volume.

GRAY MATTER

One hard and fast rule that always applies to information technology: All data and information on a computing system needs to be backed up.

When considering types of data to back up, a business needs to determine what kind of files it generates, recognize their size, and the appropriate storage size and media required to back it up, as well as the appropriate storage size for the future.

Time Available – Businesses need to determine how much time is available to backup files. If it's a 9 am to 5 pm company, they may simply start their backup process every evening at 8 pm, which means have more than twelve hours to complete the process. Backup processes do not backup computers that are currently in use, like a person working on a spreadsheet after hours which means there is a chance the spreadsheet will not be backed up at all.

Another critical issue is how long it will take to restore a file that has been backed up. If a user loses a critical spreadsheet, do they need it restored now, tomorrow, or next week? This means a business should not only prioritize their data based on type, but also on time.

How Often - Backing up a volume of data can be an extremely time consuming process even if it's automated, and it sometimes takes longer than the allotted time. Certain storage media like tape drives that access and process data sequentially are relatively slow, but typically very inexpensive. Although certain storage media may have enough space, it may be inappropriate given the time criteria, which points out the difference between archiving and backup. Archived files are typically removed from a storage volume because they become inactive, and take up storage space. These files can be ported to back up storage media and typically erased from their original location. A **backup storage plan** can be implemented that includes regularly scheduled backups. The schedule can be set to carry out backups daily, weekly, monthly, or even continuously, and based on the nature of the storage media and data volume.

Data Security - Many large organizations rely on a third party contractor that specialize in mass storage to backup and store their data and information. Rather than try to hire experts within their own company, and own millions of dollars worth of storage devices that will certainly become outdated, these companies can outsource for their storage needs, and pay on an as-needed

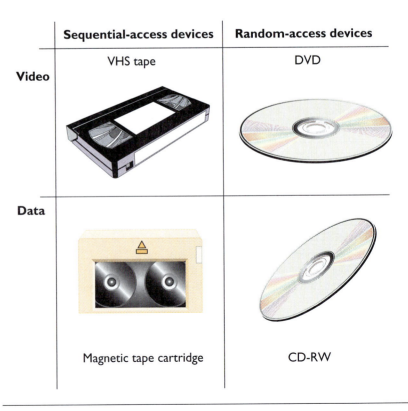

Courtesy of Prentice-Hall, Inc.

basis. When their storage needs increase, their costs will increase, and vice versa. An obvious advantage is that the business does not have to worry as much about advances in technology, because they don't actually own the technology. They also do not incur the costs of specialized employees to administer the backup technology and hardware. These advantages are sometimes balanced with concerns over access speed **and security**. Mass storage vendors have to demonstrate that their client's data is readily available, and maybe more importantly, that it is secure.

Data security is ensuring that data and information is kept safe from corruption. In computer terms, corruption is when errors occur in data retrieval or transmission and the original data contains unintended changes or is altogether unusable. Data security also ensures **privacy**, so only those intended can access it. Privacy simply refers to the developing connection between technology and the legal right to share data. All businesses store and backup extremely sensitive data and need to know that their data is extremely secure.

Disaster Recovery - Disaster recovery is when a business suffers a disaster like Hurricane Katrina and needs to regain critical control of their company, much of which is to regain access to their critical data and information. A disaster can be caused naturally or even by human error. Disaster Recovery Plans (DRPs) are critical plans that need to be in place and anticipate disasters and what to do when they occur. A business like eBay cannot afford to be off-line for very long as it costs them millions of dollars.

Courtesy of Getty Images.

WHITE BOARD

Describe several factors to consider when devising a data backup strategy.
Describe why a disaster recovery plan is so important to a business.
Why is privacy and security important when backing up and archiving data?

Summary

As mentioned in earlier chapters, organizations once again have to decide whether they are **leaders** (first adopters) or **followers** when it comes to storing data and information. For instance, a large organization may be a technology leader, deciding to upgrade their Windows XP platforms to Windows 7 the first day it becomes available. The "leader" organization is banking that 7's advantages might give them an edge in the marketplace over "follower" companies that will wait a year or two before switching from XP. The follower businesses are banking that 7 might not have enough advantages over XP to make a difference, and wait to incur the upgrade costs.

Leading and following also applies to mass storage. With solid state storage becoming cheap, readily available, and high capacity, a leader business may be tempted to switch all their "spinning" hard drives media to solid state, while the followers may hold out and see how much farther prices will come down, or if the next storage technology is even better than solid state. Many leaders early on did cost analysis and outsourced their storage needs, while followers waited to become confident that outsource was cheaper than they could do it themselves. A leader is not better than a follower and vice versa, both are simply business strategies that attempt to make the best decisions based on time and costs.

Many times information technology concepts seem somewhat intangible because computers are made up of circuit boards with electricity coursing through them, as opposed to the tangible buildings, desks, and vehicles they may own. It seems easier to imagine a business failing without their tangible assets. For instance, it is easy to imagine that a manufacturing plant simply could not operate without their conveyor belts and machinery. But the same manufacturing plant would fail miserably without its data and information. With that being said, it is critical to note that **all** of an organization's data and information needs to be backed up and archived with sound business strategies and devices.

Matching

Match each key term in the left column with the most accurate definition in the right column.

L	1. Magnetic Tape	A.	Variety of ways a computer system can store (save) data and information.
O	2. Process	B.	Includes things like desks, computers, tractors, and other physical items.
N	3. Internet Drive	C.	The legal claim a business has to names, inventions, and ideas.
M	4. RAID	D.	A concentric circular band around the disk.
K	5. DVD	E.	Pie shaped wedges.
B	6. Tangible Property	F.	Serves as a table of contents for the disk, so the read/write head knows where to store or access data and information.
C	7. Intellectual Property	G.	Very thin flexible magnetic storage disk that rotates inside a square plastic shell.
D	8. Track	H.	A storage device which stores data on rapidly rotating platters with magnetic surfaces.
A	9. Computer Storage	I.	A technology that is primarily used in memory cards for digital cameras and thumb drives.
F	10. FAT	J.	An optical disc used to store digital data.
G	11. Floppy Disk	K.	An optical disc like a CD that can be used for data storage, but more typically used to deliver high-definition movies and sound.
E	12. Sectors	L.	Data storage media packaged on reel-to-reel cartridges like a cassette tape.
H	13. Hard Disk Drive	M.	A series of stacked, spinning hard disk platters connected to one another that divide and replicate data and information to provide more reliable storage.
I	14. Flash Memory	N.	A storage service on the World Wide Web.
J	15. CD	O.	Storage of large amounts of data and information.

Multiple Choice

1. There are two main types of storage; primary storage and _____ storage.
   a. Lesser
   b. Derived
   c. Minor
   d. Secondary

2. _____ is a type of storage that allows stored data to be accessed in any order without physical movement of the storage media or device.
   a. Hard drive
   b. RAM
   c. Virtual
   d. Register

3. There are _____ bits in a byte
   a. 1
   b. 2
   c. 4
   d. 8

4. A track is a concentric circular band around the disk that is divided in to pie shaped wedges called _____.
   a. Arrays
   b. Divisions
   c. Sections
   d. Sectors

5. _____ is a technology that is primarily used in memory cards for digital cameras and thumb drives.
   a. Flash memory
   b. Sequential memory
   c. Tape memory
   d. Virtual memory

6. _____ refers to making copies of data, or computer files that can be restored in the event that the original files are lost.
   a. Data backup
   b. Copying
   c. Saving
   d. All of the above

7. Computer _____ is the variety of ways a computer system can store (save) data and information.
   a. Function
   b. Data input
   c. Storage
   d. Data output

8. Microcomputer systems are _____.
   a. Random
   b. Binary
   c. Digitized
   d. All of the above

9. _____ Property is the legal claim businesses have to names, inventions, and ideas.
   a. Tangible
   b. Intellectual
   c. Intangible
   d. All of the above

10. A storage device needs a _____ to scan across the surface of a spinning disk to record and/or access data and information.
    a. Arm
    b. Scanner
    c. Read/write head
    d. Data sweep

Blanks

Computer **storage** is the variety of ways a computer system can store (save) data and information.

Intellectual property is the legal claim a business has to names, inventions, and ideas.

Primary storage can be analogized as what a user is currently working on and **secondary** storage is where the user stores their work when they are finished.

RAM is a type of storage that allows stored data to be accessed in any order without physical movement of the storage media or device.

When eight bits are combined, they become a **byte**.

Like a record, a **track** is a concentric circular band around the disk that is divided in to pie shaped wedges called **sectors**. More than one sector comprises a **cluster**.

A **hard disk drive** is a storage device which stores data on rapidly rotating platters with magnetic surfaces.

Capacity refers to the amount of data and information a storage device can hold.

Magnetic tape is an old data storage media packaged on reel-to-reel cartridges like a cassette tape.

Most microcomputers use the **ASCII** coding scheme to represent bytes.

Short Questions

What is the purpose of a File Allocation Table?

Which storage media holds the least amount of data and information?

Name some concerns of an Internet Drive?

Why is Access Time such an important consideration as a Business Storage Strategy?

Name some of the advances in technology in storage strategy?

Why is disaster recovery such an important aspect of Business Storage Strategies?

five | applications for business productivity

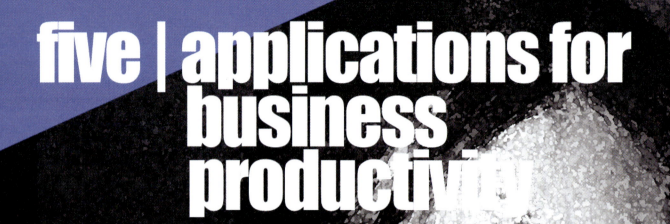

- Application Software
- Business Application Software Suites
- Word Processing Software
- Spreadsheets
- Databases
- Presentation Software
- Sharing Information
- Object Linking Business Solution
- Specialized Application Software
- Web Authoring Application Software
- Other Business Application Software
- Collaborative Application Software

Application Software

Never underestimate the power of application software. Simply enough, **application software** are programs like Microsoft Word or Adobe Photoshop that a person chooses to use as opposed to system software like an operating system that generally requires no human intervention.

Consider that Microsoft Word, the leading word processing software in today's business market, was invented in 1985. Imagine the team that invented it and the hundreds, maybe thousands of software developers, engineers and testers that have worked on it. Microsoft has thought not only of *your* basic word processing needs, but also of an absolutely amazing array of functions that most users never see. It's not just Microsoft either --companies like Adobe have a word processor called Acrobat that is so astonishing it has become the world leader in portable document files (.pdf) and can literally transform a business.

Now think of the times when you heard someone say, "Microsoft Word doesn't do what I want it to do". Perhaps you've said that yourself? Guaranteed, it will do what you're looking for, but that won't help you if you're unaware of its functionality or don't know how to access it. As with many things, your **attitude** regarding application software is what will make you a power user. Changing your attitude is up to you.

A computer is made up of physical hardware and needs **system software** to make it work correctly. In simple terms, when a computer is turned on, hundreds of system software programs run to carry out technical details that make a computer run properly and begin to become useful to the

BLACK & WHITE

One of the most important aspects of system software is that the operating system is enabled and becomes a platform for application software to work. Application software cannot work, or even exist without an operating system.

GRAY MATTER

Microsoft's latest software suite version is called Microsoft Office 2010® for Windows and also offers Microsoft Office 2008® for Mac which will work on the Mac OS platform.

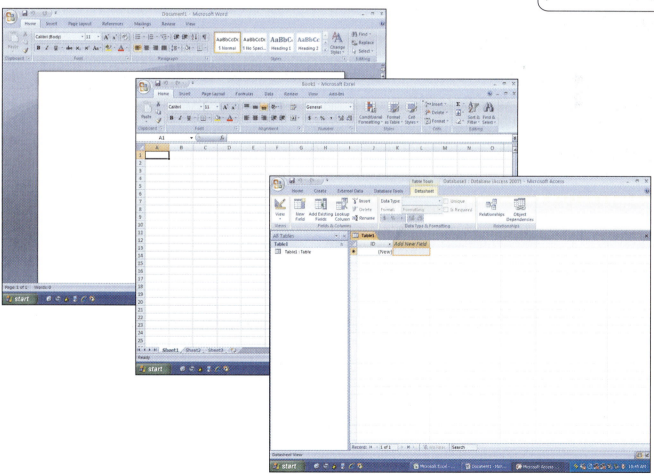

Courtesy of Cengage Learning.

CHAPTER 5 | Applications for Business Productivity

> **BLACK & WHITE**
> Application softwares are presented in windows. Multiple windows that represent multiple applications can be used at the same time, which is called multi-tasking.

> **GRAY MATTER**
> Application software is often underestimated relative to what in can and can't do. Many times, multitasking application software and using them together for one purpose can increase their productivity exponentially.

end-user. End users are simply the people that use computers. One of the most important aspects of system software is that the **operating system** is enabled and becomes a platform for **application software** to work. Application software cannot work, or even exist without an operating system.

Application software performs tens of thousands of specific tasks the end-user needs, like creating a budget for accounting, creating a resume, or making a professional presentation. If system software is a light bulb, then application software is the light. Application software is extremely powerful, and often underestimated by most computer users. Commercial application software has been developed by hundreds, even thousands of people and is constantly evolving to meet the infinite needs of the end-user, so the chances of application software not fulfilling a user's needs are remote.

Business Application Software Suites

Software manufacturers like Microsoft and Mac produce business application software and sell them in packages called software suites, or productivity suites. Software suites have three to five basic application softwares; a spreadsheet, database, word processor, presentation softwares, and project management software. Microsoft's latest software suite version is called **Microsoft Office 2010®** (**Office 2010**) **for Windows** and also offers **Microsoft Office 2008® for Mac** which will work on the Mac OS platform. All five products can work independently or together, depending on the user's application. The table below lists the Microsoft's product names for each basic business application.

Application	Microsoft	Mac
Word Processor	Microsoft Word 2010®	Word 2008®
Spreadsheet	Microsoft Excel 2010®	Excel 2008®
Database	Microsoft Access 2010®	
Presentation	Microsoft PowerPoint 2010®	PowerPoint 2008®
Project Management	Microsoft Project 2010®	

To facilitate ease-of-use, Microsoft has incorporated a similar functionality into all of their **Office** products, which give them a familiar look and feel throughout all of their products, whether they are running on Windows or Mac OS, although they may do very different things. The first of these aspects is **Microsoft Windows 7®** (**7** is Microsoft's latest operating system). Windows 7 is referred to as a **Graphical User Interface (GUI)**. A GUI is presented on the computer's screen and allows a user to interact with text, graphical images, and any other information a user requires.

All of Microsoft Office 2010's and Microsoft Office 2008 for Mac's application software are presented on the user's monitor in rectangular boxes called **windows**. All of Microsoft's applications are presented in windows, whether it's a Word document or an Excel spreadsheet. Multiple windows that represent multiple applications can be used at the same time, which is called **multi-tasking**.

In the past, older versions of Microsoft Office used menus, which were used to present certain commands a user could employ to carry out a specific task, like saving a file, or querying a database table. Microsoft Office 2010's and Microsoft Office 2008 for Mac's most notable change was to replace menus with **"ribbons"**. The ribbon is a GUI element composed of a strip across the top of the window that exposes all functions the program can perform in a single place. The ribbon replaces menus, toolbars and many other windows. Microsoft has consolidated all the related functionality in one place and therefore improves usability. The ribbon contains controls like buttons and icons that are organized with tabs, each one containing a grouping of relevant commands. Each application has different tabs for the different functionality appropriate to the application.

> **BLACK & WHITE**
>
> Spreadsheet application software presents an interface in grid of information separated by columns and rows, often financial information that is capable of calculation and graphing, and most importantly, "what-if" analysis.

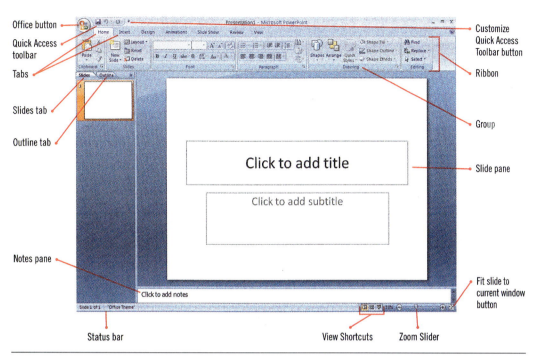

Courtesy of Cengage Learning.

> **GRAY MATTER**
>
> Spreadsheets are often the cornerstone of a business plan and forecasts to determine and estimate what will happen in the future and give a business an intelligent approximation of how to move forward with their organizations tactical and strategic decisions.

> **WHITE BOARD**
>
> What is the difference between system software and application software?
> What types of software come in a software suite?
> What is an end-user?
> Why is it important to have a good attitude regarding application software?
> What are the leading application softwares?

Word Processing Software

Word processors, like Microsoft Word 2010® and Microsoft Word 2008 for Mac allow a user to make document files. Documents can be created, updated through editing, saved to secondary storage, and eventually printed. The types of documents range from a simple one-page resume to a legal business contract that may be hundreds of pages in length to an entire novel. This textbook was written with Microsoft Word 2010®.

Word processors have endless amounts of features for an infinite amount of document applications. Word processing applications are often taken for granted because of their ease of use relative to other business software applications and the perception of singular use. In reality, a word processor offers hundreds of tools to not just make document creation easier, but far more effective. Built-in spell checkers eliminate spelling errors, and even correct misspelled words as they are typed. Grammar checkers allow document revision based on syntax and sentence structure mistakes automatically. Find and replace tools allow a user to find any word in a document, no matter how large the document is and replace it automatically.

CHAPTER 5 | Applications for Business Productivity

> **BLACK & WHITE**
> Database software is well thought-out collection of files that consist of records (rows) of data separated by fields (columns) that can be queried (questioned) to produce subsets of information.

> **GRAY MATTER**
> Querying a database may be the most powerful tool offered by a relational database management system for analysis and auditing purposes, as well as many other business functions.

Document page formatting have a nearly unlimited array of pre-loaded style sheets, fonts, templates, and layouts that can produce anything from a simple memo or a gothic diploma to a 500 page legal contract. A table of contents can be made in a word processor with very little intervention from a user.

A word processor document can also be saved as a web page for the World Wide Web, and often times in a business environment, an Intranet, which allows an organization to communicate essential information for operations. Intranet human resources manuals, policies and procedures, knowledge bases, and many other essential functions can be created in a word processor and posted directly, including images and hyperlinks.

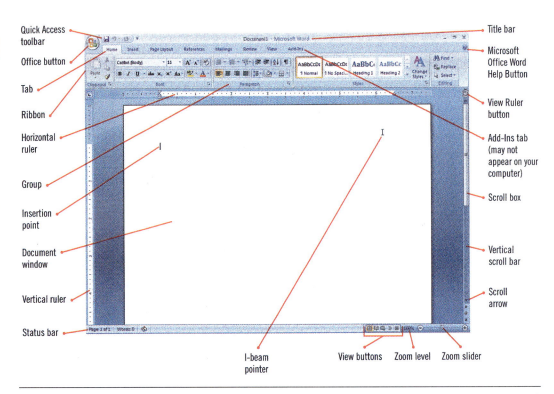

Courtesy of Cengage Learning.

Spreadsheets

Spreadsheet software like Microsoft Excel 2010® and Microsoft Excel 2008 for Mac presents an interface in grid of information separated by columns and rows, often financial information that is capable of calculation and graphing, and most importantly, "what-if" analysis. For example, a business entrepreneur could create a twelve month profit and loss projection with a spreadsheet that shows revenues, costs of sales, and expenses which in turn calculates net profit. The entrepreneur can change any of the data and instantly get feedback. What if utility costs increase? What if insurance rates go up? What if the economy takes a turn for the worse? The entrepreneur can make infinite amounts of changes to variables within the spreadsheet which will automatically calculate any changes to make an informed business decision.

The intersection of a column and row is called a **cell**. Each cell is labeled according to its column and row location, like B5. A cell holds two types of entries, either **text** or **numeric**. Text entries usually serve as labels or notes. Numeric entries obviously hold numbers, but also **formulas** and **functions**. Formulas reference other cells to create arithmetic operations, like A12-A14. In this case, the contents of cell A12 will be subtracted from the contents of the cell A14. Functions are mathematical operations supplied by the spreadsheet itself. =SUM (F14:F21) is a function that add a column of cells from F14 to F21, and places the answer in the cell where the function resides. Spreadsheets offer hundreds of prewritten formulas. Adjoining cells can be grouped together and called a **named range**. Many times a named range is used to print only a specific part of a spreadsheet, or sometimes used to add more than one column or row at a time.

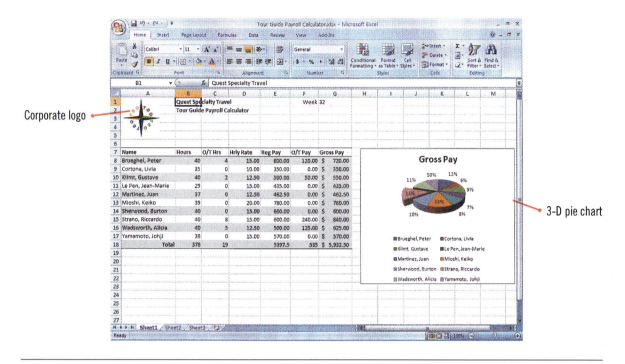

Courtesy of Cengage Learning.

All spreadsheets offer extensive graphing to get a look at numeric trends. These graphs are extremely useful in "what-if" analysis. Microsoft Excel 2010® allows for conditional formatting which is a dynamic graph based on a relationship among numbers.

Databases

Database software like Microsoft Access 2010® is well thought-out collection of files that consist of **records** (rows) of data separated by **fields** (columns) that can be **queried** (questioned) to produce subsets of information. The records retrieved by these queries become information that can be used to make business decisions. Microsoft Access 2010® and other databases are referred to as database management systems (DBMS).

In a DBMS, data is stored in computer files called tables, and tables are combined to other tables with related information, hence, a relational database. For example; a table called STUDENTS lists every student with their own row of information which is divided by columns called fields, like student ID number, last name, first name, address, etc. A table called CLASS is related, or linked to the student table by each table's student ID number field so both tables can now show an individual student and the many classes they attend, called a one-to-many relationship.

Once tables are correctly related and linked, they can be queried to find more granular information like how many students are from out of state, or which students are taking particular elective classes. Queries are only bound by the fields that exist in tables, meaning any question, or query can be asked to a database.

In business, some databases hold millions of records, like a credit card company's card holders. Related data tables house individual's credit card transactions. These businesses are able to query their database to see which of their customers may be behind in their monthly payments, or query for marketing information to see which of their customers may be likely to benefit by offering new services. Although not as powerful as querying, data tables can be sorted by any field or combination of fields. These same data tables can be combined for printed reports, like bank statements, and sorted appropriately.

Data warehousing allow businesses to store their history in relational databases, which is called a corporate memory. Data warehouses use database application software that is typically huge repositories of a business's historical data that comes from all facets of the organization, like sales figures or enrollments in a university. For instance, a business can query the data warehouse to find out how many female students attended a university from 2003 to 2005 with addresses that have a zip code that starts with an "85". As long as the information exists in a data warehouse, organizations can ask, or query an infinite amount of questions to help them make decisions.

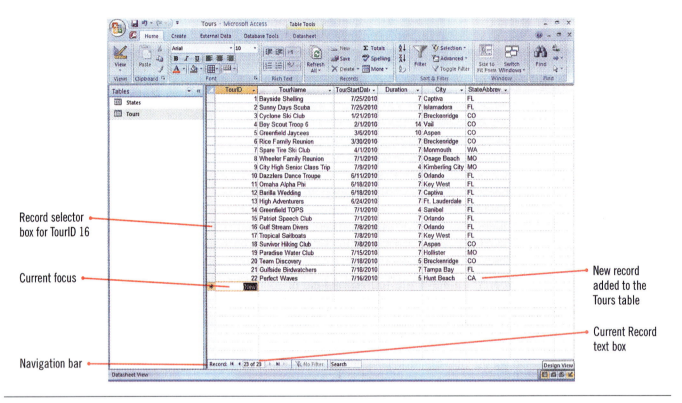

Courtesy of Cengage Learning.

Presentation Software

Presentation application programs like Microsoft PowerPoint 2010® and Microsoft PowerPoint 2008 for Mac are used to display information typically in a slide show. Presentations can be displayed on-screen, and usually are projected for an audience. Slide presentations can be created with a presentation software editor that allows a user to insert and format text, graphics, video, and hypertext and display the content. Microsoft PowerPoint 2010® has endless amounts of features like animations and clipart for an infinite amount of document applications. Businesses rely heavily on presentation softwares to communicate and collaborate in strategic and tactical meetings.

Business presentation programs are typically very easy to build, but can be ineffective if best practices are ignored. Presentations can become convoluted and confusing with too much text or crowded slides. Because a slide presentation is for an audience, its best to mix text and visuals (images) on each slide. Some audience members will be text oriented and others visually oriented. An all text presentation could be excluded a large portion of your meeting.

Effective slides have no more than seven lines of text, and each line should have no more than seven words per line. The presenter is not there to simply read the slides, they need to effectively enhance each point they are making based on the lines of text on the slide. Too much text encourages the audience to simply read the slides and lose focus on the presenter.

Presentation software allows for slides to be printed in many configurations, including handouts for the audience. Handouts allow the audience to concentrate on the presentation rather than note taking, and greatly add to the presentation's credibility. Printed handouts also can be enhanced with more detailed information that would clutter the projected slides. Lastly, slides can be printed to a portable document format (PDF), which is an electronic file that can be distributed by email or through a network, and because the file is portable, it can be read on virtually any computer.

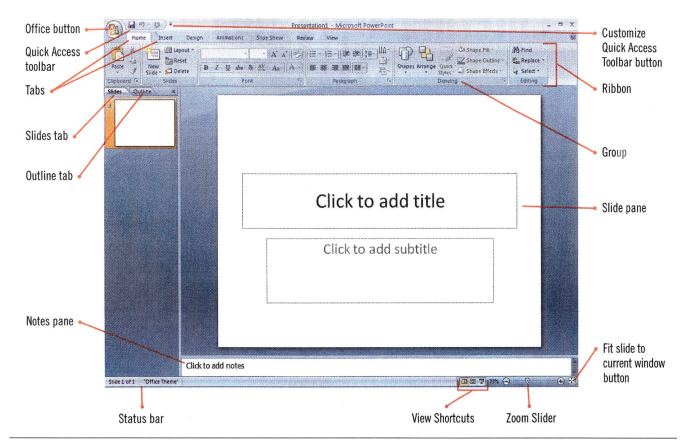

Courtesy of Cengage Learning.

WHITE BOARD

Name four basic application softwares.
Which application software is best for a "what-if" analysis?
Which software is best for data manipulation and querying?

Sharing Information

> **BLACK & WHITE**
> One of the most important aspects of application software suites is the ability to share data and information.

> **GRAY MATTER**
> One of the most important aspects of computing is the ability to share data and information that extends and enhances application software.
>
> It is important to understand how data and information is being shared.

One of the most important aspects of application software suites is the ability to **share data and information**. For example, a business plan may be made up of proposal documents created in Word and budget spreadsheets created with Excel. Many times the spreadsheet calculates budget forecast figures that also need to be included in the proposal documents. The problem is that if the Excel budget changes, does the user remember to make the associated changes in the proposal documents?

Productivity suites have three main ways of sharing information between different application softwares. The first and most basic is called "Cut and Paste". In our example, cutting and pasting allows the user to highlight or select an area in the budget spreadsheet (source data), copy the information into memory (Windows calls this memory the "Clipboard"), switch to the proposal document, and then paste it in the desired area (destination). Although this is the most straightforward method of data sharing, the copied information is static. If the source data changes in the spreadsheet, the destination data does not. The only way to update the destination document is to cut and paste the new information.

The second and third method of sharing information and data is called **Object Linking and Embedding (OLE)**. It is very important to understand the difference between object embedding and object linking.

Object embedding allows a user to select an entire area from one application and make it part of another. In the new example below (pictures), a copy of the budget spreadsheet (**source file**) can be embedded in the proposal document (**destination file**). Object embedding is static, and only takes a snapshot. When the proposal document is reopened, it can be edited, but the budget spreadsheet source file cannot. The budget spreadsheet is only as current as the last time it was embedded.

Object linking is similar to object embedding, but differs in one very important way. Object linking is dynamic. When the source file is linked into the destination file, both files stay up to date. Unlike object embedding which simply takes a picture, object linking is a dynamic link where both files are current, and both files are editable.

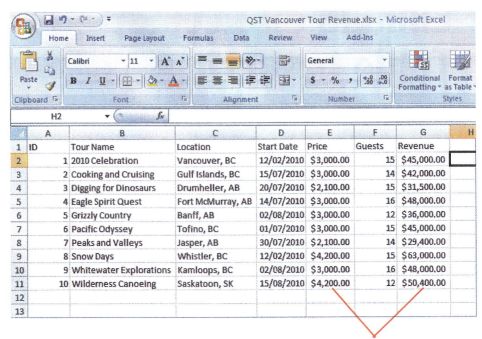

Courtesy of Cengage Learning.

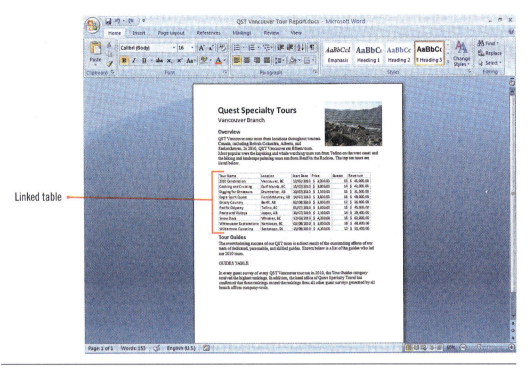

Courtesy of Cengage Learning.

Best Practice

If you open your mind regarding application software, you can affect your business in a multitude of profound ways. Once you change your attitude, you will create fluid "best practices" to transform your job as well as your business. A **best practice** is simply a recognized method to deliver a particular outcome more effectively. Organizations encourage best practices because they offer tested, reliable ways to achieve a desired outcome with the fewest problems, in the least amount of time, and with maximum accuracy. As the term suggests, it's the best way to do something at work.

Keep in mind that a best practice is today's best practice, but it may not be tomorrow's. An insight, a critical reassessment may yield an improved way of doing something, a new best practice. Software changes, people change, processes change. Good today may not be good enough tomorrow. (Eventually picking at best practices too much can yield little or no results.)

You always face competition. Someone else is making cars or running a real estate company or administering a website that offers toenail polish. How effectively you compete often hinges on how your best practices measure up to your competitor's. It's a match-up that can determine whether your business prospers or fails.

Applying Application Software to Best Practice

But how can changing your current best practice to the "best" best practice have such a profound effect in the business place? Consider the following example of a large company in Los Angeles with hundreds of employees that manage hundreds of properties all over the United States. The business does all of the typical things a national property management team does like analyzing vacancy rates, complying with state and federal governmental regulations, preparing tax statements, and much more. Keep in mind that this property management business already has every major application software at its disposal.

One of the more vexing processes in the business is dealing with legal documents, specifically legal contracts. Like many companies, they have acres of filing cabinets with an endless amount of paper, much of which are legal contracts. One of their primary problems is that these contracts have to be approved and signed by someone who may be thousands of miles away. Once the contract is sent across the country, signed and approved, it often returns to the property management company missing one little thing that might have been overlooked like a small change in some obscure paragraph of a legal document that can often be hundreds of pages. If the document returns incomplete, the process starts over, and the same costs to send it are incurred again as well as burning more time.

Case Study Problem

With over two thousand properties nationwide, the property management company has budgeted over one and a half million dollars a year on legal contract compliance alone. Much of the budget goes toward the salaries of attorneys, legal assistants, and compliance officers. Another major part of the budget is to pay FedEx charges. As near as they can figure, the property management company spends a whopping half million dollars a year for FedEx to deliver the legal contracts. The budget does *not* include the FedEx charges incurred by property that receives the legal contract to review the legal contract. The properties have to include FedEx charges in their own budgets totaling to another million dollars nationwide. Two and a half million dollars a year companywide to make sure legal documents are in order; Astounding. This is the property management company's best practice?

Before we move on, consider that everyone involved with this overweight process is well trained and exceedingly bright; the best in the business at what they do, at least the best at complying with their current best practice. The legal assistants never misfile a contract in the filing cabinet, never misprint an address on a FedEx package, and always catch compliance problems with legal contracts. As a matter of fact, the legal department is considered one of the best departments in the entire property management company. They consider the two and a half million dollars spent a year simply a cost of doing business. As a matter of fact, they will tell you it would cost a lot more if they weren't so adept at what they do. Many of them will recount the days before FedEx and UPS when legal contracts were delivered by the United States Postal Service with ground mail. Basically, they are feeling pretty good about themselves and so does the rest of the property management company.

Essentially, the entire legal department revolves around contract compliance and completion, and much of it is facilitated by FedEx. One day a 24 year old business analyst named Emily with an information technology degree arrives at the legal department and starts asking questions about their processes, poking around, and generally being a nuisance, at least the legal department thinks so. Emily has seen the budget and the amount of money spent on FedEx jumps off the page. After a few weeks of poking around, the manager of the legal department finally and begrudgingly spares a scant half hour with Emily and attempts to patronize this "green behind the ears" system analyst that thinks she know something about her business, processes, and best practice.

Emily starts by thanking the manager for her time, yet she is unimpressive, at least in the manager's eye. Emily decides to get right to the point and tells the manager she can save the legal department almost a couple of million dollars a year, minimum. The department manager can't help herself and begins to laugh out loud.

"You must be kidding!" says the department manager. "Listen Missy", she addresses Emily, "Do you have any idea how this department works or how incredibly important we are to the property management company?"

"I think I do Ma'am" replies Emily. "I have it all right here in a business plan I worked up for your department. Since you don't have time to read it because of the short duration of our meeting, would you mind if I go over the main points?"

Case Study Solution

"Please do! I have got to hear this!" replies the legal department manager. "You do realize you're talking about eliminating almost our entire budget? You do understand the term 'best practice' don't you? Our best practice has been honed over the years into a finely tuned, very efficient machine!"

"Yes Ma'am, I am aware of what 'best practice' means, and I am keenly aware of your budget" replied Emily who remained professional. "Let me start by asking a few questions and making some small suggestion. First off, I noticed all of your contracts are created and updated in Microsoft Word, is that true?"

"It's absolutely true. My people have gone to Microsoft Word training and are considered some of the best Word users in the entire company. Further, we always have the latest version. Microsoft Word is the number one word processor in the industry you know?" said the legal manager. "You're not going to suggest I change word processing software are you?" she smirked.

"As a matter of fact, that's exactly what I am suggesting." said Emily. "Have you ever heard of Adobe?" asked Emily.

"Sure!" said the manager, "you're going to tell me we should switch from the latest version of Microsoft Word to Adobe Photoshop!? Adobe makes Photoshop you know? Photoshop makes images and pictures. So we're going to take pictures of our legal documents now, is that it?" The manager's patience was almost at an end.

"No Ma'am, as you probably know, Adobe makes a word processing product called Acrobat, and Acrobat will let you create, compose, and update documents in a PDF format." said Emily. "Once you switch to Adobe Acrobat, you can port all of your legal documents to a server. The server is a centralized computer that works like a web host. Your entire department and anyone you choose would be able to access files on the server and therefore any legal document you see fit. Those who don't have access will never get in." she continued. "Rather than creating, composing, and updating your legal contracts on Microsoft Word, then printing, filing, mailing, and FedExing them all over the country, you simply create the Adobe Acrobat PDF document right on the server, as if it's just another network drive that only your staff and the appropriate people around the country have access to." finished Emily.

"Wait." replied the manager. "One of the main functions we have is to get our legal contracts so they are faultless. That's why we FedEx them back and forth until they're perfect. We're here in Los Angeles, how does someone in New York see the legal contract?" she asked.

"The same way two or more people can see the same website." Emily replied. "The files that make up a website reside on a server and it gets accessed from all corners of the planet; the same thing I am suggesting for your legal documents, except in your case only the people you choose can access them." she said.

"I'm listening. Then what happens?" said the manager in a far less patronizing tone. "You're saying that we create the legal documents essentially on this 'server' hard drive, and let someone in New York have access to that same hard drive, and its associated and appropriate documents so they can make the suitable changes, and the legal document never sees the inside of a FedEx package?" she asked. In the back of her mind, the legal manager knew Emily had just saved her a minimum of a half million dollars, the cost of FedEx. Then she started thinking of the incredible time savings. No more waiting for the FedEx guy. Everything that took days to complete could be handled in just a few hours. "Okay, but why change from Microsoft Word to Adobe Acrobat, and what's a 'PDF'?" she asked.

"A 'PDF' is an Adobe Acrobat file that means 'portable document file'. You could put your Microsoft Word documents on the server, but anyone that accessed that Word document would have to own Microsoft Word or they can't use it. Most of your offsite people probably own Word, but which version? People with Macs would probably never be able to able to open your Word files, at least not without a lot of trouble. The 'portable' part of PDF means anyone on virtually any computer that accesses your server will be able to update and read it, if you so choose." answered Emily.

Emily continued, "Adobe Acrobat also has an incredible array of tools. For instance, you know those stickers your staff uses on printed legal documents, the ones showing where something needs to be signed or updated?" she asked. "Acrobat has 'virtual' stickers that your staff can apply to the actual computer file (PDF) that represents the legal document itself. Your legal contracts are sometimes hundreds of pages. Like many word processors, PDF files are completely searchable. That means that anyone with access to your PDFs can search for a single word or name. It also means that an entire server of PDFs can be searched at one time. Let's say you were looking for PDFs that had the name 'Johnson' in them, that's extremely easy and happens in a matter of seconds. Imagine going through your 'paper' filing cabinets and doing the same thing, looking for the 'Johnson' contracts, which could take forever. Have you ever wanted to know who made the last change on one of your 'paper' legal contracts? Acrobat shows the entire history of changes throughout the life of the file, as so many application software do." said Emily.

The legal manager sat dumbfounded, staring off into space considering the paradigm this young woman had put before her. "With your solution, I wouldn't really even need to keep filing cabinets, would I?" she asked. "The server itself becomes the 'filing cabinet', doesn't It." she asked again.

"The 'server' filing cabinet becomes completely searchable. Further, the server gets 'backed up' as often as you like so you never worry about losing a legal document. The 'back ups' are actually kept offsite, so if there is a disaster, your legal contracts will remain intact." replied Emily. "By the way, all of your current Microsoft Word documents will convert easily to Adobe Acrobat PDFs" she added. "Also, the costs of conversion to the brand new 'best practice' solution is minimal especially compared to the amount of money budgeted for the old 'best practice'." She added.

Then the legal manager got a sullen look and asked Emily something profound. "First, I am sorry I treated you poorly, but this isn't the whole story is it?" she asked. "I know how many legal documents each person on my crackerjack staff can handle; it's something like 10 a day. With your solution, a legal analyst could handle thirty, maybe 50 times more legal documents in the same amount of time with none of the old associated costs, isn't that right? If that's true, which I believe it is, what do I do with my staff? I don't need five legal analysts anymore based on your solution, maybe just one, and two at the most. What do I do with the other three or four?" she asked.

"You are right, that is a big part of the story, and probably the most difficult." said Emily. "I suppose that's up to you." she ended. "Thanks very much for your time, if you have any questions I would be more than happy to help."

Improving Best Practice and Business Repercussions

Emily's 'PDF' solution seemed beyond belief, at least the results. It didn't just save 10 or 20 percent of the legal department's time and money; it literally created a whole new paradigm, a new 'best practice' that would rock the legal department to its core. Should the legal manager go forward with the solution? Start to imagine some other legal manager doing basically the same thing at some other company, your competitor. Would they adopt the same 'PDF' solution given the opportunity? Maybe they're already doing it, doing infinitely more with significantly less than your company.

Were the results of the solution astonishing? The answer is a resounding 'yes', especially to those affected Maybe a better question would be to ask if Emily's solution was difficult to implement. From an information technology view, the solution was nothing more than mechanical. Setting up a server and converting documents are nothing special, yet the solution was. It wasn't the application software that made the solution 'special', rather the 'business' solution it created and the new 'best practice' going forward.

Is Emily a genius? How can a twenty-four year old barely out of college make such a major impact on a Fortune 500 sized business? The answer is that she took time to **'know the business'**. Rather than walk in with a pre-canned computer solution, Emily spent her time understanding what the legal department actually did. She spent time understanding their 'business processes' before she even considered information technology. In a business context, activities and methods required by the business are usually called processes, or in this case, a **business process**. A business process is an assortment of associated activities or tasks to produce goods and services. Emily spent all of her time getting to know the business, getting to know the 'processes', the same processes that make up 'best practice'. By the way, she is a genius, although it doesn't take a one to analyze and implement her solution.

> **BLACK & WHITE**
> The first consideration when building a business web site is why it exists in the first place. One of the most important reasons is so a business can showcase their organization.

> **GRAY MATTER**
> A business website can be the first impression a potential customer makes. A poorly constructed website with incomplete content can lead a customer away from a business, even if the business itself is actually a well run enterprise.

> **WHITE BOARD**
> What was Emily's solution?
> Why did the solution impact the company so much?
> What would you do with the employees no longer needed?
> Why is a PDF so valuable?

Specialized Application Software

Image editing softwares like Adobe Photoshop are application programs that enable an end-user to manipulate visual images on a computer. Computer graphics are classified in two categories: **raster graphics** and **vector graphics**.

Raster graphics, or bitmaps, are image data file formats representing a rectangular grid of pixels on a computer monitor. A pixel or picture element is a singular point on a graphic image. Bitmaps have a bit for bit relationship with images displayed on a computer monitor and is characterized by the width and height of the image in pixels and by the number of bits per pixel, which determines the number of colors it can display. Vector graphics are an image data file that manipulates geometrical shapes like points, lines, curves, and polygons. These shapes are based on mathematical equations that a user can change with an image editing software to represent images on a computer.

Adobe Systems Photoshop is a graphics editing application software and the current market leader for commercial business bitmap, image, and photographic manipulation and has been described as the industry standard for graphics professionals. Photoshop is one of the few application softwares that present the same interface to a user regardless of operating system, meaning it essentially works the same on Mac OS or Microsoft Windows. (The cover of this book was designed with Photoshop.)

BLACK & WHITE

Multimedia application software is used by businesses generally to combine and manipulate text, graphics, audio, and video into a format like presentation software. Multimedia software allows a business to create an interactive training video for their new employees which can be far more effective than a simple document.

GRAY MATTER

It is important to note that multimedia software uses a tremendous amount of a personal computer's resources, specifically its random access memory (RAM). A major difference between Windows and Mac platforms is how they handle RAM, and it is generally accepted that Mac handles it far better, which makes it an ideal choice for multimedia application software.

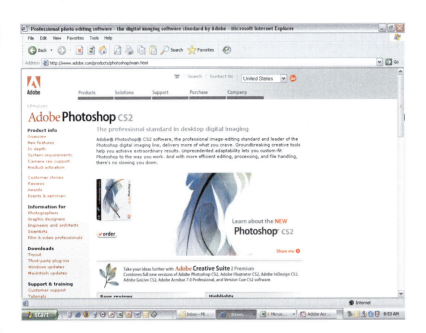

Web Authoring Application Software

Web authoring application software like **Microsoft Expression Web 2010** and **Microsoft Expression Web 2008 for Mac** software is specialized application software that allows a user to create, publish, and administer web sites on the World Wide Web through the use of a **WYSIWYG** interface. (WYSIWYG is an acronym for "What You See Is What You Get"). Web authoring programs allow users to layout images, text, video, and other elements in a GUI display without having to know HTML, or hypertext markup language, which is a standard language on the web.

The ultimate goal of web authoring programs is to post a website on the World Wide Web (WWW) or a corporate Intranet. In business, it is important to know which web authoring products are appropriate for which task. Different web authoring programs offer different features depending on the user's ultimate web site goal. For instance, a user might just want to make a website for a business to have a presence on the WWW. Products like **Adobe Macromedia** and Microsoft Expression Web focus on the needs of professional web designers to build high-quality web sites and are typically very user-friendly.

Although products like Macromedia and Expression Web are easy to use, professional web site designers must take into consideration many factors that make up a good website. For instance, the most professional looking website posted on the WWW is of little value if it does not generate traffic. The following is a list of important web design considerations:

Intention – The first consideration when building a business web site is why it exists in the first place. One of the most important reasons is so a business can showcase their organization. Business websites can provide product information and offer customer support as well as giving their customers quick and efficient access to the organization.

Viewers – An effective business website should consider who the expected users of the web site are and what their needs are before it is designed. Market segmentation analysis is often helpful in this step. A **market segment** is a subgroup of people sharing one or more characteristics that cause them to have comparable product needs.

Content – Once a web site has an intended purpose, it is important that the site contain complete and relevant information. Many businesses employ content managers to ensure appropriate and accurate information on their corporate web site.

Design Layout – Web sites should be easy to navigate. The user of the website should be able to find content easily. Visually appealing websites that engage the user and invites them to explore are far more effective than static websites. Effective design layout makes it more likely that a user will stay on the web site longer and that they will look at more content.

Search Engine Optimization (SEO) – SEO is a way of improving the volume and quality of traffic to a web site from search engines like Google and Yahoo. Webmasters and content managers use many techniques like including keywords in their websites so they are more likely to be found by random users.

One of the most powerful web authoring programs in the business environment is **Microsoft Office SharePoint Designer**. SharePoint allows corporate webmasters and content managers to create, publish, and administer web pages like other commercial web authoring software, but typically for business intranets. An **intranet** is a private computer network like the Internet that allows a business to securely share their organization's information with its employees.

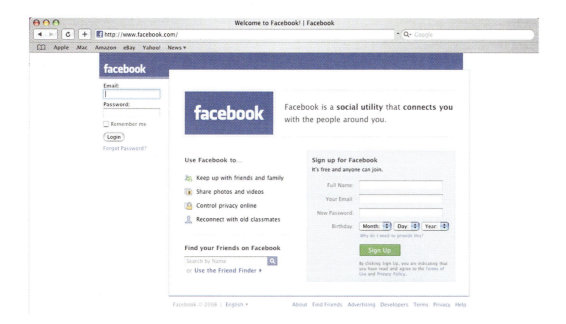

CHAPTER 5 | Applications for Business Productivity

Other Business Application Software

In business, it is important that document files can be used regardless of operating system platforms, whether they are Windows, Linux, Mac, UNIX, etc. This is referred to a **platform neutral**. Adobe is the standard for these types of platform neutral documents. Adobe's Reader and Writer application software can create **"PDF"** files that can be used in virtually any computing environment. The acronym PDF stands for "Portable Document File". For example, a business could publish legal contracts in a PDF format and reviewed at third parties computers without requiring the third party to comply with the contract's original document software format.

Multimedia application software is used by businesses generally to combine and manipulate text, graphics, audio, and video into a format like presentation software. Multimedia software allows a business to create an interactive training video for their new employees which can be far more effective than a simple document. Multimedia software is a broad category of products that range from **Adobe Photoshop** that manipulates images and photographs to **Apple iWork** that creates intuitive media-rich presentations.

It is important to note that multimedia software uses a tremendous amount of a personal computer's resources, specifically its random access memory (RAM). A major difference between Windows and Mac platforms is how they handle RAM, and it is generally accepted that Mac handles it far better, which makes it an ideal choice for multimedia application software.

Electronic mail, or **email** for short is a core business application. Microsoft Office Outlook is an example of an industry leading email application. **Email** is an electronic method of composing, sending, storing, and receiving messages over electronic communication systems. Although Outlook manages and administers email, it is actually a **personal information manager** (PIM) that facilitates tracking and managing personal information. Email applications obviously manage email functions, but also handle contact management, calendars, meeting schedules, task management, and note taking just to name a few. Email applications are really only effective in the business environment when they are used in conjunction with networked systems, whether private or the Internet, which expands their ability to communicate.

Email must be employed responsibly, especially in business. Best practice is to always consider email public. Although an email is targeted for a specific recipient, always remember that many times there is an electronic copy even after the sender and user delete it. In business, email content and structure is extremely important. The body (**message**) of an email should be well written and concise. A good email application program includes a spell checker and grammar checker. A one line **subject line** must also be concise and let the email recipient know the topic of the message. Email application program allow for file attachments like spreadsheets, and it is incumbent on the sender to alert the recipient of the attachment in the message.

BLACK & WHITE

Enterprise resource planning (ERP) systems are application software that attempts to integrate all data and processes of an entire business into one integrated system.

GRAY MATTER

Integrating all data and processes is a great idea; however, implementing this concept throughout a global enterprise is extremely difficult.

108 | **CHAPTER 5** | Applications for Business Productivity

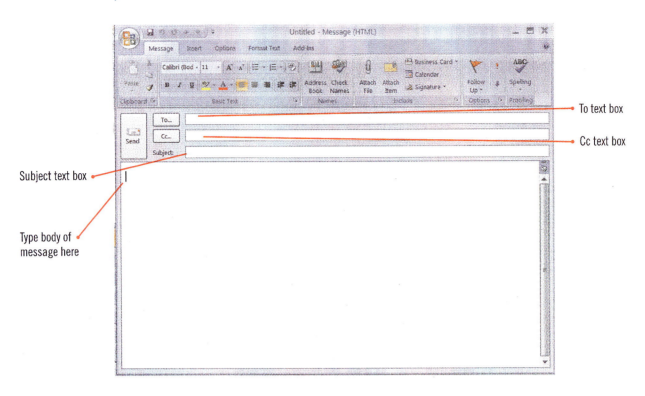

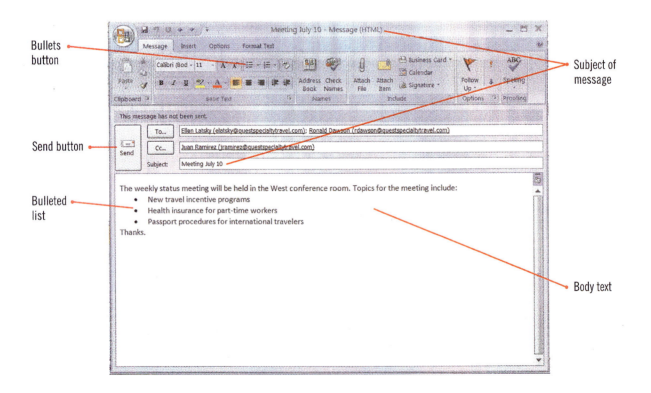

Enterprise resource planning (ERP) systems are application software that attempts to integrate all data and processes of an entire business into one integrated system. A key feature of most ERP systems is the use of an integrated database that stores data for the assorted system modules, like accounting and human resources functions. The idea is to keep information in a singular database, like an employee's name. For instance, an accounting department needs an employee's name to track their expenses and the human resources department needs the employee's name for payroll. Rather than each department administering separate databases that contain the same employee's name, the ERP has a singular database that both accounting and human resources can access.

One of the most common ERPs is manufactured by **SAP AG**, the largest software enterprise in Europe. SAP calls their application software "solutions" that are typically aimed at midsize to very large organizations. SAP creates solutions for businesses in banking, healthcare, higher education, insurance, and aerospace to name a few. Another notable and widely used ERP is **PeopleSoft**, which specializes in manufacturing, financial, human resources, and customer management. **SAS Systems** application software is also a leading ERP that facilitates decision making by enabling a business to perform statistical analysis on their ERP databases. SAS allows organizations to perform operations like business planning, forecasting, and data mining. **Data mining** is the ability to sort through large amounts of data to pick out pertinent information.

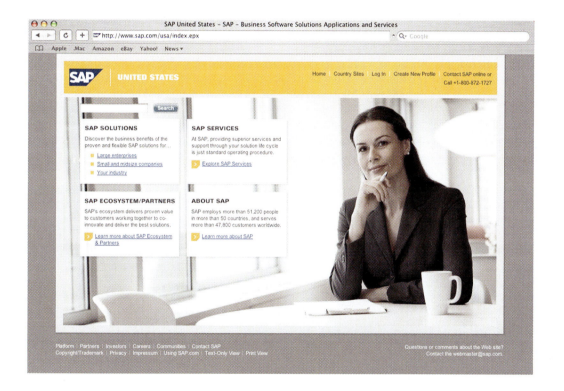

Collaborative Application Software

In business, very few work people completely alone, and those that do have find it extremely difficult to compete. The norm in business is to collaborate with coworkers to share resources and ideas. **Collaboration** is a method of mutual learning between two or more people who are working together towards a common goal.

The main form of collaboration in business is called **Conversational interaction**. Conversational interaction is basically a conversation with two or more participants to trade information and ideas, and also to build relationships. Computer communication technologies like telephony, telephones, instant messaging, and e-mail are generally adequate for asynchronous conversational interactions. A phone call is **synchronous** because both parties are participating in a conversation at the same time where other "conversations" like email and texting allow both users to participate at their leisure, which is considered **asynchronous**.

There are several collaboration softwares that are designed to help people achieve a common goal like **Microsoft's Groove** and **Lotus Notes**, which are desktop application softwares designed to make it possible to collaborate and communicate within small business groups. Collaboration software offers a shared workspace for a group of people, not unlike one very large desk with an entire project's files for anyone and everyone to access. Collaboration software reside on networks and keep the desk organized, secure, synchronized, easy to access, and provides a way for people in the same room, or around the world to work together. (Picture)

The Internet plays a significant role in business computing collaboration. Companies like Google offer online products like **Google's Docs & Spreadsheets** that provide ways to share online document editors and spreadsheets that are shared with academic and business groups.

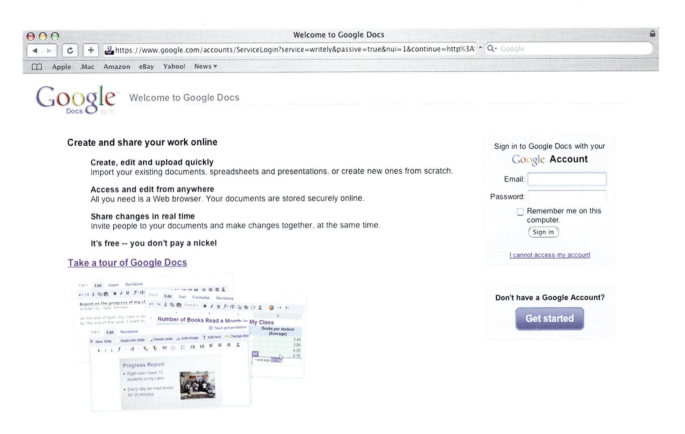

Summary

System software sets up a computer so application software can work. Application software is the work that happens on a computer. System software takes little or no user intervention, application software is a choice the user makes to create something. Other than operating system platforms, system software rarely changes whereas application software is improved constantly with an infinite array of uses.

As an individual in business, application software is one of the best places to showcase your talent and set yourself apart, but one of the most basic concepts commonly overlooked in business application software is which application software is the right one for the job, especially when it comes to choosing a database or a spreadsheet? For instance, a spreadsheet will sort and extract data and information and perform some database functions, but it is clearly the wrong tool when managing large databases with relational files. What generally happens when the wrong application software is chosen initially is that it might do some of the job well at first, but once the job is expanded it starts to fail because it does not offer the appropriate tools the right application software offers. Many businesses find themselves hamstrung with applications in the wrong software.

The answer to choosing the right software is to ask a few questions first. First, ask what you are trying to accomplish. Will you be doing a "what-if" analysis like budget and forecasting, or will you be collecting data to analyze different subsets of information?

Second, ask yourself or your business how long the application will exist. If the application is for a quick "down and dirty" job that will be done in less than a week, then choosing the right application software is still critical, but will not hurt as much in the long run. When a business process is dependent on an application for a long time, choosing the wrong application software can cost hundreds, even thousands of hours of unnecessary time and effort when the right application software would do the same job easily.

Third, look around your business and seek out applications like the one you are trying to create. Talk to other people and ask what they accomplished and how they did it. Looking outside your own organization is also a good idea, and especially the Internet. Major application manufacturers typically have enormous web resources and will almost always have help for your application.

Lastly, keep an open mind. Use the right application software even if you aren't very familiar with its use. Too many applications reside in spreadsheets because the user simply was not willing to learn a database and vice versa. Although you may have to invest time and effort up front on a "learning curve", it's a small price to pay going forward, and it's the business that pays.

Matching

Match each key term in the left column with the most accurate definition in the right column.

____ 1. Software Suite	A. One of the most important aspects of system software.
____ 2. Operating System	B. Software that cannot work, or even exist without an operating system.
____ 3. Cut and Paste	C. Usually has five basic application softwares; a spreadsheet, database, word processor, presentation softwares, and project management software.
____ 4. Database	D. Presented on the computer's screen and allows a user to interact with text, graphical images.
____ 5. Spreadsheet	E. Presented on the user interface to the user in rectangular boxes.
____ 6. Application Software	F. When multiple windows that represent multiple applications can be used at the same time.
____ 7. GUI	G. One of the most important aspects of application software suites.
____ 8. Web Authoring	H. Most basic way of sharing information.
____ 9. Window	I. Allows a user to select an entire area from one application and make it part of another.
____ 10. Word Processor	J. Allow a user to make document files.
____ 11. Object Embedding	K. Presents an interface in grid of information separated by columns and rows.
____ 12. Image Editing	L. Collection of files that consist of records of data separated by fields.
____ 13. Presentation Program	M. Displays information typically in a slide show.
____ 14. Sharing Information	N. Application programs that enable an end-user to manipulate visual images on a computer.
____ 15. Multitasking	O. Allows a user to create, publish, and administer web sites on the World Wide Web.

Multiple Choice

1. __application__ Software cannot work, or even exist without an operating system.
   a. Database
   b. Word processing
   c. System
   d. Application

2. Software is typically presented on the user interface to the user in rectangular boxes called _____.
   a. Virtual Boxes
   b. Windows
   c. GUI
   d. Spaces

3. Microsoft Office 2007's most notable change was to replace menus with _____.
   a. Top layers
   b. Tabs
   c. Inserts
   d. Ribbons

4. In a spreadsheet, the intersection of a column and row is called a _____.
   a. Intersectional space
   b. Divisional section
   c. Crosshatch
   d. Cell

5. In a spreadsheet, adjoining cells can be grouped together and called a _____.
   a. Named range
   b. Cell groups
   c. Sections
   d. Spaces

6. _____ software are application programs that enable an end-user to manipulate visual images on a computer.
   a. Image editing
   b. Photo
   c. Picture
   d. All of the above

7. _____ is a method of mutual learning between two or more people who are working together towards a common goal.
   a. Meeting
   b. Grouping
   c. Collaboration
   d. Brain storming

8. Word processors allow a user to make _____ files.
   a. Spreadsheet
   b. Document
   c. Database
   d. Presentation

9. In a DBMS, data is stored in computer files called _____.
   a. Documents
   b. Tables
   c. Spreadsheets
   d. Workbooks

10. _____ Programs are used to display information typically in a slide show.
    a. Spreadsheet
    b. Database
    c. Presentation
    d. Word processing

Blanks

Software manufacturers produce business application software and sell them in packages called __software suites__.

A __GUI__ is presented on the computer's screen and allows a user to interact with text, graphical images, and any other information a user requires.

Multiple windows that represent multiple applications can be used at the same time, which is called __multitasking__.

Microsoft Office 2010's and Microsoft Office 2008 for Mac's most notable change was to replace menus with __ribbons__.

__Database__ software is well thought-out collection of files that consist of records (rows) of data separated by fields (columns) that can be queried (questioned) to produce subsets of information.

_____ are used to display information typically in a slide show.

The first and most basic way to share data and information between applications is called __cut + paste__.

__Image editing__ softwares like Adobe Photoshop are application programs that enable an end-user to manipulate visual images on a computer.

Computer graphics are classified in two categories: __vector__ graphics and __raster__ graphics.

__Email__ is an electronic method of composing, sending, storing, and receiving messages over electronic communication systems.

Short Questions

What is the purpose of Collaboration?

What is the difference between Object Embedding and Object Linking?

What is the term when a column intersects a row in spreadsheet application software?

What are of the main differences between system software and application software?

Corporate memory refers to what type of software?

What are the most important web design considerations?

six | why the box works

- System Software
- Starting the Computer
- Administering Application Software
- Memory Management
- Device Drivers
- Interfacing and Utilities
- File Management Systems
- System Software Utilities
- Backup Utilities
- Antivirus Utilities
- System Updates

System Software

In business, there are mundane things that are simply expected to work with little or no human intervention, like a company car. The organization's employee simply expects get in the car, turn the ignition key, and go. If the company car doesn't work, the car is brought to a specialist, typically for a mechanic to fix it. With a business computer, or any computer for that matter, the same can be said of system software, the underlying computer programming that allows application software, like a spreadsheet to work. System software is simply expected to work, with very little human intervention, as well it should.

BLACK & WHITE
System software is software that manages and controls the physical hardware of a computer so that application software can work.

Application softwares are the programs that help an end-user do a particular task. The most important task system software performs is loading the operating system.

Many devices employ system software.
Courtesy of Craigmyle/Corbis Images.

Simply stated, **system software**, often called **firmware**, is software that manages and controls the physical hardware of a computer so that application software can work. **Application softwares** on the other hand are the programs that help an end-user do a particular task. When system software unexpectedly doesn't work, a specialist is brought in to fix it, just like the auto mechanic, so it begs the question; why is it important in business for anyone else besides the specialist to know how system software works?

To answer part of the question, it is important to know that the most significant task system software performs is loading the operating system. An operating system (OS) is a collection of computer programs that administers the hardware and software of a computer so it can work properly. The OS is the groundwork for all system software and performs important jobs like controlling memory, administrating input and output devices, and managing the filing system. The first and most obvious answer; especially in business is to know which operating system is right for the organization.

GRAY MATTER
Every computer is has an operating system, including the computer programming that supports your HDTV, cell phone, or even your iPhone.

A graphic design firm may be better served with an operating system like Mac's Jaguar which is ideal for imaging application softwares, photo manipulation, and logo design. On the other hand, one of Microsoft operating systems may be best for business application software like spreadsheets and databases. Many organizations choose to use both operating systems. Some operating systems are free, like Linux, but does it support the essential application software required to run a business? Some businesses, like credit card processors, require enormous amounts of computing power and choose to use an operating system called UNIX.

System software does much more than provide an operating system, it also provides essential utilities and thousands of programs running in the background that allow a computer to work properly, and even protect the system.

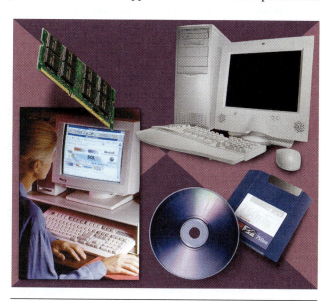

Courtesy of Prentice-Hall, Inc.

Starting the Computer

When a computer is turned on, it immediately starts loading system software to eventually provide the essential operating system, or platform. Every time a computer is powered up, it needs to know what resources it has to work with, like programming files, expansion cards, and amount of random access memory. Loading the platform into the computer's memory is called **booting**. Powering up a computer on for the first time is called a **cold boot**, and a computer that is restarted while it was already running is called a **warm boot**.

> **BLACK & WHITE**
> Loading the platform into the computer's memory is called booting. Powering up a computer on for the first time is called a cold boot, and a computer that is restarted while it was already running is called a warm boot.

> **GRAY MATTER**
> Without **BIOS**, a computer could **not** load an operating system.

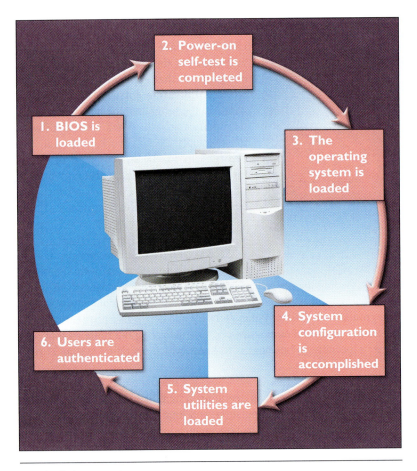

Steps to start a computer
Courtesy of Prentice-Hall, Inc.

When electricity courses through the circuits of a personal computer that has just been powered up, the first thing that happens is that system searches for the **basic input/output system (BIOS)**. BIOS is firmware programming embedded in to a computer chip, meaning the computer runs the same program every time it's turned on. The principal purpose of the BIOS is to locate the computer hardware, like a hard drives. This is so the system can make ready other software programs stored on other various media (like the hard drive originally located by BIOS) throughout the computer that in turn load, execute and assume control. The system figuratively pulls itself up by its bootstraps, which is why starting a computer is called **booting**.

On a typical business computer, once the BIOS locates a hard drive, it is able to execute instructions and programming that loads the all important operating system. The operating system in turn takes control and configures the computer's hardware to settings stored in a database called the **registry**. The registry contains settings like screen savers, appearance and personalization, and any

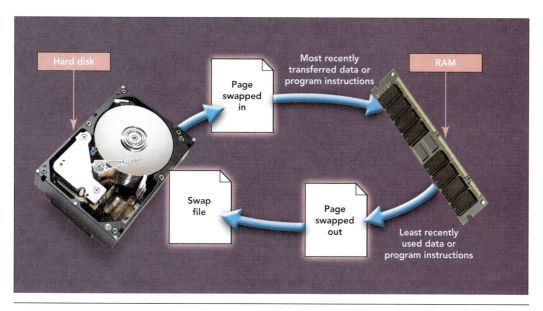

Virtual memory makes use of the hard drive as an extension of RAM
Courtesy of Pearson Education.

BLACK & WHITE
If a computer is multi-tasking or just running one application, it is the system software manages the computer's memory to make multitasking possible.

GRAY MATTER
Multitasking hasn't always been around. Operating system only allowed a computer to run single application software at a time.

other settings, whether chosen by the user or the default factory settings. Once the hardware settings are determined, the operating system loads **system utilities**, like virus protection programs.

Although not necessary on a home computer, in business, it is extremely important that the operating system **authenticates** a user to determine if they are the computer's appropriate user. The business computer authenticates users by requiring them to **login**. Logging in to a business computer is a critical process that requires a known user to type in their name (usually designated by a system administrator) and password. Once the correct name and password are verified by the system, the user's **profile** is loaded. The profile represents the user's specific preferences, like themes and styles, and what kinds of resources are available to that user. Depending on the organization, the system administrators can control a user's profile that restricts them from changing settings, like installing unknown software, or even restrict their Internet browsing capabilities. This ensures the business that the computer will be used in an appropriate manner by a known user. System administrators can also save standard profiles for new users to quickly set up a new employee.

It becomes obvious that the system administrators are a critical part of the business process, but some aspects may be a lot less obvious. System administrators in any organization are actually called network administrators; because all business requires their computers to be connected together to effectively compete in the marketplace. Network administrators are required to manage tasks like hardware setup and computer configuration, which themselves can be critical to protecting a company's assets and intellectual property, but they are also called on to be a critical part of the entire business organization. Network administrators are required to work closely with all business functions, like human resources, research and development, and accounting, to determine which employees can access any or part of an organizations second most valuable asset, its data and information. (The employee is the organizations most valuable asset.)

WHITE BOARD
What is the difference between a warm boot and a cold boot?
What is BIOS and what purpose does it serve?
What is firmware and what purpose does it serve?

Administering Application Software

Once a user has been authenticated and their user profile loaded, they are ready to use application software, like Photoshop or a spreadsheet. System software manages application software, principally, by loading it into random access memory (**RAM**) after a user makes a request to use the application software, typically by double-clicking the appropriate icon on the desktop. Sometimes a user will use multiple softwares at a time, like application software that supports document files like legal contracts, and application software that supports a database like a list of customers. The ability of the system software to support multiple softwares at a time is called **multitasking**.

Memory Management

Whether a computer is multitasking or just running singular application software, system software needs to carefully allocate and manage the computer's available memory. If the computer's available memory was water, and the computer was a bucket, it's a natural assumption to think that when the water is all used up by application software, that there is no more water to run more application software, but this isn't the case. System software somewhat fools the computer by using a clever combination of memory allocation and file switching.

For example, system software already knows how much available RAM it has to work with from when the computer was booted. Since all application software works in RAM, the system software needs to switch, or swap information in and out of RAM as needed based on the RAM's capacity. A special kind of memory is used called **virtual memory** to facilitate this technique. Virtual memory is actually the technique of breaking files requested from a secondary memory like a hard drive into smaller, more manageable files that can fit into RAM. These smaller files that represent pieces of larger files are called **pages**. If the pages exceed the capacity of the available RAM, the operating system stores temporary copies of pages on the hard drive. These files are swapped in and out of RAM as needed, hence the name **swap files**. Obviously, if the operating system has to do a lot of file swapping, the computer slows down.

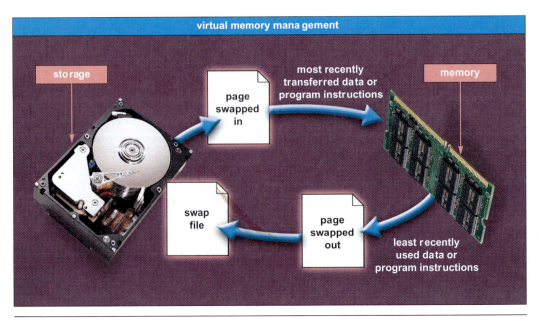

Courtesy of Prentice-Hall, Inc.

Sometimes, businesses are faced with a decision to buy new computers because they feel they are not up to the task or just too slow for their application softwares. In many cases, new computers are a sound business decision; but sometimes a less expensive alternative and more appropriate decision is to simply increase the RAM of its existing computers. To do this, a system administrator will simply install more RAM chipsets into the computer and in turn will be recognized and employed the next time the computer is booted.

RAM modules onboard the motherboard
Courtesy of Intel Corporation.

> **BLACK & WHITE**
>
> System softwares input and output information through devices like keyboards, mice, and printers.

> **GRAY MATTER**
>
> Keep in mind that computers are binary and all they really understand are extremely clever combinations of ones and zeros. If human beings understood the binary nature of a computer, system units would not have to translate its binary information into a format a human can understand, like information on a monitor or a printed document.

Device Drivers

Business computers require the critical input and output of their end users. Input is facilitated by input devices like keyboards and a mouse, whereas output is facilitated by output devices like monitors and speakers. Since a computer is a binary system that only understands machine code, it needs special programs called **drivers** to make input and output devices operate properly. Many device drivers are already included with the operating system as they have been provided by manufacturers ahead of time, and some device drivers need to be installed by the end user. All input and output devices require a driver.

> **WHITE BOARD**
>
> What do device drivers do?
> What is the purpose of a swap file?
> What does virtual memory do?

Interfacing and Utilities

All system software needs to input and output data and information to the end user in one form or another, whether through a keyboard, mouse, printer, monitor, or even a speaker. Further, because a computer operates in a binary environment that only understands a language consisting of combinations of 1s and 0s, and the end user might only understand a language like English, system software in the form of an operating system needs to serve as a translator so both the computer and end user can communicate with each other.

One of the main translating, or output devices is the computer's monitor, that displays and renders output that an end user can understand. To facilitate this output, the operating system provides a user interface that displays on a monitor. Simply put, a **user interface** is what the user sees on the monitor and provides the means in which a person can interact with the computer system, whether they are inputting to manipulate the system, or receiving output from their manipulation.

Different operating systems offer different user interfaces but have many aspects in common. The most common aspect of all major operating system user interfaces is that they present data and information in a graphical manner, and are therefore referred to as **graphical user interfaces**, or more commonly by the acronym **GUI** (pronounced "goo ē" or "gooey"). GUIs present visual indicators or special graphical elements along with text and images to communicate with its user.

CHAPTER 6 | Why the Box Works

BLACK & WHITE

One of the most important core elements of system software is its ability to store data and information on a computer and offer a system of file organization and management.

GRAY MATTER

Henry Brown, an African American inventor gave us the horizontal filing cabinet in 1886, and Edwin G. Seibels gave us the vertical filing cabinet in 1898. Other than the electronic nature of a computer, a file manager works almost identically to Mr. Brown's original invention.

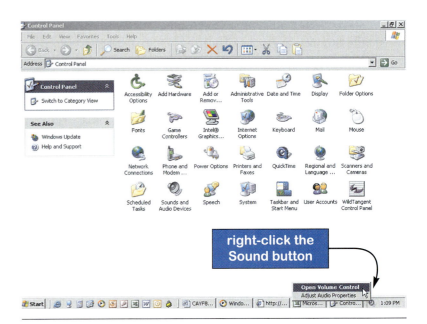

In Microsoft Windows, the Control Panel contains many options for managing system software

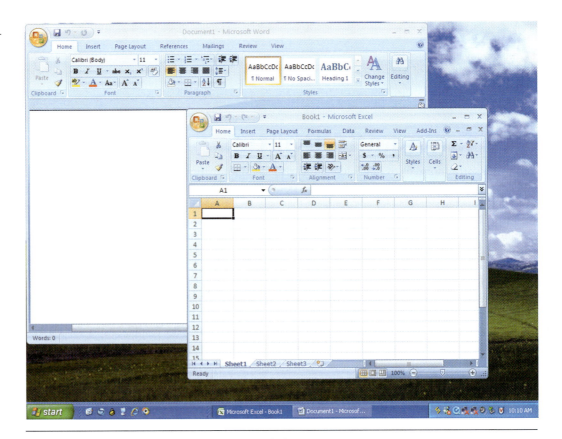

The active window is displayed on top of other open windows

In a graphical user interface, the background displayed on the monitor is considered the desktop environment, or **desktop** for short. Many times the desktop will be made of a photographic image or corporate logo chosen by the computer's user or system administrator, or often times simply an image provided by the operating system manufacturers default settings. Residing on the desktop are other graphical elements, like icons, windows, menus, ribbons, toolbars, and folders.

One of the primary functions of the GUI is to provide a way to launch, or start application software. Application software at its core is a computer program that requires computer programming to launch, or start. Rather than require a user to type in complicated programming code to launch application software, the operating system provides a visual indicator called an icon. An **icon** is a small pictogram on the desktop that the user clicks with the mouse. The clicks represent instructions, or programming that the operating system interprets and in turn launches the application program represented by the icon.

Once the application program is launched, it is rendered in a rectangular area on the desktop called a **window**. The window is a graphical user interface unto its own that outputs information and instructions so the application software residing within the window can be employed effectively.

Some common features of a window are the **"maximize"**, **"minimize"**, **"restore"** and **"close"** buttons located in the top-right corner of the window. The close button shuts the applications software off. It is important to note that the close button does not save any work done during the application's session, but will often prompt a user to do so if they chose. The maximize button expands the window to take up the entire screen, whereas the restore button reduces the size of the window. The minimize button closes the window but not the program and places it on the toolbar. Since operating systems are multitasking and allow for more than one application software to run at a time, the window the user is currently using is referred to as the **active window**.

BLACK & WHITE

File managers are easily understood when one considers a physical filing cabinet first. A physical filing cabinet, whether vertical or horizontal, is simply a large box separated by drawers. Each drawer is marked with sections of the alphabet, like "A through F", and so forth.

GRAY MATTER

Learning a file manager is the first step to becoming a competent computer user. Competent users never "lose" a file.

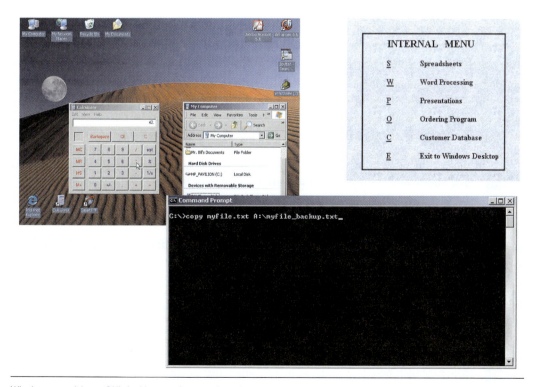

Windows provides a GUI desktop environment

Many windows offer a **menu** system to operate application software. Menus are represented by keywords that provide a list of instructions or options to operate the application software. Menus come in different configurations depending on the software's version. Many menus have associated **toolbars** to accomplish common tasks quickly like saving a document or applying a new font to text. Microsoft is moving towards replacing menus and toolbars by essentially combining both with a graphical toolbar called a **ribbon**. The ribbon consists of tabs across the top of the window that organizes common features like inserting, page layout, and viewing.

Another important feature of the desktop is **folders** which contain groups of computer files like documents and spreadsheets, and often other nested subfolders. Desktop folders act the same way as a physical folder in a filing cabinet that organize paper in a logical system.

Many times a business will provide the basic desktop configuration to its employees to ensure **standardization**, **ease of use**, and **safety**. System administrators can deliver and install their standard corporate desktop configuration, associated desktop features, and application software through a network interface to meet any particular employee's computing needs. Normally, a stand-alone computer could take many hours to configure from scratch. The business is able to rest assured that the employee has the correct tools, like virus utilities and spam blockers and that the employee did not have to do any of the installation themselves. The business also knows that the application software the employee will use has valid software licenses and complies with corporate terms of service agreements.

Some businesses will still allow their employees options to modify their desktop configurations depending on their own policies and procedures. A business may choose to allow the employee to change their desktop background and wallpaper, but not allow the employee to install any new application software themselves.

WHITE BOARD

Explain "maximize", "minimize" and "restore".
What is a user interface and what does it do?
What does a ribbon do and what does it replace?

File Management Systems

One of the most important core elements of system software is its ability to store data and information on a computer and offer a system of file organization and management. Fortunately, a file management system was invented and devised in the late 1800s whose hierarchical structure is used today in modern operating systems.

File managers are easily understood when one considers a physical filing cabinet first. A physical filing cabinet, whether vertical or horizontal, is simply a large box separated by drawers. Each drawer is marked with sections of the alphabet, like "A through F", and so forth. Inside the drawers are folders labeled with customer's names. Inside each folder are papers with the customer's information. Once employees understand the hierarchy of the filing cabinet, everyone is able to use it.

An operating system's file manager is a GUI that works the same way as the physical filing cabinet, based on a hierarchy of folders that contain computer files. Some of the computer files contained in the folders are application software files like documents, spreadsheets, and so forth, while other folders contain the actual programming files that run the application software, and even the operating system itself. Folders can contain other folders, which in turn might contain more folders to form smaller hierarchies.

Courtesy of Prentice-Hall, Inc.

Since a file management system based in an operating system is based in a GUI environment, it is able to do exponentially more than a physical filing cabinet, like searching. File management systems allow the user to search for computer files based on almost any criteria. For instance, if the end user wanted a list of all of the Microsoft Word 2007 documents on the computer, they would type "*.docx" in a search box. The "*" means find any file name, and the ".docx", which is the valid file extension for Word, means only look for Microsoft Word 2007 document files.

What if a person forgot where they stored their resume on their computer? Further, they even forgot the file name of their resume, but at least know the word "resume" is part of the file name. The user would be able to use the search utility and type "*resume*.docx" in the file manager's search box which would return any Microsoft Word 2007 that fit the criteria, like "myresume.docx", or "resume2008.docx".

File management systems also provide vital information about folders and files as well, and offer tools to navigate and organize the computer's "filing cabinet". Some common file management features are listed below:

File name — When a file is created, the user is prompted to save the file and give it a name and designate a location where it will reside on the computer's file manager. It is best practices to use meaningful names. For instance, "1stQuarter2009Budget.xlsx" would be an organization's Microsoft Excel 2007 spreadsheet containing their first quarter budget for 2009. It is also best practice to use meaningful folder names as well. For instance, a folder could be named "Budgets2009" that contains subfolders named "1stQuarter", "2ndQuarter", and so on.

Modification date — It is useful to know when the last time a file was saved or created. For instance, some files aren't modified often, like a resume. The file management system will show the last time a user's resume was updated by showing the last time the document file was saved.

File type — It is useful to know what type of file is in a folder. For instance, the subfolder "4thQuarter" might contain multiple spreadsheets, documents, and database files. File managers can display file types in the folder differentiating spreadsheets, databases, and any other resident files. File type can also show what version of software the file is, like Microsoft Excel 2003 or Microsoft Excel 2007, and even display a small icon next to the file that further indicates its file type.

BLACK & WHITE

The disk is made up of concentric circular bands called **tracks** that are separated into wedges called **sectors**.

GRAY MATTER

Defrag is a utility that that moves positive and negative charges to the innermost tracks of a disk which in turn reduce the amount of time it takes the read/write arm to save or erase data and information. Fragmented files become defragmented and more efficiently stored resulting in better and faster disk performance. The defrag utility can take hours to run depending on the amount of fragmented files on a disk.

Commonly Used Filename Extensions

Extension	File Type
.exe	Program or application
.doc	Microsoft Word
.xls	Microsoft Excel
.ppt	Microsoft PowerPoint
.mdb	Microsoft Access
.pdf	Adobe Acrobat
.txt	ASCII text
.htm or .html	Web pages
.rtf	Files in Rich Text Format
.jpeg or .jpg	Picture or image format

Figure 4C

Commonly used filename extensions.
Courtesy of Prentice-Hall, Inc.

File size — The file manager will show how big or small a file is in terms of bytes. File size lets you determine if a file is getting too big, and perhaps explain why it seems slow on your computer if it is inordinately large. File size can also help determine if a file is too large to be used as an email attachment. File managers will also let you determine the combined size of a folder and all of its contents.

The file manager will let the user sort the contents of a folder by file name, modification date, file type, and file size to better understand the computer's contents. File managers offer an array of tools and utilities to let the user manage and organize folders and files into a logical hierarchy, like "drag and drop", and "copy and paste" to name a few.

Because there are so many different file types, file managers will also display them in a wide variety of ways. For instance, image files can be displayed as small thumbnail images that display a smaller version of the image so the user doesn't have to remember what it looks like based on the file's name alone.

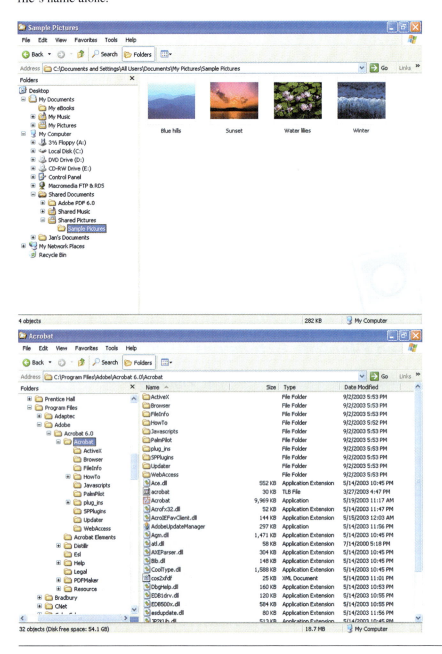

File managers show name, size, file type, date modified, and many other file details.

System Software Utilities

Defragmentation — Sometimes a computer can start to "feel" slow. One of the possible reasons is the nature in which files are saved to secondary storage, spinning media specifically. An internal hard drive is an example of spinning media. Hard drives consist of a spinning magnetic platter called a disk that has a read/write arm depositing positive and negative changes on the disk that represent saved files. Keep in mind the disk is written too frequently as well as having some of its contents erased. The disk is made up of concentric circular bands called **tracks** that are separated into wedges called **sectors**.

A single computer file's thousands of positive and negative charges that represent it can be saved all over a disk. A hard drive attempts to save and erase data and information efficiently, but after a while, positive and negative charges become scattered throughout the tracks and sectors causing the read/write arm to swing to the outermost tracks, then to the inner most, and so on. When data and information becomes scattered on a disk, it is called **fragmented**.

> **BLACK & WHITE**
> System software offers a backup utility to ensure that data and information is safe. The backup utility is a program that copies data from a computer's hard drive to a backup device.

> **GRAY MATTER**
> All files should be backed up in a timely fashion. There is never a legitimate excuse to lose data and information on a computer.

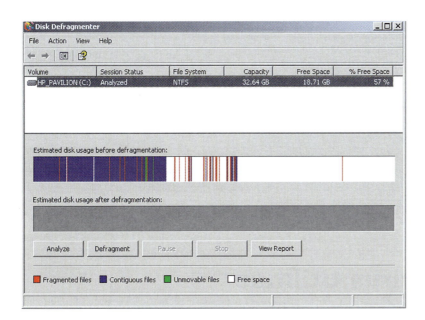

To solve the problem of fragmentation, system software offers a program called **disk defragmentation**, or **defrag** for short. Defrag is a utility that that moves positive and negative charges to the innermost tracks of a disk which in turn reduce the amount of time it takes the read/write arm to save or erase data and information. Fragmented files become defragmented and more efficiently stored resulting in better and faster disk performance. The defrag utility can take hours to run depending on the amount of fragmented files on a disk.

Backup Utilities

A business' most valuable asset is its people. Not far behind is its data and information, most of which is stored on computers. System software offers a **backup** utility to ensure that data and information is safe. The backup utility is a program that copies data from a computer's hard drive to a backup device. The backup device can be many varied types of media, like another hard drive, an optical disk, or a magnetic tape to name a few. The idea is to get the data and information copied to another device in case the computer or drive the data resides on fails.

BLACK & WHITE

Antivirus utilities are system software that identifies known viruses and attempts to block them from entering and infecting a computer system. The antivirus utility keeps a list, specifically a database of known viruses and compares the database to any incoming computer file to see if it is a virus.

GRAY MATTER

It is not a question **if** a virus will attempt to enter a computer; it is simply a question of **when**. Antivirus software is required on every computer

Backup utilities offer options like backing up during off hours when a business is closed. Other options include the ability to back up the entire contents (called a **complete backup**) of a drive (called a mirror image), or just parts of it. Many times backup utilities will back up an entire hard drive and thereafter only back up computers files that have been created or modified since the previous backup, called an **incremental backup**. It is always a good policy to do a complete backup once a month.

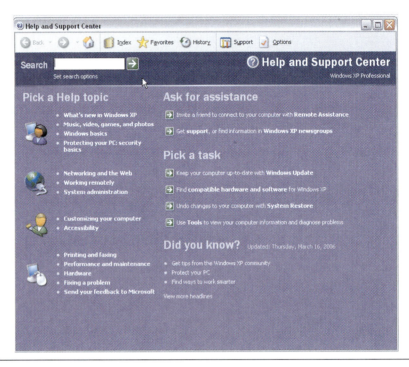

Defragmentation in progress

Antivirus Utilities

Antivirus utilities are system software that identifies known viruses and attempts to block them from entering and infecting a computer system. The antivirus utility keeps a list, specifically a database of known viruses and compares the database to any incoming computer file to see if it is a virus. This is a valuable system to check for viruses but falls short because it will not catch viruses not in the database. Virus software compensates by checking all incoming files for known patterns, or **signatures** of viruses. Since many viruses share common programming techniques, or signatures, viruses that are unknown can also be stopped.

Unfortunately, antivirus system software that examines computer files for signatures and known viruses still falls short because new viruses are developed every day. The answer is to update a computer system constantly to stay ahead of the game. Industry leaders in antivirus system software like **Norton AntiVirus** and **McAfee VirusScan** update a user's computer database through subscription services. It works like this; computer user purchases antivirus system software utilities along with a subscription which performs an initial scan of the entire system for viruses when it is first installed. Once the system is known to be virus free, the subscribed user receives updates via the Internet when the virus software manufacturers when new viruses are discovered.

Antivirus utilities don't just catch viruses; they can also repair an infected computer system by finding existing viruses and either quarantining the infected file or deleting it from the system completely and then adding the virus information to the antivirus database.

System Updates

Operating systems are the most sophisticated software installed on a personal or business computer. It is common practice for an operating system manufacturer to rush their operating systems to market, and often with many components that aren't fully functional. Some new operating systems have security flaws that entice outside hackers to attempt to enter a user's computer without their knowledge and take over their system.

To compensate for any operating system inadequacies, companies like Microsoft offer a system software utility called **system update**. For example, new or modified programming called **patches** are sent from Microsoft via the Internet to a user's computer and added to its operating system to update any deficient operating system files, or to add to features that didn't exist when the operating system was originally installed.

Not all system update patches are to compensate for operating system deficiencies; some patches might include plug and play drivers for peripheral devices like a manufacturer's newest printer, so if the user ever buys the printer, the programming to make it work properly is already onboard the user's computer.

Summary

Remember the company car from the beginning of this chapter? It comes with a spare tire, and a jack. A good company car comes with computer diagnostics to determine problems, and even anticipate them before they happen. Some cars even include satellite communications systems to put the driver in touch with the manufacturer's employees to lend assistance in case of an emergency. Further, cars have onboard navigation systems to help drivers to arrive at their destination.

To be able to operate the company car, it becomes apparent that the driver needs to know more than just how to turn the ignition key and drive. Along with safe operating techniques, the driver needs to be able to operate the car's "system software utilities" to make sure they can overcome and troubleshoot problem that might arise.

System software offers the same sort of troubleshooting as the company car. Any time the computer does something out of the ordinary, chances are the troubleshooting utilities will attempt to repair it, and often times without human interaction.

One of the main and most obvious problems is if the computer simply fails to start normally. If the computer fails to start, then the BIOS cannot search and launch the operating system, where many of the troubleshooting utilities reside. Sometimes the problem is that a new device has been added to the computer causing programming and resource conflicts. For instance, to troubleshoot this sort of problem, Microsoft Windows operating systems will start the computer in **safe mode** which uses the computer's resources at an absolute minimum. Safe mode looks like a stripped down and arcane version of windows that attempts to lead a computer's user through diagnostics and repair.

When problems are so serious that even safe mode is not available, another alternative is to insert the book disk, often a CD that attempts to boot the system by bypassing the operating system that usually resides on a computer's hard drive. If the CD boot disk works, it will present an operating system similar to safe mode and attempt to diagnose and repair the problem, or at the very least, allow the user to recover critical data and information off the computer.

It is often easy to ignore how system software works even though business is completely dependent on an infinite array of computing devices. It is a major advantage to know how a car works when dropping it off to a dealership for repair. One can become an intelligent part of a conversation and feel comfortable that the repairs will be appropriate. The same holds true for system software, whether repairing, upgrading or buying, especially when the stakes are high in a business environment.

Matching

Match each key term in the left column with the most accurate definition in the right column.

____	1. Application Software	A.	Often called firmware.
____	2. Authentication	B.	Programs that help an end-user do a particular task.
____	3. Active Window	C.	Loading the platform into the computer's memory.
____	4. Backup	D.	Determines if a user is the computer's appropriate user.
____	5. Fragmentation	E.	Represents the user's specific preferences, like themes and styles.
____	6. Toolbars	F.	The ability of the system software to support multiple softwares.
____	7. Icon	G.	A small pictogram on the desktop that the user clicks with the mouse.
____	8. Booting	H.	The window the user is currently using.
____	9. File Size	I.	Represented by keywords that provide a list of instructions or options to operate the application software.
____	10. Profile	J.	Contain groups of computer files like documents and spreadsheets.
____	11. Multitasking	K.	Last time a file was saved or created.
____	12. Modification Date	L.	How big or small a file is in terms of bytes.
____	13. Folders	M.	When data and information becomes scattered on a disk.
____	14. Menus	N.	Ensures that data and information is safe.
____	15. System Software	O.	Accomplish common tasks quickly like saving a document or applying a new font to text.

Multiple Choice

1. System software is often called _____.
   a. Multi-software
   b. Hardware
   c. Applications
   d. Firmware

2. Loading the platform into the computer's memory is called _____.
   a. Warming up
   b. Booting
   c. Starting
   d. Tasking

3. The first thing that happens is that system searches for the _____.
   a. CMOS
   b. Platform
   c. BIOS
   d. All of the above

4. Once hardware settings are determined, the operating system loads _____.
   a. System utilities
   b. Application software
   c. Drivers
   d. Windows

5. The ability of the system software to support multiple softwares at a time is called _____.
   a. Platform neutrality
   b. Connectivity
   c. Networking
   d. Multitasking

6. A user _____ interface is what the user sees on the monitor.
   a. Interface
   b. Screen
   c. Profile
   d. GUI

7. The background displayed on the monitor is considered the desktop environment, or _____.
   a. Screen saver
   b. Backdrop
   c. Slide
   d. Desktop

8. A(n) _____ is a small pictogram on the desktop that the user clicks with the mouse.
   a. Character
   b. Lettergram
   c. Icon
   d. Graphic

9. To solve the problem of fragmentation, system software offers a program called _____.
   a. Drivers
   b. GUI
   c. Defrag
   d. Help

10. To compensate for any operating system inadequacies, companies like Microsoft offer a system software utility called _____.
    a. System update
    b. Patches
    c. Disk subscriptions
    d. Compensation utility

1.01000100 | 2.01000010 | 3.01000011 | 4.01000001 | 5.01000100 | 6.01000001 | 7.01000100 | 8.01000011 | 9.01000011 | 10.01000001

Blanks

_____, often called firmware, is software that manages and controls the physical hardware of a computer so that application software can work.

Powering up a computer on for the first time is called a _____ boot, and a computer that is restarted while it was already running is called a _____ boot.

_____ is firmware programming embedded in to a computer chip, meaning the computer runs the same program every time it's turned on.

The operating system in turn takes control and configures the computer's hardware to settings stored in a database called the _____.

In business, it is extremely important that the operating system _____ a user to determine if they are the computer's appropriate user.

Since a computer is a binary system that only understands machine code, it needs special programs called _____ to make input and output devices operate properly.

A(n) _____ is a small pictogram on the desktop that the user clicks with the mouse.

Since operating systems are multitasking and allow for more than one application software to run at a time, the window the user is currently using is referred to as the _____ window.

Many menus have associated _____ to accomplish common tasks quickly like saving a document or applying a new font to text.

System software offers a _____ utility to ensure that data and information is safe.

Short Questions

What is the purpose of a System Update?

What is an incremental backup?

What are some common file management features?

What are three modes of GUI windows?

What is the purpose of a swap file?

What is the purpose of a registry?

seven | green business computing

- Green Business Computing
- Information Technology Challenges and Opportunities
- EPEAT - Electronic Product Environmental Assessment Tool
- EPEAT Criteria
- Energy Star® Specifications
- The Green PC Green Computing Business Plan
- Telecommuting

Green Business Computing

According to **National Aeronautics and Space Administration (NASA)** since the late 1800s, scientists estimate that the Earth's surface temperature has increased about 0.7° to 1.4° degrees Fahrenheit. Many of these scientist estimate that the average temperature will rise an additional 2.5° to 10.4° F by 2100. The concern is that human societies and natural ecosystems may not adapt to this rapid climate change. Many scientists have concluded that human activities like burning fossil fuels and clearing land are responsible for most of the Earth's warming. Burning fossil fuels creates carbon dioxide (CO_2) which builds up and slows the escape of heat into space, therefore creating a "**greenhouse effect**".

Some scientists, specifically at the **National Center for Atmospheric Research** look at computer climate models to predict future climate change and by their own admission claim that these models are extremely unreliable even with current climate data. These same scientists believe that computer climate models may someday be able to predict future climate change, but for right now have no confidence that change in sea ice and clouds are even remotely accurate. If the National Center for Atmospheric Research says climate models are unreliable, it raises serious questions regarding the validity of global warming conclusions.

Like many issues, the discussion of whether global warming exists requires **critical thoughtfulness**. For example, the argument of whether a Mac is better than a Personal Computer (PC) or vice versa can easily narrow into discussions of RAM usage, compatibility, and a myriad of other technical details, but the fact is, PCs dominate the market share in the business workplace. Because of this dispassionate fact, it enables one to make clearer strategic and tactical decisions when selecting a computer or information system for their business. The same holds true with global warming issues. In any walk of life it would be virtually impossible not to come across terminologies like "**green**", or "climate change". The fact is, global warming's problems, challenges, and potential sustainable solutions have gained traction and must be clearly dealt with.

BLACK & WHITE
Burning fossil fuels creates carbon dioxide (CO_2) which builds up and slows the escape of heat into space, therefore creating a "greenhouse effect".

GRAY MATTER
Regardless of the differing views, global warming has gained diffusion and acceptance as an acknowledged problem that will drive many businesses strategic and tactical decisions and sustainable solutions for many decades, creating tens of thousands of new businesses in the process.

Burning fossil fuels creates carbon dioxide (CO_2) which builds up and slows the escape of heat into space, therefore creating a "greenhouse effect."
Courtesy of PhotoLibrary/Index Stock Imagery.

Courtesy of Brian Lawrence/Getty Images.

CHAPTER 7 | Green Business Computing

BLACK & WHITE
Green computing is the practice of using computing resources efficiently while reducing the use of hazardous materials, maximizing energy efficiency, promoting the recyclability of defunct products, and reducing factory waste during the computer's manufacturing process.

GRAY MATTER
Chief Information Officers (CIOs) across the United States and Europe, those who are in charge of all of a business's computer assets, generally agree that green computing is the right thing to do, however, most would also agree that green computing is a business necessity.

Climate models may someday be able to predict future climate change, but for right now scientists have no confidence that change in sea ice and clouds are even remotely accurate.
Courtesy of Bill Bachman/Photo Researchers, Inc.

Regardless of these differing views, global warming has gained **diffusion** and acceptance as an acknowledged problem and will drive many businesses strategic and tactical decisions and sustainable solutions for many decades, creating tens of thousands of new businesses in the process. Being a core activity of business, information technology (IT) is certainly not immune to the fast and ever-changing business environment that has been furiously spawned by global warming and climate change attitudes. Every facet of IT is being rethought and reinvented to keep up with the demand for energy savings, responsible packaging, material selection, and the hundreds of other criteria important to IT consumers.

From a social perspective, environmental responsibility and global governance can simply be seen as the **right** things to do so it's easy to conclude that "greener" computing should follow suit. **Green computing** is the practice of using computing resources efficiently while reducing the use of hazardous materials, maximizing energy efficiency, promoting the recyclability of defunct products, and reducing factory waste during the computer's manufacturing process.

Courtesy of Marco Simoni/Getty Images.

Chief Information Officers (CIOs) across the United States and Europe, those who are in charge of all of a business's computer assets, generally agree that green computing is the right thing to do, however, most would also agree that green computing is a business necessity. For instance, CIOs are in charge of budgeting for all facets of information technology and computer use within a business organization, which includes the cost of power to run a business's computer assets. The cost of power as a percentage of overall IT spending ranges can from 20% for smaller enterprise data centers to 80% for very large ones. CIOs don't just purchase the most powerful and fastest computers; they must consider systems that reduce energy use which translates into millions of dollars of saving. **Green Computing is a necessity**.

CHAPTER 7 | Green Business Computing

Courtesy of John Lamb/Getty Images.

Information Technology Challenges and Opportunities

Computers use power, lots of it. Since virtually all businesses use computers, they need to be **concerned with overall energy costs** and ways to reduce these costs. Consider just the **cost for air conditioning enormous** data centers and computer rooms that house one or many businesses critical data and information. Finding a solution to reduce the heat computers put out by only a few degrees can equate to millions of dollars of cost savings. The IT industry will also have to be concerned with government imposed levies and statutes on **carbon production in the computer manufacturing** process as well as **regulations on power consumption and waste**. The IT industry will have to comply with these governmental regulations which will only get more stringent with time.

BLACK & WHITE

In 2006, the Environmental Protection Agency (EPA) funded a grant that developed the Electronic Product Environmental Assessment Tool or EPEAT for short managed by the Green Electronics Council (GEC).

GRAY MATTER

The idea for the computer manufacturer would be to meet as many of the criteria as possible and in turn be awarded one of EPEAT's Gold, Silver, or Bronze environmental performance designations so the consumer is able to differentiate which products are environmentally sound, and which ones are not.

Computers are made up of all sorts of chemicals, whether it is in the manufacturing process, the actual computer itself, or the disposal of a computer when it is no longer useful. The need for an **environmentally responsible way to dispose of old software and hardware** becomes a paramount challenge to all businesses.

Working, sustainable solutions, when applied to all of these challenges will yield vast benefits for the environment, information technology and the businesses and people that use them. The adoption of energy efficient and green practices will save businesses trillions of dollars.

Courtesy of Matti Niemi/Getty Images.

WHITE BOARD

What are some concerns in Green Computing?
Why are Chief Information Officers concerned with Green Computing?
Is adopting Green Computing practices the right thing to do and why?
Is adopting Green Computing practices a necessity and why?

BLACK & WHITE

Energy Star® is a joint program of the U.S. Department of Energy and the U.S. Environmental Protection Agency (EPA) that attempts to help businesses and consumers save money and protect the environment by identifying energy efficient products and practices.

GRAY MATTER

Energy Star® claims that if all computers sold in the United States meet the Energy Star® requirements, the savings in energy costs alone will grow to about $2 billion each year and greenhouse gas emissions will be reduced by the equivalent of those from 2 million cars.

EPAT - Electronic Product Environmental Assessment Tool

In 2006, the **Environmental Protection Agency (EPA)** funded a grant that developed the **Electronic Product Environmental Assessment Tool** or **EPEAT** for short managed by the **Green Electronics Council (GEC)**. EPEAT is an easy-to-use online tool that helps large institutions purchase, select, and compare computer desktops, laptops and monitors based on their environmental attributes.

EPEAT evaluates electronic products, many of which are business computers relative to 51 environmental criteria, 23 of the criteria are required and 28 of the criteria are optional. The idea for the computer manufacturer would be to meet as many of the criteria as possible and in turn be awarded one of EPEAT's Gold, Silver, or Bronze environmental performance designations so the consumer is able to differentiate which products are environmentally sound, and which ones are not. To even qualify for registration as an EPEAT product, a product must conform to all the required criteria listed below:

EPEAT Criteria

Reduction or elimination of environmentally sensitive materials: Computers use chemicals like cadmium, mercury, chromium, and many others in their manufacturing process as well as in the finished product which can potentially harm the environment. EPEAT's first criterion encourages manufacturers to reduce the amount of chemicals or eliminate them altogether whether in the manufacturing process or when the computer is discarded.

Materials selection: Materials selection informs the consumer of the percentage of recycled plastics and offers a declaration of the percentage of renewable/bio-based plastic material content. The materials selection criterion also offers the consumer the weight of the product. The consumer can then compare products like computers based on materials which may sway their final decision.

Design for end of life: Design for end of life means that computer manufacturers, as well as all electronics manufacturers, inform their consumers about the special handling needs while disposing of their product when it is no longer useful. Manufacturers are discouraged from using paints and special coatings that are not compatible with recycling. They are also encouraged to make products that are easier to disassemble, mark components for easier identification, and identify hazardous parts, all which promote the recycling process.

Product longevity/life cycle extension: Product longevity/life cycle extensions encourage manufacturers to make extended warranties available to their consumers so their products last longer, and also to design the product so it can be upgraded with common tools.

End of life management: End of life management asks manufacturers to make provisions to take their product back at the end of the product's life cycle. For example, computer manufacturers would have to set up programs that would let their customers' mail their old computers in when they are no longer needed and the manufacturer would dispose of the product responsibly. Manufacturers would also have to set up provisions to take back old batteries.

Corporate performance: Corporate performance means that a manufacturer must demonstrate a sound corporate environmental policy consistent with International Organization for Standardization and have self-certified environmental management systems for in place for the design and manufacturing.

Courtesy of Andrew Paterson/Getty Images.

Packaging: Packaging criteria requires computer and electronics manufacturers to reduce or eliminate intentionally added toxins in packaging as well as having separable packing materials with a declaration of recycled content.

Energy conservation: Energy conservation asks manufacturers to adopt the government's Energy Star® specifications which are discussed later in the chapter.

The Electronic Product Environmental Assessment Tool (EPEAT) asks manufacturers to do a lot, much of which dramatically increases their manufacturing costs. If their costs increase, their profits will suffer, so will they be willing to participate in a program that depends on an educated consumer that knows to look for a bronze, silver, or gold EPEAT seal? Are consumers conscientious enough to pay more for a product with an EPEAT gold star that may save them money and help the environment or will they opt for a less expensive computer that is more harmful to the environment? Should the government mandate EPEAT for all computers sold in the United States? It is important to weigh environmental responsibility with solid business concepts.

All EPEAT Criteria (R-Required O-Optional)
4.1 Reduction/elimination of environmentally sensitive materials
R 4.1.1.1 Compliance with provisions of European RoHS Directive upon its effective date
O 4.1.2.1 Elimination of intentionally added cadmium
R 4.1.3.1 Reporting on amount of mercury used in light sources (mg)
O 4.1.3.2 Low threshold for amount of mercury used in light sources
O 4.1.3.3 Elimination of intentionally added mercury used in light sources
O 4.1.4.1 Elimination of intentionally added lead in certain applications
O 4.1.5.1 Elimination of intentionally added hexavalent chromium
R 4.1.6.1 Elimination of intentionally added SCCP flame retardants and plasticizers in certain applications
O 4.1.6.2 Large plastic parts free of certain flame retardants classified under European Council Directive 67/548/EEC
O 4.1.7.1 Batteries free of lead, cadmium and mercury
O 4.1.8.1 Large plastic parts free of PVC
(continued)

All EPEAT Criteria (R-Required O-Optional) Cont.

4.2 Materials selection

- **R** 4.2.1.1 Declaration of postconsumer recycled plastic content (%)
- **O** 4.2.1.2 Minimum content of postconsumer recycled plastic
- **O** 4.2.1.3 Higher content of postconsumer recycled plastic
- **R** 4.2.2.1 Declaration of renewable/bio-based plastic materials content (%)
- **O** 4.2.2.2 Minimum content of renewable/bio-based plastic material
- **R** 4.2.3.1 Declaration of product weight (lbs)

4.3 Design for end of life

- **R** 4.3.1.1 Identification of materials with special handling needs
- **R** 4.3.1.2 Elimination of paints or coatings that are not compatible with recycling or reuse
- **R** 4.3.1.3 Easy disassembly of external enclosure
- **R** 4.3.1.4 Marking of plastic components
- **R** 4.3.1.5 Identification and removal of components containing hazardous materials
- **O** 4.3.1.6 Reduced number of plastic material types
- **O** 4.3.1.7 Molded/glued in metal eliminated or removable
- **R** 4.3.1.8 Minimum 65 percent reusable/recyclable
- **O** 4.3.1.9 Minimum 90 percent reusable/recyclable
- **O** 4.3.2.1 Manual separation of plastics
- **O** 4.3.2.2 Marking of plastics

4.4 Product longevity/life cycle extension

- **R** 4.4.1.1 Availability of additional three year warranty or service agreement
- **R** 4.4.2.1 Upgradeable with common tools
- **O** 4.4.2.2 Modular design
- **O** 4.4.3.1 Availability of replacement parts

4.5 Energy conservation

- **R** 4.5.1.1 ENERGY STAR®
- **O** 4.5.1.2 Early adoption of new ENERGY STAR® specification
- **O** 4.5.2.1 Renewable energy accessory available
- **O** 4.5.2.2 Renewable energy accessory standard

4.6 End of life management

- **R** 4.6.1.1 Provision of product take-back service
- **O** 4.6.1.2 Auditing of recycling vendors
- **R** 4.6.2.1 Provision of rechargeable battery take-back service

(continued)

All EPEAT Criteria (R-Required O-Optional) Cont.
4.7 Corporate performance
R 4.7.1.1 Demonstration of corporate environmental policy consistent with ISO 14001
R 4.7.2.1 Self-certified environmental management system for design and manufacturing organizations
O 4.7.2.2 Third-party certified environmental management system for design and manufacturing organizations
R 4.7.3.1 Corporate report consistent with Performance Track or GRI
O 4.7.3.2 Corporate report based on GRI
4.8 Packaging
R 4.8.1.1 Reduction/elimination of intentionally added toxics in packaging
R 4.8.2.1 Separable packing materials
O 4.8.2.2 Packaging 90% recyclable and plastics labeled
R 4.8.3.1 Declaration of recycled content in packaging
O 4.8.3.2 Minimum postconsumer content guidelines
O 4.8.4.1 Provision of take-back program for packaging
O 4.8.5.1 Documentation of reusable packaging

> **BLACK & WHITE**
>
> In many instances, computer products that display the Energy Star® seal are more expensive to purchase but are far more efficient and cost effective in the long run.

> **GRAY MATTER**
>
> The Energy Star® program asks computer makers to focus on three PC modes: Active Use, Sleep Mode and "Off", or Standby Mode.

Had you ever heard of EPEAT until now? If you were in your local electronics store and saw one of EPEAT's gold environmental performance designation stickers on a personal computer, would you have any idea what it is or what it means? Even if you knew what it meant, would it be the most important criteria in your buying decision? A 'gold' EPEAT computer is obviously going to cost a significant amount more to manufacture. For argument sake, let's say the EPEAT box costs $200 more than a non-EPEAT box. Both boxes have exactly the same specifications (same hard-disk size, same RAM, etc.). Do you want to save the planet? Pay $200 extra if you do, at least you'll make less of an environmental impact. Does it mean you don't love the planet if you decide on the non-EPEAT box and save $200?

Now consider your federal and state governments who are pushing to become more 'green'. What if they decide to mandate that all of the computers must be EPEAT compliant, specifically with gold environmental performance designations? If they do, that government can claim to be greener to a certain extent. Governments don't buy computers one at a time; on the contrary, they buy them thousands at a time. Now consider the added cost of the EPEAT computers. Will the government raise taxes so they can be greener? Maybe they will actually save money in the long run. Hopefully they will use less electricity as a result of the EPEAT's Energy Star's compliance. Maybe they will avoid the cost of end-of-life computer disposal when the boxes are no longer useful. Either way, becoming 'greener' costs money.

> **WHITE BOARD**
>
> What is EPEAT?
> Why are some EPEAT criteria?
> What does the acronym EPEAT mean?
> What government body started EPEAT?

BLACK & WHITE

The process of power conversion is actually very inefficient so Energy Star® standards required that a PC's power supply convert 65% of its AC power into DC current, and revised that standard in 2007 to 80%. The EPA calls this the "80 Plus" standard.

GRAY MATTER

Green Computing Business Plans are based on the idea that businesses can become environmentally friendly, more profitable, and socially responsible through a series well-though out implementations of sustainable policies and procedures and future information technology purchasing.

Energy Star® Specifications

In 1992 the (EPA) introduced **Energy Star®** as a voluntary labeling program designed to identify and promote energy-efficient products, like business computers, to reduce greenhouse gas emissions. Computers and monitors were the first labeled products. The Energy Star® label is now on over 50 product categories including major appliances, office equipment, lighting, and home electronics. The idea is to design products like chips, motherboards, and other computer components to use far less electrical wattage than conventional computers.

Energy Star® is a joint program of the **U.S. Department of Energy** and the **U.S. Environmental Protection Agency (EPA)** that attempts to help businesses and consumers save money and protect the environment by identifying energy efficient products and practices. The idea is that if a computer manufacturer complies with a series of energy saving criteria, they will be awarded the Energy Star® seal that informs consumers which computing systems are energy efficient. The Energy Star® logo is far more recognizable to the consumer than EPEAT. Energy Star® claims that if all computers sold in the United States meet the Energy Star® requirements, the savings in energy costs alone will grow to about $2 billion each year and greenhouse gas emissions will be reduced by the equivalent of those from 2 million cars.

Central processing unit (CPU) manufacturers like **Intel®** and **AMD®** spend huge amounts of time and resources researching better ways to make their chips more energy efficient which will, in turn, allow them to display the Energy Star® seal on their products. Intel claims that by shrinking transistor size from 65nm to 45nm and using different transistor materials, they can dramatically increase the performance and efficiency of its core micro-architecture. Intel's 45nm processors are produced using a lead-free process and use Hi-k silicon technology for reduced transistor leakage, enabling more energy-efficient, high-performance processors. These products result in sleeker, smaller and more energy-efficient desktops, notebook PCs, mobile devices and server designs.

Courtesy of Getty Images.

In many instances, computer products that display the Energy Star® seal are more expensive to purchase but are far more efficient and cost effective in the long run.

The Green PC

Personal computer (PC) makers are working diligently to develop more environmentally friendly systems called **Green PCs**. The question is what constitutes a Green PC? EPEAT and Energy Star® programs outline various standards, but generally, a Green PC includes the following:

- Include energy-efficient power supplies.
- Include power supplies and processors that consume minimum amounts of electricity.
- Attempt to do away with or at least minimize environmentally harmful components.
- Make use of aluminum or plastic parts made from post-consumer, recycled materials.

The most important factor in a Green PC is energy efficiency. The Energy Star® program asks computer makers to focus on three PC modes: **Active Use, Sleep Mode** and **"Off"**, or **Standby Mode**. Active Use simply means a computer is on and being used. Sleep mode a special low-power mode where power to certain areas of the computer is shut off after a designated period of time, and Standby mode is when a computer turns off automatically when it has not been used for a specific amount of time designated by the user.

In the Active Use mode, a PC uses about 50 watts and a laptop uses 14. In Sleep Mode, a PC uses 4 watts, and a laptop uses about 1.5. In the Standby mode, a PC uses 2 watts and a laptop uses 1 watt. Obviously, the shorter the time period a user designates to enter these modes, the more energy or cost savings. Many businesses have focused only on criteria like size, portability, and cost in the past to decide whether to buy a business PC or a laptop, so it is also important for them to note that laptops use far less energy, which could be a major factor in their purchasing decisions.

Energy Star® also focuses on the power that enters the business computer. PC power supplies convert AC power to DC power. The process of power conversion is actually very inefficient so Energy Star® standards required that a PC's power supply convert 65% of its AC power into DC current, and revised that standard in 2007 to 80%. The EPA calls this the **"80 Plus"** standard. Energy Star® also sets power conversion standards for when a PC and computer monitor enters Sleep mode. Energy Star® standards require a PC to enter Sleep mode after 30 minutes of inactivity and a monitor to enter Sleep mode after 15 minutes of inactivity.

Computer makers like **Apple** have been extremely aggressive by reducing and eliminating toxic substances like polyvinyl chloride (PVCs) in their manufacturing process. **Hewlett-Packard** (HP) claims their computers produce less heat and reduce cooling energy by 15% to 30%, and use up to 75% less energy in Sleep mode. PC maker **Lenovo** offers 42 PC models that are EPEAT compliant, many of which have EPEAT's gold rating. **Dell** claims their computers use 25% less energy than they did only a few years ago.

Businesses have always had to consider a myriad of criteria when deciding which computers to purchase. Criteria that must also be considered are the benefits of Green PCs. Green PCs benefits can be categorized as either socially responsible or purely economic. From the socially responsible standpoint, a business can feel good about "doing the right" thing by purchasing Green PCs but also needs to weigh the benefits from the purely economic standpoint to make a fiscally responsible purchasing decision. The trick is to do both while still gaining a competitive advantage.

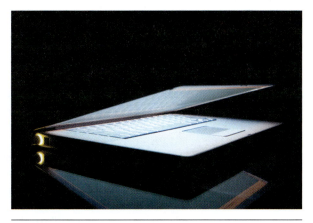
Courtesy of Scott Heiner/Getty Images.

BLACK & WHITE
By choosing a manufacturer that offers a recycling service at the time of purchase, a business can rest assured that they can send the old computer or peripheral device back and it will be recycled or disposed correctly, many times according to EPA and EPEAT standards.

GRAY MATTER
Reducing paper consumption is a corporate attitude that must be adhered to. It's not practical to never print, but many techniques can greatly reduce paper use like widening margins on documents, reducing font size, and printing on both sides of paper.

WHITE BOARD
Describe some Green PC criteria.
What does the term "80 Plus" mean?
Which computer manufacturers are producing Green PCs?

Green Computing Business Plan

Green Computing Business Plans are based on the idea that businesses can become environmentally friendly, more profitable, and socially responsible through well-though out implementations

BLACK & WHITE

Telecommuting is essentially a work arrangement where employees benefit from flexibility in working location and hours. Telecommuting typically does not require an employee to physically commute to a central location to work and is replaced by some form of computer telecommunication link, like the Internet.

GRAY MATTER

In many cases, telecommuters work from their own home office and may not ever visit their businesses physical conventional offices at a central location for months. In some instances, some telecommuters never meet their boss or fellow employees in person.

of sustainable policies and procedures and through future information technology purchasing. Businesses start developing Green Computing Business Plans with the following baseline consideration:

- Organizational Policies and Procedures
- Best Practice Considerations
- Long-term, Sustainability Considerations
- Reduction of Power Usage and Paper Consumption
- Recycling Policies and Procedures
- Used Computer Software and Hardware Disposal
- Governmental Guidelines (EPEAT & Energy Star®)
- Green Computer Equipment Purchasing Recommendations

Courtesy of Getty Images.

It may seem obvious, but one of the most important aspects of a Green Computing Business Plan is to actually do it, and keep doing it. Developing a plan is admirable, but without implementation and continued enforcement of policies and procedures, it's just talk. Top level management must back the Green Computing Business Plan for it to be successful. As with other types of business plans, the Green Computing Business Plan must outline tangible benefits like the ones listed below:

Responsible Recycling: Reusing paper is a good start, but in information technology, recycling involves discarding old computers in very conscientious ways because they are filled with harmful chemicals and toxins. By choosing a manufacturer that offers a recycling service at the time of purchase, a business can rest assured that they can send the old computer or peripheral device back and it will be recycled or disposed of correctly, many times according to EPA and EPEAT standards. One of the easiest ways to recycle older computer equipment is to donate it to schools or charities which can be advantageous depending how a business accounts and depreciates this equipment.

Follow EPEAT and Energy Star® Guidelines: Include the bronze, silver, and gold EPEAT logos, as well as Energy Star® seals, for computer purchasing criteria to evaluate, compare, and select computers. EPEAT's online resource is a good baseline for comparative computer purchasing as well as for identifying top EPEAT manufacturers. Energy Star® standards assure computer purchasers of a direct cost savings through efficient energy use and conservation. Include business-wide computer standards for Active Use Mode, Sleep Mode and Standby Mode as well as corporate policies regarding when it's appropriate to turn off computers altogether.

Courtesy of Kevin Lanthier/Getty Images.

Decrease or Eliminate Paper Consumption: The easiest way to decrease or eliminate paper consumption is simply to not print documents, ever. Although this notion may seem severe, it's not. Computing systems are designed to distribute and disseminate information efficiently, using things like emails and monitors. Reducing paper consumption is a corporate **attitude** that must be adhered to. It's not practical to never print, but many techniques can greatly reduce paper use like widening margins on documents, reducing font size, and printing on both sides of paper.

Economic Considerations: It is gratifying to implement a Green Computing Business Plan as well as fostering a socially responsible corporate environment; however, do not ignore economic implications for the sake of being "Green". Business plans *must* demonstrate clear economic benefits to become sustainable corporate policies and procedures.

> **WHITE BOARD**
>
> What is a Green Computing Plan?
> Why are some of the considerations when making a Green Computing Plan?
> What is one of the most important aspects of a Green Computing Plan?

Telecommuting

One popular way to promote a green business environment is to allow employees to telecommute. **Telecommuting** is essentially a work arrangement where employees benefit from flexibility in working location and hours. Telecommuting typically does not require an employee to physically commute to a central location to work and is replaced by some form of computer telecommunication link, like the Internet. One of the main benefits of telecommuting is that it typically reduces an employee's "**carbon footprint**", which is the measure of the impact human activities have on the environment relative to the amount of greenhouse gases produced, measured in units of carbon dioxide". One environmental benefit of telecommuting is the reduction of traffic congestion, which in turn reduces air pollution and petroleum use.

In many cases, telecommuters work from their own home office and may not ever visit their businesses physical, conventional offices at a central location for months. In some instances, telecommuters may never meet their boss or fellow employees in person. The minimum tools of telecommuting are normally a phone and a computer with Internet access. The employee is able to field work requests from both devices which mean a business does not have to provide space for them at a central location. With bandwidth increasing exponentially and Internet access becoming less expensive; the cost to connect a telecommuter to their employer's intranet and network has become negligible when compared with the operating costs of providing space in a conventional office.

Telecommuting research conducted in 2008 shows that 33 million Americans hold jobs that could be done from their own home office. If they did, the U.S. could make major cuts in oil dependency. The Environmental Protection Agency and the Department of Transportation suggest that expanding telecommuting in the United States to those not currently doing so can reduce oil imports by as much as 48%.

Courtesy of Siri Stafford/Getty Images.

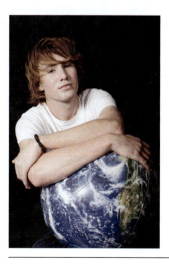

Courtesy of David Freund/Getty Images.

Summary

Green Business Computing is the practice of applying computing resources resourcefully while reducing the use of hazardous materials, increasing energy efficiency, promoting recycling, and reducing waste created during a computer's manufacturing. It is important to realize that Green Business Computing is not just the right thing to do, but a necessity from both a business and environmental perspective.

There are many **Information Technology Challenges and Opportunities** that are concerned with energy costs, carbon production, power utilization, governmental regulations, and waste. The need for an environmentally accountable way to dispose of outdated software and hardware is a challenge to all businesses. These challenges must be met with sustainable solutions to reap the benefits for the environment, information technology and the businesses and people that use them.

The Electronic Product Environmental Assessment Tool (EPEAT) and its stringent criteria are an online tool designed to inform consumers about electronic products which includes computing systems and their peripheral products, like printers and scanners, and rates which ones are the most environmentally friendly. The **Energy Star®** Program sets out criteria to computer manufacturers that rate computers according to their energy efficiencies. Both programs are effective ways to lay out standards where both the computer manufacturers and consumers can understand which products are environmentally responsible as well as cost effective.

Green PCs include energy efficient power supplies and processors that attempt to use a minimum amount of electricity and attempt to at least minimize the use of harmful components. Manufacturers of Green PCs use materials like aluminum and plastics to make the recycling process more efficient when the computer is no longer useful to a business. **Green Computing Business Plans** help businesses become environmentally friendly, more profitable, and more socially responsible through the implementation of policies and procedures. Businesses can start developing Green Computing Business Plans by considering their organizational policies and procedures, best practices, reduction of power usage and paper consumption, recycling policies, and following EPEAT and Energy Star® standards.

Telecommuting is an agreement between employers and their employees where the employee benefits from flexible working locations and hours and the employer benefits from reduced overhead expense and increased employee satisfaction. Telecommuting does not require an employee to physically commute to a central location; rather it is replaced by some form of computer telecommunication link, like the Internet. One of the main benefits of telecommuting is that it reduces an employee's carbon footprint.

Please be good to the Earth.

Matching

Match each key term in the left column with the most accurate definition in the right column.

____	1. EPEAT	A.	Manufacturer must demonstrate a sound corporate environmental policy.
____	2. GEC	B.	Manufacturers to make provisions to take their product back at the end of the product's life cycle.
____	3. Design for end of life	C.	Central processing unit (CPU) manufacturers
____	4. Materials selection	D.	Introduced in 1992 by the EPA
____	5. End life management	E.	Claims their computers use 25% less energy than they did only a few years ago.
____	6. Corp. performance	F.	The most important factor in a Green PC
____	7. Packaging	G.	Criteria requires computer and electronics manufacturers to reduce or eliminate intentionally added toxins in packaging.
____	8. Energy Star®	H.	The Energy Star® program asks computer makers to focus on
____	9. Intel® and AMD®	I.	Claims their computers produce less heat and reduce cooling energy by 15% to 30%, and use up to 75% less energy in Sleep mode.
____	10. Green PCs	J.	A work arrangement where employees benefit from flexibility in working location and hours.
____	11. Energy efficiency	K.	Informs the consumer of the percentage of recycled plastics.
____	12. Three PC modes	L.	Personal computer (PC) makers are working diligently to develop more environmentally friendly systems.
____	13. Telecommuting	M.	Special handling needs while disposing of their product when it is no longer useful.
____	14. Hewlett-Packard	N.	Green Electronics Council.
____	15. Dell	O.	Electronic Product Environmental Assessment Tool.

Multiple Choice

1. Like many issues, the discussion of whether global warming exists requires _____.
   a. Balance
   b. Media
   c. Critical thought
   d. All of the above

2. _____ is the practice of using computing resources efficiently while reducing the use of hazardous materials, maximizing energy efficiency, promoting the recyclability of defunct products, and reducing factory waste during the computer's manufacturing process.
   a. EPEAT
   b. Green Computing
   c. Active mode
   d. Standby mode

3. _____ across the USA and Europe, those who are in charge generally agree that green computing is the right thing to do.
   a. CEOs
   b. CFOs
   c. CIOs
   d. All of the above

4. _____ is a necessity.
   a. Green computing
   b. EPEAT
   c. Energy Star
   d. All of the above

5. EPEAT is managed by the _____.
   a. SEC
   b. Government
   c. EPA
   d. GEC

6. _____ informs the consumer of the percentage of recycled plastics.
   a. Materials selection
   b. EPEAT
   c. EPA
   d. All of the above

7. _____ means that computer manufacturers inform their consumers about the special handling needs while disposing of products.
   a. Green computing
   b. Telecommuting
   c. Materials selection
   d. Design for end of life

8. In 1992, the EPA introduced _____.
   a. Green computing
   b. EPEAT
   c. Energy Star
   d. All of the above

9. Which is not a PC mode?
   a. Active
   b. Sleep
   c. Inactive
   d. Standby

10. _____ is essentially a work arrangement where employees benefit from flexibility in working location and hours.
    a. Telecommuting
    b. Modem surfing
    c. Internet
    d. All of the above

Blanks

Like many issues, the discussion of whether global warming exists requires _____.

According to _____ since the 1800s, scientists estimate that the Earth's surface temperature has increased about 0.7° to 1.4°.

_____ is the practice of using computing resources efficiently while reducing the use of hazardous materials, maximizing energy efficiency, promoting recyclability.

_____ use chemicals like cadmium, mercury, chromium, and many others in their manufacturing process.

_____ encourage manufacturers to make extended warranties available to their consumers so their products last longer.

_____ make provisions to take their product back at the end of the product's life cycle.

_____ means that a manufacturer must demonstrate a sound corporate environmental policy.

_____ criteria requires computer and electronics manufacturers to reduce or eliminate intentionally added toxins in packaging as well as having separable packing materials with a declaration of recycled content.

_____ is a joint program of the EPA that attempts to help businesses and consumers save money and protect the environment by identifying energy efficient products and practices.

Personal computer (PC) makers are working diligently to develop more environmentally friendly systems called _____.

Short Questions

What are the three PC modes the Energy Star® program is concerned with?

What is the 80 Plus Standard?

What does the acronym EPEAT stand for?

Who started EPEAT and why?

How does telecommuting promote a greener environment?

What is a carbon footprint?

eight | networks

Networks
Building a Computer Network
Network Operating Systems
Network Topology
Types of Computer Networks
Network Security

Networks

A **computer network** is two or more computers connected together to communicate and share resources. The shared resources refer to computer files, folders, software, and also peripheral hardware like printers, scanners, webcams, etc. The advantages of a computer network over a stand-alone system are so significant that businesses cannot compete effectively in the marketplace without a network of some kind, even if the business is a sole proprietorship.

BLACK & WHITE

A computer network is two or more computers connected together to communicate and share resources. The shared resources refer to computer files, folders, software, and also peripheral hardware like printers, scanners, webcams, etc.

GRAY MATTER

Can a business survive without a network? The answer is clearly no. A stand-alone computer can be powerful, but a network is exponentially more useful.

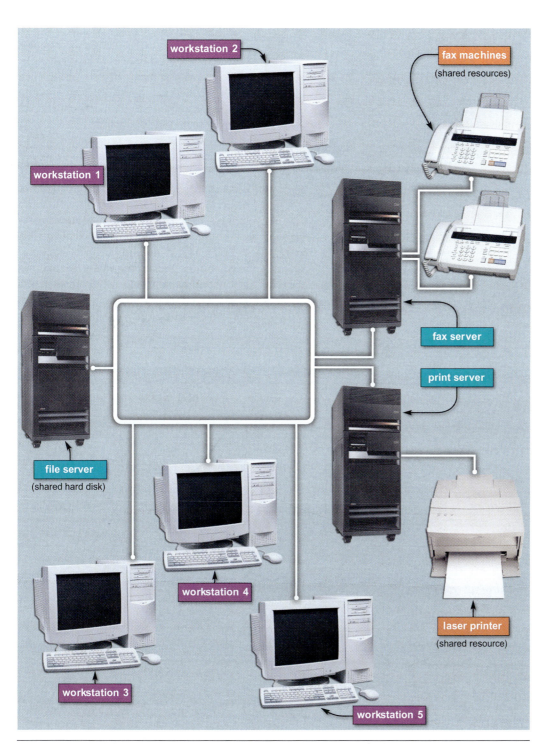

Courtesy of IBM Corporation; and courtesy of Pearson Education.

CHAPTER 8 | Networks

To further understand computer networks, consider the figure below. This is a computer network made up of three computers, called **clients**, which are connected to a central computer called a **server**. Notice the server is connected to two **peripheral devices**, a printer and a scanner. Consider this computer network is used by a small three person business, and as you read on, consider the alternatives of not using a network. Every device connected to a network is called a **node**.

To start to get a small idea of network advantages, consider a three person business called Net Pros that decides to invest in a network, and another three person business called No Net that decides a network is an unnecessary expense. Refer to the *Table 1* below to compare startup costs of both companies.

Notice that No Net's startup costs are considerably lower ($4,600) than Net Pros because they did not have to pay for a server or network, but did have to buy two extra printers. (The network allows all three computers to use the same printer). Although Net Pros initial start up costs seem counterintuitive at first glance, the many advantages below will demonstrate why computer networks are far more valuable:

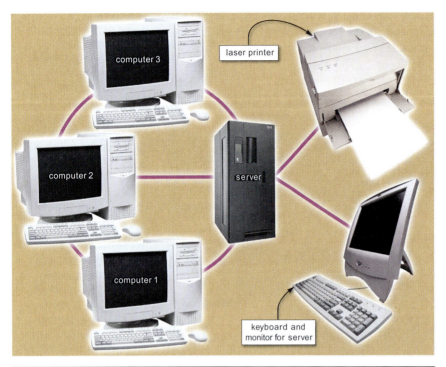

Courtesy of Prentice-Hall, Inc.

BLACK & WHITE
A computer network is an absolute necessity for any size business, even a sole proprietor who must at least be connected to the Internet, the world's largest computer network.

GRAY MATTER
Most computing systems assume that they will be connected to a network, at the very least the Internet.

Table 1

Net Pros	Quantity	Price	Total
Desktop Computer (Clients)	3	$1,500	$4,500
Server Computer	1	$3,000	$3,000
Printer	1	$500	$500
Scanner	1	$200	$200
Network	1	$3,000	$3,000
			$11,200
No Net	**Quantity**	**Price**	**Total**
Desktop Computer	3	$1,500	$4,500
Server Computer	n/a		
Printer	3	$500	$1,500
Scanner	3	$200	$600
Network	n/a	$0	
			$6,600

Economics — *Table 1* shows that No Net had to buy three printers and three scanners instead of just one printer and one scanner. Everyone at Net Pros has the ability to print and scan a document at the same peripheral printer and scanner, whereas No Net had to buy two extra printers, and two extra scanners to have the same capabilities. Although No Net was able to absorb these extra costs and still have less initial capital outlay than Net Pros, they will continue to incur these costs on a go-forward basis.

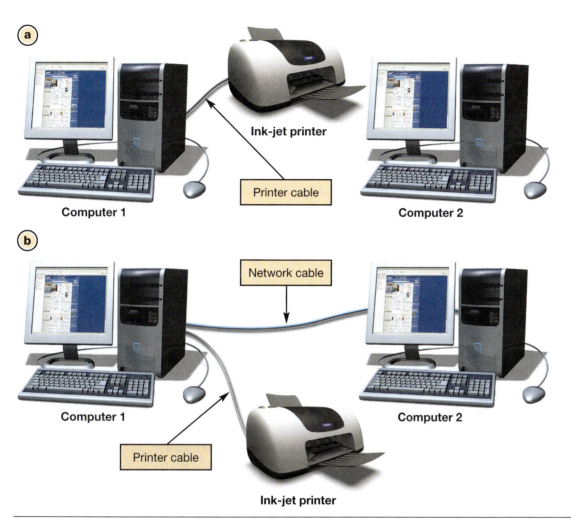

(a) Computers 1 and 2 are NOT networked so computer 2 cannot access the printer. (b) Networking allows both computers to share one printer.
Courtesy of Pearson Education.

Peripherals — Suppose both companies want to upgrade to a new $700 printer? Net Pros will simply spend $700 one time for one printer that all its employees can use, whereas No Net will have to buy three printers for $2,100 to match capabilities. No Net can certainly decide that they will purchase only one printer, but only one of their employees will be able to use it. Net Pros will always have this decided advantage anytime the need a peripheral device.

Courtesy of Canon U.S.A., Inc.

Courtesy of Microsoft Corporation.

Software — Assume both companies use the same system and application software, like Microsoft Vista and Microsoft Office 2007. Net Pros will install the software one time on their server where it can be used by all the client computers, and No Net will have to install the same software three times on three different computers. The cost for the software is the same for both companies (Net Pros needs to purchase 3 licenses), yet the time involved to install Not Net's software is far greater. If both companies want to upgrade their software, Net Pros will upgrade once on the server and all of the clients will benefit, whereas No Net will have to upgrade all three computers individually. Net Pros can also be assured that everyone in the company is on the same page because they know everyone is using standard software.

Collaboration — Both companies have an expectation that their employees will collaborate on certain projects, which may mean sharing spreadsheets or any other computer files from time to time. Net Pros is able to set up a folder on a networked drive on their server, and put all the appropriate files in one place on the server where all three of their employees can access them. Because No Net's computers are independent of one another, only one of their employees will be able start the project, and then have to copy any computer files associated with the project to some sort of media, like a flash drive to share it with their cohorts. Their cohorts in turn will copy the flash drive's information to their computer and then update the files and will only be able to share their work by recopying to the flash drive's updated contents and give it to whoever needs the information next. This can be very arduous and error prone.

BLACK & WHITE

The Network Interface Card is plugged into a slot on the motherboard inside of the computer that allows a network cable to be plugged in so it can interface, or communicate with other computers.

GRAY MATTER

Most computers sold come with a network interface card on board which is an indication of how valuable it is to be attached to a network.

Back Up — Every computer system needs to be backed up on a regular basis to assure no computer files are lost. Since No Net is using independent computers, it is incumbent on each of the three users to back up their system themselves, and also restore lost computer files when need be. Net Pros on the other hand know that computer files that they saved to the network server are backed up on a regular basis automatically, and so don't need to be concerned with this mundane but critically important chore.

Internet — One peripheral benefit of a network is that a single Internet line can be wired to the server and all of the clients can then connect. No Net's three employees must pay for three separate Internet lines for each individual computer, a far more costly and complicated proposition. Because Net Pros is able to leverage a single Internet connection that services all of the client computers, it can take advantage of an email system and instant messaging as well.

Courtesy of Associated Press.

Although the example above is oversimplified, it illustrates just some of the few benefits of networks and points out that although initial start up costs for a network can be greater than without, the benefits of a network far outweigh having individual, stand alone computers. Even if a business is a sole proprietorship, it must make use of network to compete, and many times that network is the Internet, the world's largest network. Keep in mind that the example was small, and some networks are made up of thousands of computers, so the advantages are exponential.

WHITE BOARD

What advantages do Net Pros hae over No Net?
Why does Net Pros have an economic advantage over No Net even though their startup costs were larger?

Building a Computer Network

Network Interface Card (NIC)
Courtesy of Prentice-Hall, Inc.

There are four basic components all networks require besides the computers themselves. The first part is a **Network Interface Controller (NIC)** card for each computer. The NIC is plugged into a slot on the motherboard inside of the computer that allows a network cable to be plugged in so it can interface, or communicate with other computers. Most computers today are purchased "network ready" as they already come with an NIC, and the most common NIC is called an Ethernet Card. Ethernet cards provide a unique 48-bit address called a **MAC address** for the computer, meaning no two Ethernet cards have the same address; therefore, each computer on a network can be uniquely identified.

With Ethernet cards installed which connect computers and allow them to communicate, a standard form of communication, or language must exist, called a **protocol**, which is the second basic component of a network. If people from different countries speaking different languages met for a business conference, they would have to arrive at a common language or protocol in order to communicate effectively. A network protocol provides that common language and rules for communication. A network protocol is a convention or standard that controls or allows communication and data transfer between two computers. Simply stated, a network protocol is the rules governing network communication. Network protocols are governed by hardware, software, or an arrangement of both.

BLACK & WHITE

The most common network protocol is called Transmission Control Protocol / Internet Protocol (TCP/IP).

GRAY MATTER

Transmission Control Protocol / Internet Protocol packets are commonly broken down into 8000 kilobytes "files" and then reassembled when they reach their destination.

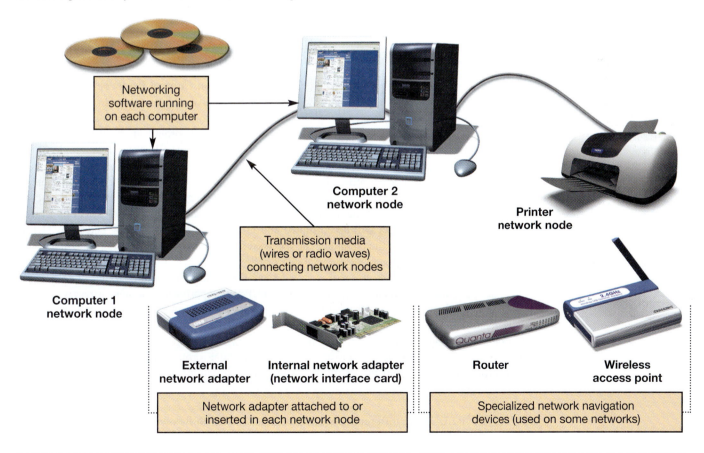

Network components
Courtesy of Pearson Education.

BLACK & WHITE

TCP/IP and UDP are different network protocols, each with its own advantages and disadvantages, and neither being better than the other. Networks choose the appropriate protocol for the appropriate usage.

GRAY MATTER

A video computer file is potentially made up of thousands of frames of pictures that are streamed to its end user. If one of the thousands of frames is lost in network transmission, will it significantly affect the video? The answer is no. Since TCP/IP is too restrictive for video, UDP protocols are used instead.

The third component that all networks have in common is the physical cables that connect them together. **Network cables** are specialized wires with adapters to plug into the NIC, and the most common type of cable is called twisted pair. Twisted pair is a specialized wire that cancels out electromagnetic interference from other electronic devices and increases reliability. The most commonly used network cable is Ethernet Cable. (Note: networks can be connected together wirelessly without the need for cables and NICs, but generally are used for smaller networks that may not be appropriate for large businesses.)

A network **Hub** is the fourth common component of a computer network, and the most common hub is an Ethernet hub. The hub as the term suggests is a central location of the computer network that serves as a traffic cop for network connection and communication. Hubs insure that computer traffic does not run into each other and eliminates collisions. Cables from network computers and other devices are plugged into a Hub.

Once the four basic network elements are in place and operational, computers and peripherals can begin to communicate and share data. For instance, a business wants all of its employees to be able to access a human resources (HR) database located on their intranet (a type of web-based network). The HR database allows employees to search internal job postings and is located on a singular computer. Since the singular computer has a MAC address provided by its Ethernet NIC, the network is able to direct users to the appropriate location on the network.

Since all of the employees (clients) on the network share the same protocol(s), or rules governing data transfer and communications within the network, they are able to receive information that their computers will understand. Data and information on a network travels through network cables as pulses of electricity that represent binary information (1s and 0s) and is translated into a form the receiving computer can understand and then translated by an output device like a display screen or printer that the end user can understand.

Data and information travelling through network cables is governed by the hub so it does not collide with other data and information and then directed to the appropriate computer on the network.

The most common network protocol is called **Transmission Control Protocol / Internet Protocol (TCP/IP)**. An example of the way the TCP/IP network protocols or network rules work is the following: A Finance Department of a global organization may choose to distribute a yearly forecast budget spreadsheet file for approval to its home office sent through its businesses' network. Because of the spreadsheet's large file size, the network breaks the file down into smaller, more manageable pieces, called packets. Packets are sent to the receiving computer on the network and then reassembled it the correct order. The home office computer translates the file into the spreadsheet once it is correctly received and reassembled. TCP/IP checks to see that the receiving computer receives all of the packets that make up the spreadsheet and that the packets are in the correct order, if not, the spreadsheet will be corrupted and not usable for the receiving end user. TCP/IP guarantees the reliability of the computer file received by the network's end user.

Another common network protocol is called **User Datagram Protocol (UDP)**. For some common file types like documents and spreadsheets, TCP/IP is appropriate because a receiving computer cannot afford to lose a packet, however, some file types can. A video computer file is potentially made up of thousands of frames of pictures that are streamed to its end user. If one of the thousands of frames is lost in network transmission, will it significantly affect the video? The answer is no. Since TCP/IP is too restrictive for video, UDP protocols are used instead. Because UDP protocols simply send the entire file at once in a streaming fashion, it is much faster than TCP/IP. However, UDP does not guarantee a file's reliability.

TCP/IP and UDP are different network protocols, each with its own advantages and disadvantages, and neither being better than the other. Networks choose the appropriate protocol for the appropriate usage.

> **WHITE BOARD**
>
> List the four basic elements of a computer network.
> What is a network protocol?
> What is the most common network protocol?
> Where does UDP have an advantage over TCP/IP?

Network Operating Systems

An operating system (OS) on a stand-alone computer is software that administers the hardware and software of a computer so it works properly. The OS, often called a platform, performs important jobs like controlling memory, input and output devices, and managing the files. Most operating systems run with little or no user interaction. A **network operating system (NOS)** is software that controls an entire network. The NOS is responsible for network traffic control, administering packets, file management, administering certain functions like backup, and security.

A network operating system is similar to a stand-alone operating system in that both provide features like automatic hardware detection, so when a new device is attached on to a network, the NOS is able to recognize it, and install it as part of the network. Network operating systems also support multi-processing which allows multiple processes to occur at the same time.

One of the more important aspects of the NOS is that it needs to know who is using the network, or who its end user is. Unlike a stand-alone OS, which may or may not require a user password to access the computer, a network operating system provides security which requires its users to preregister with a network administrator before being allowed to use the network. A **network administrator** is responsible for smooth network operations, network performance and implementation of new nodes or even new networks. Once a user is registered with the network, they must provide a password to log on to the network which in turn authenticates their identity and controls access to certain areas of the network.

> **BLACK & WHITE**
>
> Topology refers to the mapping of a physical network and logical interconnections between nodes. Simply stated, it is the way a network is arranged and laid out. A node is any device that is connected as part of a computer network, including computers, hubs, printers, switches, etc.

> **GRAY MATTER**
>
> Choosing the right network topology can be determined with cost, space, scalability, and reliability.

Courtesy of Darren Modriker/Corbis Images.

A network administrator is required to have a strong business sense and familiarity with their organization, and specifically, the organizational structure. Most businesses are separated by functional areas, like human resources, accounting, research and development, production, and marketing. Within the functions, hierarchies exist which determines who is in charge. Often times a network administrator will determine network access and grant more access to a manager of a functional area than to the employees of the same functional area. Network access is often determined by the businesses corporate hierarchy.

Network Topology

Topology refers to the mapping of a physical network and logical interconnections between nodes. Simply stated, it is the way a network is arranged and laid out. A **node** is any device that is connected as part of a computer network, including computers, hubs, printers, switches, etc. The most common of these basic types of topologies are as follows:

CHAPTER 8 | Networks

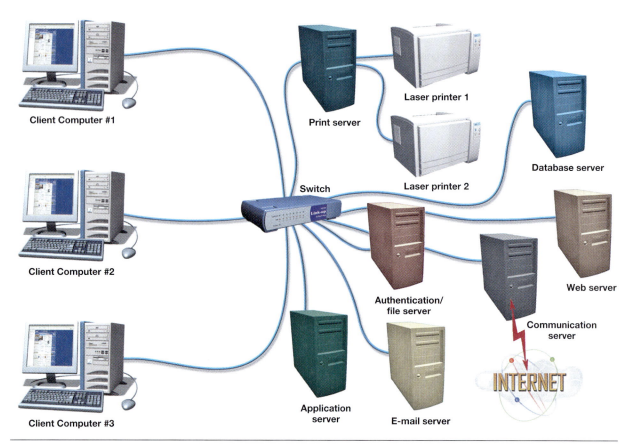

Typical large scale client/server network with dedicated servers.
Courtesy of Pearson Education.

BLACK & WHITE

Unlike the networks described above, P2P does not have the concept of clients and servers, rather a group of clients that act as their own individual servers and share their resources. P2P networks are relatively easy to set up and are very common for sharing audio and video.

GRAY MATTER

Some file sharing networks, specifically networks that share MP3 music and video files use peer-to-peer networks for greater reliability and low cost.

Bus Topology — a bus topology or linier bus is a network topology where all of the nodes of the network are connected to a common linear backbone with two endpoints. Data is transmitted between the two endpoints and the nodes are connected to this backbone. One advantage of a bus topology is that all nodes can receive data virtually simultaneously. A disadvantage is that if the backbone is down, all nodes on the backbone are down as well.

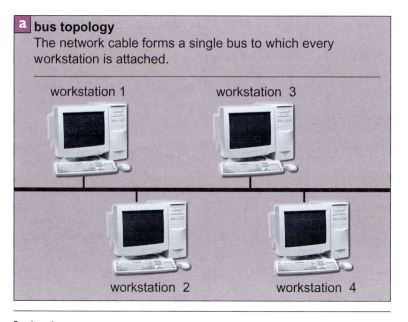

Bus topology
Courtesy of Prentice-Hall, Inc.

Star Topology — a star topology gets its name from its star shape with all of the nodes connected to a common central node in a hub and spoke-like fashion. The center of the star is the hub which attach to the nodes with spokes. Many times the hub is a server with the networked computers and nodes as clients, thus, a client / server model. Star topologies have the disadvantages as a linear bus; if the central hub fails, every node attached to the hub fails.

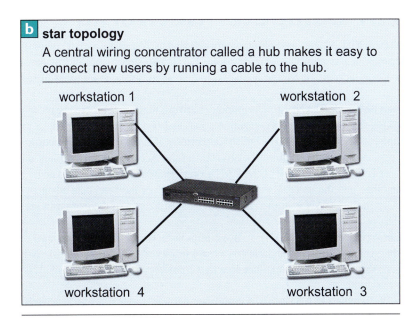

Star topology
Courtesy of Prentice-Hall, Inc.

Ring Topology — a ring topology is shaped like a ring where each computer (node) is connected to two other computers in the network and with the first and last computers being connected to each other. Data is transmitted between computers from one to another in a circular manner. Ring topologies are the least used topology with microcomputers.

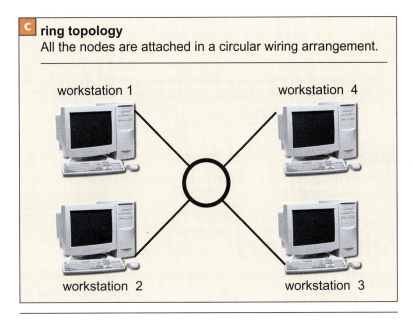

Ring topology
Courtesy of Prentice-Hall, Inc.

> **WHITE BOARD**
>
> What is a topology when referring to a computer network?
> Which is the most popular computer topology and why?

Types of Computer Networks

Local Area Network (LAN) is a computer network that is relatively small, typically in a single building, but sometimes as small as a single room. LANs can serve smaller businesses, and many times they serve smaller parts of a large business, like an accounting department or sales division.

Campus Area Network (CAN) — is a computer network that connects two or more LANs located on a campus, like a university, or an organization's national headquarters, or even an industrial complex. For example, a CAN connects an English Department's LAN to a Math Department's LAN so they can share resources. Business campuses can connect the Accounting Department's LAN with the Human Resources LAN. Typically, all of the LAN's on a business campus or university are connected in one way or another, and the more they are connected, the more they can take advantage of networking in general. Generally, a CAN is limited in size to the specific size of the campus it serves.

Metropolitan Area Network (MAN) — is a computer network that connects two or more LANs or CANs together, but within the boundaries of a town or city. An example of a MAN is a bank with different locations throughout a metropolitan area that connects all of its branches LANs together.

Wide Area Networks (WAN) — is a computer network over a wide geographical area that connects LANs, CANs, and MANs together. Many times, WANs rely on a telephone company's transmission facilities to connect the smaller networks together. Many large organizations rely on MANs to centralize data and information from its satellite office spread all over a country, and sometimes the world. For example; airlines rely on Centralized MANs so ticketing agents can access flight information. Centralized MANs consist of the network itself connected to dumb terminals. A dumb terminal is a computer whose only job is to connect to the network and cannot be employed to do anything else, like develop a spreadsheet or presentation.

Peer to Peer Networks (P2P) — is a computer network that generally connects computers directly to one another without the use of a server. Unlike the networks described above, P2P does not have the concept of clients and servers, rather a group of clients that act as their own individual servers and share their resources. P2P networks are relatively easy to set up and are very common for sharing audio and video.

Internet — is the world's largest network connecting thousands of networks together, including LANs, CANs, MANs, and WANs. The interconnection of public, private, commercial, industrial, and governmental networks is called internetwork.

> **WHITE BOARD**
>
> List the different types of computer networks and their appropriate usage.
> What is the world's largest network?

Network Security

Network security starts with a solid understanding of network threats, and the primary threat is an unwanted user. Network administrators need to adopt policies and procedures that define rules for network access, that determines who is allowed to use the network and to what extent.

Network rules and protocols should be documented to clearly defined and cover every eventuality. Network rules and protocols need to be based on what is available on a computer network and then base appropriate policies and procedures regarding them. Some of the following considerations for network security are the following:

Passwords — A password is a secret word, or combination of keyboard characters typed in by a user to authenticate their identity to a computer network. Obviously, if the password falls into the wrong hands, the computer network security is easily breached. Network policies and procedure documents need to outline what constitutes a strong password. A strong password has a specific amount of characters with mixed case, and many times requires letters and numbers, and in some cases special characters.

Strong passwords have mixed results in their effectiveness. For instance, although strong passwords are more difficult to guess because of their complexity, a user may have a more difficult time remembering it and may be tempted to write the password down in the general vicinity of their network computer.

Password policies should also outline the longevity of a password and require network users to change it on a regular basis for security reasons. This too has its advantages and disadvantages. On one hand, network security is more difficult to breach with constantly changing passwords, and on the other hand, the network user may find it inconvenient and continue to write the password where it can be undermined.

A network administrator needs to have a close relationship with their human resources department to change passwords for employees that have been terminated from an organization. A disgruntled former employee can wreak havoc on a businesses' network by deleting files or stealing private company information.

Web browsing — Network security policies should outline user's web access as well as web browsing habits of a user if web access is indeed granted. Some organizations choose to restrict web browsing altogether to avoid potential problems. One advantage of completely restricting web browsing is that an organization can insure their employees will not visit malicious or inappropriate websites that might compromise network security or even create liability for the organization itself. Many websites can install malicious cookies onto a network user's computer. The cookie can be in the form of a small program or computer file designed to gather company data and information from the computer network. Because website content is cached, or stored on a user's (client) computer, it can contain potentially undesirable content. Because the user is an employee of a business, and therefore a representative, the organization can be liable.

It is clear to see why many organizations choose not to allow employees to browse websites from their computer network given all of the pitfalls. If they do allow web browsing, network security policies need to clearly outline what is and is not appropriate as well as install web browsing filters which can filter out undesirable content.

Email / Instant Messaging — Email policies and procedures are similar to web browsing policies in that users need to be trained and educated on proper usage. For instance, a company employee needs to understand that an organization's email and instant messaging systems are to be used for business only, and not for personal use. Email systems residing on a computer network must also have strong tools in place to avoid malicious content like computer viruses. It is imperative the network policies and procedures include that email is to be used in the organization's best interest and only for the organization.

> **BLACK & WHITE**
> Network security policies should outline user's web access as well as web browsing habits of a user if web access is indeed granted. Some organizations choose to restrict web browsing altogether to avoid potential problems.

> **GRAY MATTER**
> Keep in mind that websites "visit" the client computer that requested the information which means any content requested can be resident on a business computer. This means undesirable content can reside on a business computer if an employee surfs to an inappropriate web site.

CHAPTER 8 | Networks

BLACK & WHITE

A firewall is specialized hardware and software that insures that only authorized personnel within an organization can use an organization's Intranet.

GRAY MATTER

A firewall is like having a security guard at a business' building. The security guard insures that only valid employees enter the building and keeps out those who are not.

On an intranet, the difference is that hardware and software that make up a firewall are used to keep unauthorized people from entering.

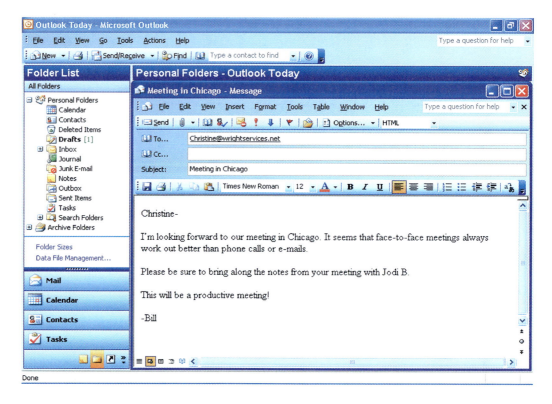

Courtesy of Prentice-Hall, Inc.

Permissions — Most computer networks refer to network access as permissions, essentially restricting or granting access to specific files and folders on a computer network to a user or group of users. Network administrators must work closely with human resources departments as well as specific departments to understand their organizational structure and hierarchy, and then potentially base network permissions on these constructs. For instance, a middle manager of a production plant may be granted permission to access all of her employee's computer folders and files, but the employees would only be granted permission to view their own computer folders and files.

Firewall — A firewall is specialized hardware and software that insures that only authorized personnel within an organization can use an organization's Intranet. An intranet is a like a private version of the Internet that works the same way as the Internet, but is confined within an organization. Intranets contain company policies, computer files, and a host of other business resources. Many companies choose to let their employees work from locations other than a home office, saving valuable time and resources, as well as increasing productivity by employing an intranet. Telecommuting employees can log on to their businesses' computer network and access its intranet from home which is a great advantage. Network security policies and procedures must insure that proper compliance of the intranet is clear and safe for the business and its users.

WHITE BOARD

What is the purpose of a firewall?
What is a strong password and why is it important?

Summary

Can a business survive without a network? The answer is clearly no. Although a stand-alone computer is extremely powerful, a network is exponentially more powerful.

Imagine trying to run any organization without telephones. Can it be done? Technically, it can. Perhaps a business can run with postal mail, faxes, and even FedEx to communicate with vendors, suppliers, and other organizations. Even if one was to give this business the benefit of the doubt and recognize that they employ best practices when using the post office, faxes, and FedEx, the obvious question is why?

The answers lay in an economic theory called opportunity cost. In economics, opportunity cost is the cost of the highest forgone alternative and its benefit(s) that a business did not choose. Simply put, opportunity cost is the cost of what a business decided not to do as compared to what they actually did, or the cost of choosing to save money by not using telephones compared to the cost of using them. Add up all the costs and benefits of using telephones and compare it to not using telephones. In the case of our business, they chose not to use telephones. Now imagine the costs and benefits the same business would have reaped had they chosen to use telephones. Would they have been better off choosing to use telephones?

Apply the theory of opportunity cost to a business that chooses not to use a computer network, or even a business that owns a network but has deployed it poorly. Although the organization initially saves money by not purchasing a network, opportunity cost suggests that in the long run, the benefits of a network far outpaces not having one at all.

Matching

Match each key term in the left column with the most accurate definition in the right column.

G	1. Hub	A.	Two or more computers connected together to communicate and share resources.
M	2. Network Administrator	B.	Every device connected to a network.
N	3. Topology	C.	The most common Network Interface Card.
K	4. NOS	D.	Unique 48-bit address.
A	5. Computer Network	E.	Convention or standard that controls or allows communication and data transfer between two computers.
O	6. Peer-to-Peer	F.	Most common type of cable.
L	7. Hardware Detection	G.	Central location of the computer network.
C	8. Ethernet	H.	Most common network protocol.
E	9. Network Protocol	I.	Broken down file into smaller, more manageable pieces.
D	10. MAC	J.	Protocol that sends the entire file at once in a streaming fashion.
B	11. Node	K.	Software that controls an entire network.
F	12. Twisted Pair	L.	When a new device is attached on to a network, the NOS recognize it.
J	13. UDP	M.	Responsible for smooth network operations, network performance.
I	14. Packets	N.	Mapping of a physical network and logical interconnections between nodes.
H	15. TCP/IP	O.	Network that generally connects computers directly to one another without the use of a server.

Multiple Choice

1. A _____ refers to the mapping of a physical network and logical interconnections between nodes.
   a. Topology
   b. Site Map
   c. Client
   d. Server

2. A _____ is specialized hardware and software that insures that only authorized personnel within an organization can use an organization's Intranet.
   a. Bus
   b. Firewall
   c. Node
   d. Protocol

3. A _____ is a secret word, or combination of keyboard characters typed in by a user to authenticate their identity to a computer network.
   a. Protocol
   b. Password
   c. Code Word
   d. Key Word

4. Most computer networks refer to network access as _____.
   a. User-friendliness
   b. Accessibility
   c. Permissions
   d. Open architecture

5. Network _____ starts with a solid understanding of network threats, and the primary threat is an unwanted user.
   a. Architecture
   b. Administration
   c. Security
   d. Governance

6. The most common type of cable is called _____.
   a. Twisted pair
   b. Chained
   c. Optical cable
   d. Copper wire

7. A _____ is two or more computers connected together to communicate and share resources.
   a. Server
   b. Client
   c. Interconnected hub
   d. Computer network

8. A _____ is a computer network that generally connects computers directly to one another without the use of a server.
   a. Peer to Peer Network
   b. WAN
   c. MAN
   d. LAN

9. A _____ password has a specific amount of characters with mixed case, and many times requires letters and numbers, and in some cases special characters.
   a. Precise
   b. Detailed
   c. Explicit
   d. Strong

10. A. _____ Area Network is a computer network that is relatively small, typically in a single building, but sometimes as small as a single room.
    a. Local
    b. Metropolitan
    c. Campus
    d. Wide

1.01000100 | 2.01000010 | 3.01000011 | 4.01000001 | 5.01000100 | 6.01000001 | 7.01000100 | 8.01000011 | 9.01000011 | 10.01000001

Blanks

A __computer network__ is two or more computers connected together to communicate and share resources.

The __NIC__ is plugged into a slot on the motherboard inside of the computer that allows a network cable to be plugged in so it can interface, or communicate with other computers.

Ethernet cards provide a unique 48-bit address called a __MAC address__.

__Network cables__ are specialized wires with adapters to plug into the NIC, and the most common type of cable is called twisted pair.

__Hubs__ insure that computer traffic does not run into each other and eliminates collisions.

The most common network protocol is called __TCP/IP__.

The __NOS__ is responsible for network traffic control, administering packets, file management, administering certain functions like backup, and security.

A __network administrator__ is responsible for smooth network operations, network performance and implementation of new nodes or even new networks.

__Topology__ refers to the mapping of a physical network and logical interconnections between nodes.

__Peer to Peer__ is a computer network that generally connects computers directly to one another without the use of a server.

Short Questions

What is the world's largest network?

What are the pros and cons of a strong password?

What hardware and software is used to protect a network from an unauthorized outside user?

Which network topology is the most common?

What sort of protocol is best for delivering video files over a network?

What are name of any device connected to a network?

nine | internet

- Internet History
- World Wide Web Structure
- Website Address
- Websites
- Browsers
- Browser Features
- Internet Service Providers (ISP)
- Search Engines
- E-commerce
- Security
- E-mail
- Voice over Internet Protocol (VoIP)
- Intranet

Internet History

To understand the Internet, it is important to first know where it came from and why. In the late 1960's, scientists working for the U. S. Air Force needed a way to get data and information from one computer to another in the most efficient way possible. This network of computers also had to be highly robust and survivable, that is to say if one of the computers on the network failed, the network itself would not.

In 1969 at the University of California at Los Angeles (UCLA), **ARPANET** (Advanced Research Project Agency Network) was born, one of the precursors to today's Internet. In the early years, other similar networks were connected to each other to form larger networks that would eventually come to be known as the Internet in the 1990s. Until then, the Internet was still the domain of scientists and academicians until Tim Berners-Lee at **CERN** (Center for European Nuclear Research) invented a standard programming language called **HTML** (Hypertext Markup Language) and the protocol to move information through the Internet called **HTTP** (Hypertext Transfer Protocol). Once this was accomplished, the **World Wide Web** (WWW) was born. It is important to know that the WWW is a part of the Internet.

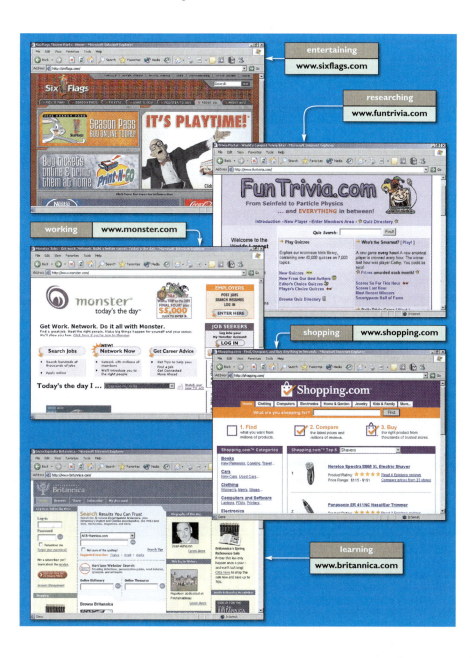

BLACK & WHITE

In 1969 at the University of California at Los Angeles (UCLA), ARPANET (Advanced Research Project Agency Network) was born, one of the precursors to today's Internet. In the early years, other similar networks were connected to each other to form larger networks that would eventually come to be known as the Internet in the 1990s.

GRAY MATTER

Everyone in America knows that Al Gore claimed to invent the Internet. He actually never made that claim, rather saying, "During my service in the United States Congress I took the initiative in creating the Internet". Gore can certainly claim that he was indeed in the forefront of legislative initiatives to create the Internet.

BLACK & WHITE

A browser is application software that provides an interface which lets a user display and interacts with text, images, and other information located on the World Wide Web.

GRAY MATTER

Because browsers essentially only read and organize hypertext markup language and arrange it on an interface for presentation, it is not necessarily "strong" application software.

Web site developers understand that their web pages will potentially be displayed on multiple platforms, screen resolutions, and browsers and therefore need to program for standard common denominators.

When Berners-Lee invented HTML, he knew the language would have to be standard, so it would work on almost any kind of computer on the World Wide Web, whether it was a Personal Computer (PC), Mac, or any other computer. HTTP was developed for the same purpose, to transfer information in a standard fashion that all computers on the Internet could receive. Once all of this was in place, websites sprung up on the Internet by the millions.

Internet and World Wide Web Structure

Comprehending the Internet and World Wide Web's scope can be daunting so it's best to start small. Imagine just 10 computers in a star topology all connected by wire to an eleventh computer in the center. (Figure 4.1, Star Topology)

The Internet is a network called a **"Client / Server"** model. A computer on a network that stores webpages is called the **server** or host, and the computer on the network that requests those webpages is called a **client**. A computer can be both a client and a server at the same time.

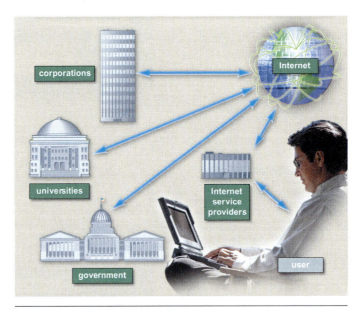

Courtesy of Prentice-Hall, Inc.

Each computer is numbered from 1 to 11, which represents each computer's **Internet address**. Since each computer is connected to every other computer, at least indirectly, web pages on one computer can be accessed by another. Notice computer number 7 (**server or host**) stores a file, or web page on it called index.html. (**Note:** Websites typically have a **homepage** called "index". The "html" means the page is a Hypertext Markup Language document.) Suppose computer 2 (**client**) requests a copy of index.html transferred from computer 7. Computer 2 would first have to call the address where the file resides and then the file name, (7/index.html). Computer 2 will receive the copy of index.html to be translated and viewed with **browser application software**.

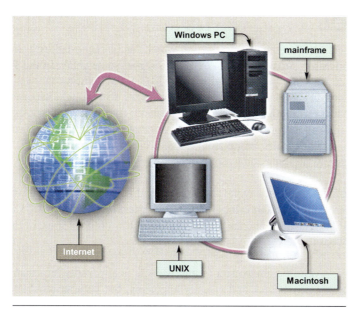

Courtesy of Prentice-Hall, Inc.

Now take the simple example above and multiply it by millions of clients, servers, networks, and addresses spread worldwide, and you can start to comprehend the enormity and implications of the World Wide Web. The WWW is the most dominant, dynamic resource on the planet with infinite implications on a global scale. The World Wide Web is also growing at an incredible rate, with millions of new users monthly.

> **WHITE BOARD**
>
> What is a client / server model?
> What is ARPANET and why was it started?

Internet Address

Figure 4.1 shows a very simplistic view of the World Wide Web in size and complexity. With millions of computers connected to the Web, it becomes important to come up with an address system or an **Internet Protocol address (IP)** in order to identify and communicate throughout the network. Websites have address called **Uniform Resource Locators** or URLs like http://www.yahoo.com. The components of these URLs are as follows: **Http** refers to the standard protocol, or the rules of exchanging files from a server to a client on the Internet. **WWW** refers to the World Wide Web. (Remember, the WWW resides on the Internet.) www.yahoo.com is the **domain name** of the website and **.com** is the domain code or extension. The **.com** refers to "Commercial". Other common domain codes include: **.edu** (Education), **.gov** (Government), **.mil** (Military), and **.org** (Organization).

Top-Level Domain Name	Used By
.com	Commercial businesses
.biz	Businesses
.edu	Educational institutions
.info	Information
.gov	Government agencies
.pro	Professionals
.mil	Military
.aero	Aviation
.net	Network organizations (such as ISPs)
.coop	Cooperatives
.org	Nonprofit organizations
.museum	Museums
.name	Names

Courtesy of Prentice-Hall, Inc.

protocol | server | path | resource name
http://www.microsoft.com/windows/ie/default.asp

Courtesy of Prentice-Hall, Inc.

Websites

> **BLACK & WHITE**
>
> Users often associate a poorly designed websites with an inferior business, whether they know it or not. Extensive website usability studies have shown that a user loses confidence in a business by seeing only the poorly designed homepages and poorly rendered graphics, regardless of whether the business is good or bad.

> **GRAY MATTER**
>
> All browsers essentially do the same thing; render text, graphics, video, and other elements in a user interface.
>
> The difference is that different browsers offer different features and claims of different levels of security.

A website is a collection of web pages on a server which can be requested by a client and displayed with **browser application software** which exist on a server somewhere on the World Wide Web. Most web pages are typically programmed with HTML. HTML allows the web pages to display text, images (pictures), videos, and much more. Web pages also include hyperlinks. A **hyperlink** (sometimes called **link**), is a clickable navigation element, (typically text, but can be images) in a webpage to another webpage of the same website, or even a completely new website. Hyperlinks access the address and document name from another computer on the WWW. Web pages have information on virtually anything and everything. (Figure 4.2 Website Pictures)

With modern software, almost anyone can produce and post a website to the WWW. People that produce websites are called **web developers**, or **webmasters**. However, just because one can produce a website, doesn't make the site any good. The list below outlines some of the more important aspects of a good website.

Content — The most important aspect of any website is always its information, or content. A web site may be technically sound, and visually appealing, but without reliable and original content, it is simply inadequate. Many organizations and businesses employ full-time **content managers** to avoid this problem by keeping their websites updated regularly and populated with relevant information. A growing trend is to let the web site users themselves submit original content. Examples include http://www.facebook.com and http://www.YouTube.com.

Interactivity — A website that engages the user makes it memorable. A website needs to be interesting enough for an initial visit, but also interesting enough to make a user return. A good website involves the user with a sense of participation.

Design — Users often associate a poorly designed websites with an inferior business, whether they know it or not. Extensive website usability studies have shown that a user loses confidence in a business by seeing only the poorly designed homepages and poorly rendered graphics, regardless of whether the business is good or bad. This points out the significance of good design, and that a website can be a customer's initial impression of a business.

> **WHITE BOARD**
>
> What are some of the considerations that go into good business website?
> Why is content so important in a web site?

Browsers

A **browser** is application software that provides an interface which lets a user display and interacts with text, images, and other information located on the World Wide Web. Essentially, a browser is used to display information from the WWW onto your computer screen. It is often said that you visit a web site, which is actually a misnomer. Web sites visit you, the client. When you request a web page or files from a different computer or server, like in figure 4.1, that page, or HTML file(s) is visiting your computer, and the browser translates and organizes that information so it is readable for a human being.

CHAPTER 9 | Internet 173

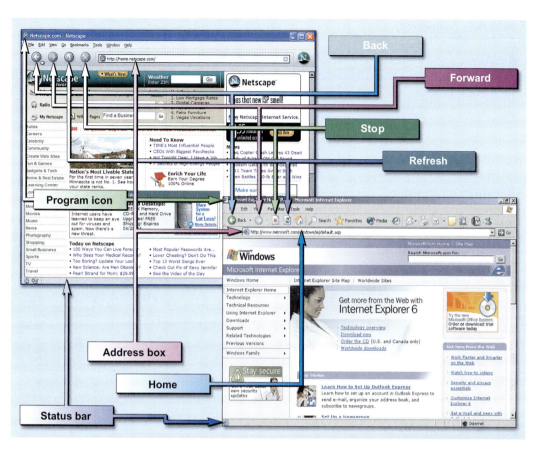

Courtesy of Prentice-Hall, Inc.

There is more than one brand of browser. **The table below** shows which browsers are used the most.

Table 4.1

Ranking	#1	#2	#3	#4	#5
	Firefox	Google Chrome	Internet Explorer	Opera	Safari
Tabbed Browsing	•	•	•	•	•
Integrated Search Engine	•	•	•	•	•
Smart Toolbar	•	•	•	•	•
Thumbnail Preview		•	•	•	
Save Tabs	•		•	•	•
Customize	•		•	•	•
Frequently Visited Webpage's List	•	•	•	•	
RSS Feeds	•	•	•	•	•
					(continued)

Table 4.1 *(continued)*

Ranking	#1 Firefox	#2 Google Chrome	#3 Internet Explorer	#4 Opera	#5 Safari
Automatic Updates	•	•	•	•	•
Password Manager	•	•	•	•	•
Synchronize		•	•	•	
Find On Page	•	•	•	•	•
Zoom	•	•		•	
Parental Controls	•		•		
Add-ons	•		•	•	•
Spell Check	•			•	•
Mouse Gestures				•	
Voice Interaction				•	
Open Source Development	•	•			
Download Manager	•	•		•	
Security					
Pop-Up Blocker	•	•	•	•	•
Anti-Spyware	•	•	•	•	•
Anti-Virus	•	•	•	•	•
Anti-Phishing	•	•	•	•	
Clear History	•	•	•	•	•
Private Mode	•	•	•		
Support					
Telephone Support			•		
Email Support	•		•	•	
Online Help	•	•	•	•	•
Tutorials	•	•	•	•	•
FAQs	•	•	•	•	•
User Forums	•	•	•	•	•

Browser Features

Different browsers have different features as well as different versions. Older versions support fewer features while newer versions are constantly upgraded for newer, faster, and more complex features and technologies. Browser companies are constantly fighting browser wars to get more market share. The following are common features of most browsers on the market today.

Bookmarks — Bookmarks are also called **"Favorites"**. Many times a URL is long and hard to remember, like "http://www.facebook.com" and you find yourself accessing it often. A browser will catalog, or bookmark your favorite URLs that the user has visited or plans to visit, so the user doesn't have to remember the page URL.

Caching is when the browser stores copies on a user's computer of previously viewed web pages that a user has already accessed so it does not have to find it again on the World Wide Web or request it again from the originating server. Cached web pages display much quicker because they already reside on the client's computer.

Cookies are text files sent to a browser and then sent back unchanged by the browser to the originating server. Cookies are used for tracking and maintaining specific information about users, such as site preferences and the contents of their electronic shopping carts.

Graphic files (GIF, JPEG) — Web browsers display images with Joint Photographic Expert Group (JPEG, pronounced JAY-peg) and Graphics Interchange Format (GIF) file formats.

JavaScript — Some browsers are able to understand a programming language called JavaScript as well as HTML. JavaScripts are client-side (user) programs that allow the browser to run small applications, like clocks and calendars that show up on a web page.

Does it really matter what browser a business uses? Browsers are essentially free; they either come with an operating platform, like Microsoft Internet Explorer, or are easily downloaded from the World Wide Web, like Firefox. Beside their common features, browsers also have different consideration that need close attention when choosing the right one for your business. Some important considerations include the following:

Security — The Internet and the World Wide Web are public, which means that your browser and computer can be compromised by outside hackers. Microsoft's Internet Explorer (IE) is integrated into its operating system like Windows Vista, which many experts say is a security issue. If an outside user breaches the IE browser, experts say that the operating system can be breached as well. Firefox on the other hand is a stand-alone, or independent browser, so does not suffer from the same exposure. Either way, security features are a major concern when choosing a browser.

Popup Blockers — Popups are separate browser windows that are programmed by website designers to open extra browser windows without user interaction, typically an advertisement, while accessing a website. Unwelcome popups can be annoying and slow browser performance. Although there are legitimate reasons for popup windows, a good browser should have settings to disallow popups

Usability — A major consideration when choosing any software is its usability and ease of use, and a browser is no exception. A good browser should be able to display and render any website as the web designer intended, as well as having a robust set of tools the user can utilize to easily modify personal browser settings.

> **WHITE BOARD**
>
> List browser features and what they do.
> What is JavaScript and what does it do?

> **BLACK & WHITE**
>
> Connectivity is when one computer can connect to another or many computers and share information and resources. Without connectivity, the Internet would not exist, nor would any other network.

> **GRAY MATTER**
>
> If Gordon Moore is correct and processing speed as well as Internet speed continues to double every year and a half or so, will a browser continue to need cache?
>
> Browsers cache web pages to avoid rerequesting the same web page that was previous viewed, but if Internet speed continues to increase, caching and refreshing may become unnecessary.

Internet Service Providers (ISP)

Connectivity is when one computer can connect to another or many computers and share information and resources. Without connectivity, the Internet would not exist, nor would any other network. To gain connectivity on the Internet, it is imperative to find a provider to do so.

Type	Price Range per Month	Speed of Access (receiving data)	Advantages	Disadvantages
Dial-up	$5 to $25	Slow (56 Kbps)	Availability	Slow speed Reliability
DSL	$20 to $60	Medium (256 to 1,500 Kbps)	Speed Reliability	Availability High user cost
Cable	$30 to $60	Fast (up to 20 Mbps)	Speed Reliability	Availability High user cost
Satellite	$60 to $100	Medium (700 Kbps)	Availability Speed	High user cost Reliability
Network	Usually free to the user	Fast (in excess of 54 Mbps)	Low user cost Speed	Availability

Courtesy of Prentice-Hall, Inc.

An **Internet service provider (ISP)** is a business or organization that provides people a way to access the Internet and World Wide Web. ISPs can be started by just about anyone with the money and expertise. ISPs use various technologies such as dial-up and Digital Subscriber Line (**DSL**), and may provide a combination of services including domain name registration and hosting, web hosting. Customers pay ISPs for Internet access which allows them to connect to the Internet. There are many thousands of ISPs, some doing business worldwide like **Cox Communications** and **Qwest**, while others provide services regionally, and even locally. Some important ISP considerations include the following:

Broadband Internet access, shortened to "**broadband** is a high data-transmission rate Internet connection. DSL and cable modem are popular consumer broadband technologies, are typically capable of transmitting faster than a dial-up modem. Different broadband technologies include Cable and Wireless.

Internet hosting service runs Internet servers, which are then available to serve content such as webpages to the Internet, or clients. A common kind of hosting is web hosting. Websites need to reside somewhere on the World Wide Web, so ISPs "rent" or host space to website owners and offer domain name registration so that they can be found on the Internet by clients, or users. This is called "**Web Hosting**". Web hosting services usually offer e-mail hosting and a variety of other services.

In business, it is always best to review costs and investigate cost reduction and ISPs are no exception to this rule. The ISP market is extremely competitive and services and costs are changing all the time. It is best to review these costs on a regular basis.

Search Engines

Once you are on the World Wide Web, how do you find what you want? The answer is **search engines**. A search engine is a website that lets a user type in specific **keywords** or phrases and then returns a list of hits (hyperlinks) that best match the search criteria. Popular search engines include **Yahoo!**, **Google**, and **AltaVista**.

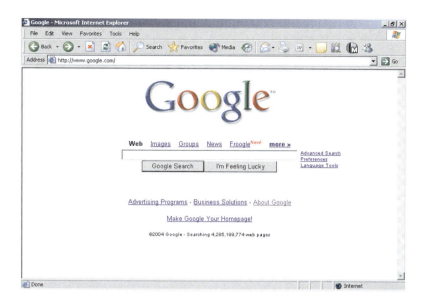

Not all search engines work alike or return the same results. Some search engines, called "**keyword search engines**" only require the user to type in the keyword or phrase. Many of these same search engines are organized into directories like medicine, or automotive so the user can search only within a particular area. As the name implies, these are called **directory searches**. **Metasearch engines** look and work like keyword searches, but return the results of many search engines at once and eliminate duplicates hits.

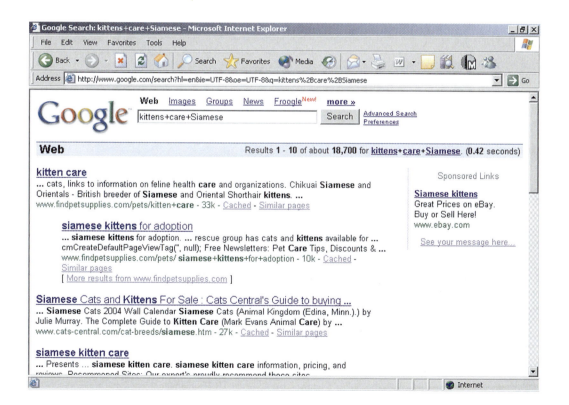

E-commerce

> **BLACK & WHITE**
>
> Electronic Commerce is the distributing, buying, selling, advertising, and marketing of goods or services over the Web.

> **GRAY MATTER**
>
> E-commerce is a paradigm and has had a dramatic and profound effect on how retailers conduct their business.

Electronic Commerce is the distributing, buying, selling, advertising, and marketing of goods or services over the Web. Instead of a physical storefront, e-commerce relies on a web site. In simplest terms, e-commerce is doing business on the Web. Large established retail organizations can enhance their scope and reach beyond physical boundaries by opening **virtual storefronts** on the Web. Many businesses that have no retail outlets or even specific locations can launch virtual storefronts, like Amazon.com. The three main types of seller-customer relationships in e-commerce are as follows.

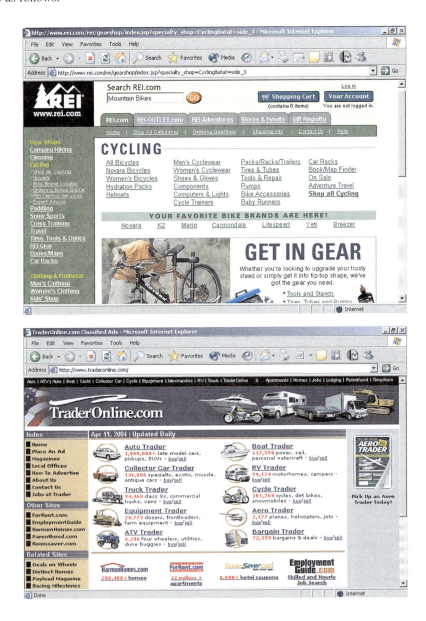

Business-to-business (B2B) is businesses distributing, buying, selling, advertising, and marketing of goods or services over the Web to other businesses. B2B transactions are inclined to take place within specific categories. For example, a business dealing with medical products will search for a bulk buyer within the agriculture category.

Business-to-consumer (B2C) is where commercial organizations sell to consumers. Examples include REI.com, overstock.com, and buy.com.

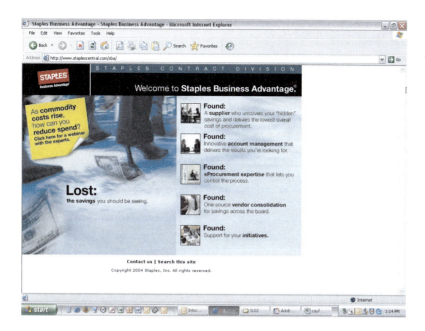

Consumer-to-consumer (C2C) involves e-commerce between consumers, usually facilitated some third party. Online auction websites are the most common example, like eBay.com where consumers place their products for sale and other consumers can bid to buy them. EBay.com makes their money by charging buyers and sellers a flat fee or commission.

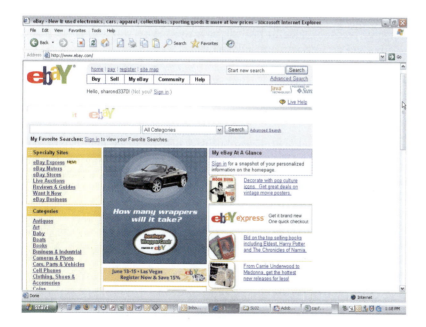

The promises of e-commerce are limitless, so it is extremely important to remember that e-commerce is still the process of "**doing business**" on the Web, and therefore, all **rules of business** still apply. A good business still needs a very capable management team, a well-organized business structure, good customer service, inventory controls, and much more. Like any business, e-commerce requires a good, lucent **business plan**. The following are just a few important considerations for a successful e-commerce business:

Market research — Who is your customer? Who are your competitors? What's your product? Is there demand for your product? These are just some of the many questions any business needs to for success. E-commerce alone does not guarantee success and is not exempt from **market analysis**.

Information technology (IT) competencies — Modern web-authoring software provides easy ways to construct a website and post it on the World Wide Web, but e-commerce requires many more considerations when it comes to website design, and needs to be on the cutting edge of technology. E-commerce websites need to provide an easy, secure way to handle transactions while remaining attractive and very easy to use and navigate.

Streamlined business process — E-commerce demands that a business investigates how it does business on the web. It is imperative to have a complete understanding of the products and services offered, and how they will be delivered in the marketplace.

Agility — Many times, a brick-and-mortar business may be aware that they need to update their storefronts, but time constraints and costs may keep them from doing so. E-commerce offers unique management and information technology agility that allows for website reengineering, and even an entire business facelift far faster than conventional businesses.

All business rules still apply in e-commerce. In many cases, an e-commerce company will not survive not only based on its product, but by not having a competent management team, poor post-sales services, poorly organized business structure, lack of network infrastructure and a non-secure, badly designed website.

> **WHITE BOARD**
>
> How does e-commerce affect traditional business without e-commerce?
> What is the most popular form of e-commerce?

> **BLACK & WHITE**
>
> Browser hijacking is when the browser's settings are modified by Malware. Malware is software designed to damage a computer's system without the owner's knowledge. The changes made are typically very difficult to reverse.

Security

Many users of the World Wide develop a false sense of security by trying to stay off malicious websites and remain "low-key", and if they do so, will not fall prey to any harmful consequences, like viruses. Unfortunately, staying vigilant is not enough. Browsers can be hijacked without the user ever knowing, and if and when they do, it is typically too late.

Browser hijacking is when the browser's settings are modified by **Malware**. Malware is software designed to damage a computer's system without the owner's knowledge. The changes made are typically very difficult to reverse. Various software packages exist to prevent such alterations. The following are malwares.

> **GRAY MATTER**
>
> Everything benefits someone or something. Malware obviously benefits computer criminals, but does it also benefit anti-virus software manufacturers?

Viruses — A **computer virus** is a malicious computer program that can copy itself and infect a computer, typically without the user being aware of it. Viruses range from programs that can be annoying that simply display a message to programs that destroy entire computer systems. Because so many programs are self-replicating, they can spread extremely quickly though out the Internet.

Worms — A worm is like a virus in that it spreads quickly and is extremely harmful, but does not need to attach itself to an existing program. Worms are self-replicating (they copy themselves) programs. It sends copies of itself to other computers on a network without any user participation or knowledge. Worms typically harm networks, whereas viruses infect or damage files on a targeted computer systems.

Courtesy of Prentice-Hall, Inc.

Trojan horse — A Trojan horse is usually a harmless or interesting looking program that when executed, unleashes harmful viruses into a users system. Many times Trojan horses are even more insidious in that their viruses are released based on time. A user many use the original program until the Trojan horse releases it viruses at a future date.

Spyware — Spyware is software that installs itself on a user's system without permission and gleans personal data and information about a user without their knowledge or permission. Normally, spyware attempts to steal information like credit card numbers, social security numbers, passwords, and any other data that can lead to identity theft.

Adware — Adware is software which routinely displays advertising to a computer system after the software is installed, usually without the users consent. On the World Wide Web, it is usually displayed in a browser as a popup window.

Tens of thousands of malwares exist so it is important to protect your system with ad-blocker, anti-virus and spyware prevention programs like Norton and McAfee.

E-mail

> **BLACK & WHITE**
>
> Communication is the most common use of the Internet, and a large part of that is accomplished through electronic mail.

> **GRAY MATTER**
>
> Always consider that any communication on the Internet is recorded somewhere and should be conducted with that in mind.

Communication is the most common use of the Internet, and a large part of that is accomplished through **electronic mail (e-mail)**. E-mail is a "store and forward" system of composing, sending, storing, and receiving messages over electronic communication systems like the Internet.

E-mail actually works much the same way as postal mail. A user first sends an electronic message to an **e-mail server** on the Internet the same way a letter you mail goes initially to a post office. In the case of the post office, they route the letter from the post office to the appropriate street address. E-mail is slightly different because it is incumbent on the intended recipient of the email to visit the e-mail server and request their e-mail. The process is technically more complicated, but nonetheless a straightforward procedure.

An e-mail has several important basic aspects that allow a user to send effective communications. **The figure below** shows the **e-mail address** of the person who will receive the email. This e-mail address consists of user's name, a domain code, and a domain name, not unlike a URL. Below the email address is the **subject**, which is typically a small one line description of the nature of the email. Below the subject is an optional **attachment**, which allows the user to attach a computer file(s) that is delivered with the email. These files are typically documents and graphics. The e-mail address, subject, and attachment together comprise the **header**. The body of the e-mail is the actual **message** itself.

Other options e-mail offers are the ability to copy more than one recipient by using the **carbon copy (Cc)** option. This option lets all of the recipients know who else has received the same email. The **blind carbon copy (BCC)** distribution option works like the carbon copy except none of the recipients know who else received the same email, or whether anyone other than them received it at all. **E-mail lists** help facilitate e-mailing by storing common e-mail contacts.

Whether sending personal or business e-mail, there are some extremely important protocols of e-mail that must be recognized. The first and most important aspect is that it is best to understand that all **e-mail should be considered public**. Most e-mail servers are owned by private entities, businesses, or universities, so the transmission of electronic mail messages through these systems makes the ultimate ownership of the message their domain. E-mail server owners will almost always have a **Terms of Service Agreement (TOS)** that specifically outlines e-mail usage and protocols. A rule of thumb is to never say or type anything in an e-mail that you wouldn't be willing to say in public.

Email Security. It is always important to know where an email came from. Many times, criminals will fraudulently send out millions of legitimate looking emails in the hopes that a user will comply with requests for data and information. For example, this technique, called **phishing** sends an email that looks like it is from a legitimate bank, when in reality, it is a ruse that attempts to fool the user into voluntarily typing their social security numbers, bank passwords, and pin numbers. The unsuspecting user might think they are updating their own bank's records, when in reality they are giving up extremely sensitive data.

Spam — Any unwanted mail like phishing is called spam. Spam emails can range from simple advertising to phishing schemes. A simple rule is to never answer a spam email, or even open it. Sometimes spam offers the user the ability to remove themselves from the originating spam's email list giving them the false sense that they will never receive this unwanted spam again. Unfortunately, when the user attempts to use the "remove" link, they are actually verifying that the spam made it to a legitimate email address, and they will most like receive even more spam. **Spam filters** can be installed to combat the millions of spam emails sent out daily. Because spam is so abundant, it slows down computer systems and causes administrators enormous amounts of time to combat it.

Voice over Internet Protocol (VoIP)

Voice over Internet Protocol (VoIP) is the routing of voice conversations, or typically, phone calls over the Internet. Simply stated, it's a phone system that uses the Internet as its phone lines instead of traditional phone lines. VoIP is a subset of **telephony**. Companies providing VoIP, like Skype, Vonage, and CISCO, are referred to as providers, and used to carry voice signals over the Internet.

If it's any indication of the future of VoIP telephones, consider that in September of 2005, eBay paid $2.6 billion to acquire Skype, the pioneers of Internet telephone services. VoIP to VoIP phone calls are usually free, which has remarkable cost reduction implications to organizations that provide phones to their employees. VoIP telephony doesn't necessarily even need an actual phone, just a microphone and a speaker attached on to a microcomputer that has access to the Internet. This means that people can communicate globally a little or no cost.

VoIP technology has a way to go to improve and claim its market share, but its promises to affect business in the future seem boundless.

Intranet

An **intranet** is a like a private version of the Internet that works the same way as the Internet, but is confined within an organization. The same concepts and technologies of the Internet apply, such as clients and servers running with Internet protocols that are used to build an intranet. Intranets

> **BLACK & WHITE**
> Voice over Internet Protocol (VoIP) is the routing of voice conversations, or typically, phone calls over the Internet. Simply stated, it's a phone system that uses the Internet as its phone lines instead of traditional phone lines.

> **GRAY MATTER**
> If voice over internet protocol telephones employs the Internet as their networks, will traditional phone companies be able to compete?

> **BLACK & WHITE**
> An intranet is a like a private version of the Internet that works the same way as the Internet, but is confined within an organization.

> **GRAY MATTER**
> Without a firewall, an Intranet is just another part of the Internet. Would a business be willing to post their secrets, policies, procedures, and operational matters on the Internet? The answer is clearly no.

still use the same HTTP, browsers and e-mail protocols, along with other Internet common protocols. The key aspect of an Intranet is **privacy**. A **firewall** is specialized hardware and software working together that insures that only authorized personnel within an organization can use the Intranet. Firewalls keep public networks like the Internet from accessing private networks like an Intranet. Without a firewall, an Intranet is just another part of the Internet.

In business, an Intranet can dramatically reduce costs if not eliminate them altogether. For example, consider what a global organization like ExxonMobil did in the past to produce and distribute their human resources (HR) policies and procedures manuals. If you take into account only basic costs to print the HR manual and mail it to every one of ExxonMobil's 92,000 employees worldwide you can begin to imagine what an expensive and daunting task it is.

An Intranet can go a long way towards eliminating these costs. Instead of incurring the cost of printing human resource manuals, why not just create a website on ExxonMobil's private intranet

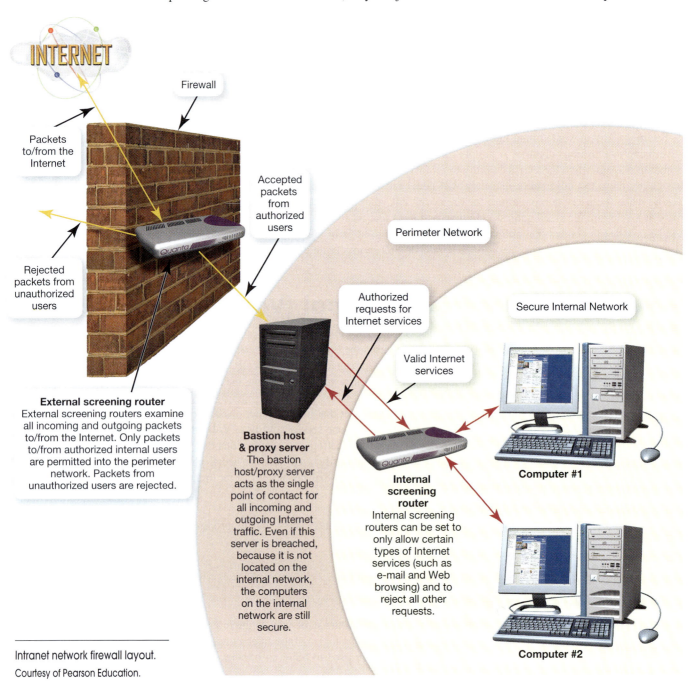

Intranet network firewall layout.
Courtesy of Pearson Education.

with the same human resources information? The cost of printing manual is no longer necessary, so these costs will be eliminated. Since every employee has a desktop computer with access to the Intranet, the cost of distributing a physical HR manual worldwide will be eliminated as well.

What if ExxonMobil updates their human resources, which they will inevitably do? In the past, it meant starting the incredibly expensive printing and distribution process again, even if it were only one updated page of the human resources manual. Consider another major cost; the extraordinary amount of **time** it took to get human resource manuals worldwide to employees pre-Intranet. With an Intranet, it is as simple as updating the HR website in a singular location on a web server and every employee receives the changes instantly.

Now that ExxonMobil's human resources manual is online, safely within its Intranet, is it a better product? Since the online HR manual is web based, employees can now do quick searches, navigate with hyperlinks, access e-mail addresses, and much more.

These "Intranet" cost reductions only consider printing, distribution, and time, and only for a human resources manual. What about employing your Intranet for posting online Annual Reports, organizational news, and the hundreds of other core informational needs every company requires? The cost reductions are staggering.

Summary

Business Intranets can also be used for knowledge exchange by setting up **knowledge systems** or **knowledge bases**. A knowledge system lets employees exchange ideas and content within their own organizations. Fundamentally, if an employee in an organization has a good idea, they can post it to the business' knowledge base where every other employee can access it. Eventually, a large collection of these collaborative ideas become searchable within the organization's Intranet.

If an employee or group of employees are faced with a task they have never undertaken, they can first search their company's intranet knowledge base with the hopes that someone else in the organization has already done it. If so, the reduction of time for the given task becomes obvious. Many times, employees find good ideas randomly that may improve efficiency by searching through new intranet postings. They may find ideas they might not have considered or even thought about.

Matching

Match each key term in the left column with the most accurate definition in the right column.

O	1. Cookie	A.	Can claim taking legislative initiative to create the Internet.
J	2. Javascript	B.	Standard programming language for a browser.
N	3. Caching	C.	Started In 1969 at the University of California at Los Angeles.
L	4. Hyperlink	D.	Invented HTML
M	5. Webmasters	E.	Resides on the Internet.
I	6. Browser	F.	The computer on the network that requests webpages.
E	7. World Wide Web	G.	Websites addresses.
B	8. HTML	H.	Refers to a Commercial website
K	9. Connectivity	I.	Software that displays websites.
D	10. Berners-Lee	J.	Client-side programs that allow the browser to run small applications.
C	11. ARPANET	K.	When one computer can connect to another or many computers and share information and resources.
F	12. Client	L.	Clickable navigation element.
G	13. URL	M.	People that produce websites.
H	14. .com	N.	When the browser stores copies on a user's computer of previously viewed web pages.
A	15. Al Gore	O.	Used for tracking and maintaining specific information about users.

Multiple Choice

1. The Internet is a network called a _____ model.
   a. Computer
   b. International
   c. Networked
   d. Client / Server

2. A website is a collection of web pages on a server which can be requested by a client and displayed with a _____.
   a. Workbook
   b. Browser
   c. Window
   d. GUI

3. A _____ is a clickable navigation element in a web page.
   a. Cursor
   b. Icon
   c. Hyperlink
   d. All of the above

4. People that produce websites are called _____.
   a. Webmasters
   b. Gurus
   c. Web surfers
   d. All of the above

5. A website that engages the user makes it memorable is said to be _____.
   a. Subtle
   b. Interesting
   c. Dynamic
   d. Interactive

6. The most popular browser is _____.
   a. Windows Internet Explorer
   b. Firefox
   c. Mozilla
   d. Netscape

7. _____ are text files sent to a browser and then sent back unchanged by the browser to the originating server.
   a. Text pads
   b. Word pads
   c. Notepads
   d. Cookies

8. _____ is when one computer can connect to another or many computers and share information and resources.
   a. Wireless
   b. Networkable
   c. Connectivity
   d. Resourceful

9. VoIP is often referred to as _____.
   a. Phone service
   b. Voice band
   c. Telephony
   d. Electronic voice mail

10. A(n) _____ is a like a private version of the Internet that works the same way as the Internet, but is confined within an organization.
    a. Intranet
    b. VoIP
    c. Network
    d. Firewall

Blanks

The Internet is a network called a __client/server__ model.

A website is a collection of web pages on a server which can be requested by a client and displayed with __browser__.

A __hyperlink__ is a clickable navigation element, in a webpage to another webpage of the same website, or even a completely new website.

The most important aspect of any website is always its information, or __content__.

__Caching__ is when the browser stores copies on a user's computer of previously viewed web pages that a user has already accessed so it does not have to find it again on the World Wide Web.

__Cookies__ are text files sent to a browser and then sent back unchanged by the browser to the originating server.

Some browsers are able to understand a programming language called __JavaScript__ as well as HTML.

__Connectivity__ [application software] is when one computer can connect to another or many computers and share information and resources.

__E-commerce__ is the distributing, buying, selling, advertising, and marketing of goods or services over the Web.

A __virus__ is a malicious computer program that can copy itself and infect a computer, typically without the user being aware of it.

Short Questions

What is a trojan horse?

What is the point of a blind carbon copy in an email system and how does it work?

Why do email server owners have Term of Service Agreements?

What can be done to reduce or eliminate spam?

What sort of products use telephony?

What is the difference between the Internet and an Intranet?

Business Website Alternatives

What if you needed a website for your new small florist shop? The problem is that you have no idea where to start. You call around to local web developers you found on Google and get all sorts of quotes for website costs and hear a lot of other terminologies and acronyms you're not quite familiar with like 'Search Engine Optimization' and 'ODBC'. You do your homework the best you can and get five different quotes for seemingly five different things and tell yourself all you really want is a website and become more confused than when you started. Some of the quotes are really inexpensive and some are way more than you budgeted for. Even if you decide to buy the services of a web developer you're still never really confident that you went with the right company.

Consider an alternative to hiring a web development company and doing it yourself. You may be a competent computer user but you still have to admit you have no idea where to start. What software do you need to actually make webpages? Where does the website go once it's finished even if you do invest the time and effort to learn the 'webpage' software? How do you know anyone will ever see it if you can actually get it up and running on the World Wide Web (WWW)? Another problem is that you didn't start your business to be a website developer, you're a florist, and you know a lot about running a flower business. What if there was a place on the WWW that would let you make a fully functioning website with no special software and a minimum amount of expertise? That place actually exists and it's called Blogger (http://www.blogger.com) which is a service provided by Google.

'Blogs' have been around for a long time. **Blogs** were originally called 'web logs' but the term was shortened as it came into the vernacular of the web. A blog is a website usually maintained by an individual with regular entries of commentary, descriptions of events, or other material such as graphics or video. Many people use blogs as a way to communicate information like family news, political opinions, and a variety of other uses. One thing many have overlooked is that 'blogger.com' (Blogger) will make a fully functioning website with any special software and very little expertise.

To make a blog 'website', you don't need any special software, just a browser. Blogger provides premade templates that are easily modified and countless ways to make your site unique. With a little research and elbow grease, blogs can look like large corporate websites with many of the same tools by simply dragging and dropping 'gadgets' into your website. Blogs don't require the extra cost of a web host provider either, so there are no added costs. The Internet and World Wide Web are expanding at a dizzying pace as are the capability of its online tools, like Blogger. It's worth a try.

Early Website Technology

When the Internet was in its early stages from the early 1970s through the 80s, it was still the domain of computer enthusiasts, academicians, and über-geeks. It wasn't that the general populace and business was unaware of the Internet; it was simply that it had not evolved enough to be useful for everyone. High speed Internet lines didn't exist, finding an Internet provider was difficult at best, and websites didn't really exist. Application programming software to make webpages and websites didn't even exist until after Tim Berners-Lee invented **Hypertext Markup Language** (HTML) in 1990 HTML even when they did, they were difficult and cumbersome to use. With the dawn of HTML, the **World Wide Web** was born.

Ideas like facebook.com were thought of long ago, they just weren't feasible when the web was born.
Courtesy of Lucas Racasse/Getty Images.

Websites and webpages could have used many languages or applications like Microsoft Word to generate them, and webpages would have had extensions like http://www.domain.com/homepage.**doc** (document files) instead of the http://www.domain.com/homepage.**html** (HTML file) that we have today. Berners-Lee knew that although many computers had Microsoft Word, not all of them did. If they didn't have Microsoft Word, they would not be able to view websites at all. Even if a client did have Word, he knew there were many different versions, so there was no guarantee that a "Word Document" webpage would render correctly. What Berners-Lee actually did was genius. He invented a **standard**; platform neutral language that all computers could read called hypertext markup language (HTML). Basically, **platform-neutral** means that HTML can be read and rendered correctly by any browser that exists on any platform, like Windows 7, Mac, Linux, or UNIX.

You don't visit a website, a website visits you.
Courtesy of Lucas Racasse/Getty Images.

A **website** is an assortment of Web pages that can include text, images, videos, and other elements that is hosted on a web server accessible via the Internet. In the early 90s, it was almost unheard of to show videos on websites, although it was possible. Internet transmission speeds were so slow and video files were so big it simply wasn't worth the time or effort it took for download-

> **BLACK & WHITE**
>
> A website is an assortment of Web pages that can include text, images, videos, and other elements, which is hosted on a web server that is accessible via the Internet.

> **GRAY MATTER**
>
> Platform neutral means that HTML can be read and rendered correctly by any browser that exists on any platform, like Windows 7, or Mac, or Linux, or UNIX.

ing. A **web server** is a dedicated computer connected to the Internet that accepts **Hypertext Transfer Protocol (HTTP)** requests from Internet users (clients) and fulfills the request by sending (serving) HTML documents, or web pages via HTTP. Simply put, when someone is surfing the Web, the act of clicking on a link, or hyperlink, is an HTTP request for a webpage to be sent from a web server where the desired content, typically the homepage of a website exists, to the user's computer.

There are a lot of misnomers when it comes to website terminologies, for instance, you don't visit a website: it visits you. When a client clicks on a hyperlink to make an HTTP request for a webpage residing on a web server, the webpage is sent to the client's computer, or more simply, the webpage visits the client, not the other way around. Even to suggest that a web "page" is sent from a web server to a client is technically incorrect. What is really sent is pure HTML that is turned into a webpage by the client's web browser. Webpages really don't even exist until they are resolved and rendered by the client's browser, for example, Microsoft Internet Explorer or Mozilla Firefox; however, it is commonplace to say a web server sends web pages to the client.

What is on the cache of your computer?
Courtesy of ImageZoo/Getty Images.

Consider that a web page is simply a "programmed document" that is located on a computer (web server) connected to the World Wide Web. The "programmed document" doesn't even become a web page until a web browser like Microsoft Internet Explorer or Mozilla Firefox receives a *copy* of the "programmed document" from the server and then makes sense of its programming and then arranges it all on a user's (client's) computer's monitor so that the user (client) that requested it can make heads or tails out of it. One of the key words in this transaction is "copy", and that copy ends up residing on a user's computer. The word "copy" in terms of a web browser is actually referred to as cache. **Cache** is actually data that was duplicated from data on another computer, in this case, a web page.

WHITE BOARD

Why is the Internet different from the World Wide Web?
What is the main language of the World Wide Web?
What is a request?
Why did Tim Berners-Lee decide HTML should be standard?

If web pages that visited a client's computer are cached, which they typically are, that means all the content a client looked at on the WWW resides on the client's computer, typically called "**history**". Web browsers allow for client's to review their history based on the client's cache. Now consider that the client computer is a business computer, and the user is an employee of that business, and the user has recently seen a website with objectionable content. This means that copies (cache) of the objectionable content now reside on the business' computer system. Because of this, businesses many times monitor and filter websites that their employees can see, and many times do not let their employees "surf" the web at all because of the liability "cache" can create. Having a firm grasp on how websites and the World Wide Web technically function can make a big difference in a business environment, and on the decisions they are called upon to make.

HTML is the basic language of the Internet.
Courtesy of John Foxx/Getty Images.

Hypertext Markup Language

HTML is the acronym for **Hypertext Markup Language** which is the principal programming language resolved and rendered by browsers to display Web pages. **Hypertext** refers to text on a computer that will lead the user to related information and a **markup language** is a computer programming language using a set of annotations that give browsers the instructions to display text, images, and other web elements on a web page. An HTML document typically has a filename extension of ".htm" or ".html", so an HTML web page document for instance might be *homepage.htm* or *index.html*.

HTML is represented in the form of tags called **elements** that are enclosed by angle brackets like "<" and ">". The brackets help browsers know where information like hyperlinks, paragraphs, lists, colors should be located on a web page, and controls the general appearance of the overall page. Basically the bracketed elements of HTML are the method used to portray the arrangement of text-based information in a web page document. For instance, a "title" tag encloses the title of a website like <title>Yahoo!</title> which lets the browser display "Yahoo!" on the top left corner of a browser window's title bar. Notice that the title tag starts with a bracketed tag that says the word "title" and uses the same word to end the title tag by including a slash before the word "title." This is common throughout all HTML elements. Some common HTML elements can be categorized as follows:

Head Elements typically define a web document's title, style, and additional information about the document's author, page description, and keywords to help search engines find the web page. Typical head element tags are as follows:

<title></title> tags define the web page's title like <title>McCarthy Custom Homes</title> which places the words "McCarthy Custom Homes" in a browser window's title bar.

<style></style> tags define an overall style for a webpage by describing fonts, colors, and other design elements. For instance, the following HTML tells the browser that the background color for a web page should be black (#000000), the font for the web page should use "Geneva", and the font size should be 14 point.

```
<style>
    background-color: #000000;
    font-family: Geneva;
    font-size: 14px;
</style>
```

<meta> tags are additional pieces of information about the web page's author, web page description, and keywords, to help search engines find the web page like the following:

<meta name="description" content="McCarthy Custom Homes is one of Utah's top custom home builders and remodeler."><meta name="keywords" content="McCarthy, McCarthy Custom Homes, Salt Lake City, Draper, Park City, Deer Valley, Sandy">

> ### BLACK & WHITE
> **HTML** is the acronym for **Hypertext Markup Language** which is the principal programming language resolved and rendered by browsers to display web pages.

> ### GRAY MATTER
> Will web browsers ever get more powerful so they can support platform-neutral application software like spreadsheets, word processors and databases?

Static websites are fairly easy to construct, even with a tool as simple as Microsoft Notepad.
Courtesy of John Foxx/Getty Images.

"Meta" descriptions provide a description of a web site.
Courtesy of ImageZoo/Getty Images.

The "meta" description above provides a description of the web site when it is found by a search engine like Google so a user can read what the website is about before clicking on its URL. The "meta" name keywords provide search engines with words to match on which a user might type into the search engine looking for a type of website, in this case, a custom home builder.

Link Elements create elements that can become hyperlinks which allow web page users to navigate to different parts of a web site, or different parts of the World Wide Web. The following is an example of a link element:

<a href="http://www.mchut.com">McCarthy Custom Homes</a>

The previous link element would look like "McCarthy Custom Homes" in a browser window and should a user click on it, it would take them to that location on the WWW.

Image Elements use special tags to help the browser window display pictures, photographs, and images typically using the GIF or JPEG file formats like the following: <img src="meadow.gif" alt="meadow"/>. The previous tag shows an image called "meadow.gif" on a browser and if the user places their mouse on the image, it will display the word "meadow".

As the Internet increases in speed and size, so do the images on websites.
Courtesy of ImageZoo/Getty Images.

Structural (Block) Elements are designed to tell a browser how to display and align elements like lists, headings and paragraphs. Like word processing programs, structural HTML elements can align, center, and manipulate text and images into place so the browser can render a more readable webpage. For instance, one of the main tag elements creates a table with the <table></table> tags with the <tr></tr> tags creating rows and the <td></td> tags creating cells within a row.

Presentational Elements are like <style> head elements but are used in the body of a webpage and allow the HTML to create presentational effects like italics, bold, and emphasis. For instance, McCarthy Custom Homes would render the text between the "bold" tags like the following: **McCarthy Custom Homes** on a browser.

It is important to know that there are many HTML tags and elements that can be used to make a web site, and that while HTML is the main language of the World Wide Web, others exist. Another language that a browser can read is called JavaScript, which extends a web site's usability. **JavaScript** is a programming language that is considered a client-side language in reference to websites. Web developers can insert a JavaScript program in an HTML document that might show the user how many days until the New Year on the browser. The client's browser must be "**java enabled**" for the program to run, and since browsers exist on the client side of the client/server model of the Internet, JavaScript programs only work on the "client side". Another language that is popular for web sites is called **Adobe Flash** which can integrate video on a browser, add animations, promote interactivity, and develop rich Internet applications.

> **BLACK & WHITE**
>
> **Presentational Elements** are like <style> head elements but are used in the body of a webpage and allow the HTML to create presentational effects like italics, bold, and emphasis.
>
> **GRAY MATTER**
>
> Another language that a browser can read is called **JavaScript**, which extends a web site's usability. JavaScript is a programming language that is considered a client-side language in reference to websites.

BLACK & WHITE

Static websites styles rarely if ever change their content and displays its information the same way to all users.

Dynamic website styles actually generate a web page directly from the server depending on the context of the user.

GRAY MATTER

It is virtually impossible for a static website to gain any sort of popularity because it is too much of a chore to update its content.

Although static websites are easy to make, a good website must be dynamic in nature.

WHITE BOARD

Why are elements important in Hypertext Markup Language?
What is the main function of JavaScript?
Name some common HTML elements.
What does it mean to be "java enabled"?

Website Styles & Categories

Websites can be broken down into specific styles and categories depending on their purpose. Website style simply refers to whether a website's content is static or dynamic, and categories are subsets of styles which include personal, commercial, governmental, and Intranet.

Static websites styles rarely, if ever, change their content and display their information the same way to all users. Sometimes static websites are referred to as **brochure websites** or **classic websites** and are typically written purely with HTML. Static websites can take advantage of JavaScript and Flash, and include all the bells and whistles, but it is the fact that the content never changes that defines it as static. Static websites are also the easiest type of website to build, and can use simple text editors like Microsoft Notepad, or WYSIWYG programs like **Microsoft FrontPage** or **Adobe Dreamweaver**. Just because a website is static does not means it's not valuable. Some businesses simply use websites on the WWW the same way they would put their contact information in a phone book. These sites typically look like well laid-out brochures and many times encourage the user to contact their business through email or telephone.

Websites can be broken down into specific styles and categories depending on their purpose.
Courtesy of ImageZoo/Getty Images.

Dynamic website styles actually generate a web page directly from the server depending on the context of the user. For instance, facebook.com requires a user to authenticate or identify them self by typing in their email address and password, and then, based on this information, literally writes a web page, much of which is HTML, for that particular user, with content that is specific to them. The information about the authenticated user is generally stored in a database, and when the user (client) signs in and requests a web page, the database is queried for that user's information, then automatically writes the web page and serves it to the client. Although dynamic websites are much more difficult to program, in the end, they are much easier to maintain, and many times actually use fewer webpages. Dynamic webpages are built as single templates that can serve many thousands of users, like facebook.com, while populating different information into that template depending on the user.

Categories of websites include personal, commercial, governmental, and Intranet websites. **Personal** websites are just that; webpages created by an individ-

Some businesses simply use websites on the WWW the same way they would put their contact information in a phone book.
Courtesy of Getty Images.

Although dynamic websites are much more difficult to program, in the end, they are much easier to maintain, and many times actually use fewer webpages.
Courtesy of Lucas Racasse/Getty Images.

ual that contain content of a personal nature. **Commercial** websites are a collection of webpages that support a business enterprise for the purpose of e-commerce or as a brochure type website to incent a user to employ the business. **Governmental** websites are typically a website platform for informational purposes that support their citizens. **Intranets** are websites about a company to support its employees and guarded by firewalls to authenticate its users. Whether a website is personal, commercial, governmental, or Intranet, it can still be static or dynamic depending on its purpose.

> **WHITE BOARD**
>
> What makes a website 'dynamic'?
> What makes a website 'static'?
> Name some common categories of websites.
> What is an 'intranet' and what does it do?

> **BLACK & WHITE**
>
> Websites have an almost infinite amount of uses, but can be classified by type. The type of website actually varies depending on the user's perspective.

> **GRAY MATTER**
>
> Blog websites are one of the most popular websites on the World Wide Web. 5,000 to 10,000 new blogs are published on the web each day.

Types of Websites

Websites have an almost infinite number of uses, but can be classified by type. The type of website actually varies depending on the user's perspective. Below are just some of the many types of websites:

Blog – A blog is essentially an online diary, originally called a "web log" and shortened to blog. The owner of the blog is called a **blogger** and many times invites the website's readers to post their own comments on discussion forums.

Content Website – Content sites typically dispense original content and are often supported by advertising. Many content sites contain news and opinions and have a staff of contributors and generally do not accept content from outside sources like a blog.

Courtesy of Tom Grill/Getty Images.

Corporate Website – Corporate sites should not be confused with a corporate Intranet. Corporate sites distribute information about a business to provide background information about their goods and services for public consumption whereas corporate Intranets provide on information to its employees and use authentication and firewalls to keep its information private from the general public.

Commerce Website – A commerce site is often called an eCommerce site whose sole purpose is to sell goods and services online.

Directory Website – Directory sites are also called search engines that provide users content that is divided into categories for ease of use.

Employment Websites – Employment sites are a popular way for multiple businesses to post their jobs online to the public. Prospective employees can search employment sites with tools that allow them to efficiently sift through thousands of jobs and employers can extend their reach beyond what a newspaper advertisement would provide.

Gaming Website – Typically gaming sites are games unto themselves and require extensive plug-ins like Adobe Flash, JavaScript, and ActiveX. Gaming sites characteristically have many advertisements and encourage their users to buy the game they're playing.

News Website - similar to information sites, but is devoted to providing news and commentary. News websites have had an enormous impact on the distribution of printed newspapers by markedly reducing their market share.

Courtesy of Stockbyte/Getty Images.

Personal Website – Personal websites often take advantage of online blog software and are administered by people or families to include information and content that the individual wishes to share with their friends and family.

School Website - a school website is used by teachers, students, parents, and administrators to post information about their school's current events, schedules, and homework.

Video Sharing Website - A video sharing website lets user to upload videos for a wider audience to view and often includes ratings and search tools. Video sharing sites use User Datagram Packet (UDP) protocols instead of Transmission Control Protocol / Internet Protocol (TCP/IP).

Search Engine Website – A search engine site offers general information and research and is intended as an entryway for other websites. Search engine sites offer the user the ability to type in "keywords" about the subject matter they are looking for in a website.

> ### WHITE BOARD
> Find three blog websites on the World Wide Web.
> Find three corporate websites on the World Wide Web.
> Find three commerce websites on the World Wide Web.
> Find three employment websites on the World Wide Web.
> Find three news websites on the World Wide Web.
> Find three personal websites on the World Wide Web.
> Find three school websites on the World Wide Web.
> Find three search engine websites on the World Wide Web.

Website Online Software

Relative to other computer programming languages and platforms, HTML is not all that powerful, and web browsers as a computer program delivery method for a complex networked business computing systems are not all that strong either. That is not to say anything good or bad about HTML, but it is inherently weak as a programming language because it needs to remain *standard* so most platforms and browsers can use it. Microsoft Access is an extremely powerful database application program with an exceptionally powerful interface and programming language, and web browsers like Microsoft Internet Explorer and Mozilla Firefox pale in comparison. Once again, this is simply the nature of what these two application softwares are called on to do, and for the most part Microsoft Internet Explorer and Mozilla Firefox are set up simply to render and resolve HTML on a computer's monitor.

Courtesy of Stockbyte/Getty Images.

In terms of operating on a client/server network, a distributed database application program written with Microsoft Access would be considered a **fat client** which typically provides rich functionality on the client side independent of a central server. In broad terms it means that when server on a network stores data files and serves them up to its clients, the clients would be required to have Microsoft Access or some other type of database application program (fat client) installed to read and work with the data. Conversely, web browser application software is considered a thin client. A **thin client** is a client computer or client software like a web browser in client/server network that depends on the server for computer processing which in turn serves up the information to the client.

Courtesy of Tom Merton/Getty Images.

Businesses typically use fat client programs on client/server networks like Local Area Networks (LAN) which are restricted in size. Fat clients have far greater functionality than thin clients. Once a business starts to use the fat client on a larger network, it starts to struggle because it requires the server to serve up and process more information to more client computers than it can handle. Another problem is that fat clients are typically more expensive relative to web browsers which are thin clients.

Businesses find themselves in a bit of a conundrum distributing information over large networks. The bigger the network, the less they can depend on the enormous functionality fat clients enjoy which forces them to depend on thin clients where functionality is far less. On the other hand, the temptation for a business to distribute a computing software system on the Internet is massive. The Internet is the world's largest network which means a business can essentially distribute their systems worldwide for very little cost, but it also means that the business will be forced to use a thin client or web browser for their system. Part of the temptation for a business to distribute a computing software system on the Internet is that virtually all computers have web browsers, which means the business will not have to purchase or develop additional fat client software.

BLACK & WHITE

A **thin client** is a client computer or client software like a web browser in client/server network that depends on the server for computer processing which in turn serves up the information to the client.

GRAY MATTER

Relative to other computer programming languages and platforms, HTML is not all that powerful, and web browsers as a computer program delivery method for a complex networked business computing systems are not all that strong either.

BLACK & WHITE

The bigger the network, the less they can depend on the enormous functionality fat clients enjoy which forces them to depend on thin clients where functionality is far less. On the other hand, the temptation for a business to distribute a computing software system on the Internet is massive.

GRAY MATTER

Obviously, website online software has to be a dynamic website that generates and processes web pages directly from the server, called server-side processing.

Courtesy of Jeffrey Hamilton/Getty Images.

Using web browsers as thin clients while their servers do all the work has another marked disadvantage relative to fat clients; they typically need to be refreshed often which means it is incumbent on the user to make sure the information they see on their monitor is current. For instance, if a user of thin client software sees an airline offering a round-trip ticket for $714 on a web browser, what happens if the airline changes the price for that same ticket on their server? If the user does not hit their refresh button on the web browser, they will not see the change which can cause great confusion between the customer and the airline. Obviously, website online software has to be a **dynamic website** that generates and processes web pages directly from the server, called **server-side processing**. Although data and information are processed on the server side, it still does not ensure that the information on the client side is current because of the nature of a web browser's refresh button.

Overall, many businesses take advantage of the Internet to distribute their computing systems, but have to be keenly aware of the advantages and disadvantages of fat client vs. thin client computing.

Courtesy of Martin Poole/Getty Images.

BLACK & WHITE

Online advertising is a form of sponsorship that uses the World Wide Web for delivering business marketing messages to catch the attention of its customers.

WHITE BOARD

What are some advantages to thin clients?
What are some advantages to fat clients?
Is website online software static or dynamic and why?
What is "server side processing"?

GRAY MATTER

When a business advertises online, they expect or at least hope that a user will click on their ad and pursue their product or service. Unlike other forms of advertising, they can get general statistics on how many people have clicked on their ads.

Online Advertising

It is not unusual to see a website with online advertising, as a matter of fact, it seems to be the norm. Many websites are a commercial enterprise (".com" means *commercial*) and depend on advertising dollars to support their business. **Online advertising** is a form of sponsorship that uses the World Wide Web for delivering business marketing messages to catch the attention of its customers. One of the key benefits of online advertising is that the content and information being advertised is published immediately on the World Wide Web. Because of the nature of the WWW, advertisers know that their content is not restricted by geography, like a printed newspaper. Online advertising can be very effective because the viewer made a conscious choice to interact with the advertiser and many times can interact with them through email, chat, or phone. There are many different examples of online advertising that include the following:

Search Engine Results – Search engines offer a user results that are technically called a Search Engine Results Page or SERPs. SERPs are the listing of hits, or web page hyperlinks, returned by a search engine in response to a keyword query. When a search engine like Google.com returns its results, their SERPs include Sponsored Listings which are basically small classified, contextual advertisements purchased by businesses to entice the user to click their link which usually shows up towards the top right corner of a web page.

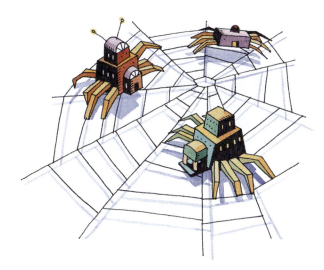

Social Network Advertising – Social network advertising is focused on social network websites like facebook.com and myspace.com. Facebook.com users typically fill out information about their own demographics like age, interests, and location. Social network advertisers can then place their ads for the demographics they feel best suited for their products and services.

Banner Advertisements – Banner Ads or web banners are online advertising that entails embedding a JPEG or GIF image advertisement into a web page that attracts traffic to a website by linking to the website of the advertiser.

When a business advertises online, they expect or at least hope that a user will click on their ad and pursue their product or service. Unlike other forms of advertising, they can get general statistics on how many people have clicked on their ads. A billboard on the side of a freeway can only give general information on how many cars pass that billboard daily. A website can give information on how many viewers view the website as well as how many of their viewers click on ads. Many times websites can use popup ads that open in a new web browser which forces the user to either read the ad or change their settings. Because of these dynamics, businesses purchase their advertising online in three basic ways:

Courtesy of Mike Kemp/Getty Images.

Cost Per Click (CPC) – Cost per click is when an online advertiser only pays the website owner if a viewer clicks on their advertisement. The advertiser only pays for the ad when it's clicked on.

Cost Per Thousand Impressions (CPM) – Cost per thousand impressions actually means "*cost for every thousand impressions or hits*". The "M" in cost per thousand impressions actually represents the Roman numeral "one thousand". Basically, the advertiser is paying to advertise on a website with a particular audience and charged for every thousand viewers.

Cost Per Action (CPA) – Cost per action advertising is when the website publisher only charges the advertiser when a specific action is completed by the viewer like completely filling out an online form or purchasing a product.

Summary

Once you understand how websites and the Internet work, you can start to understand where it's headed. For instance, it's not difficult to make the case that the Internet is still in its infancy and relative to a fat client, it is actually extremely slow. Fat clients reside on servers that get information sent to them automatically without actually having to request it, like a thin client browser. It's not unusual for a fat client's interface to get automatically updated information every three seconds. (Fat clients are typically in the same locale as their server so updates are not that process-intensive) This insures that if someone else on the same network updates information, all users on the network get the change, like airline reservation networks.

Imagine a thin client on the Internet trying to do the same, automatically updating every three seconds. That means one thin client would request information from its server 1,200 times an hour, and if the online software system had 500 users, it means the server get 600,000 hits an hour, which would completely overwhelm it. Keep in mind that servers on the Internet can be on the other side of the planet and data and information travels through myriads of routers just to make it to the thin client. A fat client's server is typically in the same building, or at least the same business campus.

Moore's Law tells us that the Internet will eventually catch up in speed to match the advantages of fat clients, but that's still a long way off. Start to imagine what the Internet of the future looks like with that kind of speed. Consider Google Earth, which updates every few months and then apply Moore's Law. Will it be possible for Google Earth to go live? Will the technology exist where someone could go online and see a live shot of their house from outer space? The answer is that the technology does exist today, and we are simply waiting for Internet speeds to increase exponentially, which they will certainly do. What about HTML? Will we even need it when the Internet's speed increases? Why not just stream video as a website? From a business standpoint, it is always wise to remember how websites and the Internet work, and where it is headed in the future.

Matching

Match each key term in the left column with the most accurate definition in the right column.

O	1. HTML	A.	HTML is represented in this form.
N	2. Platform neutral	B.	Data that was duplicated from data on another computer.
M	3. Web server	C.	Special tags to help the browser window display pictures.
K	4. Website	D.	Create elements that can become hyperlinks.
B	5. Cache	E.	An online diary.
A	6. Tags	F.	Rarely change their content and display their information the same way to all users.
G	7. Head elements	G.	Define a web document's title, style, and additional information.
D	8. Link elements	H.	Generates a web page directly from the server depending on the context of the user.
C	9. Image elements	I.	Websites about a company to support its employees and guarded by firewalls to authenticate its users.
L	10. Flash	J.	Collection of web pages that support a business enterprise.
F	11. Static website	K.	An assortment of Web pages that can include text, images, videos, and other elements that is hosted on a web server accessible via the Internet.
H	12. Dynamic website	L.	Another popular language for websites.
J	13. Commercial website	M.	Dedicated computer connected to the Internet that accepts Hypertext Transfer Protocol (HTTP).
I	14. Intranets	N.	Means that HTML can be read and rendered correctly by any browser.
E	15. Blog	O.	Tim Berners-Lee invented it.

Multiple Choice

1. He invented Hypertext Markup Language (HTML).
   a. Steve Wozniak
   b. Ray Ozzie
   c. Bill Gates
   d. Tim Berners-Lee

2. _____ means that HTML can be read and rendered correctly by any browser.
   a. Standard
   b. Platform neutral
   c. Normal
   d. All of the above

3. A _____ is a dedicated computer connected to the Internet.
   a. Database server
   b. Firewall
   c. Web server
   d. All of the above

4. _____ is data that was duplicated from data on another computer.
   a. Cache
   b. HTML
   c. HTTP
   d. Flash

5. HTML is represented in the form of tags called _____.
   a. Protocols
   b. HTTP
   c. CSS
   d. Elements

6. _____ elements are designed to tell a browser how to display and align elements.
   a. Structural
   b. Image
   c. Text
   d. None of the above

7. _____ websites generate a web page directly from the server depending on the context of the user.
   a. Fast
   b. Ordinary
   c. Static
   d. Dynamic

8. When an advertiser only pays the website owner if a viewer clicks on their advertisement.
   a. CFC
   b. CPS
   c. CPC
   d. None of the above

9. When the website publisher only charges the advertiser when a specific action.
   a. CPC
   b. CFC
   c. CPA
   d. CPS

10. Another language that a browser can read is called _____.
    a. JavaScript
    b. C
    c. C+
    d. All of the above

Blanks

A __webserver__ is a dedicated computer connected to the Internet that accepts Hypertext Transfer Protocol (HTTP) requests.

A __website__ is an assortment of Web pages that can include text, images, videos, and other elements that is hosted on a web server accessible via the Internet.

__cache__ is actually data that was duplicated from data on another computer, in this case, a web page.

HTML is represented in the form of tags called __elements__ that are enclosed by angle brackets like "<" and ">".

The client's browser must be __java enabled__ for the program to run, and since browsers exist on the client side of the client/server model of the Internet, JavaScript programs only work on the "client side".

__Static__ websites styles rarely, if ever, change their content and display their information the same way to all users.

__Dynamic__ website styles actually generate a web page directly from the server depending on the context of the user.

A __thin client__ is a client computer or client software like a web browser in client/server network that depends on the server for computer processing which in turn serves up the information to the client.

__Online advertising__ is a form of sponsorship that uses the World Wide Web for delivering business marketing messages to catch the attention of its customers.

__Cost per click (CPC)__ is when an online advertiser only pays the website owner if a viewer clicks on their advertisement.

Short Questions

What is the difference between a thin client and a fat client?

What is cache and what does it do?

Why were videos so scarce when the Internet started?

What is the basic language of the Internet?

Explain what elements do in HTML?

List types of websites and their purpose?

eleven | security

- System Security & Computer Privacy
- Business System Threats
- Firewalls
- Malware Threats
- Malware Solutions
- Passwords
- Internet Fraud
- Computer Privacy
- Identity Theft

System Security & Computer Privacy

Computer security is concerned with risk management, confidentiality, integrity and the availability of the electronic information that is processed and stored on a computing system. In a computing system, **risk management** is the recognition, consequences, and assessment of risk to a computer's assets, and developing strategies to manage and protect them. It is important to identify that every computer is at risk, and understand the enormous penalties for ignoring these problems.

A computer is an extremely attractive target for an intruder or hacker as they hold valuable information like credit card numbers, passwords, bank account information, music files, and sensitive business data. A **hacker** is often someone who attempts to evade or disable a computer's security measures, and then steals computer resources at their leisure. Computer hackers are not just after information, many times they attempt to hijack heavily sought after computing processing cycles and speed, as well as storage space.

BLACK & WHITE
Computer security is concerned with risk management, confidentiality, integrity and availability of electronic information that is processed and stored on a computing system.

GRAY MATTER
Consider the data and information on a computer the same way you would consider any other tangible asset.
Would you leave the key to your car in the ignition? Would you leave priceless jewelry out in the open?

Fireware hardware and software are just a few tools to keep an information system safe.
Courtesy of Symantec Corporation.

An **unsecure computer** is an extremely easy to breach, especially by a seasoned hacker. Many times these computers are connected to the Internet, so they receive emails with malicious attachments, like viruses, worms, and malware. Sometimes just reading an email can initiate an undetectable program that can take over the whole computer system, and many times the end user remains completely unaware. Entire networks of computers can fall prey to the same fate. Unfortunately, this is only one of thousands of scenarios that can and does happen every day. It is better to assume a computer will be attacked regardless of security measures and take preemptive measures to prevent them than it is to naively ignore computer security altogether.

Business System Threats

Businesses commonly take advantage of the Internet by setting up intranets. An intranet is a businesses' private version of the Internet that works the same way as the Internet, but is confined within the business. The same concepts and technologies of the Internet apply, such as clients and servers running with Internet protocols. Intranets still use the same hypertext transfer protocols (HTTP), browsers and e-mail. The key aspect of an Intranet is **privacy**. A **firewall** is specialized hardware and software working together that insures that only authorized personnel and employees within a business can use their Intranet.

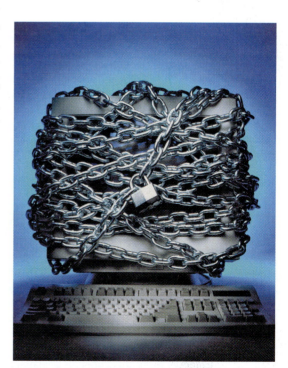

Courtesy of Mangiat/Corbis Images.

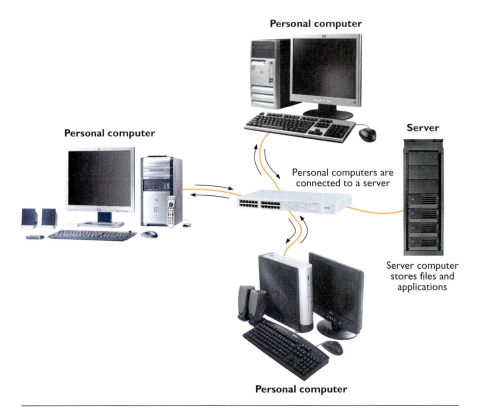

Courtesy of Prentice-Hall, Inc.

BLACK & WHITE

A Trojan horse program often seems harmless and possibly interesting until it is executed. When the program is executed, it may release one or many harmful viruses, worms, or any other sort of malicious program into a computer or networked system.

GRAY MATTER

Trojan horse viruses are extremely hard to detect and deploy themselves typically months and sometimes years after they have entered a computer system which points out the importance of a good, up to date virus protection program.

Businesses keep all sorts of data and information on their networks. An intranet can contain financial information, human resources policies and procedures, specialized accounting systems, research and development secrets, and an endless array of other computer information.

Firewalls

Firewalls keep unauthorized Internet users out of private intranets. Without a firewall, an Intranet is just another part of the Internet. To protect any network, including a business intranet, a combination of hardware devices and software are employed to create a firewall. In simple terms, a **firewall** is configured to deny or permit network users, (many times Internet users) or data into a computer network with different levels of trust. Any communications in or out of an intranet pass through a special security computer called a **proxy server** as a precaution to protect from any external threats.

A firewall's job is to control the flow of data and information between computer networks by opening or closing ports for the various transmission protocols like http, email, ftp, etc. A common business example is the relationship of the Internet which is a zone with no trust to an intranet which is a zone of very high trust.

A firewall's function in a network is like a fire door in a building, used to keep the threat of a fire out, or at least from spreading. A network firewall is used to prevent intrusion to the private network. Like a fire door, called a port, it's used to contain and delay structural fire from spreading to contiguous buildings.

Without proper configuration, a firewall can often become worthless. Standard security practices dictate a "default-deny" firewall ruleset, in which the only network connections which are allowed are the ones that have been explicitly allowed. Unfortunately, such a configuration

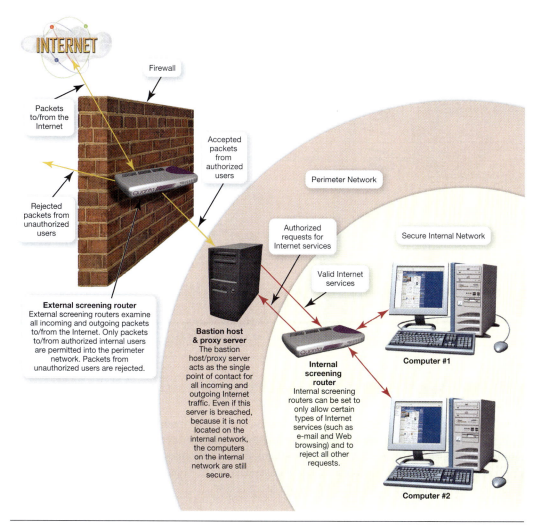

Courtesy of Prentice-Hall, Inc.

> **BLACK & WHITE**
>
> Operating system vendors like Microsoft and Mac OS are constantly vigilant to protect their user's operating systems by automatically offering online updates, or system patches that have been identified as security threats in the operating system itself.

> **GRAY MATTER**
>
> A computer system always needs to be backed up and have up to date good antivirus software.
>
> It is important to know that files being restored from backup were also protected from viruses or one can inadvertently restore a virus.

requires detailed understanding of the network applications and endpoints required for the organization's day-to-day operation. Many businesses lack such understanding, and therefore implement a "default-allow" ruleset, in which all traffic is allowed unless it has been specifically blocked. This configuration makes inadvertent network connections and system compromise much more likely.

> **WHITE BOARD**
>
> What is a risk management?
> What is proxy server and what purpose does it serve?
> What is a firewall and what is it for?
> What is 'risk management'?

Malware Threats

Computer Virus – The term virus comes from biology. Computer viruses are computer files that reproduce by making copies of them self in a computer's memory, storage, or on a network, called metamorphic viruses, similar to what a biological virus does. Unlike a biological virus, computer

BLACK & WHITE
Internet fraud is a broad term that refers to any fraudulent activity regarding online activity. Internet fraud can occur through email systems, message boards, chat rooms, or websites.

GRAY MATTER
Fraudulent Internet schemes are devise all the time so it is important to always be vigilant when conducting business with any Internet entity.

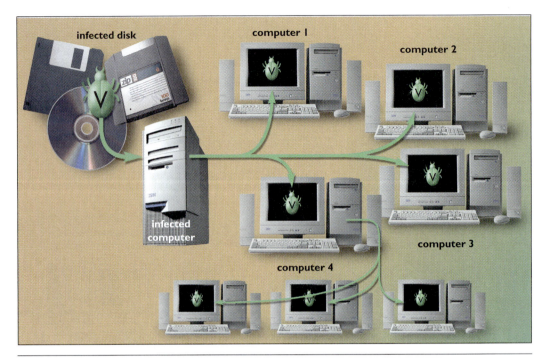

Courtesy of Prentice-Hall, Inc.

viruses do not simply evolve themselves; computer viruses are intentionally created by programmers for a wide variety of reasons. Viruses are malicious and are actually categorized by a broader terminology called **malware**. Malware is programs specifically intended to penetrate or damage a computer system without the end user's knowledge. There is a wide array of motivations for a programmer to create malware, many of which are listed below.

Some malware has been written as research projects to further understand how to combat them, while others are pranks and vandalism. Malware is often used for financial gain, whether it's from identity theft or to plant spyware, which can monitor another computer's actions, and it is even used for extortion.

Worms - A computer worm is like a virus in that it is self-replicating but many times far more insidious in that it does not need to attach itself to an existing program to spread. Worms use networks to travel by sending copies of itself to other parts of the network without a user's knowledge or intervention. A worm can do a variety of harm to a computing system, from slowing a systems performance to erasing files to damaging physical hardware.

Trojan horse – The term Trojan horse originates from the myth of the Trojan War and its infamous Trojan horse. A Trojan horse program often seems harmless and possibly interesting until it is executed. When the program is executed, it may release one or many harmful viruses, worms, or any other sort of malicious program into a computer or networked system. Often, Trojan horses need no user intervention, but instead wait for a particular computer action, or even a particular date.

Spyware – Spyware is a computer program that is installed covertly on a computer to capture or take control of the computer, without a user's knowledge or consent. As the name suggests, spyware secretly monitors a user's keystrokes and behavior, but can also install new software, often more spyware or programming to divert a computer to third party advertising websites. Unfortunately, many users who discover spyware will buy "spyware cleaning software" on the Internet only to find they are actually enabling a third party to install their own version of spyware, and unwittingly think the computer problem is solved.

Courtesy of Image.com/Corbis Images.

Adware – Adware or advertising-supported software is typically more irritating to a user as it is not usually as malicious. Adware are programs that automatically display or downloads advertising to a computer. Many times adware is installed from Internet web sites without user intervention or knowledge. One reason adware programmers are motivated is economic. Like spyware, a user might be given an option to purchase a software package that can eliminate the original adware.

Spamming – Spam or junk email is the abuse of an email system to arbitrarily send typically millions of unsolicited bulk messages. These email messages range from advertising, to chain letters, to criminal schemes. Any unsolicited email should be considered spam and treated as a threat to a computer system. Computers are not just the domain of spam, as faxes, mobile phones, blogs, and newsgroups can fall prey as well.

Denial-of-service attack (DoS attack) (▲) is an attempt to make a computer or any of its resources unavailable to its intended users. A DoS attack can come in the form a malicious program downloaded as an email attachment that runs constantly without the user's knowledge and requires an enormous amount of processing power of the computer. The computer slows down because of the extra computing cycles being used up and many times simply stops running altogether effectively denying use of the computer. Many times DoS attacks will target something as large as an entire network or simply deny use of a website or software.

Reverse Phishing / Keylogging - A relatively newer form of malware, keylogging is when a perpetrator logs on to a computer workstation and installs a program that simply records every keystroke made at the workstation's keyboard. The computer criminal waits for a legitimate user to sign in, and then the keylogging software records their login ID, password, and any other sensitive information. Once the keystrokes are recorded, the criminal is able to play them back and breach the workstation's security.

BLACK & WHITE

Antivirus softwares are computer programs that attempt to identify, prevent and eliminate computer viruses and malware, and typically before they reach a computing system or network.

GRAY MATTER

Operating system vendors like Microsoft and Mac OS are constantly vigilant to protect their user's operating systems by automatically offering online updates, or system patches that have been identified as security threats in the operating system itself.

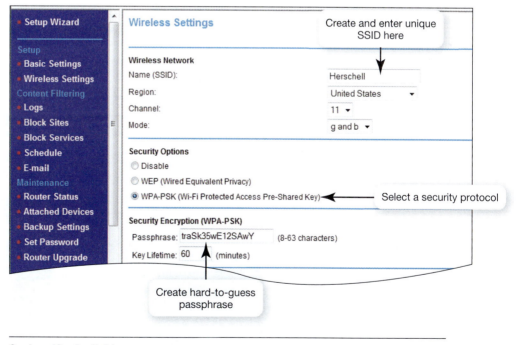

Courtesy of Prentice-Hall, Inc.

WHITE BOARD

What is a virus and why does it exist?
List several types of viruses and how they work.

BLACK & WHITE

Privacy can be defined as the ability of an individual to keep their personal information out of public view. For an individual, computer privacy has much to do with an expectation of remaining anonymous.

GRAY MATTER

Some may argue that privacy does not exist when using the Internet.

Malware Solutions

Every computer system, whether stand-alone or network must have an anti-virus software installed. **Antivirus softwares** are computer programs that attempt to identify, prevent and eliminate computer viruses and malware, and typically before they reach a computing system or network. Antivirus software programs examine computer files and match them to known viruses stored in a database and also monitor a computing system for suspicious activities that might indicate that a computer is already infected. Two of the more popular antivirus programs are Symantec Corporation's Norton AntiVirus and McAfee's VirusScan which are constantly updated with the latest downloads to ward off the newest viruses.

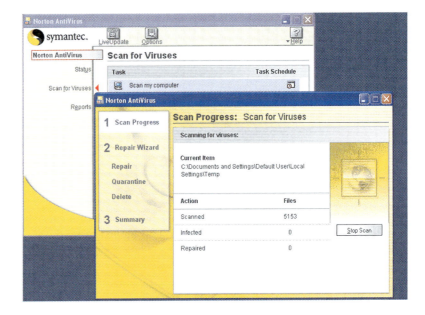

Operating system vendors like Microsoft and Mac OS are constantly vigilant to protect their user's operating systems by automatically offering online updates, or **system patches** that have been identified as security threats in the operating system itself. As computer criminals become more sophisticated, operating system vendors must constantly improve their systems to thwart these threats.

Courtesy of IBM Corporation.

All files on a computer should be **backed up**, but realistically, it's important to back up files with high priority and those that cannot be easily recreated. It is very important to also have the original CDs that was used to install both system and application software in the case of a catastrophic computer failure. Backups should be done on a regular basis based on how often they are accessed. It is extremely important to know when to restore files to a system as a user may have backed up the very infected file that caused the problem in the first place. Antivirus software should be employed to scan back up storage media as well as the computer. Email and their attachments are a great source of malware so it is important to know which ones are harmful. A malevolent attachment often times is an executable program that waits for an event for the program to run, and often the event is simply downloading it from an email. The attachment might be a virus, malware, Trojan horse, or many other types of harmful malware. This points out the importance of antivirus software, but sometimes it isn't enough, as new viruses are spawned daily. It also points out the importance of common sense when dealing with any email attachment, or downloading any software.

> **BLACK & WHITE**
>
> Phishing is a criminal activity using social engineering techniques and attempts to deceptively gain private information, like usernames, PIN numbers, passwords and credit card details, by masquerading as a legitimate business organization typically in a legitimate looking email.

Passwords

A **password** on a computing system can be helpful to deter computer criminals, but it's important to understand that it's best to use a **strong password**. Strong passwords are longer in length than ordinary passwords, typically eight to twelve characters. They also use mixed case letter, and many times numbers and special characters. Strong passwords should be completely unrelated from anything in the computer's surroundings but also easy enough to remember so a user can remember it without having it written down. An example of a strong password is: "aR1z0nA".

> **GRAY MATTER**
>
> Computer privacy can be defined in many ways depending on a point of view. Privacy can be defined simply enough as the ability of an individual to keep their personal information out of public view.

Internet Fraud

Internet fraud – Internet fraud is actually a very broad term that refers to any fraudulent activity regarding online activity. Internet fraud can occur through email systems, message boards, chat rooms, or websites. Typically, this type of fraud is through criminal solicitation followed by transferring the proceeds to the perpetrators. Some of the more serious crimes committed on the Internet include stealing credit card numbers and intercepting wire transfers.

Most Internet fraud is done by stealing stolen credit card data by simply copying information from online retailers. Stealing credit card information constitutes **identity theft**. Hackers attempt to locate large databases online that store credit card information, and then sell the data to other online criminals. Credit card information is normally encrypted as it travels online, but eventually needs to be decrypted back to plain ordinary text and hackers see this step as another opportunity to intercept credit card information. Sometimes credit card information is stolen by employees of companies that process the original purchase, and the employee in turn sells the information to criminals.

Click fraud - One of the newer Internet fraud schemes is called click fraud. Online businesses like Google offer advertising networks, like Google AdSense. Websites that participate in Google's AdSense can contextual advertising to their sites, and the website's visitors can choose to visit the advertiser's website. The idea is that when the visitor clicks to the advertiser's website, Google pays the owner of the original website a per click fee. It's important to note that it is at the website visitor's discretion whether to click to a

Courtesy of Craigmyle/Corbis Images.

214 CHAPTER 11 | Security

Norwegian teenager Jon Johansen released the computer program DeCSS, which enabled Linux computers to play movies stored on DVDs. The program violated the Digital Millennium Copyright Act's prohibition against circumventing encryption measures. Norwegian authorities twice prosecuted Johansen, but he was acquitted both times.

German teenager Sven Jaschan created the Sasser worm, which infected about 18 million Windows computers in April 2004, disrupting operations at Delta Air Lines, Australian railroads, and other businesses. A juvenile court sentenced Jaschan to one and a half years' probation and 30 hours of community service.

Briton Philip Cummings worked for Teledata Communications (TCI), an American company that makes instant credit-check devices for banks, car dealers, and other businesses. He participated in an identity-theft ring that affected 30,000 people. After pleading guilty, Cummings was sentenced to 14 years in federal prison.

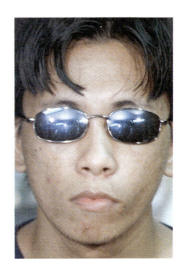
Filipino computer science student Onel de Guzman allegedly wrote The Love Bug virus, which infected millions of computers worldwide. At the time the virus was created, the Philippines had no laws against computer hacking, and he was never prosecuted.

American David L. Smith created the Melissa virus and posted it on an alt.sex.usenet group using a stolen AOL account. The virus infected hundreds of thousands of computers. Smith was sentenced to 20 months in federal prison, required to do 100 hours of community service, and fined $5,000.

American Jeanson J. Ancheta created the Trojan horse program rxbot, which spread to thousands of Internet-connected computers. He sold access to infected computers to customers who used them to distribute spam or launch distributed-denial-of-service attacks. He was sentenced to 57 months in federal prison. In addition, he paid $15,000 in restitution and surrendered his computers, a car, and $60,000 in cash.

Courtesy of Associated Press; courtesy of David Images/Getty Images; courtesy of Associated Press; courtesy of Associated Press; courtesy of Associated Press; and courtesy of Corbis Images.

new website or not. Fraudulent schemes have been developed by hackers by writing programs inserted into advertising network websites that automatically pass a user to the advertiser whether they had any intention of visiting or not, and collecting the ill gotten per click fee.

Purchase scams – Purchase scams are the most uncomplicated type of Internet fraud. Purchase scams involve a buyer typically in another country that approaches merchants via spam and asks if they can pay for shipping with a credit card. The computer criminal will write a professional looking letter with a credit card number that is most likely stolen, but has the capacity to cover the requested order. Once the order is shipped, the credit card is cancelled and the shipping company receives a charge back and loses all of their money from the order.

Phishing - Phishing is a criminal activity using social engineering techniques and attempts to deceptively gain private information, like usernames, PIN numbers, passwords and credit card details, by masquerading as a legitimate business organization typically in a legitimate looking email. Phishing occurs mostly when an outside entity or phisher deceptively represents themselves as a financial institution like a bank. (PayPal and eBay are two very common targets for phishing schemes) For example, a phisher may send millions of emails that look like they're from a particular bank to unsuspecting users and look perfectly legitimate but are in fact a conduit to collect sensitive information. Because millions of emails were sent, the phisher knows that many of the email recipients will almost certainly bank at whatever institution is being fraudulently represented. The email will likely say that some information about a user's account was lost and almost certainly ask the email recipient for their name, account number, and PIN. If an unsuspecting user complies with the phishing email, the phisher has exactly what they want; control of the bank account.

It is extremely important to note that no institution will ever ask for any account information, ever. Legitimate entities should not even have the ability to look up their own customer's passwords; only reset them, and only after getting consent from their customers based on specific information.

> **BLACK & WHITE**
>
> The United States Department of Justice defines identity theft as follows: Identity theft and identity fraud are terms used to refer to all types of crime in which someone wrongfully obtains and uses another person's personal data in some way that involves fraud or deception, typically for economic gain.

> **GRAY MATTER**
>
> Always check your credit score and bank statements for clues of identity theft.

> **WHITE BOARD**
>
> What are some Internet frauds and how do they work?
> Why can phishing be such an effective Internet fraud?

Computer Privacy

Computer privacy can be defined in many ways depending on a point of view. **Privacy** can be defined simply enough as the ability of an individual to keep their personal information out of public view. For an individual, computer privacy has much to do with an expectation of remaining anonymous. **Anonymous** means that one's personal identity is not known.

Many individuals have the false impression of privacy or anonymity when they using the Internet and may not realize they are participating in their own loss of privacy. For instance, a user may choose to purchase a book from a popular, legitimate book selling website and feel comfortable that they can type in personal information including name, address, and credit card number to complete an online purchase. The user might return to the same website and be greeted by a personal greeting and a selection of books like the one they purchased a few days earlier. The question is; how did the book website know so much about you when you returned?

Courtesy of The Image Bank/Getty Images.

BLACK & WHITE

For a business, computer privacy refers to protecting one of its most important assets; its data and information.

GRAY MATTER

History files are a list of stored or cached websites on a user's computer that are essentially an account of where and what a user's web browser has visited on the web. If an employee wants to protect their privacy at work, they need to assume they are always being monitored, whether on the web, email, or telephone.

The answer is called a **tracking cookie**. Remember that you don't visit a website; it visits you. A copy of a webpage was sent from the book seller's server to your computer (client). Along with the webpage copy, the server also sent a small text file called a cookie that the user is typically unaware of. When the user typed their personal information into the webpage, it is also being copied to the cookie. Unless the cookie is deleted after the user is finished with the webpage, it stays on the client's computer so that the next time they visit the bookseller's website, the cookie fills in information like a personal greeting along with the user's name, address, and credit card information so it does not have to be re-entered.

Courtesy of Corbis.

The advantage of a cookie is that the user does not have to fill out tedious information twice into the same webpage, and they buying experience is much easier. The bookseller is able to leverage information from the cookie by comparing the original book purchase to their databases and make legitimate book suggestions that the user might actually appreciate, increasing the potential of more sales.

The disadvantage of cookies is that they can be used for tracking website browsing behavior. The bookseller has information about your browsing habits, how much you've spent, and other information that could potentially compromise your privacy.

Cookies can also be used for data mining. **Data mining** is when experts extract useful data and information from recorded data, like a cookie. Keep in mind all of the personal information you typed into a website, for instance your email address resides in a cookie. What if the bookseller uses the cookie to add your information to their database for market analysis? Once you are in their database, do they sell your information? Is it a coincidence that you start receiving unwanted emails from other businesses after you made the original book purchase after your information were sold? If your information was sold, your privacy was most certainly compromised.

Browser application software allows users to decide whether to accept cookies, but if the user decides to reject a cookie, it typically renders the webpage unusable. The lesson is that that no matter how careful a user is on the Internet, or a network for that matter, total anonymity does not really exist.

For a business, computer privacy refers to protecting one of its most important assets; its data and information. A business' data and information in the wrong hands can spell disaster. Compromised financial information, research and development ideas, and employee records are just some examples of business data and information that has to remain private.

A business needs to scrutinize their employee's access to data and information regularly and consistently, including web browsing habits, emails, software usage, and even phone calls. Businesses also need to make their employees aware of clearly outlined policies and procedures regarding appropriate data and information access behavior, including making employees know their activities will be monitored regularly. The employee in turn will need to fully understand the implications of these policies and procedures, and that their employers have the right to monitor their activity.

Some businesses may choose to not allow an employee to surf the web at work for fear they will acquire a malicious tracking cookie or virus, or end up with undesirable content in their computer's cache. Businesses can install web browsing filters to avoid undesirable content, and also routinely check an employee's browser history files. **History files** are a list of stored or cached websites on a user's computer that are essentially an account of where and what a user's web browser has visited on the web. If an employee wants to protect their privacy at work, they need to assume they are always being monitored, whether on the web, email, or telephone.

Identity Theft

Identity theft is a crime concerning the unlawful practice of assuming another individual's identity, and it is one of the fastest growing crimes in the United States and Canada. The key piece of information a criminal needs to steal one's identity is their social security number. One of the many things a criminal in possession of another person's social security number can attempt is to apply for credit.

The United States Department of Justice defines identity theft as follows: **Identity theft** and **identity fraud** are terms used to refer to all types of crime in which someone wrongfully obtains and uses another person's personal data in some way that involves fraud or deception, typically for economic gain. Below is a list of several ways a criminal can acquire personal information about an individual:

Shoulder surfing – Although a quaint term, shoulder surfing is exactly what it sounds like; a criminal in a public place will simply glance over their victims' shoulder and watch them dial a phone number, or type in a password on a laptop, or simply listen for a credit card number. One example that most people can relate too is when they type their PIN number into an ATM, they typically look around to make sure no else is looking.

Dumpster Diving – A lot of information is simply thrown away around homes and offices, like copies of checks, bank statements, credit card statements which usually bear your name, address, and sometimes even your phone number. It's not uncommon to throw away pre-approved credit card applications that arrive in the mail, the post offices' version of spam. Criminals know this and are willing to simply sift through trash to get it.

Spam – Criminals send a legitimate looking email representing themselves as perhaps a bank. The spam email might explain that your account information has been compromised, and for security purposes you need to provide your username and password to rectify the situation. Once the unknowing user complies with the phony email, they have literally handed the information over.

Armed with enough information about an individual, the criminal can assume a person's identity and commit many types of crimes, like falsely applying for loans or credit, fraudulently withdraw money out of the victims' bank account, illegal use of telephone calling cards, and obtaining goods and privileges the criminal might not ordinarily get if they were to use their own names. Perhaps the worst thing about identity theft is that a business or individual only becomes aware of identity theft after the damage has been done, and this only assumes that they ever become aware of it. Reversing the damage like ruined credit or loss of money is often a very long and arduous task.

For protection against identity theft, the United States Department of Justice urges people to remember the acronym "**SCAM**". SCAM stands for the following: Be "**Stingy**" about giving out personal information. Treat all of your personal information on a "need to know" basis. "**Check**" your financial information on a regular basis and look what should and shouldn't be there. "**Ask**" periodically for your credit report. It is a good idea to check your credit score on a regular basis as a barometer of your financial status and watch for any unusual fluctuations. "**Maintain**" careful records of your banking and financial records.

BLACK & WHITE

A lot of information is simply thrown away around homes and offices, like copies of checks, bank statements, credit card statements which usually bear your name, address, and sometimes even your phone number. It's not uncommon to throw away pre-approved credit card applications that arrive in the mail, the post offices' version of spam. Criminals know this and are willing to simply sift through trash to get it.

GRAY MATTER

Criminals send a legitimate looking email representing themselves as perhaps a bank. The spam email might explain that your account information has been compromised, and for security purposes you need to provide your username and password to rectify the situation. Once the unknowing user complies with the phony email, they have literally handed the information over.

Summary

If you remotely suspect you have been a victim of identity theft, act immediately to minimize the damage. If appropriate, close bank accounts and cancel credit card accounts. Assume that all of your information has been compromised, even if it looks like it has not. Contact the Federal Trade Commission to report your situation at 1-877-ID-THEFT.

The United States Congress passed the **Identity Theft and Assumption Deterrence Act in 1998** that created a new offense of identity theft that prohibits knowingly transferring or using another person's identity and defined identity theft as a federal crime and carries a maximum term of 15 years in prison. Always take mistaken identity and identity theft seriously and take the appropriate actions to avoid them.

Matching

Match each key term in the left column with the most accurate definition in the right column.

O	1. Data Mining	A.	Concerned with risk management, confidentiality, integrity and the availability of the electronic information that is processed and stored on a computing system.
N	2. Phishing	B.	Recognition, consequences, and assessment of risk to a computer's assets.
M	3. Antivirus Software	C.	Someone who attempts to evade or disable a computer's security measures.
K	4. Spam	D.	Private version of the Internet
B	5. Risk Management	E.	Specialized hardware and software working together that insures that only authorized personnel and employees within a business can use their Intranet.
A	6. Computer Security	F.	Key aspect of an Intranet.
G	7. Proxy Server	G.	Special security computer.
D	8. Intranet	H.	Broader terminology for viruses.
C	9. Hacker	I.	Virus in that it is self-replicating.
L	10. DoS	J.	Computer program that is installed covertly on a computer to capture or take control of the computer.
F	11. Privacy	K.	Junk email.
H	12. Malware	L.	Attempt to make a computer or any of its resources unavailable to its intended users.
J	13. Spyware	M.	Computer programs that attempt to identify, prevent and eliminate computer viruses and malware.
I	14. Worm	N.	Criminal activity using social engineering techniques and attempts to deceptively gain private information.
E	15. Firewall	O.	When experts extract useful data and information.

Multiple Choice

1. A _____ is often someone who attempts to evade or disable a computer's security measures.
   a. User
   b. Prankster
   c. Firewall
   d. Hacker

2. A _____ as a precaution to protect from any external threats.
   a. Backup
   b. Proxy server
   c. Server
   d. Firewire

3. Viruses are malicious and are actually categorized by a broader terminology called _____.
   a. Application software
   b. System software
   c. Malware
   d. All of the above

4. _____ is a computer program that is installed covertly on a computer to capture or take control of the computer.
   a. Spyware
   b. Platform
   c. Plug and Play
   d. Hardware

5. A _____ attempts to make a computer or any of its resources unavailable to its intended users.
   a. Switch
   b. Trojan horse
   c. Security shield
   d. DoS

6. _____ is when experts extract useful data and information from recorded data, like a cookie.
   a. Data mining
   b. Hacking
   c. Tracking
   d. Cracking

7. _____ is a crime concerning the unlawful practice of assuming another individual's identity.
   a. False Identity
   b. Incorrect identity
   c. Mistaken identity
   d. Identity theft

8. All files on a computer should be _____
   a. Documents
   b. Database
   c. Backed up
   d. Deleted

9. _____ are programs that automatically display or downloads advertising to a computer.
   a. Compuware
   b. Key ware
   c. Adware
   d. System trackers

10. A(n) _____ is configured to deny or permit network users or data into a computer network with different levels of trust.
    a. Firewall
    b. Motherboard
    c. Intranet
    d. All of the above

Blanks

Computer **Security** is concerned with risk management, confidentiality, integrity and the availability of the electronic information that is processed and stored on a computing system.

A **hacker** is often someone who attempts to evade or disable a computer's security measures, and then steals computer resources at their leisure.

A(n) **unsecure computer** is an extremely easy to breach, especially by a seasoned hacker. Many times these computers are connected to the Internet, so they receive emails with malicious attachments, like viruses, worms, and malware.

A **firewall** is specialized hardware and software working together that insures that only authorized personnel and employees within a business can use their Intranet.

Communications in or out of an intranet pass through a special security computer called a **proxy server** as a precaution to protect from any external threats.

Viruses are malicious and are actually categorized by a broader terminology called **malware**.

Some browsers are able to understand a programming language called **cookies** as well as HTML.

Antivirus Software are computer programs that attempt to identify, prevent and eliminate computer viruses and malware, and typically before they reach a computing system or network.

Internet fraud is actually a very broad term that refers to any fraudulent activity regarding online activity.

Phishing is a criminal activity using social engineering techniques and attempts to deceptively gain private information, like usernames, PIN numbers, passwords and credit card details.

Short Questions

What is a tracking cookie and what purpose does it serve?

How is a strong password different than a regular password?

Why is a Denial of Service (DoS) so dangerous and what does it do?

What can be done to reduce or eliminate spyware and adware?

What sort aspects are covered when a business does a risk assessment analysis?

What is a system patch and where do they come from?

twelve | information systems in business

- Information Systems Role in Business Departments
- The Accounting Department
- The Human Resources Department
- The Marketing Department
- The Research and Development (R&D) Department
- The Production Department
- Information Systems Collaboration
- Business System Reporting

Business Functions

Jack lives in Portland, Oregon and makes extra money by shaping and selling kiteboards. Although building kiteboards started out as a hobby, he found that people really liked his **product** and he could make a few bucks to supplement is regular job as an information systems analyst. Jack doesn't have any aspirations of building a kiteboard empire, he just likes kiteboarding, hanging out in the Columbia River Gorge, and talking with fellow kiters.

At first, Jack only produced kiteboards for himself, but friends kept asking if he'd make them boards. Jack decided to start a small business and named his new venture 'Jack Attack Kiteboards'. Pretty soon Jack had a few thousand dollars from kiteboard sales, but had no idea what they cost to produce or even how much he should be selling them for. He knew he had capital outlay for foam blanks, fins, and fiberglass, but knew he needed to find out if he was actually making a profit.

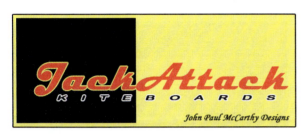

Jack opened a separate bank account for his new business and started to **account** for his money. After analysis of his deposits and withdrawals, he was able to start formulating a **price** of what his kiteboards cost. With the information he gathered from his bank account, he was able to determine the price kiteboards he hadn't even produced should cost, based on costs and labor.

As Jack got better at producing kiteboards, he started **collaborating** with fellow kiteboard manufacturers and discussed new **research and designs** methods. Some of the new techniques he learned were helpful, and others not so much. One aspect of Jack's business was advertising 'Jack Attack Kiteboards' by leaving flyers around the Columbia River Gorge corridor and **marketing** to anyone who would listen.

After a few years of passion and hard work, Jack ended up with a life changing decision. Jack Attack was very successful and was getting beyond Jack's ability to run it by himself. If he was going to 'go for it', Jack would have to quit his information systems job and work at Jack Attack full time and probably have to **hire some employees**.

Jack's story simply points out that all businesses, no matter how large or small have to do five business functions; accounting, production, research & development, human resources, and marketing.

Information Systems Role in Business Departments

Thousands of colleges and universities worldwide prepare women and men for careers in business. Some schools are more highly regarded than others, some choose to focus on specialized subject matter, and some prefer to take a broader approach. The one thing most of these schools agree on is that most businesses share the same core business functional behaviors, or departments, whether it is a global enterprise, or a sole proprietorship. The five business departments are listed below:

- Accounting Department
- Human Resource Department
- Marketing Department
- Research & Development Department
- Production Department

BLACK & WHITE

Will you own your own business someday? Your success could hinge on whether you can apply information systems correctly and successfully.

GRAY MATTER

All businesses, no matter how large or small have to do five business functions; accounting, production, research & development, human resources, and marketing.

BLACK & WHITE

Business departments need to communicate with one another through data and information sharing called collaboration.

GRAY MATTER

Even as a sole proprietor, whether defined or not, every business needs to account for its money, employ at least on human (themselves), market their wares, stay apprised of the business environment through research, and produce something.

BLACK & WHITE

How organizations account for their money is usually mandated by rules and regulations, and in the United States these rules are called generally accepted accounting principles (GAAP).

Traditional roles of human resource departments involve recruiting and hiring new employees, evaluating and managing personnel, tracking personnel data, administering payroll and pensions, and sometimes providing advice to employees regarding work-related issues.

GRAY MATTER

Accounting is the mathematics of business and information technology can greatly enhance it practices and accuracy.

People are the most important asset any company has, and it's the role of the human resource department to administer them.

Consider for a moment how interrelated the five business departments are and the how much information technology is brought to bear to make critical business decisions. For instance, imagine an automobile manufacturer that produces thousands of parts to produce just one car. The production department needs to know exactly how many cars to produce. If they make too many, the extra cars sit around in costly lots as excess inventory and have to be sold at a discount. If they make too few, the car manufacturer misses an opportunity to sell cars and is not at maximum profitability.

But who knows how many cars to make? The accounting department knows how many cars need to be sold for the business to be profitable. The marketing department knows what kind of cars certain people are most likely to buy and what the car's appropriate price should be. The human resources department knows how many people it takes to make a car. The research and development department is betting that their new innovations will sell more cars and the production department knows how many cars their department can produce.

Business departments need to communicate with one another through data and information sharing called **collaboration**. Collaboration is simply two or more people working towards a common goal, and in the case of the automobile manufacturer, five business departments working towards a common goal. Before collaboration and collaborative software can be discussed, it's important to discuss the roles of the five business departments.

Courtesy of Tom and Dee Ann McCarthy/Corbis Images.

The Accounting Department

A broad definition of a **business** is that is an organized entity designed to sell goods and/or services, usually in an endeavor to make a profit. **Business functional behaviors** therefore can be defined as the necessary core activities required to operate a successful business. For instance, whether a business is a diversified worldwide with tens of thousands of employees or just a single person selling antique books on eBay, both must account for their profits and losses. It stands to reason that the **first** department, often is accounting, which is perhaps the most important. **Accounting** measures and provides financial information about an organization primarily for its decision makers, investors, and taxing authorities. Accounting is often referred to as the language, or mathematics of business.

How organizations account for their money is usually mandated by rules and regulations, and in the United States these rules are called **generally accepted accounting principles (GAAP)**. GAAP are accounting rules for preparing, presenting, and reporting financial statements so the organization and its investors can have a standard set of reports regarding a business' well being. Some of these financial statements include balance sheets, income statements, earning statements, and cash flow reports. To insure the accuracy and fair reporting of these financial statements, laws like the **Sarbanes-Oxley Act of 2002 (SOX)** were enacted to counter fraudulent reporting.

To facilitate the accounting reporting process, information systems including hardware and software play a vital and critical role. Accounting often requires the collaborative efforts of many individuals and the appropriate application software in a networked system to get the job done. How the job gets done can often determine a business' profitability which can be leveraged into a competitive advantage.

Courtesy of Jose Pelaez/Corbis Images.

> **WHITE BOARD**
>
> Describe the role of an accounting department.
> Describe some rules and regulations that accounting departments must comply with.
> What is GAAP?
> What is SOX?
> Accounting is the _____ or _____ of business.

The Human Resources Department

Economic terms like "firm-specific human capital" and even "human resources" suggest that people are a commodity, which is true by some definitions. What is true is that people are the most important asset in any business, and it's the job of human resources departments to administer people. **Human resources** are the **second** core business functional behavior primarily involved with administration of a business' personnel. Traditional roles of human resource departments involve recruiting and hiring new employees, evaluating and managing personnel, tracking personnel data, administering payroll and pensions, and sometimes providing advice to employees regarding work-related issues. Human resources departments track enormous amounts of information about the people that work for a business, and even the people who are no longer employed by that business.

Human resources departments must be fully aware of an entire organization's structure. Businesses are often defined with an organizational chart that shows a visual representation of essentially who works for who, and who is in charge of who. Human resources departments must be aware of all of the aspects of these intra-departmental relationships, and define them clearly. For instance, human resources departments will outline job titles, training, pay ranges, job requirements, and other work-related aspects of all personnel on the organizational chart, which in itself is a daunting task.

> **BLACK & WHITE**
>
> Simply stated, marketing is the promotion of a business' products and is the third core business functional behavior. Marketing departments focus on customers and have core responsibilities like advertising and branding a business' products and services.

> **GRAY MATTER**
>
> The best product in the world is useless and has no value if no one knows about it and it's a marketing department's job to let the world know about it.

Courtesy of Jose Juis Pelaez/Corbis Images.

Businesses have certain expectations of their employees that have to be clearly communicated at the outset of their employment. The way to communicate these expectations is to have the human resources department develop and provide an employee manual to all employees. Applying information systems correctly or not can have enormous implications on this process. Human resources departments can leverage Internet technologies and develop an intranet to disseminate their employee manual, or follow a traditional path of actually printing the employee manual on paper.

> **WHITE BOARD**
>
> Describe the role of a human resources department.
> Describe some challenges that human resources departments face.
> Why are information systems important to HR?

The Marketing Department

Simply stated, **marketing** is the promotion of a business' products and is the third core business functional behavior. Marketing departments focus on customers and have core responsibilities like advertising and branding a business' products and services. Marketing is the **third** of the core business functional behaviors.

E. Jerome McCarthy, a professor at Michigan State University best defined marketing by coining the term "The Four Ps of Marketing". McCarthy's Four Ps concept is universally accepted as the necessary activities to run a successful marketing department. The first "P" is product. **Products** are the actual goods and services a business produces and how they relate to customer's needs including warranties, guarantees, and customer support. **Pricing** refers to what a product costs, or at least what a business is willing to exchange for their products. **Promotion** is the advertisement of a business' products and services, as well as promotion and publicity. Finally, **placement** is how a product or service is delivered to a customer. How, where, and to who a product is delivered describes placement.

Marketing departments have their hands full with products alone, having to know every aspect of all products and services a business offers, and then effectively communicate this information to their customers. Careful analysis is required to price products. Prices can actually vary on the same product. For instance, marketing departments need a firm grasp on economic theory; a business will charge less on a product where the supply of the product is plentiful, and charge more for the same product in a region where the product is scarce. Promotion and placement can also vary for the same product, perhaps depending on regional statues that may or may not allow for certain types of advertising.

Information technology plays a critical role in all four Ps of marketing. For instance, a business needs to make the appropriate market segment aware of products they are most likely to purchase. It wouldn't make sense to advertise an Xbox and gaming products in a retirement community. Finding a suitable market segment can involve complex database analysis and risk assessment to make sure products are introduced to suitable customers.

Courtesy of Warren Morgan/Corbis Images.

> **BLACK & WHITE**
>
> Research and development (R&D) departments take a creative and systematic approach to evolve a business' original idea and devise new ones.

> **GRAY MATTER**
>
> Research and development requires a mix of imagination, critical thinking, and a systematic approach to be successful in a business environment.

> **BLACK & WHITE**
>
> Part of an R&D department's systematic approach is to consider if their ideas are feasible, and if they can be implemented. R&D departments need to have a broad grasp of the business they serve and its industry as well.

> **GRAY MATTER**
>
> Production departments make these goods and services to be sold commercially. Production departments focus their efforts on which goods and services to produce, how to produce them, and what it's going to costs to produce them.

> **WHITE BOARD**
>
> Describe the role of a marketing department.
> Describe some challenges that marketing departments face.
> What are the "P's" of marketing?

The Research and Development (R&D) Department

A common axiom is that if a business isn't growing, it's dying. One of the main focuses of a R&D department is to keep a business growing. Businesses start with an idea, and then develop that idea into products and services that meet the needs of customers. **Research and development** (R&D)

CHAPTER 12 | Information Systems in Business

Courtesy of Charles Grupton/Corbis Images.

departments take a creative and systematic approach to evolve a business' original idea and devise new ones. Research and development is the **fourth** of the core business functional behavior. Sometimes, R&D departments will refer to what they do as "brainstorming", a collaborative thought process by many people to come up with ideas and directions for the business and many times without a predetermined outcome but always with a commercial yield in mind.

Part of an R&D department's systematic approach is to consider if their ideas are feasible, and if they can be implemented. R&D departments need to have a broad grasp of the business they serve and its industry as well. Implementing new ideas can mean hiring new people which means collaborating with the human resources and marketing departments. New ideas also involve working closely with the accounting department to get a firm grasp on what the idea will ultimately cost by creating forecast budgets. Ultimately, the production departments will have to create the new products and services from the R&D department's original ideas.

Information systems like networked collaboration software plays a key role in research and development. Global enterprises often have R&D departmental meetings using video conferencing, webcasts, and "whiteboard" software that allow participation from people spread across the world.

WHITE BOARD

Describe the role of a research and development department.
Describe some challenges that research and development departments face.
Why is it so important that R&D Departments collaborate with other departments?

The Production Department

Many businesses make tangible products like cars and machinery that are called "goods". Others create intangible products called "services", like the advice from an attorney or consulting from a financial advisor. **Production departments** make these goods and services to be sold commercially. Production departments focus their efforts on which goods and services to produce, how to produce them, and what it's going to **costs** to produce them.

Obviously, production departments also focus their attention on the most efficient and cost effective way to produce goods and services to maximize profits. For instance, a production department that makes coat hangers may become aware of a manufacturing machine that will triple their output of hangers. Production departments need to weigh many factors when deciding to purchase the new machine. First, what does the machine cost and what will it cost to operate? If the machine is purchased, where does the business store three times as many hangers (inventory)? Can the business effectively distribute the three times the hangers to their customers? These are just a few of many factors that go into the production department's decision process.

What if the business only offers services like financial advice? Can they leverage the global distribution of the Worldwide Web by posting their services on web sites? Is a website even an appro-

BLACK & WHITE

Data and information exchange software and techniques can be categorized as electronic computing tools whereas collaborative software and techniques can be categorized as management tools.

GRAY MATTER

Imagine the impact the World Wide Web has on industries like travel. If a **webinar** is truly effective, does an organization ever need to send their employees on business trips for corporate meetings? Do webinars and other form of electronic collaboration affect the airline industry?

priate vehicle to distribute their services and if so, how secure is the information? Once again, these are just a very small part of the considerations a production department has when determining how, what, where, and when to produce goods and services.

With so many factors involved in production, information systems and technology must be leveraged effectively. For instance, one of the many tools in a production department's decision process is a spreadsheet to perform a "what-if" analysis to consider all factors and determine if a decision is correct, like purchasing a coat hanger machine. Like every other department, production departments need to collaborate closely with accounting, marketing, R&D, and human resources to further understand their own determining factors that go into their decisions.

Courtesy of Prentice-Hall, Inc.

WHITE BOARD

Describe the role of a production department.
Describe some challenges that production departments face.
What's the difference between tangible and intangible products?

Information Systems Collaboration

Since the five business departments are interrelated it is imperative that they share data and information. The fact is business departments need to do more than just share data and information to be successful; they need to **collaborate** with one another. Although sharing data and information can take many forms, like an annual budget printed on paper or an electronic database file, it is important to understand that data and information is simply a tool used for decision making. For instance, a bicycle company's research and development department gets information from their production department detailing whether their current manufacturing machines will be able to produce the R&D department's new bicycle designs. In the mean time, they receive marketing department information outlining what bike models are most desirable in the marketplace. When the R&D department understands the information, they are able to make decisions on what sort of new bike models designs they should pursue.

It is important to know that there is a difference between data and information exchange and collaboration. Business collaboration is two or more people, or two or more departments working towards a common business goal. Collaboration is facilitated by the exchange of data and information. In the case of the bicycle company, the R&D department might decide they are limited to what they can design based on the data and information from the production department and their manufacturing limitations. Collaboration goes beyond data and information exchange. Although the production department informed the R&D department of their limitations, the two departments can collaborate on what is possible. Although the R&D department had their sights set on developing a certain bike frame, the production department can collaborate in the bike's design by suggesting new ideas to the R&D department that don't have production limitations, which goes a long way towards overall business goals.

Courtesy of Chen/Corbis Images.

Information technology (IT) has to be leveraged efficiently when sharing data and information to encourage collaboration. Keep in mind that IT collaboration and data exchange almost always assumes the use of a network, whether it is private, or even the Internet. Understanding the distinctions between data and information exchange and collaboration helps define information technology's role in business. Data and information exchange software and techniques can be categorized as **electronic computing tools** whereas collaborative software and techniques can be categorized as **management tools**.

Electronic computing tools provide data and information exchange to facilitate decisions. One of the oldest of these business tools is an Internet **discussion board**. A discussion board, sometimes called a forum, allows a virtual community of interested users post electronic messages to a web page. The first post to a discussion board is typically a comment that starts a thread. Others posts follow in chronological order based on the original **thread**. Anyone in the virtual community can start a new thread. Discussion boards and threads are often used for online education and often used within a business' **intranet**. (An intranet is a like a private version of the Internet that works the same way as the Internet, but is confined within a business organization.)

Instant messaging and **online chat** is another way to collaborate by exchanging data and information. Instant messaging is similar to email except that it is real-time computer communication. Businesses can use instant messaging across an office environment, or across the world. Unlike email, instant messaging systems let users know if their party is available, and many users consider it less intrusive than using a telephone and in many cases cheaper and less intrusive. Online chat is not just restricted to personal computers, many devices offer mobile instant messaging often called **texting**.

Video and data conferencing allow businesses to collaborate through a network by allowing two or more locations interact via video and exchange data during the conference often called a **webinar**. Webinars typically allow for collaboration and participation between an audience and a presenter. A major advantage to these types of conferencing is that participants are not required to travel. Video conferencing is sometimes called virtual collaboration. Data conferencing is when two or more users share the same computer as if they were sitting side by side, but from different locations. For instance, two users can collaborate on the same computer and look at the same spreadsheet from different networked locations, which are sometimes called **application sharing**.

Project Management Software provides a business a collaborative road map for organizing and managing resources to schedule a project from start to finish. **Microsoft Project** is project management software that provides a spreadsheet-like GUI input screen to list every aspect and goal to complete a business project, and assign people responsible for these aspects and goals. The output from Project is a concise, collaborative schedule of all activities, deadlines, milestones, and completion dates to efficiently complete a project. Further, Microsoft Project outputs graphical representation of the project with a **Gantt chart** that looks very similar to a road map. The output from project management software is sometimes called the **system development life cycle (SDLC)**. When a business wants to outsource a computer programming job, they will often use project management software called **Unified Modeling Language (UML)**.

BLACK & WHITE

Electronic computing tools provide data and information exchange to facilitate decisions. One of the oldest of these business tools is an Internet **discussion board**. A discussion board, sometimes called a forum, allows a virtual community of interested users post electronic messages to a web page.

GRAY MATTER

Video and data conferencing allow businesses to collaborate through a network by allowing two or more locations interact via video and exchange data during the conference often called a webinar.

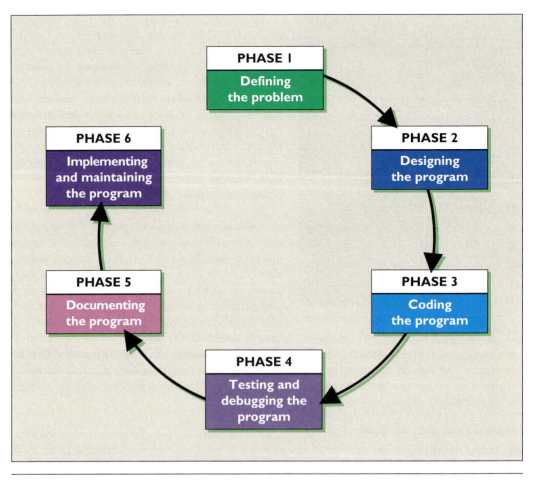

Courtesy of Prentice-Hall, Inc.

Knowledge Management Systems (KM) are collaborative systems that organize, create and distribute a business' collective knowledge. A common example of a knowledge management system within a business starts with distributing ideas, called **knowledge transfer**. An employee of a nationwide organization might come up with a great idea and want an efficient way to distribute it so other employees can take advantage of it. Businesses set up web sites similar to search engines like Google on their private intranet which insures that only other employees can access the knowledge management system. The employee posts their idea to the "Google-like" KM so other employees can find it when they search the system, which in turn distributes knowledge to the rest of the company. Some businesses incent their employees to post their idea with bonuses if the idea has merit, and sometimes if the idea saves the company money pay the employee a percentage of the savings.

Knowledge management systems become more valuable with time because of accumulated amount of knowledge. The KM serves as a repository that organizes every idea ever posted into searchable categories making them easy to access company wide.

One of the newer online collaboration systems is called **online application software**. For instance, two or more users can access the same spreadsheet, word processor, or presentation software and share its data and information. Google offers this free service called **Google Docs & Spreadsheets** and is widely used by businesses and universities for the purpose of collaboration.

CHAPTER 12 | Information Systems in Business

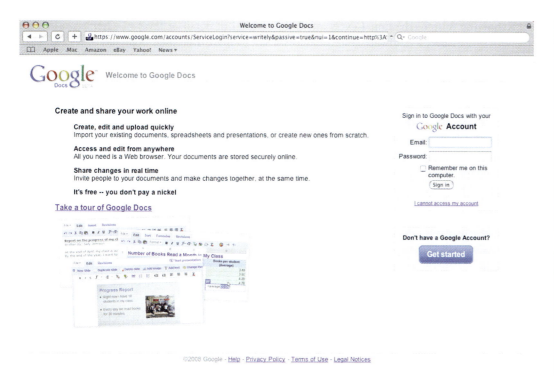

BLACK & WHITE
Business System Reporting or reporting for short is informational output from an information system to facilitate decision making. Reporting can be output in many formats, including display information on a monitor or printed output on paper.

GRAY MATTER
Reports are as good as the data and information they are made up of. A well formatted and organized report is worthless if the information is inaccurate and not reconciled.

WHITE BOARD
Why is collaboration in the business environment so important?
Describe some collaborative tools used in organizations.
What effect does the World Wide Web have on collaboration?
Why are knowledge management systems valuable to an organization?

Business System Reporting

Business System Reporting or reporting for short is informational output from an information system to facilitate decision making. Reporting can be output in many formats, including display information on a monitor or printed output on paper. Most reports are **periodic** in nature, meaning that they are produced at given intervals, sometimes daily, weekly, monthly, etc. Reports can also be **demand** reports, meaning that they can be produced whenever they are needed. Demand reports are sometimes called **ad hoc** reports. The ultimate purpose for all business reporting is to make sound business decisions.

Courtesy of Kaufman/Corbis Images.

Reports help businesses analyze information and can be predictive in nature to make strategic and tactical decisions. **Strategic decisions** refer to long-term planning designed to achieve a specific goal, whereas **tactical decisions** are specific actions that serve a larger purpose. Some reports can lead to both tactical and strategic decisions. There are three main aspects of reporting and they are all interrelated:

- Reporting Summarization Levels
- Analysis & Predictive Reporting
- Management Level Reporting

BLACK & WHITE
Strategic decisions refer to long-term planning designed to achieve a specific goal, whereas tactical decisions are specific actions that serve a larger purpose.

GRAY MATTER
Reports can lead to intelligent strategic and tactical decision making as well as verify and validate them. Budget, forecast, and variance reports are good examples of reports that lead to solid business decisions.

Reporting Summarization Levels refers to the level of detail or level of summarization in a report. For instance, a hardware store produces a sales report from their computerized cash registers on a daily basis. The computerized cash register has software installed called a **transaction processing system (TPS)** that collects and stores data (typically in a database) about the hardware store's daily sales. When all of the daily transactions are printed on paper (or displayed on a monitor), the result is a highly detailed report about every transaction for a given day, like Report 7.1. All businesses have a TPS report that can provide this level of detail. Imagine how much paper one day of TPS reporting is used for Home Depot that sells millions of products every day. Many large organizations never commit their TPS reports to paper and simply leave their TPS data stored in a large database. Transaction processing systems and the data they provide are the groundwork for all other reports.

Report 7.1 shows the hardware store's ten transactions for July 14th, 2009 from its TPS database that is sorted by the time they occurred. Notice that each product is categorized. Report 7.1 shows the highest level of detail. Report 7.1 is generally an accounting report, although each of the five business departments has similar reports. For instance, human resources can generate a report of all employees and their salaries on a given day. The most important question is whether report 7.1 is strategic or tactical? Report 7.1 would be considered tactical because it incents the hardware store manager to take specific actions, in this case, order new inventory to replace what was sold.

Report 7.1—Detailed Daily Transactions—July 14th, 2009			
Time	**Product**	**Category**	**Price**
7:14 AM	Claw Hammer	Tools	$ 24.95
8:03 AM	Flathead Screwdriver	Tools	$ 12.15
8:03 AM	10 Flathead Screws @ .03/Screw	Hardware	$ .30
9:01 AM	Hedge Clippers	Gardening	$ 16.20
10:20 AM	Plastic Garbage Bags (100 per box)	Hardware	$ 11.95
12:03 PM	Hacksaw	Tools	$ 14.90
1:00 PM	Needle Nose Pliers	Tools	$ 12.95
2:30 PM	Grass Seed (10 pound bag)	Gardening	$ 25.90
4:16 PM	20 2 x 4 (15 foot length, $2.00 per)	Lumber	$ 40.00
5:55 PM	15 2 x 4 (15 foot length, $1.50 per)	Lumber	$ 22.50
		Total	$181.80

The same TPS database that produced report 7.1 can also produce a more summarized report that shows transactions sorted, summarized, and totaled by category as shown in report 7.2. Notice that the two gardening sales (Hedge Clippers and Grass seed) in Report 7.1 are now combined and totaled in report 7.2, as are all the categories. Also notice that the overall total of $181.80 is the same for both reports because they came out of the same TPS database, and are therefore **reconciled** with each other. In business, reconciliation is the process of matching and comparing figures in accounting records, and in this case, matching and comparing reports 7.1 and 7.2. Report 7.2 could be considered both strategic and tactical. It does point out specific actions (tactical) in general terms because of its summarization, but can also start to be useful for long term planning (strategic) like which category of the hardware store can be expanded to take advantage of increased sales if it was compared to the same report the month before.

Report 7.2—Daily Transactions Summarized by Category—July 14th, 2009		
	Category	Price
	Gardening	$ 42.10
	Hardware	$ 12.25
	Lumber	$ 62.50
	Tools	$ 64.95
	Total	**$181.80**

Report 7.2 can be summarized even further by combining its category totals as shown in Report 7.3 which simply shows the overall total for July 14th, 2009. Once again, it is important to note that all three reports were produced by the same TPS database and therefore always reconciled to each other. Reports that are completely summarized are generally always strategic in nature, especially when they are compared to the same report within a different time frame. Notice Report 7.3 is a daily report. Combining a year's worth of summarized, daily reports like 7.3 can start to reveal trends and lead to long term planning and goal setting for a business.

Report 7.3—Daily Transactions Total—July 14th, 2009		
	Total	**$181.80**

Reports 7.1, 7.2, and 7.3 demonstrate reporting summarization levels by distilling the hardware store's TPS database into reports that will eventually lead to business decisions. Reporting summarization levels can be used in an infinite amount of combinations. For instance, if the hardware store had thousands of sales that encompassed hundreds of categories, Report 7.2 would have still shown the same level of summarization but would have been a lot longer. What if the hardware store manager was interested in the same level of summarization provided by Report 7.2 but was only interested in a few categories for July 14th, 2009? Database systems offer tools to query the TPS database and pick only the data and information for the hardware store's manager to eventually make a business decision. Summarized reports lend themselves to **graphical** reporting which can reveals trends within a business. Different software can graph summarized data into many different configurations revealing trends that static numbers cannot.

Analysis & Predictive Reporting reports refer to reports that analyze information and are predictive in nature to make strategic and/or tactical decisions. Analysis reports use the TCP as a foundation and also can be summarized, but go a step further. Reports can begin to reveal trends or tendencies in a business, called **trend reporting**. For instance, report 7.2 for July 14th, 2009 can be combined and compared with previous "7.2" reports to create a "5 Day Trend Report" as shown below. (Note: the report below is still reconciled with the original "7.2" report above. The "14th" column that totals $181.80 reflects the same total on Report 7.2)

BLACK & WHITE

Analysis & Predictive reporting reports refer to reports that analyze information and are predictive in nature to make strategic and/or tactical decisions.

GRAY MATTER

Analysis & Predictive Reporting reports can reveal trends in a business. For instance a report can show whether or not sales are increasing or decreasing, and depending on the level of summarization, which specific products are perform well or not.

Report 7.2—Daily Transactions Summarized by Category— 5 Day Trend Report/July 10th–14th						
Category	10th	11th	12th	13th	14th	Totals
Gardening	$70.01	$63.55	$34.89	$50.90	$42.10	$261.45
Hardware	$56.90	$34.56	$30.90	$24.98	$12.25	$159.59
Lumber	$239.89	$211.08	$205.45	$129.90	$62.50	$848.82
Tools	$43.98	$50.44	$52.98	$60.02	$64.95	$272.37
Totals	$410.78	$359.63	$324.22	$265.80	$181.80	$1,542.23

With a quick visual inspection, the hardware store's manager can see trends developing over a five day period. Although five days is typically not enough time to make a decision, it does point out a trend. Notice sales in all categories except Tools have gone down over the five-day period, and total sales have as well. The manager might react to this trend by putting Gardening, Hardware, and Lumber products on sale, just one of many decisions she can make based on the downward trend. Keep in mind that the manager needs critical thinking skills to make a sound business decision. For instance, the downward trend could simply be seasonal which may require no decision at all.

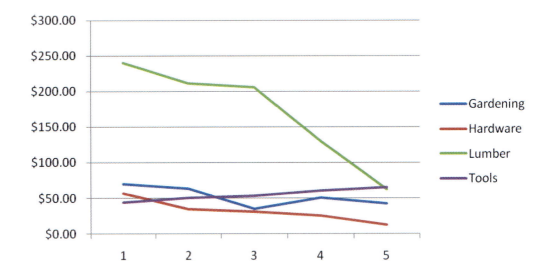

To enhance the effectiveness of the 5 Day Trend Report, the same information can be represented graphically as shown above. Because of their visual nature, graphical reports are sometimes much more appropriate and can point out trends that numeric reports cannot.

Analysis and predictive reports include combinations of **Budget, Forecast, and Variance Reports**. Businesses need to know what has happened in their past, what's happening now, and try to intelligently forecast what is going to happen in the future. Time specific budget reporting does this by combining all three aspects that can lead to both tactical and strategic decisions. Consider the budget report below for the hardware store: (Note: the report below is still reconciled with the original "5 Day Trend" report above. The "Actual" column that totals $1,542.23 reflects the same "Totals" column on the 5 Day Trend Report)

Report 7.2—Daily Transactions Summarized by Category—Variance Report/July 10th–14th						
	Actuals			Forecast		
Category	Actual	Previous	Variance	Actual	Forecast	Variance
Gardening	$261.45	$254.90	$6.55	$261.45	$300.00	($38.55)
Hardware	$159.59	$212.23	($52.64)	$159.59	$200.00	($40.41)
Lumber	$848.82	$714.09	$134.73	$848.82	$700.00	$148.82
Tools	$272.37	$345.90	($73.53)	$272.37	$300.00	($27.63)
Totals	$1,542.23	$1,527.12	$15.11	$1,542.23	$1,500.00	$42.23

The variance report above although still simplistic in nature shows two main headings: "Actuals" and "Forecast".

The **Actuals** heading shows three columns:

- **Actual**: Shows what happened, or what was sold over the course of the last five days in the hardware store between July 10th and July 14th of 2009.
- **Previous**: Shows what transpired over the previous five day period from July 5th to July 9th of 2009.
- **Variance**: Shows the difference between the Actuals and Previous columns.

The Actuals headings show "what happened" from one time period to another and the variance between the two time periods.

The **Forecast** heading shows three columns:

- **Actual**: Shows what happened, or what was sold over the course of the last five days in the hardware store between July 10th and July 14th of 2009.
- **Forecast**: Shows what was projected to happen, or forecast during July 10th and July 14th of 2009.
- **Variance**: Shows the difference between the Actuals and Forecast columns.

The Forecast headings show "what was projected to happened" from one time period to another and the variance between the two time periods. Generally, business managers can make tactical decisions and take specific actions based on the Actuals information, and strategic decisions and do long term planning based on the Forecast information.

Management Level Reporting refers to the level of detail or summarization appropriate for a certain levels of employee regardless of report type. All businesses have a hierarchy, or a chain of command. In a business organization, this hierarchy can be broken down many different ways and many different levels. A typical hierarchy is as follows:

- Executives
- Managers
- Supervisors
- Laborers

With the exception of the Laborers, all levels have supervisory responsibilities for the level below them. Executives supervise managers; managers are responsible for supervisors and supervisors are responsible for laborers. Different levels of management require different reporting as outlined on the next page:

Courtesy of Prentice-Hall, Inc.

In business, top level **executive reporting** require very little detailed reporting, like transaction processing system reports. Executives are interested in the big picture, with reports that offer complete summarization and are highly graphical. Executives are not just interested in their own organization; they must keep an eye on their competition which means the information in their reporting requires internal and external information. Executive reporting facilitates strategic decision making, which leads to long term planning and goal setting. (Note: Executive reports are summarized from Management reports)

Management reporting is summarized from the TPS reports and can sometimes be used for strategic decisions, but generally is used for tactical decisions that require specific actions. Management reports exclusively use internal information. (Note: Management reports are summarized from Supervisory reports which are generated from the transaction processing system.)

Supervisory reporting is highly detailed and generated directly from the transaction processing system, and is rarely used for decision making.

Summary

Successful businesses are successful because of their people, not their computers. Successful businesses understand that computers are simply tools, but also understand that computers and information technology offer an infinite array of possibilities for their organizations and leverage computing for an advantage over their competitors. As mentioned in previous chapters, people are smart, ingenious, open-minded, and imaginative and are able to use information technology to enhance these traits and ultimately run successful businesses.

By the way, Jack went for it.

Matching

Match each key term in the left column with the most accurate definition in the right column.

H	1. Pricing	A.	Two or more people working towards a common goal.
O	2. Knowledge System	B.	Organized entity designed to sell goods and/or services, usually in an endeavor to make a profit.
M	3. Thread	C.	Measures and provides financial information.
D	4. GAAP	D.	Accounting rules for preparing, presenting, and reporting financial statements.
C	5. Accounting	E.	Law that insures the accuracy and fair reporting of these financial statements.
N	6. Gantt Chart	F.	Involved with administration of a business' personnel.
B	7. Business	G.	Involved in the promotion of a business' products
K	8. Production	H.	Refers to what a product costs.
L	9. Computing Tools	I.	Advertisement of a business' products and services, as well as promotion and publicity.
G	10. Marketing	J.	Takes a creative and systematic approach to evolve a business' original idea and devise new ones.
J	11. R&D	K.	Focuses their efforts on which goods and services to produce.
A	12. Collaboration	L.	Data and information exchange software and techniques.
E	13. Sarbanes/Oxley	M.	The first post to a discussion board.
F	14. Human Resources	N.	Looks very similar to a road map.
I	15. Promotion	O.	Collaborative system that organizes, create and distribute a business' collective knowledge.

Multiple Choice

1. Business departments need to communicate with one another through data and information sharing called _____.

   a. File sharing
   b. Memo
   c. Email
   d. Collaboration

2. An organized entity designed to sell goods and/or services, usually in an endeavor to make a profit is called a _____.

   a. Community
   b. Business
   c. Organization
   d. Seller

3. The _____ insures the accuracy and fair reporting of financial statements.

   a. Privacy Act
   b. Freedom of Information Act
   c. Sarbanes-Oxley Act of 2002
   d. All of the above

4. _____ is the promotion of a business' products.

   a. Marketing
   b. Human resources
   c. Research
   d. Accounting

5. Data and information exchange software and techniques can be categorized as _____.

   a. Apps
   b. Drivers
   c. System tools
   d. Electronic computing tools

6. _____ are collaborative systems that organize, create and distribute a business' collective knowledge.

   a. Knowledge Management Systems
   b. Internets
   c. Portals
   d. Information systems

7. Another name for a demand report is a(n) _____ report.

   a. Starter
   b. Accounting
   c. Periodic
   d. Ad hoc

8. _____ Decisions refer to long-term planning designed to achieve a specific goal.

   a. Thoughtful
   b. Tactical
   c. Strategic
   d. Computing

9. _____ Decisions are specific actions that serve a larger purpose.

   a. Thoughtful
   b. Strategic
   c. Tactical
   d. Computing

10. _____ measures and provides financial information about an organization.

    a. Accounting
    b. Human resources
    c. Research & Development
    d. Marketing

Blanks

A broad definition of a _business_ is that is an organized entity designed to sell goods and/or services, usually in an endeavor to make a profit.

GAAP are accounting rules for preparing, presenting, and reporting financial statements so the organization and its investors can have a standard set of reports regarding a business' well being.

Accounting measures and provides financial information about an organization primarily for its decision makers, investors, and taxing authorities.

_HR_ are a core business functional behavior primarily involved with administration of a business' personnel.

Marketing is the promotion of a business' products and is the third core business functional behavior.

Production are the actual goods and services a business produces and how they relate to customer's needs including warranties, guarantees, and customer support.

Promotion is the advertisement of a business' products and services, as well as promotion and publicity.

_R+D_ departments take a creative and systematic approach to evolve a business' original idea and devise new ones.

Data and information exchange software and techniques can be categorized as _____ tools whereas collaborative software and techniques can be categorized as _Knowledge_ tools.

The first post to a discussion board is typically a comment that starts a _thread_.

Short Questions

What is the purpose of a Gantt Chart? _Road map_

What is stored in Knowledge Management Systems and what purpose do they serve?

What is a webinar?

What are five core Business Functional Behaviors?

What is the purpose of the Sarbanes-Oxley Act?

What are the four "Ps" of marketing?
Product
Pricing
Promotion
Placement

thirteen | careers

- Information Technology Careers
- Business Information Technology Perception
- Information Technology Jobs
- Knowing the Business
- Enterprise Resource Planning Solutions
- ERP Advantages
- ERP Disadvantages
- Unified Modeling Language
- System Development Methodologies

Information Technology Careers

It's been said that you don't really choose a career, a career chooses you, and the information technology (IT) field is no exception. For example, a person with a geography degree might find themselves thrust into a geography job that requires better than average IT skills, ends up excelling at the job's IT aspects and eventually evolves into a purely IT career, whereas an IT professional might do the opposite, and perhaps evolve away from IT and more into marketing. Some people simply choose a career they want to pursue early on, and others fall into careers by happenstance. Whichever the case, information technology as a career choice is somewhat unique in that it arguably offers **broader opportunities throughout business** because it courses throughout every aspect of the business world. Often times the IT professional has an easier time changing careers than many other types of business professional. The reason: information technology is everywhere in every aspect of business, so in a sense, IT professionals have seen and done it all.

BLACK & WHITE
Information technology as a career choice is somewhat unique in that it arguably offers broader opportunities throughout business.

GRAY MATTER
IT professionals are business professionals first that can be found through all core business functional behaviors and attempt to improve these business processes through value-added activities.

Courtesy of Mark Richards/PhotoEdit.

Consider a fleet of cars, each one representing the core business functional behaviors of accounting, human resources, marketing, research & development, and production. In this analogy, some would be tempted to think IT professionals are the people that fix the motors and mechanical aspects in all of these cars, but that would be a misnomer. There are certainly careers for people who are interested in "fixing motors" called the polytechnic aspects of computing, like making sure a server stays online or repairing a motherboard, but business information technology careers are different. Information technology enhances business, so IT professionals would be people that make the cars go faster and run as efficiently as possible.

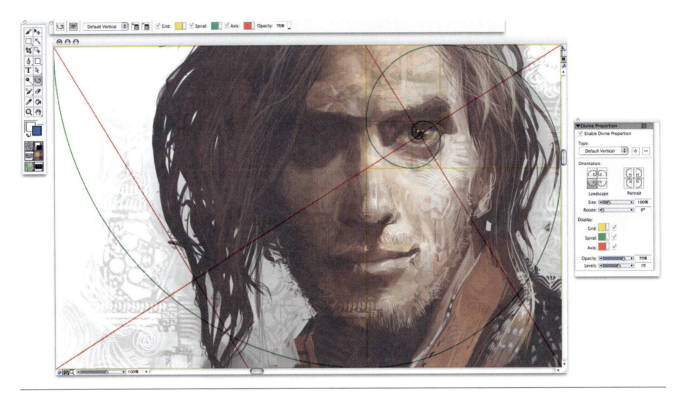

Technology careers are endless, like graphic design with tools that are boundless in imagination.
Courtesy of Pearson Education.

The key is that IT professionals need to know about the cars first and foremost before they can even attempt to enhance them with technology. A common axiom for IT professionals is "**know the business**". IT professionals need a deep understanding into the inner workings of how a business works and what it does before they can start applying information technology solutions. **IT professionals are business professionals first** that can be found throughout all core business functional behaviors and attempt to improve these business processes through value-added activities. **Value added** refers to the added value of a product or service over the cost of products and services used to produce it from the previous stage of production. For example, "value-added" can be applying information technology to an existing process like printing and distributing monthly paper reports and improving the process by distributing the same reports electronically online through an intranet.

Business Information Technology Perception

Although many businesses have IT departments, they remain outside of the core business functional behaviors. Information technology departments are responsible for servicing and enhancing all computing and technical assets and intellectual property of a business organization. This is a broad and ambiguous definition that sometimes causes problems with perception. Some aspects of IT departments are responsible for simply servicing and maintaining computer assets while others employ business analysts that serve as a type of business IT consultants throughout an organization. There are typically two types of IT professionals within an information technology department; **service** and **IT consulting**. Many organizations have people that serve both roles simultaneously. Many times, this can cause confusion. For instance, the human resources department of the organization may have misplaced expectations of a service individual that only deals with hardware concerns or answers phones at a help desk and can't answer a business problem. The opposite can happen to the IT consulting individual that can't fix a printer when their real expertise is business consulting.

The perception problem is generated because IT departments are outside the core business departments and are somehow deemed not as important to the organization. The fact is, IT is outside the core business departments, which is neither a good or bad thing. The problem is making the mistake that IT is not as important as accounting, human resources, marketing, research & development, and production. None of the core business departments can even function without information technology. It becomes tempting to say IT is more important than the departments, but that too would be a mistake. Information technology has a **symbiotic** relationship with all departments. Departments don't function without IT, and business IT doesn't exist with the departments to service. Many times information technology provides the conduit departments need to communicate with each other, so one could make the case that IT is the "bond" that holds an organization together.

Information Technology Jobs

Chief Information Officer (CIO) is a job title for the board level head of an information technology department within a business organization. The CIO normally reports to the Chief Operations Officer (COO) or Chief Executive Officer (CEO). The importance of the CIO position has risen significantly in the last decade as information technology has become a more significant part of business. The CIO is usually a member of the executive board of a business. The job title "CIO" started in the United States and is slowly replacing the older "IT Director" title that is more common throughout the world.

CIO is the highest paying information technology position in business, sometimes making as much as seven figures. CIOs come will typically have degrees and backgrounds in computer information systems, engineering, and computer science and a massive amount of business experience. One of the most important qualifications for a CIO is expertise in business and leadership, which is why many of them have master's degrees in business administration (MBAs). CIOs sometimes make tactical business decisions, but frequently their expertise and focus is their strategic decision and project management skills.

Head Applications Developers are in charge of software application development teams that development, design, program, and test software applications. Try to image the complexities that go into managing multiple programmers, testers, and users to generate an application that runs an airline's reservation system, and what's at stake if it doesn't work, or not delivered on time. Head applications developers typically have at least a bachelor's degree in computer information systems and must have superior project management skills and often use tools like Microsoft Project to organize their teams. Along with project management skills, they also must possess extremely good communication skills and a lot of application development experience.

Head applications developers also use software development tools and techniques like SDLC and UML. **SDLC** is an acronym for System Development Life Cycle which is a process for creating and altering computer applications through an approach that includes planning, system analysis, design, implementation, and system maintenance. Many times head applications developers are given the task of modifying an existing system, which are called **legacy systems**. Often legacy systems are more difficult to deal with that developing a brand new system because they are typically already in use by an organization which means the system needs to keep working to support the business. **UML** is an acronym for Unified Modeling Language which includes a set of graphical notation techniques to create computer models and applications. UML is sort of a "blueprint" for developing an application, and can be used with the team or outsourced.

Applications Architects design parts of applications like screen interfaces, middleware and programming infrastructure that complies with head applications developer's design principles as

---

BLACK & WHITE

There are typically two types of IT professionals within an information technology department; service and IT consulting.

GRAY MATTER

The core business functional behaviors of accounting, human resources, marketing, research & development, and production don't function without IT, and IT doesn't exist with these departments to service.

> **BLACK & WHITE**
>
> Senior Web Developers prepare, plan and implement web-based software applications. These applications include everything from shopping carts for online stores to advanced intranet deployment.

> **GRAY MATTER**
>
> **Business Intelligence Analysts** make sense out of an organizations data and information, as well as external data and information to present to senior staff for the purpose of making tactical and strategic decisions.

well as falls into line with their SDLC. Middleware is the computer programming and software that connect the components an applications architect designs and programming infrastructure are the actual programming language components that help and application work correctly and as designed.

Applications need to work well as well as being intuitive to the end user. Applications architects need to be thoughtful in their designs so the end product meets the head applications developer's vision and requirements and typically learn these skills in colleges and universities on their way to a bachelor's degree majoring in computer science or computer information systems that are typically attached to a business school. Once out of school, it takes between five and eight years experience to become an applications architect and can be a very lucrative career.

Data Modelers, often called **Database Administrators (DBAs)** categorize data requirements and create the database entities and models that ensure accurate and smooth flowing information throughout a business. DBAs can work on a head applications developer's team but often work on existing legacy systems. A bachelor's degree in computer science, information technology and several years of database experience is required to become a database administrator with a strong focus on mathematics.

Network Administrators are directly responsible for the smooth operations and maintenance of the business' networks and networking technology which includes its hardware and software. They often work in partnership with network engineers and network architects to implement and deploy new networks, expand old ones, or integrate an existing network with another existing network. Remember that networks are one of the most important aspects of business computing in that they connect people and resources so network administrators are highly paid and in high demand. Network administrators typically have bachelor degrees but are often trained by network software companies like Novell and Microsoft which offer certification in all aspects of networking. Generally network administrators have years of experience with smaller networks until they are trusted to be in charge of a large LAN or WAN.

Information Technology Auditors sometimes called **Senior IT Auditors** make sure computing systems are being used correctly in specific industries within given set of regulations and compliance issues. IT auditors develop, test and evaluate computer systems for efficiency, accuracy, and security. Often IT auditors will be challenged by their clients to break in to their systems to see were security flaws exist. Information technology auditors often have advanced degrees in computer information system as well as a background in accounting. Big Four accounting firms like KPMG often hire and pay IT auditors very well to help their clients and their computing systems become Sarbanes-Oxley compliant.

Senior Web Developers prepare, plan and implement web-based software applications. These applications include everything from shopping carts for online stores to advanced intranet deployment. Senior web developers differ greatly from web designers that typically only deploy websites. Many times a business will identify a legacy system and ask senior web developers to rewrite it completely and make it browser based so it can be deployed on the World Wide Web for worldwide distribution. Web designers can gain experience to become senior web developers but must know multiple technologies and platforms and hold at least a bachelor's degree in computer science or computer information systems. Senior web developers are one of the most sought after and highly paid positions in the information technology field.

Business Intelligence Analysts make sense out of an organizations data and information, as well as external data and information to present to senior staff for the purpose of making **tactical** and **strategic** decisions. Many times they analyze, review, communicate, and distribute reports on paper, via intranet, or even the Internet and make recommendations to senior management.

Business intelligence analysts must have a very strong analytical background as well as sharp business knowledge. They are required to know what data and information a business needs and how to format it so it makes sense, and have an eye for detail to make sure their reports are always accurate. They also need to be agile to create new ways to present information upon request. Business intelligence analysts usually have several years of experience plus a bachelor's degree in computer information systems with a strong emphasis on business.

Information Technology Staff Consultants must have great communication skills as they are the conduit between IT and the rest of the organization. Although information technology staff consultants are highly trained with technology backgrounds, they must be able to bridge the gap between IT departments and perhaps a marketing department. For instance, a marketing department may need a special application developed and deployed but may not have the technology skills to do so. The IT department that develops the application may not have marketing experience so it becomes the information technology staff consultant's role to be a conduit between the two. As one would expect, this position requires a technology based background with a bachelor's degree in business and superior communication skills as well as two or three years experience.

Knowing the Business

Information technology professionals, specifically IT consultants are always striving to increase efficiency in businesses. The simple approach is to first **understand a business** and what it does and then apply information technology. This sounds straightforward enough, but often with unexpected results, some good, and some not so good depending on your point of view.

Imagine an accounting department for a large property management company who is in charge of finance for 1,000 apartment complexes throughout the country. Each one of these apartment complexes requires capital on at least a daily basis for things like landscaping maintenance, repairs, and employee salaries. Every time an apartment complex needs money they have to request a disbursement from the property management company who in turn approves or disapproves the request, and if approved, transfers the funds to the apartment complex's bank account. The property management company needs to track each and every disbursal. In the past, when the property management company only had 50 or so apartment complexes, they tracked disbursals on a spreadsheet, specifically on Microsoft Excel.

As the property management company flourished and acquired new apartment complexes it quickly became apparent that a spreadsheet had its limitations. With 50 properties, each requesting funds on a daily basis, the spreadsheet started to grow beyond its capabilities. 50 properties times at least one disbursement per day takes at least 50 rows of an Excel spreadsheet. 50 rows a day for a year is 18,250 rows. 100 properties in one year takes a minimum of 36,500 rows and their current portfolio of a 1,000 properties take a minimum of 365,000 rows!

An IT consultant points out to the property management company that Microsoft Excel is probably a bad choice of application software because of the nature of a spreadsheet. 365,000 rows of disbursement information loaded into RAM will make any computer sluggish, but that's just the beginning. The property management company needs to know specific information that is difficult to draw out of the spreadsheet. For instance, what is the total amount of disbursements for properties in the 85258 zip code during July of 2009? Although the information can be gleaned from the spreadsheet with a lot of sorting and summing, it is difficult at best.

Maybe the biggest problem is that the spreadsheet needs to reconcile with the property management company's bank accounts, so they employ three full time accountants for this purpose alone. These accountants spend their days sharing the spreadsheet on a network. Because of the nature of a spreadsheet, only one accountant can use it at a time. To get around this problem, they have broken the original spreadsheet into three spreadsheets based on different regions of the country, West.xlsx, Midwest.xlsx, and East.xlsx. Each accountant combines their data and information with one large master spreadsheet at month's end to get an overall picture of all 1,000 apartment complexes and perhaps to get some analytical data.

The IT consultant suggests exporting the data and information to a database like Microsoft Access and points out some astounding advantages. First, instead of having three large spreadsheets that need to be combined, the database can be in one singular relational database that all three accountants can use at the same time. Secondly, a database can check data input to make sure a user enters "high-quality" data. For instance, the database can make sure that zip codes, states, and dates and other information will always be in the correct format with the correct spelling, a chore a spreadsheet either can't do or would struggle to do. Because of this, reconciliation issues would be reduced greatly. Third, one database form can easily be developed to show all disbursements of each individual property, something a spreadsheet could never hope to do.

Perhaps the biggest advantage to a database is the ability to query information. The property management company could now "ask" their disbursements database questions it could never hope a spreadsheet could answer. The company's ability to ask these myriad of new questions would greatly enhance their ability to make tactical and strategic decisions. It would allow them to know where their money is going and for what purpose, and when.

Changing a spreadsheet to a database has countless advantages, at least in the case of the property management company. It's not unusual for a business to use the wrong application software for one reason or another. In the case of the property management company, they simply "outgrew" their spreadsheet system. The property management company was using a tool that cost them extra employees to manage and denied them the ability to thoughtfully analyze and manage their data efficiently.

Once the information technology consultant ports the spreadsheet data to a database and launches the new database system the property management company's problems are solved, right? Yes and no, depending on your point of view within the company. The property management company no longer needs three accountants to manage the disbursements, now they only need one, which yields and enormous cost savings in salaries. If you're among the two accountants that got laid off because they're no longer needed, maybe you're not so thrilled about the new database system.

The previous example points out how important it is that the IT professional needs to **know the business** first before they can apply any technology solutions. In the case of the property management company, the IT professional has a responsibility to inform the company of all of the benefits of the database system or any information technology solution and its repercussions. Did two accountants really need to be laid off? In business, employees are always a company's biggest asset. Perhaps with better planning up front, the two accountants could have been reassigned and retained their employment. Part of "knowing the business" is know what effects technology will have on a business.

Enterprise Resource Planning Solutions

Enterprise resource planning (ERP) software is a business-wide computer system used to administer and organize all the computer resources and information for functional departments of a business from shared data stores, or database residing on a local area network. Simply stated, it's an overall software solution that attempts to get functional departments in a business on the same page when it comes to software allowing them to share information and more easily collaborate with each other.

The advantage to a central database in an ERP solution is that it includes all an organization's information in one centralized location that can be more easily shared throughout a business, at least that's the idea. Accounting has a lot of information in the ERP database that Production needs as well. For instance, both departments might each have an employee that enters customer names, address's, zip codes, etc. Instead of an Accounting person and a Production person entering the same data in separate proprietary databases, the ERP solution only requires one person to enter data which also enhances data integrity. Data integrity is a term that means data is whole or complete.

ERPs are somewhat of a "Holy grail" when it comes to overall business solutions and extremely difficult to implement. Keep in mind that when an information technology consultant or even a team of consultants looks at business technology solutions, they must first investigate the business process of an organization, and in many cases, businesses already have a "way" of doing things and further have legacy systems. Many times, a business needs to conform to what an ERP offers by re-engineering as opposed to software conforming to a business, which is counterintuitive. This is one of the main disadvantages of ERPs, so in a sense changing the software means changing the business as well.

IT consultants need to be fully aware of the advantages and disadvantages of Enterprise Resource Planning solutions and make their clients fully aware of both. Some of the advantages and disadvantages are listed below:

ERP Advantages

- Functional departments increase production, collaboration, and efficiency by sharing information
- Revenue cycle and order tracking is more easily available across functional departments which enhances tactical and strategic decision making
- Information is available at a more granular level, meaning information can be analyzed to a much finer degree.

ERP Disadvantages

- Businesses often have to re-engineer their own processes to fit ERP solutions. (Keep in mind this is not necessarily a bad thing as the new processes may be vastly improved, but still difficult to do.)
- Because they are business wide, ERPs can be very expensive. Costs, training, implementation, and business process re-engineering across all functional departments is extremely costly.
- If only one person on an ERP database enters information, they must be extremely accurate or the entire organization suffers with inaccurate data.
- ERP systems are very difficult to modify or customize after they are fully implemented.

Unified Modeling Language

Information technology professionals are always thinking of better ways to do things, from business processes to existing legacy systems. IT careers in business takes an incredible imagination and the ability to think and plan critically. That being said, IT consultants can't simply apply technology without a specific plan, and that's where Unified Modeling Language helps.

Unified Modeling Language (UML) is a standardized visual modeling language for developing computer software. UML includes a set of graphical notation tools and techniques to create what basically amounts to a blueprint for constructing a computer application. Many times software developers will use UML to outline how to build their software and in what order it should be built and then outsources the project for another computer programmer to finish.

When developing software systems IT professionals employ UML by first investigating an organization's business processes and identifies who will be involved with the project, like end-users. Those that will be involved with a new system are called actors. UML is typically used with Object oriented programming languages, a type of programming language which encourages the programmer to reuse parts of an application like forms, programming modules, and code. There are four basic steps in UML:

- **Use Case Scenarios** are an explanation of a computer system's behavior as it receives and responds to requests that start off from outside of that system. Essentially, a use case says "who" can do "what" with the system. Use cases capture a system's behavioral requirements by detailing what will happen when a computer program runs.
- **Object Oriented Analysis (OOA)** requires the computer programmer to start analyzing what a new system will need and applies object-modeling techniques to analyze the functional requirements for a system. OOA is focused on what a computer system does.
- **Object Oriented Design (OOD)** takes the OOA diagrams and information and expands it to make implementation specifications. OOD is focused on how a computer system does what it does.
- **Sequence Diagrams** are a kind of relational illustration that shows how computer processes relate and interact with each another and in what order. Sequence diagrams are sometimes called timing diagrams because they visually represent what should happen in a computer program and in what order.

System Development Methodologies

IT consultants need a systematic approach to developing an entire software solution like a business-wide enterprise resource planning (ERP) system or any system for that matter. It is important in the beginning stages and every stage of every computer project that the IT consultant or team of consultants be in control of every detailed step of development. To do this, system developers choose a methodology. The following outlines three different methodologies as well as their advantages and disadvantages:

- **System Development Lifecycle (SDLC)** is the process of creating or altering systems that takes a strict step by step approach to every phase of development. SDLCs vary in steps depending on the software developer and scope of the project. Below are a general guideline of SDLC steps and their descriptions. (Note: steps must be completed in order):

    1. **Initiation** starts with high-level brainstorming of an intended project that tries to determine the goals of the project and whether it is even *feasible*. Part of initiation means developing a feasibility study that answers whether a new or existing system is economically, technically and operational achievable.
    2. **Concept Development** is a stage in the SDLC that is only started if initiation is complete and determined feasible. Concept development starts to define the scope of a project like how big or small it will be and what part of an organization it will affect. One of the more important documents produced in this step in the Cost and risk analysis statements which outline cost benefits and risks should a business undertake the project.
    3. **Planning** stages are for developing a project management plan. It is common to use Microsoft Project that allows a project manager to allocate resources and make sure who is in responsible for completing each step of the overall project. Microsoft Project can also help in cost analysis and provide a visual representation in a Gantt chart.
    4. **Requirements** stages often break the intended or existing system down to analyze problems or even potential problems by employing diagrams like the ones produced in the unified modeling language (UML).
    5. **Design** is the stage where a computer system starts to look like a computer system. Screen layouts, process diagrams, business rules as well as other documentation are constructed as *subsystems* that will eventually become the system itself.

6. **Development** takes the subsystems from the design stage and converts them to an overall system by installing them on their appropriate operating system and conducting preliminary testing.
7. **Testing and Integration** starts when the development stage is complete to make sure it conforms to the previous requirements of the SDLC.
8. **Implementation** is the introduction of the new or improved computer system into the production environment. Implementation also resolves problems indentified from the testing and integration phase.

It's important to know that if any phase of the system development lifecycle fails, the information technology consultant building the computer system is required to go back one step and start over. For instance, if the **development phase's** subsystems don't work, the problem lies in the previous **design** stage. Many times the SDLC process will require computer developers to back up one phase because the original project sponsor will request a **change order**, essentially rendering any one of the SDLC's steps incomplete. It is important to note that beyond the structured step-by-step approach that the SDLC provides, it also provides **documentation** of how the computer system evolved and how it works.

Compared to other methodologies, SDLC is more time consuming which translates into a more expensive computer system. SDLC typically requires more staff to implement

- **Rapid Application Development (RAD)** is a computer system development methodology which takes a minimalist approach. Computer software developed with RAD is more or less a "develop as you go" approach which allows systems to be developed much faster than the SDLC approach, and makes it more flexible to change in requirement.
- **Software Prototyping** is a methodology that can be used during software development by creating software prototypes. In this case, a prototype is an incomplete version of the software being developed. Sometimes these prototypes are called vaporware because they only simulate a few aspects of the final version of the software. Software prototyping lets software developers evaluate different aspects of the software's eventual implementation and also allows end-users to give their input. End-users end up becoming an important aspect of software development as they can offer suggestions that the developer may not have considered and it also makes them closer to the project.

Summary

Are people in the information technology field geeks? The answer is yes. The successful ones are also extremely well-paid and satisfied with their careers. But the IT field is not just the domain of geeks; it is filled with men and women from all walks of life around the globe working in a myriad of different industries. Perhaps one of the best aspects of the information technology field is that it can serve a person well in and out of the IT field. Either way, learning IT will give any businessman or businesswoman a marked advantage in their career.

Matching

Match each key term in the left column with the most accurate definition in the right column.

H	1. Applications Architect	A.	Offers broader opportunities throughout business.
O	2. Use Case Scenario	B.	A deep understanding into the inner workings of how a business works and what it does before they can start applying information technology solutions.
M	3. Data Integrity	C.	Refers to added value of a product or service over the cost of products and services used to produce it from the previous stage of production.
D	4. Symbiotic	D.	Type of relationship IT has with all business departments.
C	5. Value Added	E.	Job title for the board level head of an information technology department within a business organization.
N	6. UML	F.	In charge of software application development teams that development, design, program, and test software applications.
B	7. Knowing The Business	G.	More difficult to deal with that developing a brand new system.
K	8. Web Developer	H.	Designs parts of applications like screen interfaces, middleware and programming infrastructure.
L	9. ERP	I.	Categorize data requirements and create the database entities and models that ensure accurate and smooth flowing information throughout a business.
G	10. Legacy System	J.	Responsible for the smooth operations and maintenance of the business' networks and networking technology which includes its hardware and software.
J	11. Network Admin.	K.	Prepare, plan and implement web-based software applications. These applications include everything from shopping carts for online stores to advanced intranet deployment.
A	12. IT Careers	L.	Business-wide computer system used to administer and organize all the computer resources and information for functional departments of a business from shared data stores.
E	13. CIO	M.	Term that means data is whole or complete.
F	14. Head Apps Developer	N.	Standardized visual modeling language for developing computer software.
I	15. DBA	O.	Explanation of a computer system's behavior as it receives and responds to requests that start off from outside of that system.

Multiple Choice

1. _____ are directly responsible for the smooth operation and maintenance of a business network.
   a. Maintenance Coordinator
   b. Web Developer
   c. CIO
   d. **DBA**

2. _____ is business wide system software to administer and organize computer resources for functional departments.
   a. UML
   b. **ERP**
   c. TCP/IP
   d. DBA

3. _____ is a standardized visual modeling language for developing computer software.
   a. Software
   b. ERP
   c. **UML**
   d. All of the above

4. _____ is a relational illustration that shows computer processes and their interactions with each other.
   a. **Sequence Diagram**
   b. UML
   c. OOA
   d. OOD

5. _____ is a programming language that encourages developers to reuse parts of an application.
   a. HTML
   b. Cobol
   c. Basic
   d. **Object Oriented**

6. _____ is an older existing system.
   a. **Legacy System**
   b. Application software
   c. Inheritance System
   d. None of the above

7. The highest level of IT jobs is the _____.
   a. CfhC
   b. CFO
   c. CEO
   d. **CIO**

8. _____ refers to the added product importance.
   a. Level Addition
   b. Magnitude
   c. **Value Added**
   d. None of the above

9. Data _____ is a term that means data is whole or complete.
   a. Veracity
   b. Base
   c. **Integrity**
   d. Computing

10. ERP Systems are very _____ to modify after they are fully implemented.
    a. **Difficult**
    b. Easy
    c. "Simple Switch"
    d. None of the above

Blanks

IT professionals are business people __first__ that can be found throughout all core business functional behaviors.

There are typically two types of IT professionals within an information technology department; __Service__ and __IT Consulting__.

__CIO__ is a job title for the board level head of an information technology department within a business organization.

Business __Intelligence__ Analysts make sense out of an organizations data and information.

Data __Integrity__ is a term that means data is whole or complete.

Because they are business wide, ERPs can be very __expensive__.

Unified __Modeling__ Language is a standardized visual modeling language for developing computer software.

__RAD__ is a computer system development methodology which takes a minimalist approach.

__Implementation__ is the introduction of the new or improved computer system into the production environment.

__SDLC__ is the process of creating or altering systems that takes a strict step by step approach to every phase of development.

Short Questions

What is the purpose of a SDLC?

What is the point of UML?

What are the disadvantages of ERP?

What are the stages of the SDLC?

What are the advantages of ERP?

Why is it so important to "know a business"?

fourteen | database

Database Definition
Database Structure
Business Database Advantages
Structured Query Language
Business Database Scenario and Implications
Business Database Scenario Advantages
Business Database Scenario Disadvantages

Database Definition

Database software is well thought-out collection of computer files called tables that consist of records (rows) of data separated by fields (columns) that can be queried (questioned) to produce subsets of information. The records retrieved by these queries become information that can be used to make business decisions. Databases are referred to as database management systems (DBMS). In a DBMS, data is stored in computer files called tables, and tables are combined to other tables with related information, hence, a relational database. Business databases are always distributed on a computer network for multiple users.

BLACK & WHITE
Database software is well thought-out collection of computer files called tables that consist of records (rows) of data separated by fields (columns) that can be queried (questioned) to produce subsets of information.

GRAY MATTER
At its core a database is made up of files called tables that are related to each other. Other files that exist within a database like reports that display database information on screen or on paper, saved query files that are used to find specific populations of a databases, and forms which overlay data tables and queries for more specific views of data.

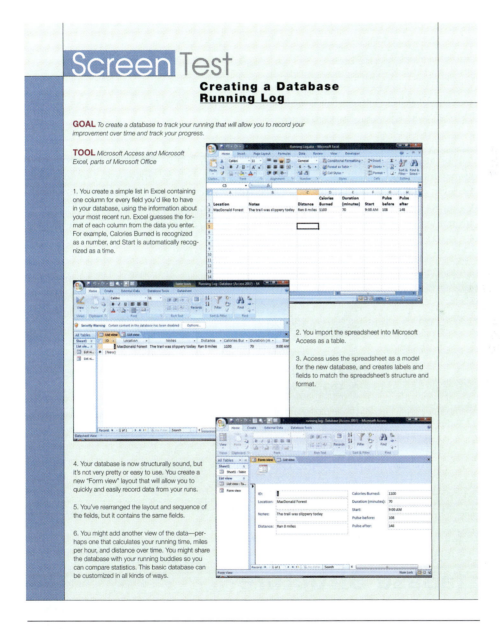

Creating a simple database.
Courtesy of Pearson Education.

Software	Company
Access 2003	Microsoft
dBASE PLUS	dBASE, Inc.
DB2	IBM
Lotus Approach	IBM/Lotus
Oracle Database 10g	Oracle, Inc.
Paradox	Corel
R:BASE 7.1	R:BASE Technologies, Inc.
Visual FoxPro	Microsoft

Commercial Database Management System Software.
Courtesy of Prentice-Hall, Inc.

It can be argued that the first database management systems were filing cabinets. A typical filing cabinet might have three drawers marked with alphabetical characters. For instance, the top drawer might be labeled "A through H". Once a drawer is opened, alphabetical tabs separate folders. Within each folder exists information; perhaps about a customer or property. Database systems are extremely similar to filing cabinets in that they organize information based on a set of rules.

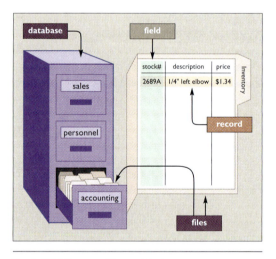

The first DBMS was a filing cabinet.
Courtesy of Prentice-Hall, Inc.

Database Structure

At its core a database is made up of files called **tables** that are related to each other. Other files that exist within a database like **reports** that display database information on screen or on paper, saved **query** files that are used to find specific populations of a databases, and **forms** which overlay data tables and queries for more specific views of data.

A form lies on top of a table to give a user a more useful view of data.
Courtesy of Prentice-Hall, Inc.

Database designers construct databases by using **entity relationship diagrams (ERM)** which is a database-modeling method to construct a theoretical and conceptual representation of data to produce a **schema**. A database schema is a "map" of data tables and their relationships to each other. Simply stated, an ERM is a picture of a database's tables and how they relate to each other.

Database	One or more data files
Data File (or Table)	A collection of records
Record	The combined fields about a person, place, thing, or event
Field	One or more characters
Character	8 bits (the letter M = 01001101)
Bit	0 or 1

Courtesy of Prentice-Hall, Inc.

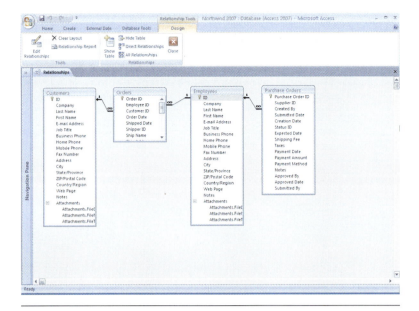

Entity relationship diagrams help database designers create schemas.

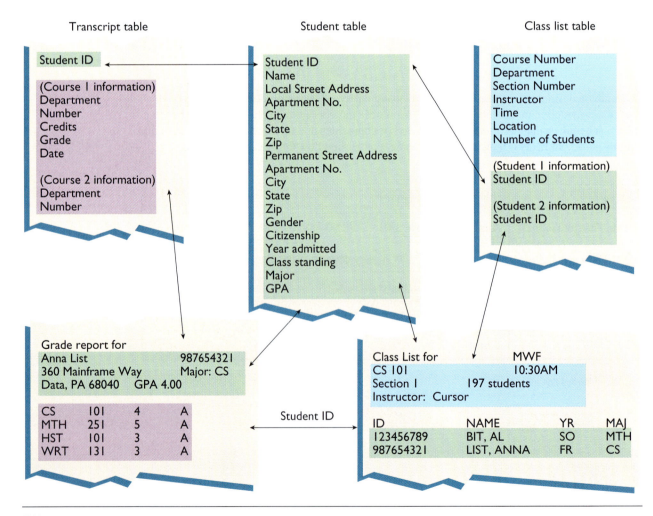

ERM
Courtesy of Prentice-Hall, Inc.

Database designers need to **know a business**. They first start out finding out what a business does and how they do it. For instance, a business may have "customers" which tells the designer that the database will need a "Customers" table. The database designer finds out what is **unique** to those customers like their first name, last name and where they live and then includes these pieces called **fields** (columns) of information in the "Customers" table on the ERM. Once the structure of the "Customers" table is complete, the database designer may find out that the business's customers place orders with them, and sometimes more than one order. The database designer will construct an "Orders" table with fields like "Order Date", "Shipped Date", etc. When the Orders table is complete, the database designer designates its relationship to the Customers table by understanding that "one" customer can place "one or many" orders called a "One to Many" relationship. Once the conceptual structure of the ERM is complete, the designer can start making the tables in the database.

The database designer is also required to know what a business' expectations are of its DBMS. What are the business' report needs? Does the business need to display information on screens in certain configurations? What sort of "questions" or queries will the business require? What are the security concerns of the database? Often, more experienced designers will **consult** a business to help them realize the vast potential of a well organized DBMS.

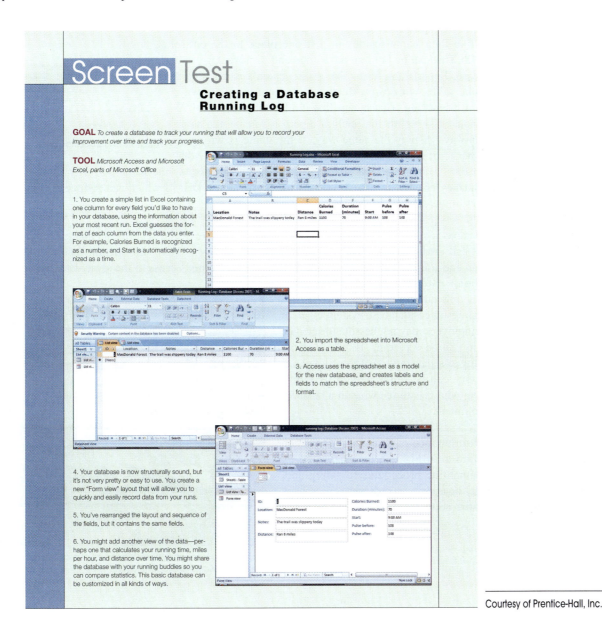

Courtesy of Prentice-Hall, Inc.

Business Database Advantages

> **BLACK & WHITE**
> Data integrity techniques attempt to avoid data input errors like typing errors.

At first glance, a DBMS seems restrictive, especially relative to other business application software. Most business application software like word processors or spreadsheets present the end user with a blank file that is ready for use. For instance, one can start Microsoft Excel, select "File", "New" and simply start inserting formulas and layout. Database software is different, requiring the end user to create their own files starting with tables, and then relating them to each other. Once the table structure is complete, the user is required to understand possible valid entries in a table's field (column). For instance, a "Zip Code" field can be set up to ensure that a user only enters five digits or ten digits (85714 or 85714-1201) and only accept numeric figures. Once a field has a "**data validation**", it ensures **data integrity**. Data integrity techniques attempt to avoid data input errors like typing errors.

> **GRAY MATTER**
> Avoiding data redundancy ensures accuracy system wide throughout a DBMS which can reduce reconciliation errors immensely.

Technique	Result
Alphabetic check	Ensures that a field contains only letters of the alphabet.
Numeric check	Ensures that a field contains only numbers.
Range check	Verifies that entered data fall within a certain range.
Consistency check	Determines if incorrect data have been entered.
Completeness check	Determines if a required field has been left empty.

Data validations
Courtesy of Prentice-Hall, Inc.

The nature and structure of a well thought out database management system helps a business **avoid data redundancy**. For instance, only a **singular table** holds personal information about a person. A person's unique information like their name resides in just one place in the entire DBMS. This can be both an advantage and disadvantage in a database. Reports and forms that use a person's name from a singular table will *always* display that name the same way, even if it is wrong. That means that if a DBMS consists of 23 forms and 124 reports that include a person's name, the name will always display the same way. If the name is wrong, it only has to be corrected in one singular place; on the table that holds the "name" data and all forms and reports will display the name correctly. Avoiding data redundancy ensures accuracy system wide throughout a DBMS which can **reduce reconciliation errors** immensely.

Databases store all kinds of sensitive information, like social security numbers, employee pay rates, and credit scores. DBMS systems have the ability to store information securely by giving certain end-users access to data, and other end-users limited access to the same data. For instance, a human resource director may have rights and complete access to all of a human resources database system whereas her employees may not be able to see data in the same system, like a fellow employee's pay rate. Different levels of **security** can be implemented by determining who gets to see what in a business environment.

> **BLACK & WHITE**
> Maintenance of data and information residing a DBMS can be performed by implementing procedures to safely add, delete, or update records as well as back up entire networked database systems.

Maintenance of data and information residing a DBMS can be performed by implementing procedures to safely add, delete, or update records as well as back up entire networked database systems.

Courtesy of Mark Richards/PhotoEdit.

> **GRAY MATTER**
> **Structured Query Language (SQL)** is the most widely used standard computer language for relational databases that allows a programmer to manipulate and query data.

Structured Query Language

Structured Query Language (SQL) is the most widely used standard computer language for relational databases that allows a programmer to manipulate and query data. One of the most common uses of SQL is to query a table(s). For instance, a table might have the names of 10,000 book titles and their prices. If a person wanted to know which books in the data table cost more than $100.00 they could set up a SQL statement like the following:

SELECT Title
FROM Book
WHERE Price > 100
ORDER BY Title

> **BLACK & WHITE**
> Structured Query Language (SQL) has been around since the 1980s.

> **GRAY MATTER**
> Structured Query Language (SQL) is going to be one of the most important tools for accounting majors in that much of their auditing will be performed on data tables.

The first line of the SQL statement "Selects" which field in the table should be in the query's results, in this case, the "Title" field. The second line (FROM) determines which data table to query, which holds the "Title" field. The last line determines what criteria should be applied, in this case to another field called "Price" that resides in the "Book" table. The criterion in the third line of the SQL finds books where cost is greater than $100.00. Once the SQL is run, the fourth line will sort the results.

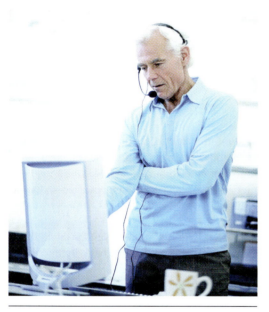
Courtesy of Altrendo Images/Getty Images.

The SQL above is very simplistic, yet *exceptionally* powerful. Data is fluid because it changes all the time. New books can be added and deleted to the data table in the above example. Book prices can change as well. SQLs like the one above can be saved to ask the same question to fluid data for different results. Many SQLs include more than one table in their query as well as multiple criterions.

Structured Query Language is not just for querying. Imagine a data table with 100,000 records that includes products, product category, and their prices. What if a business wants to increase prices by five percent on products that are considered "Hardware"? One way to solve the problem is to have someone go through all 100,000 records, check if its hardware, update the price by increasing it by five percent. Obviously this process would take hours, maybe days to complete. Even when the manual process was complete, did the data entry clerk with this arduous job do it correctly? Did they recalculate the price accurately? Did they make sure only hardware items were affected? A very simple SQL like the one above could be written to do the entire job in seconds. It would actually take longer to write the SQL (a few minutes) than it would to process the job. The SQL would take a matter of seconds to do what would take days manually. The SQL would, given it is written accurately, be perfectly accurate. The same SQL could be saved and modified.

Business Database Scenario and Implications

Zach is considered good at his job. He works at a large banking institution and is in charge of compiling facts and information on his bank's foreclosed real estate. When he first started, the bank had about 50 properties in foreclosure so his job was manageable, but as the economy soured, that number ballooned to almost five hundred. One of the main aspects of Zach's job was to produce a "REO Fact Sheet" for each and every property. (REO is an acronym for "Real Estate Owned"). The REO Fact Sheet has 75 individual facts about each property like REO number, property name, address, property type, property value, etc. and is distributed bank wide.

When Zach first started, he took over for a person who was actually producing the fact sheets on a typewriter so he transferred the information to Microsoft Word documents. Although it was chore to hand-type the information into Word and make sure it was accurate, he knew it would make his **business process** more efficient in the long run. (He considered scanning the old documents with OCR technology but decided hand-typing would be best). Now that he had the fact sheets in word processing documents, he was able to be more organized. For instance, he named his Word documents after the property's REO number, like 121714.docx. Zach saved all the REO Fact Sheet Word documents in an "REO Documents" folder on his personal computer's hard drive. His Windows 7 Explorer allowed him easy searching and sorting capabilities so accessing a fact sheet became infinitely easier than searching through a filing cabinet of typewritten documents.

Zach's corporate life will change dramatically over the coming weeks.
Courtesy of BananaStock/Jupiterimages.

When Zach had to start a new fact sheet, which was unfortunately becoming more and more frequent, he was able to access a blank REO Fact Sheet template on his hard drive he'd named "template.docx". He simply inserted a new property's information in the template and used the "Save As" function in Word to name the new document file after its associated REO number. (He sorted his Word documents in the Windows 7 Explorer to find out what the next available REO number was.)

Although the bank was piling up properties, Zach kept up. Every month he would print all of his *completed* documents, make copies, and distribute them to different parts of the bank by interoffice mail. Departments like the Property Management Group depended on Zach's REO Fact Sheets heavily to budget how many properties they were now in charge of. The Finance Department used the fact sheets to compile numbers like "Total Bank Owned Property Value".

One of the most important things Zach's predecessor told him during his initial training was to *never, ever* distribute an incomplete REO Fact Sheet. To avoid distributing incomplete REO Fact Sheets, Zach decided to have two separate folders, one called "Complete" and the other called "Incomplete". 400 REO Fact Sheet documents were in the complete folder, and the other 100 were in the incomplete folder. As an REO Fact Sheet became complete, Zach would simply drag the document from the incomplete to the complete folder.

One day Zach was called into his boss's office and told he needed to modify the REO Fact Sheet. Executive Vice Presidents had requested more information. As Zach left his boss's office, he was overwhelmed by what he knew would be a daunting chore. Zach knew he would have to open up each and every REO Fact Sheet Word document, all 500. Once the document was opened, he would have to make the requested changes and then save the document. In his head, he couldn't even imagine how long that would take. Even when and if he got the chore complete, he wondered if the document would ever be changed in the future and if he'd have to do the process all over again.

Zach knew there was no way he could do his job effectively with the specter of the currently requested configuration changes to the REO Fact Sheet. He also knew he would inevitably have requested changes in the future. He would have to change his business process completely, but to

Is Abby giving Zach good advice?
Courtesy of iStockPhoto.com.

what? Zach called his friend Abby at the bank's Information Technology department who suggested he try the "**Mail Merge**" function offered in Microsoft Word. Abby described a way that Zach could modify his existing REO Fact Sheet template to mail merge with only one other Word document. She suggested he call the new document "Information.docx". All of the data in Zach's 500 REO Fact Sheets could be imported to the new information.docx file and configured in such a way that a separate template document file could read them one at a time. Zach could modify his existing "template.docx" and insert fields that could read data within the "information.docx. This would mean Zach would only need to deal with two Word files to produce the exact same results. If anyone requested a change to the REO Fact Sheet, it would only have to be done to the template.docx file.

Although Zach knew he had a lot of work ahead of him stripping data out of the 500 Word files into a new information.docx document, he also knew that once he done, his new business process would be a lot more efficient as well as more easily modified. Abby gave Zach something else to consider. Instead of having one Microsoft Word file merging with another Microsoft Word file, why not have the Microsoft Word template.docx merge with a Microsoft Excel spreadsheet? Abby told Zach that although the "Word to Word" mail merge would work, it still may be difficult to manage the data in the information.docx document. The disadvantage of the information.docx is that its file size would be extremely big, the data is in no particular order, and typically its data is arranged somewhat awkwardly.

Abby described how data in an Excel spreadsheet could be arranged in **records** (rows) separated by tabular **fields** (columns). The template.docx Word document could be attached to the new spreadsheet. Once the template was up and running, Abby explained all of the benefits of the spreadsheet. All Zach would have to do to enter a new REO foreclosed property was to simply add a row in the Excel spreadsheet. The spreadsheet could be sorted, counted, and summed in infinite ways and perhaps even new reports could be developed. Zach was sure this was the best route to go.

Abby wanted Zach to consider one more idea. Although mail merging the template.docx to a spreadsheet would work, it too would have its disadvantages. She reminded Zach of the terms she'd used to describe data in a spreadsheet like "records" and "rows". This was database terminology. The real answer to Zach's dilemma was to transfer all 500 REO document's data to a database like Microsoft's Access. Abby agreed to help with the data migration from Word to Access and promised Zach he would see the immediate benefits of a database.

Zach trusted Abby's judgment and decided to give the database idea a try although he still had deadlines, and the changes to the REO Fact Sheet will still not complete. Abby assured Zach that she could write a program that would open all 500 REO Word documents. The REO document files would be opened one at a time by Abby's program, and safely transferred to a database table. Zach showed Abby where all of the REO documents resided on his hard drive, both complete and incomplete. Abby mentioned that information this sensitive was probably better suited on one of the network's drives where network administrators could make sure it was backed up on a regular basis. Zach was still lukewarm on the whole idea. He was still no closer to making the changes on the REO Fact Sheet that had been requested from his boss. Abby told him she would write the program to migrate the data and that they would meet tomorrow.

Zach was nervous the next day when he met Abby. He wanted to know things were getting accomplished, especially the new configuration of the REO Fact Sheet that had been requested the day before. Abby told Zach that the data transfer from Word to Access went well, but she found a few problems. She showed Zach the new Microsoft Access data table which he'd mentioned looked just like a spreadsheet. Abby agreed but told Zach that the comparisons ended there. She said that in this case a database is much more appropriate for his **application**, and substantially more powerful.

As Abby showed Zach the Access data table he thought it looked nothing like his REO Fact Sheet, and Abby agreed which made Zach even more nervous. Abby had named the database "REO" and the data table "Properties". Abby had also included an extra column in the data table called "Complete or Incomplete" which obviously determined the status of an REO. She had a "C" in the field (column) for completed REOs and an "I" for incomplete.

Abby had mentioned there were some problems with the data. For instance, some of the zip codes of the REO properties were wrong. Zach wondered how in the world Abby would know that and was fairly certain she was wrong. Zach had always prided himself on the very careful way he input information into his 500 REO Fact Sheets, so doubted Abby's claim. She showed Zach the zip code field (column) that she had labeled "Zip Code". Two of the zip codes only had four digits, when they should have had five. Zach found the REO numbers and quickly opened the associated Word documents from where the data had been imported. Sure enough, the Word documents had the exact same four digit zip codes. Zach was somewhat embarrassed but Abby assured him errors in the database were easy to avoid.

Zach wondered what other data was wrong and asked Abby how she found it so easily. She explained she had sorted some of the fields like "Zip Code", and the two offending zip codes sorted right to the top of the data table. Zach said a spreadsheet will do the same kind of sort. Abby agreed, but mentioned a spreadsheet is a lot more trouble to sort compared to a data table, and is really difficult to deal with on higher echelon sorts. She also mentioned the inherent danger of sorting in a spreadsheet. She asked Zach what would happen if he sorted a spreadsheet without highlighting the entire range of data and then saved. Zach knew the spreadsheet would be ruined. Abby assured Zach that that never happens with data tables.

Abby showed Zach the data in the "State" field and said although the data was technically right, it was inconsistent. She showed Zach how to perform an elementary query that asked the data table to produce the unique records in the State field. Some of the records that indicated a property was in Arizona were marked "Az" and some said "AZ". The "State" field had four other states with inconsistent data like the Arizona properties. Zach asked if there was a way to fix the "State" data. Abby showed Zach another easy query that took care of the whole "State" field. She quickly mentioned that a spreadsheet could not do this.

It took Abby and Zach just under an hour of easy queries and sorts to audit and "clean" all 75 fields of data in the new Access data table. (75 fields represented the original 75 individual pieces of information in the REO Fact Sheet previously in 500 Word documents.) Zach was amazed how many subtle mistakes existed, but more amazed how easily they were spotted and fixed. Then Abby showed Zach something she knew a spreadsheet couldn't do. She asked Zach if he wanted to make sure that zip codes were always input correctly. Zach rightfully told Abby that there were only two correct formats for zip codes: five digits and nine digits with a dash. Abby switched the data table from View mode to Design mode and found the "Zip Code" field in the data structure, or **schema** as she called it. Abby showed Zach a way to insert a "field mask" on the "Zip Code" field that restricted data input. Abby switched back to the "View" mode and showed Zach that the Zip Code field now only accepted input of five digit zip codes or nine digit zip codes with a dash. Zach quickly wondered what other fields could benefit from field masks. Abby told him almost all fields could have field masks, like "State". Abby told Zach that he could set up his data table to type only capitol letters in the "State" field even if the Cap Lock on his keyboard was off. He could even make the field present him with a list of all of the states when he was inputting data in the "State" field.

Zach had now committed to a database and asked Abby if they could focus on the REO Fact Sheet, after all, that's what this whole exercise was all about. Abby showed Zach how to make a "form". A form overlaid the data table to show information in a more organized manner. Zach's new form would look exactly like the REO Fact Sheet. It only took Zach a few hours to make the form and when he was done, he now had a powerful tool that changed the very nature of his job. What Zach didn't know was that his new database would change the entire bank.

Business Database Scenario Advantages

Zach started to realize that most of the time he'd spent on REO Fact Sheets in the past was now unnecessary. His new database was on a network drive now so he didn't have to worry about backups, which he rarely did anyway. His business process had completely transformed. He no longer had to manage 500 individual Word document files. He simply had one place where all of the REO information was held. He was able to input and update information on his new REO Fact Sheet form in his data table. Zach's database easily found and eliminated past input errors from his Microsoft Word days and kept him from making errors in the future. Zach could also print his form and distribute it by simply querying complete REOs. If his boss requested changes to the REO Fact Sheet's configuration, Zach would make them in minutes.

Abby stopped by to check up on Zach's progress. He was in the midst of printing completed REO Fact Sheets to distribute them to appropriate departments throughout the bank. Then Abby asked Zach something that stopped him in his tracks. She asked why he bothered printing REO Fact Sheets at all. As Zach started to explain the nuances and extreme importance of departments throughout the bank needing the information he produced in a timely manner, she stopped him. She reminded Zach that his database was now on a network drive. She told Zach that if he chose too, other people throughout the bank on the same network could look at his REO Fact Sheet form. She described a few modifications to the form so no one but Zach could edit the underlying database. Instead of ever printing on paper, REO Fact Sheets and their associated information would be distributed completely electronically through the bank's network.

Zach started to realize that other than updating and inserting new bank REO information into his networked database, he had all but eliminated every other aspect of his job. His data was infinitely more accurate and distributed the on the bank's network the instant his database was updated bank wide. Abby asked Zach something else. She wanted to know why he distributed information only in the REO Fact Sheet form configuration. She suggested he could configure his data in an almost infinite variety of ways like reports and new forms that would be distributed on the network and eliminate the need for other bank departments to compile and make their own reports.

Once Zach's REO database was up and running, he started setting up meetings with other business departments. He decided to sit down with his customers, the very departments he had been distributing his REO Fact Sheets to. Every department he met with was more than willing to let Zach take on their reporting responsibilities once they knew Zach had all of the REO data in one single repository. They had basically been duplicating Zach's efforts by taking his REO Fact Sheets and configuring the data into their own reports and then spending an inordinate amount of time making sure what was entered from the fact sheet reconciled to their configurations. Some departments had entered REO Fact Sheets into their own Word documents while others entered into Excel spreadsheets.

Zach had to convince the bank's departments he could do what they felt was an overwhelming chore. In reality, Zach knew that all he had to do was make new reports based on what bank departments were already doing. For instance, the Property Management Department had a report that used 60 of Zach's 75 existing database columns (fields). The Property Management Department would also specify which properties it wanted reported so Zach would base the new report on a specified query. Each department Zach dealt with would verify the report was sound and adopt it. Zach's REO database was quickly becoming a colossal money-saver for the bank. He had eliminated enormous amounts of distribution, reconciliation, and duplication of efforts.

Zach's database system was in constant flux, what started as a single form on a single data table grew and evolved. When Abby was showing Zach some database techniques, she'd mentioned "filtering", the ability to add a filter to a data table that would only display specific information. For instance, a filter could easily be added to the "State" field by inserting "AZ", and in turn the data table would only display information for Arizona. Zach knew exactly where he needed a filter from the moment how knew how the technique worked. From the very beginning of his database system, Zach included a filter in the "Complete or Incomplete" field to only display REO's that had complete information. This meant that any REO without complete information was hidden from all users, and all reports.

Business Database Scenario Disadvantages

One day Zach was called into his boss's office. Zach boss introduced him to department heads of the bank. Zach could somehow tell this was not going to be a pleasant meeting. Zach was introduced as the person that had developed a networked database system that had saved so much time and money throughout the bank, which was a good thing, at least he thought so. One of the department heads asked why a particular property was not showing up in any of Zach's forms or reports. The department head explained that she knew of a commercial property that had just been foreclosed on by the bank, yet it was no where to be seen in Zach's REO database. Zach recognized the property's name and knew it was in his database and also knew exactly why it didn't show up and explained that the information for the property was not complete. Zach was waiting a few more fields of information that simply weren't available when the property was foreclosed and explained the property would "display" in his database as soon as it was "complete". Zach even went as far to explain how the "Complete or Incomplete" field's filter worked and that it had been in play since the inception of the REO database system. It was important for Zach to also explain that it was made clear to him by his predecessor to *never* report an REO property until all 75 pieces of data had been gathered.

Zach meets the brass.
Courtesy of Lehrstuhl fur Wirtschaftsinformatik.

Zach's explanation did not seem to assuage the palpable tension in the room, on the contrary, it felt worse. The department heads asked Zach how many REO properties were actually being reported to which he responded, "about 400". They asked how many properties were "Incomplete" and not being reported and Zach said about 100. The tension in the room turned worse. Bank executive were just realizing that their problems were 20% worse than they'd even known. They had essentially been budgeting for a 400 REO property problem when they really had a 500 REO property problem. For instance, the Property Management Department had enough staff to manage 400 properties (based on Zach's database) and was just finding out that there were actually 500. They wondered aloud how long ago the other 100 properties had been foreclosed and they had no idea.

At the end of what was an extremely uncomfortable meeting, they asked Zach to remove the filter from the "Complete or Incomplete" field which he did upon returning to his office. Throughout that afternoon Zach's phone was ringing off the hook. People bank wide who depended on Zach's REO database wanted to know how their numbers increased by 20%! People wondered where all these new properties came from. Most people in the bank simply assumed the database was wrong or had some "bug", but Zach and the department heads knew differently. The data was right, and had always been right. Everything changed in an instant as one arcane policy of not reporting incomplete REOs ended by deleting a database filter in a field.

Zach was called into his boss's office late that afternoon and was sure he would be fired. One thing that stayed in Zach's head was that throughout evolving his Microsoft Word REO Fact Sheet to a new networked Access database that he had done his job correctly. To Zach's surprise his boss asked for a few new ad hoc reports from the new REO database system. He told Zach that no one was happy about finding out that the bank had a bigger REO problem than was first thought, but at least now everyone knew what the bank was really facing. It was Zach's networked REO database that uncovered what was really happening bank wide and the business could start preparing and more accurately budgeting for the future to make tactical and strategic decisions. Zach's boss did ask if there were any more "surprise" filters on the REO database. Zach said no.

Summary

Zach's experience is not uncommon in business, so where did he go wrong? He successfully navigated his business process through an evolving computer-based system to arrive at a "**best practice**". He saved the bank enormous amounts of money and time, so what's the problem. The first problem was the word processing mess he inherited when he started his job. Keep in mind that Zach started his database "journey" *only* because someone requested a change to a poorly thought out word processing system that could not efficiently react. A **competent computer user** would have already recognized that the word processing system was insufficient before it failed.

Zach's database story points out a **failure in business, not computing**. What might have been most disturbing was the failure of the business to recognize its own deficient policies and procedures. Zach was right to follow the "complete / incomplete" policy but should have had the **critical thinking** skills to question it and what effect it could have on the bank. The bank's total number of REOs weren't even known until the database system exposed the arcane policy, and all the while it was inappropriately operating and budgeting. What about Zach's boss, was he culpable? The answer is a resounding "yes". Zach's boss didn't need to be a micro-manager to recognize a business situation that became inflamed as it was exposed by an infinitely more efficient database system. Zach's boss should have also had the computer competency and **business awareness** to recognize that one of his employees was doing their job completely wrong.

How about Abby, should she share some of the blame? The answer is yes. Perhaps a computing system audit before the whole debacle would have exposed Zach's deficient word processing system. Further, as a computer professional, Abby should have known that Zach's system should have been migrated directly to a database instead of wasting time on poorly thought out ideas like "mail merge" and spreadsheets.

In business, **best practice** is a management process, technique, or method that is most effective at arriving at a desired outcome, or best outcome than any other process, technique, or method, and it was obviously ignored. In the end, **placing blame is a valueless pursuit**. Zach's story simply points out the how extremely crucial it is to be a competent computer user and more importantly, competent in business.

Matching

Match each key term in the left column with the most accurate definition in the right column.

____	1. Query	**A.**	A well thought-out collection of tables that consist of records of data separated by fields.
____	2. Integrity	**B.**	At its core a database is made up of files called _____ that are related to each other.
____	3. SQL	**C.**	Database designers construct databases by using _____.
____	4. Know	**D.**	Database designers need to _____ a business.
____	5. ERMs	**E.**	A row in a data table.
____	6. Redundancy	**F.**	A column in a data table.
____	7. Tables	**G.**	A file that overlays a data table for a specific view.
____	8. Access	**H.**	It refers to questioning a data table.
____	9. Network	**I.**	A theoretical and conceptual representation of data.
____	10. Form	**J.**	An advantage to a database.
____	11. Security	**K.**	Microsoft's DBMS.
____	12. Database	**L.**	Business databases are always delivered on a _____.
____	13. Record	**M.**	A standard query method.
____	14. Field	**N.**	Eliminated in a DBMS.
____	15. Schema	**O.**	A name for high quality data.

Multiple Choice

1. A database is made up of files called _____ that are related to each other.

   a. Spreadsheets
   b. Queries
   c. Forms
   d. Tables

2. Database designers construct databases initially by using _____.

   a. SQL
   b. ERM
   c. Access
   d. HTML

3. Database designers need to _____.

   a. Start with tables first
   b. Start with forms first
   c. Know a business
   d. All of the above

4. Business databases are *always* distributed on a computer _____ for multiple users.

   a. Network
   b. Server
   c. DBMS
   d. None of the above

5. Which of the following is a business database advantage

   a. Integrity
   b. Lack of Redundancy
   c. Security
   d. All of the above

6. Database designers find out what is _____ when designing tables.

   a. Unique
   b. Wrong
   c. Right
   d. Important information

7. A row in a data table is called a _____.

   a. Trace
   b. Form
   c. Field
   d. Record

8. A column in a data table is called a _____.

   a. Trace
   b. Form
   c. Field
   d. Record

9. A file overlaid on a data table for viewing is called a _____.

   a. SQL
   b. Report
   c. Form
   d. Query

10. SQL is used to _____ data.

    a. Query
    b. Sort
    c. Erase
    d. None of the above

1.01000100|2.01000010|3.01000011|4.01000001|5.01000100|6.01000001|7.01000100|8.01000011|9.01000011|10.01000001

Blanks

A general definition of _____ software is that it is a well thought-out collection of computer files called tables that consist of records of data separated by fields.

At its core a database is made up of files called _____ that are related to each other.

_____ are DBMS files that overlay data tables and queries for more specific views of data.

Database designers construct database systems by using _____ which is a database-modeling method.

The nature and structure of a well thought out database management system helps a business avoid data _____.

Different levels of _____ can be implemented by determining who gets to see what in a business environment.

_____ is the most widely used standard computer language for relational databases that allows a programmer to manipulate and query data.

Database systems are extremely similar to filing cabinets in that they organize information based on a _____.

Once a field has data _____, it ensures data integrity.

Avoiding data redundancy ensures accuracy system wide throughout a DBMS which can reduce _____ immensely.

Short Questions

How does a DBMS avoid data redundancy?

What is the purpose of an entity relationship diagram?

What is a schema?

What are some advantages of a DBMS?

How does a DBMS differ from a spreadsheet?

Why is it important that a database designer "know a business"?

Glossary
DEFINITIONS

@ In an e-mail address, a symbol used to separate the user name from the name of the computer on which the user's mailbox is stored (for example, frodo@bagend.org). Pronounced "at."

10baseT An Ethernet local area network capable of transmitting 10 megabits of data per second through twisted-pair cabling.

100baseT See Fast Ethernet.

1394 port See FireWire port.

.NET passport A free service Microsoft introduced as part of its .NET strategy in which users create a .NET Passport profile that stores an e-mail address and a password as well as allowing the option to choose whether profile information will automatically be shared with participating Web sites to provide personalized services.

A

Accelerated Graphics Port (AGP) A port specification developed by Intel Corporation to support high-speed, high-resolution graphics, including 3D graphics.

acceptable use policy (AUP) An Internet service provider (ISP) policy that indicates which types of uses are permissible.

acceptance testing In information systems development, the examination of programs by users. See also application testing.

access point See network access point.

access speed The amount of time that lapses between a request for information from memory and the delivery of the information. Also called access time.

access time See access speed.

account On a multiuser computer system, a user information profile that includes the user's name, password, and home directory location. Unlike a profile on a consumer-oriented operating system, an account provides basic security features that prevent users from accessing or overwriting each others' files.

active monitoring In online banking, a security measure in which a security team constantly monitors the system that holds account information for the telltale signs of unauthorized access.

ActiveX control A small program that can be downloaded from a Web page and used to add functionality to a Web browser. ActiveX controls require Microsoft Windows and Microsoft Internet Explorer and are usually written in Visual Basic (VB).

Ada A programming language that incorporates modular programming principles, named after Augusta Ada Byron.

adapter 1. A circuit board that plugs into an expansion slot in a computer, giving the computer additional capabilities. Synonymous with card. Popular adapters for personal computers include video adapters that produce video output, memory expansion boards, internal modems, and sound boards. 2. A transformer that enables a computer or peripheral to work with line voltage that differs from its electrical requirements.

Add or Remove Programs An icon in a computer operating system's control panel that allows for proper installation and uninstallation of programs.

ADSL (Asymmetric Digital Subscriber Line) A type of Digital Subscriber Line (DSL) service for Internet access. ADSL enables download speeds of up to 1.5 Mbps.

adware A type of Internet spyware created by advertising agencies to collect information about computer users' Internet habits.

algorithm A mathematical or logical procedure for solving a problem.

all-in-one computer A system unit that contains all of the computer's components, including input components and the display.

alphabetic check Ensures that only alphabetical data (the letters of the alphabet) are entered into a field.

analog signal A signal sent via continuous waves that vary in strength and quality, such as those that phones and phone lines send and receive. See digital signal.

anonymity On the Internet, the ability to post a message or visit Web sites without divulging one's identity. Anonymity is much more difficult to obtain than most Internet users realize.

anonymous FTP An Internet service that enables you to contact a distant computer system to which you have no access rights, log on to its public directories, and transfer files from that computer to your own.

antivirus software A utility that checks for and removes computer viruses from memory and disks.

applet 1. A small- to medium-sized computer program that provides a specific function, such as emulating a calculator. 2. In Java, a mini-program embedded in a Web document that, when downloaded, is executed by the browser. Both leading browsers (Netscape Communicator and Microsoft Internet Explorer) can execute Java applets.

application service provider (ASP) A third-party commercial firm, nonprofit, or government entity that provides software-based services and solutions to companies that want to outsource some or almost all of their information technology needs.

application software Programs that enable you to do something useful with the computer, such as writing or accounting (as opposed to utilities, which are programs that help you maintain the computer).

application testing In information systems development, the examination of programs individually, and then further examination of the programs as they function together.

application window The area on-screen that encloses and displays a launched application.

application workspace The area within an application window that displays the document.

archive A file that contains two or more files that have been stored together for convenient archiving or network transmission.

argument set In spreadsheet programs such as Microsoft Excel, the part of a mathematical function that contains its passable parameters or variables.

arithmetic-logic unit (ALU) The portion of the central processing unit (CPU) that makes all the decisions for the microprocessor, based on the mathematical computations and logic functions that it performs.

arithmetic operations One of the two groups of operations performed by the arithmetic-logic unit (ALU). The arithmetic operations are addition, subtraction, multiplication, and division.

arrow keys See cursor-movement keys.

artificial intelligence (AI) A computer science field that tries to improve computers by endowing them with some of the characteristics associated with human intelligence, such as the capability to understand natural language and to reason under conditions of uncertainty.

artificial system A collection of components constructed by people and organized into a functioning whole to accomplish a goal.

ASCII (American Standard Code for Information Interchange) A standard computer character set consisting of 96 uppercase and lowercase letters along with 32 nonprinting control characters. Developed in 1963, ASCII was the first computer industry standard.

assembler A program that transforms source code in assembly language into machine language readable by a computer.

assembly language A low-level programming language in which each program statement corresponds to an instruction that the microprocessor can carry out.

authentication In computer security, a method of preventing unauthorized users from accessing a computer system, usually by requesting a password.

Reprinted from Bill Daley, *Computers Are Your Future,* Ninth Edition (Prentice Hall, 2008).

automation The replacement of human workers by machines.

autosave A software feature that backs up open documents at a user-specified interval.

auxiliary storage See storage.

B

back door A secret decoding mechanism that enables investigators to decrypt messages without first having to obtain a private key.

backbone In a wide area network (WAN), such as the Internet, a high-speed, high-capacity medium that transfers data over hundreds or thousands of miles. A variety of physical media are used for backbone services, including microwave relay, satellites, and dedicated telephone lines.

background application In a multitasking operating system, any inactive application. Compare with foreground application.

backside cache See secondary cache.

backup software A program that copies data from a secondary storage device (most commonly a hard disk) to a backup medium, such as a tape cartridge.

bad sector In magnetic storage media such as hard drives, a sector of the disk's surface that is physically damaged to the point that it can no longer store data safely.

bandwidth The amount of data that can be transmitted through a given communications channel, such as a computer network.

banner ad On the World Wide Web, a paid advertisement—often rectangular in shape, like a banner—that contains a hyperlink to the advertiser's page.

bar code reader An input device that scans bar codes and, with special software, converts the bar code into readable data.

BASIC Acronym for Beginner's All-Purpose Symbolic Instruction Code. An easy-to-use high-level programming language developed in 1964 for instruction.

basic input/output system (BIOS) Read-only memory (ROM) built into the computer's memory that contains the instructions needed to start the computer and work with input and output devices.

batch processing A mode of computer operation in which program instructions are executed one after the other without user intervention. Batch processing uses computer resources efficiently but is less convenient than interactive processing, in which you see the results of your commands on-screen so that you can correct errors and make necessary adjustments before completing the operation.

baud rate The maximum number of changes that can occur per second in the electrical state of a communications circuit. An early modem's data transfer rate may have been given in baud, but a modem's data transfer rate is now correctly measured in bits per second (bps).

beta version In software testing, a preliminary version of a program that is widely distributed before commercial release to users who test the program by operating it under realistic conditions.

binary digit See bit.

binary numbers A number system with a base (radix) of 2, unlike the number systems most of us use, which have bases of 10 (decimal numbers), 12 (feet and inches), and 60 (time). Binary numbers are preferred for computers for precision and economy. Building an electronic circuit that can detect the difference between two states (high current and low current, or 0 and 1) is easy and inexpensive; building a circuit that detects the difference among 10 states (0 through 9) is much more difficult and expensive. The word *bit* derives from the phrase binary digit.

biological feedback device A device that translates eye movements, body movements, and brain waves into computer input.

biometric authentication A method of authentication that requires a biological scan of some sort, such as a retinal scan or voice recognition.

bit Short for binary digit, the basic unit of information in a binary numbering system.

bit-mapped graphics Images formed by a pattern of tiny dots, each of which corresponds to a pixel on the computer's display. Also called raster graphics.

bits per second (bps) a measurement of data transmission speed. In personal computing, bps rates frequently are used to measure the performance of modems and serial ports.

BLOB (binary large object) In databases, a data type for very large objects, such as an entire spreadsheet file or a picture file, that may be several megabytes or more in size.

blue screen of death A feared error message with a blue background that appears when Microsoft Windows NT has encountered an error condition; typically resolved only by system rebooting.

Bluetooth A trademarked personal area network (PAN) technology, conceived by cell phone giant Ericsson and named after a 10th-century Viking, that allows computers, mobile phones, printers, and other devices within a certain range of each other to communicate automatically and wirelessly.

Boolean search A database or Web search that uses the logical operators AND, OR, and NOT to specify the logical relationship between search concepts.

boot To start the computer. See cold boot and warm boot.

booting The process of loading the operating system to memory.

boot disk See emergency disk.

boot sector virus A computer virus that copies itself to the beginning of a hard drive, where it is automatically executed when the computer is turned on.

bots Miniprograms capable of carrying out a variety of functions on the Internet, such as greeting newcomers to Internet chat groups.

branch control structure See selection control structure.

branch prediction A technique used by advanced CPUs to prevent a pipeline stall. The processor tries to predict what is likely to happen.

broadband Refers to any transmission medium that transports high volumes of data at high speeds, typically greater than 1 Mbps.

broken link On the World Wide Web, a hyperlink that refers to a resource (such as a sound or a Web page) that has been moved or deleted. Synonymous with dead link.

browser See Web browser.

bubble-jet printer See inkjet printer.

bug A programming error that causes a program or a computer system to perform erratically, produce incorrect results, or crash. The term *bug* was coined when a real insect was discovered to have fouled up one of the circuits of the first electronic digital computer, the ENIAC. A hardware problem is called a glitch.

build-or-buy decision In the development of information systems, the choice of building a new system within the organization or purchasing it from an outside vendor.

bus See data bus.

bus topology The physical layout of a local area network that does not use a central or host computer. Instead, each node manages part of the network, and information is transmitted directly from one computer to another.

business process reengineering (BPR) The use of information technology to bring about major changes and cost savings in an organization's structure. Also called reengineering.

business processes Activities that have an identifiable output and value to the organization's customers.

business skills Skills such as teamwork, project management skills, communication skills, and business savvy.

business-to-business (B2B) e-commerce A type of e-commerce where one business provides another business with the materials and supplies it needs to conduct its operations.

byte Eight bits grouped to represent a character (a letter, a number, or a symbol).

C

C A high-level programming language developed by Bell Labs in the 1970s. C combines the virtues of high-level programming with the efficiency of assembly language but is somewhat difficult to learn.

C++ A flexible high-level programming language derived from C that supports object-oriented programming but does not require programmers to adhere to the object-oriented model.

cable modem A device that enables a computer to access the Internet by means of a cable TV connection. Some cable modems enable downloading only; you need an analog (POTS) phone line and an analog modem to upload data. The best cable modems enable two-way communications through the cable TV system and do not require a phone line. Cable modems enable Internet access speeds of up to 1.5 Mbps, although most users typically experience slower speeds due to network congestion.

cache memory A small unit of ultra-fast memory used to store recently accessed or frequently accessed data, increasing a computer system's overall performance.

call center A computer-based telephone routing system that automatically connects credit card authorization systems to authorization services.

callback system A method of network control that serves as a deterrent to system sabotage by verifying the user ID, password, and telephone number of the individual trying to access the system.

carpal tunnel syndrome (CTS) A painful swelling of the tendons and the sheaths around them in the wrist due to injury caused by motions repeated thousands of times daily (such as mouse movements or keystrokes).

case control structure In structured programming, a logical construction of programming commands that contains a set of possible conditions and instructions that are executed if those conditions are true.

category 5 (cat-5) A type of twisted-pair cable used for high-performance digital telephone and computer network wiring.

cathode ray tube (CRT) A vacuum tube that uses an electron gun to emit a beam of electrons that illuminates phosphorus on-screen as the beam sweeps across the screen repeatedly.

Cave Automated Virtual Environment (CAVE) A virtual reality environment that replaces headsets with 3D glasses and uses the walls, ceiling, and floor to display projected three-dimensional images.

CD/DVD Jukebox An enterprise storage device that offers multiple DVD-ROM and CD-ROM drives to store and give users network access to all of an enterprise's digital content.

CD-R Compact disc-recordable storage media that cannot be erased or written over once data has been saved; they're relatively inexpensive.

CD-R drives Compact disc-recordable devices that can read standard CD-ROM discs and write data to CD-R discs.

CD-ROM See compact disc read-only memory.

CD-ROM drive A read-only disk drive that reads data encoded on compact discs and transfers this data to a computer.

CD-RW Compact disc-rewritable storage media that allows data that has been saved to be erased or written over.

CD-RW drive A compact disc-rewritable drive that provides full read/write capabilities using erasable CD-RWs.

cell 1. In a spreadsheet, a rectangle formed by the intersection of a row and a column in which you enter information in the form of text (a label) or numbers (a value). 2. In telecommunications, a limited geographical area in which a signal can be broadcast.

cell site In a cellular telephone network, an area in which a transmitting station repeats the system's broadcast signals so that the signal remains strong even though the user may move from one cell site to another.

cellular telephone A radio-based telephone system that provides widespread coverage through the use of repeating transmitters placed in zones (called cells). The zones are close enough so that signal strength is maintained throughout the calling area.

centralized structure When technology management is centered in the IT department, and everyone within the organization works with standardized technology solutions in their everyday work.

central processing unit (CPU) The computer's processing and control circuitry, including the arithmetic-logic unit (ALU) and the control unit.

certification An endorsement of professional competence that is awarded on successful completion of a rigorous test.

channel In Internet Relay Chat (IRC), a chat group in which as many as several dozen people carry on a text-based conversation on a specific topic.

character Any letter, number, punctuation mark, or symbol produced on-screen by the press of a key or a key combination.

character code An algorithm used to translate between the numerical language of the computer and characters readable by humans.

check-screening system A computer system used in point-of-sale (POS) terminals that reads a check's account number and accesses a database of delinquent accounts.

chip An integrated circuit (IC) that can emulate thousands or millions of transistors.

chipset A collection of supporting components that are all designed to work together smoothly on a computer motherboard.

ciphertext The result of applying an encryption key to a message.

circuit switching A type of telecommunications network in which high-speed electronic switches create a direct connection between two communicating devices. The telephone system is a circuit-switching network.

citing sources Providing enough information about the source of information you are using so that an interested or critical reader can locate this source without difficulty.

class In object-oriented (OO) programming, a category of objects that performs a certain function. The class defines the properties of an object, including definitions of the object's variables and the procedures that need to be followed to get the object to do something.

click-and-mortar In electronic commerce, a retail strategy in which a Web retail site is paired with a chain of local retail stores. Customers prefer this strategy because they can return or exchange unwanted goods more easily.

clickstream The trail of links left behind to reach a particular Web site.

client 1. In a client/server network, a program that runs on users' computers and enables them to access a certain type of data. 2. On a computer network, a program capable of contacting the server and obtaining needed information.

client/server A method of organizing software use on a computer network that divides programs into servers (programs that make information available) and clients (programs that enable users to access a certain type of data).

client/server computing A software application design framework for computer networks in which software services are divided into two parts, a client part and a server part.

client/server network A computer network in which some computers are dedicated to function as servers, making information available to client programs running on users' computers.

Clip Organizer In Microsoft Office, a repository of clip art and images that can be inserted into a document or presentation.

clipboard See Office clipboard.

Clipper Chip A microprocessor that could encrypt voice or data communications in such a way that investigators could still intercept and decode the messages.

clock speed The speed of the internal clock of a microprocessor that sets the pace at which operations proceed in the computer's internal processing circuitry.

cluster On a magnetic disk, a storage unit that consists of two or more sectors.

CMOS (complementary metal-oxide semiconductor) A special type of nonvolatile memory used to store essential startup configuration options.

coaxial cable A high-bandwidth connecting cable in which an insulated wire runs through the middle of the cable.

COBOL (Common Business-Oriented Language) An early, high-level programming language for business applications.

code The written computer instructions that programmers create.

code of conduct A set of ethical principles developed by a professional association, such as the Association for Computing Machinery (ACM).

codec Short for compression/decompression standard. A standard for compressing and decompressing video information to reduce the size of digitized multimedia files. Popular codecs include MPEG (an acronym for Motion Picture Experts Group), Apple's QuickTime, and Microsoft's AVI.

cold boot A system start that involves powering up the computer. Compare with warm boot.

collision In local area networks (LANs), a garbled transmission that results when two or more workstations transmit to the same network cable at exactly the same time. Networks have means of preventing collisions.

command A user-initiated instruction that tells a program which task to perform.

command-line user interface In an operating system, a variety of user interface that requires users to type commands one line at a time.

commercial software Copyrighted software that must be paid for before it can be used.

Common Object Request Broker Architecture (CORBA) In object-oriented (OO) programming, a leading standard that defines how objects can communicate with each other across a network.

communications The high-speed movement of data within and between computers.

communications channel (also referred to as links) In communications, the path through which messages are passed from one location to the next.

communications device Any hardware device that is capable of moving data into or out of the computer.

compact disc read-only memory (CD-ROM) A standard for storing read-only computer data on optical compact discs (CDs), which can be read by CD-ROM drives.

compact disc-recordable (CD-R) A "write-once" optical storage. Once you've recorded on the disc, you can't erase the stored data or write over the disc again. You can play the recorded CD on most CD-ROM drives.

compact disc-rewritable (CD-RW) A read/write optical storage technology that uses a CD-R drive to record data on CD-RW discs. You can erase the recorded data and write new data as you please. Most CD-ROM drives can read the recorded data. CD-RW drives can also write to CD-R discs, but you can write to CD-R discs only once.

CompactFlash A popular flash memory storage device that can store up to 128 MB of digital camera images.

compatible The capability to function with or substitute for a given make and model of computer, device, or program.

compatible computers Computer systems capable of using the same programs and peripherals.

competitive advantage A condition that gives an organization a superior position over the companies it competes with.

compiler A program that translates source code in a third-generation programming language into machine code readable by a computer.

completeness check Determines whether a required field has been left empty. If so, the database prompts the user to fill in the needed data.

Component Object Model (COM) In object-oriented (OO) programming, a standard developed by Microsoft Corporation that is used to define how objects communicate with each other over networks.

computer A machine that can physically represent data, process this data by following a set of instructions, store the results of the processing, and display the results so that people can use them.

computer crimes Actions that violate state or federal laws.

computer ethics A new branch of philosophy dealing with computing-related moral dilemmas.

computer information system (CIS) A computer system in which all components are designed to work together.

computer network See network.

computer science (CS) A scientific discipline that focuses on the theoretical aspects of improving computers and computer software.

computer security risk Any event, action, or situation—intentional or not—that could lead to the loss or destruction of computer systems or the data they contain.

computer system A collection of related computer components that have all been designed to work smoothly together.

computer virus A program, designed as a prank or as sabotage, that replicates itself by attaching to other programs and carrying out unwanted and sometimes dangerous operations.

computer-aided software engineering (CASE) Software that provides tools to help with every phase of systems development and enables developers to create data flow diagrams, data dictionary entries, and structure charts.

computer-based training (CBT) The use of computer-assisted instruction (CAI) programs to educate adults.

conditional control structure See selection control structure.

congestion In a packet switching network, a performance interruption that occurs when a segment of the network experiences overload.

connectivity The ability to link various media and devices, thereby enhancing communication and improving access to information.

connector A component that enables users or technicians to connect a cable securely to the computer's case. A male connector contains pins or plugs that fit into the corresponding female connector.

consistency check Examines the data entered into two different fields to determine whether an error has been made.

contention In a computer network, a problem that arises when two or more computers try to access the network at the same time. Contention can result in collisions, which can destroy data.

contention management In a computer network, the use of one of several techniques for managing contention and preventing collisions.

control module In a program design tool called a structure chart, the top module or box that oversees the transfer of control to the other modules.

control structure In structured programming, a logical element that governs program instruction execution.

control unit A component of the central processing unit (CPU) that obtains program instructions and sends signals to carry out those instructions.

convergence The coming together of information technologies (computer, consumer electronics, telecommunications) and gadgets (PC, TV, telephone), leading to a culmination of the digital revolution in which all types of digital information (voice, video, data) will travel over the same network.

cookie A text file that is deposited on a Web user's computer system, without the user's knowledge or consent, that may contain identifying information. This information is used for a variety of purposes, such as retaining the user's preferences or compiling information about the user's Web browsing behavior.

cooling fan A part of the system unit that prevents components from being damaged by heat.

copy-protected software Computer programs that include some type of measure to prevent users from making unauthorized copies.

copyright infringement The act of using material from a copyrighted source without getting permission to do so.

copyright protection scheme A method used by software manufacturers to ensure that users cannot produce unauthorized copies of copyrighted software.

corporate espionage The unauthorized access of corporate information, usually to the benefit of one of the corporation's competitors.

cost/benefit analysis An examination of the losses and gains, both tangible and intangible, related to a project.

cracker A computer user obsessed with gaining entry into highly secure computer systems.

crash An abnormal termination of program execution.

cross-platform programming language A programming language that can create programs capable of running on many different types of computers.

cumulative trauma disorder (CTD) An injury involving damage to sensitive nerve tissue. See carpal tunnel syndrome.

cursor A flashing bar, an underline character, or a box that indicates where keystrokes will appear when typed. Also called insertion point.

cursor-movement keys A set of keys on the keyboard that move the location of the cursor on the screen. The numeric keypad can also move the cursor when in the appropriate mode. Also called arrow keys.

customer relationship management (CRM) Enterprise software that keeps track of an organization's interactions with its customers and focuses on retaining those customers.

custom software Application software designed for a company by a professional programmer or programming team. Custom software is usually very expensive.

cybercrime Crime carried out by means of the Internet.

cybergang A group of computer users obsessed with gaining entry into highly secure computer systems.

cyberlaw A new legal field designed to track developments in cybercrime.

cyberstalking A form of harassment in which an individual is repeatedly subjected to unwanted electronic mail or advances in chat rooms.

D

data The raw material of computing: unorganized information represented for computer processing.

data bus A high-speed freeway of parallel connections that enables the CPU to communicate at high speeds with memory.

data dependency A microprocessor performance problem in which a CPU is slowed in its functioning by the need to wait for the results of instructions before moving on to process the next ones.

data dictionary In information systems development, a collection of definitions of all data types that may be input into the system, including field name, data types, and validation settings.

data diddling A computer crime in which data is modified to conceal theft or embezzlement.

data file A named unit of information storage that contains data rather than program instructions.

data flow diagram A graphical representation of the flow of data through an information system.

data glove A device that translates hand and arm movements into computer input.

data independence In a database, the storage of data in such a way that it is not locked into use by a particular application.

data integrity In a database, the validity of the stored data; specifically, its freedom from error due to improper data entry, hardware malfunctions, or transmission errors.

data maintenance Includes procedures for adding, updating, and deleting records for the purpose of keeping a database in optimal shape.

data mart A large database that contains all the data used by one of the divisions of an organization.

data mining The analysis of data stored in data warehouses to search for previously unknown patterns.

data redundancy In a database, a design error in which the same data appears more than once, creating opportunities for discrepant data entry and increasing the chance that the data will be processed incorrectly.

data security Ensuring that the data stored in a database isn't accessible to people who might misuse it, particularly when the collected data are sensitive.

data transfer rate 1. In secondary storage devices, the maximum number of bits per second that can be sent from the hard disk to the computer. The rate is determined by the drive interface. 2. The speed, expressed in bits per second (bps), at which a modem can transfer, or is transferring, data over a telephone line.

data type In a database or spreadsheet program, a particular type of information, such as a date, a time, or a name.

data validation In a database, a method of increasing the validity of data by defining acceptable input ranges for each field in the record.

data warehouse A very large database, containing as many as a trillion data records, that stores all of a firm's data and makes this data available for exploratory analysis (called data mining).

database A collection of information stored in an organized way.

database management system (DBMS) An application that enables users to create databases that contain links from several files. Database management systems are usually more expensive than file management programs.

database program An application that stores data so that needed information can be quickly located, organized, and displayed.

database server software In a client/server database system, software that runs on a LAN and responds to remote users' requests for information.

dead link See broken link.

debugging In programming, the process of finding and correcting errors, or bugs, in the source code of a computer program.

decision support system (DSS) A program that helps management analyze data to make decisions on semistructured problems.

default In a computer program, a fallback setting or configuration value that is used unless the user specifically chooses a different one.

default value The setting in a database field that is automatically selected unless another value is provided.

deliverable In the development of an information system, the outcome of a particular phase of the systems development life cycle (SDLC).

denial of service (DoS) attack A form of network vandalism that attempts to make service unavailable to other users, generally by flooding the service with meaningless data. Also called syn flooding.

desktop The portion of the graphical user interface (GUI) that appears after the operating system finishes loading into memory.

desktop computer A personal computer designed for an individual's use. Desktop computers are increasingly used to gain access to the resources of computer networks.

device driver A program file that contains specific information needed by the operating system so that a specific brand or model of device will function.

dialog box In a graphical user interface (GUI), an on-screen message box used to request information from the user.

digital camera A camera that records an image by means of a digital imaging system, such as a charged-coupled device (CCD), and stores the image in memory or on a disk.

digital cash system A method for using smart cards and prepaid amounts of electronically stored money to pay for small charges such as parking and tolls.

digital certificate A form of digital ID used to obtain access to a computer system or prove one's identity while shopping on the Web. Certificates are issued by independent, third-party organizations called certificate authorities (CA).

digital divide The racial and/or income disparity in computer ownership and Internet access.

digital light processing (DLP) projector A computer projection device that employs millions of microscopic mirrors, embedded in a microchip, to produce a brilliant, sharp image.

digital modem See ISDN adapter.

digital signal A signal sent via discontinuous pulses, in which the presence or absence of electronic pulses represents 1s and 0s, such as computers send and receive. See analog signal.

digital signatures A technique used to guarantee that a message has not been tampered with.

digital telephony Telephone systems using all-digital protocols and transmission, offering the advantage over analog telephony of noise-free transmission and high-quality audio.

digital video camera Camera that uses digital rather than analog technologies to store recorded video images.

digital video disc (DVD) The newest optical disc format, DVD is capable of storing an entire digitized movie. DVD discs are designed to work with DVD video players and televisions.

digital video disc-RAM (DVD-RAM) A digital video disc (DVD) format that enables users to record up to 2.6 GB of data.

digital video disc-ROM (DVD-ROM) A digital optical disc format capable of storing up to 17 GB on a single disc, enough for a feature-length movie. DVD is designed to be used with a video player and a television. DVD discs can be read also by DVD-ROM drives.

digitization The transformation of data such as voice, text, graphics, audio, and video into digital form, thereby allowing various technologies to transmit computer data through telephone lines, cables, or air and space.

Direct Broadcast Satellite (DBS) A consumer satellite technology that offers cable channels and one-way Internet access. To use DBS for an Internet connection, a modem and phone line are required to upload data.

direct conversion In the development of an information system, the termination of the current system and the immediate institution of the new system throughout the whole organization.

disaster recovery plan A written plan, with detailed instructions, specifying an alternative computing facility to use for emergency processing until a destroyed computer can be replaced.

discrete speech recognition A speech recognition technology that is able to recognize human speech only when the speaker pauses between words.

disintermediation The process of removing an intermediary, such as a car salesperson, by providing a customer with direct access to rich information and warehouse-size selection and stock.

disc A portable storage optical media, such as CD-ROM.

disk A portable storage magnetic media, such as floppy disks, that provides personal computer users with convenient, near-online storage.

disk cache A small amount of memory (up to 512 KB), usually built into the electronics of a disk drive, used to store frequently accessed data. Disk caches can significantly improve the performance of a disk drive.

disk cleanup utility A utility program that removes unneeded temporary files.

disk defragmentation A program used to read all the files on a disk and rewrite them so that files are all stored in a contiguous manner. This process almost always improves disk performance by some degree.

disk drive A secondary storage mechanism that stores and retrieves information on a disk by using a read/write head. Disk drives are random-access devices.

disk scanning program A utility program that can detect and resolve a variety of physical and logical problems related to file storage.

diskette See disk.

distributed hypermedia system A network-based content development system in which individuals connected to the network can each make a small contribution by developing content related to their area of expertise. The Web is a distributed hypermedia system.

distributed structure When technology management is decentralized and users are able to customize their technology tools to suit their individual needs and wants.

document A file created with an application program, such as a word processing or spreadsheet program.

documentation In information systems development, the recording of all information pertinent to the development of an information system, usually in a project notebook.

domain In a computer network, a group of computers that are administered as a unit. Network administrators are responsible for all the computers in their domains. On the Internet, this term refers to all the computers that are collectively addressable within one of the four parts of an IP address. For example, the first part of an IP address specifies the number of a computer network. All the computers within this network are part of the same domain.

domain name On the Internet, a readable computer address (such as www.microsoft.com) that identifies the location of a computer on the network.

domain name registration On the Internet, a process by which individuals and companies can obtain a domain name (such as www.c34.org) and link this name to a specific Internet address (IP address).

Domain Name System (DNS) The conceptual system, standards, and names that make up the hierarchical organization of the Internet into named domains.

dot-com The universe of Internet sites, especially those doing electronic commerce, with the suffix com appended to their names.

dot pitch On a monitor, the space (measured in millimeters) between each physical dot on the screen.

dot-matrix printer An impact printer that forms text and graphic images by hammering the ends of pins against a ribbon in a pattern (matrix) of dots. Dot-matrix printers produce near–letter quality printouts.

double data rate (DDR) SDRAM A type of SDRAM that can both send and receive data within a single clock cycle.

download To transfer a file from another computer to your computer by means of a modem and a telephone line. See upload.

downsizing In corporate management, a cost-reduction strategy involving layoffs to make a firm leaner and more competitive. Downsizing often accompanies technology-driven restructuring that theoretically enables fewer employees to do the same or more work.

drawing program An application program used to create, edit, and display vector graphics.

drill-down A technique used by managers to view information in a data warehouse. By drilling down to lower levels of the database, the manager can focus on sales regions, offices, and then individual salespeople, and view summaries at each level.

drive activity light A light on the front panel of most computers that signals when the hard disk is accessing data.

drive bay A receptacle or opening into which you can install a floppy drive, a CD-ROM or DVD-ROM drive, or a removable drive.

driver A utility program that is needed to make a peripheral device function correctly.

DSL (Digital Subscriber Line) A general term for several technologies that enable high-speed Internet access through twisted-pair telephone lines. Also called xDSL. See ADSL (Asymmetric Digital Subscriber Line).

DSL modem Similar to a traditional telephone modem in that it modulates and demodulates analog and digital signals for transmission over communications channels, but does so using signaling methods based on broadband technology for much higher transfer speeds.

dumpster diving A technique used to gain unauthorized access to computer systems by retrieving user IDs and passwords from an organization's trash.

DVD-R Digital video disc-recordable optical storage media that, like CD-R discs, cannot be erased or written over once data has been saved.

DVD-RAM See digital video disc-RAM.

DVD-ROM Optical storage media that can hold up to 17 GB of data.

DVD-ROM drive A read-only disk drive that reads the data encoded on DVD-ROM discs and transfers this data to a computer.

DVD+R A recordable optical storage media that enables the disc to be written to one time and read many times.

DVD+RW discs Digital video disc-read/write optical storage media that allow you to write, erase, and read from the disc many times.

DVD-RW Optical storage media on which you can write, erase, and read from the disc many times.

dynamic random access memory (DRAM) A random access memory chip that must be refreshed periodically; otherwise, the data in the memory will be lost.

E

e-book A book that has been digitized and distributed by means of a digital storage medium.

e-book reader A book-sized device that displays an e-book.

e-commerce See electronic commerce.

ECMA Script (Java Script) A scripting language for Web publishing, developed by Netscape Communications, that enables Web authors to embed simple Java-like programming instructions in the HTML text of their Web pages.

economic feasibility Capable of being accomplished with available fiscal resources. This is usually determined by a cost/benefit analysis.

e-learning The use of computers and computer programs to replace teachers and the time–place specificity of learning.

electrical engineering (EE) An engineering discipline that is concerned with the design and improvement of electrical and electronic circuits.

electronic commerce The use of the Internet and other wide area networks (WANs) for business-to-business and business-to-consumer transactions. Also called e-commerce.

electronic data interchange (EDI) A communications standard for the electronic exchange of financial information through information services.

electronic mail See e-mail.

electronic vault In online banking, a mainframe computer that stores account holders' information.

element In HTML, a distinctive component of a document's structure, such as a title, heading, or list. HTML divides elements into two categories: head elements (such as the document's title) and body elements (headings, paragraphs, links, and text).

e-mail Electronic mail; messages sent and received through the use of a computer network.

e-mail address A series of characters that precisely identifies the location of a person's electronic mailbox. On the Internet, e-mail addresses consist of a mailbox name (such as jsmith) followed by an at sign (@) and the computer's domain name (as in jsmith@hummer.virginia.edu).

e-mail attachment A computer file that is included with an e-mail message.

emergency disk A disk that can be used to start the computer in case the operating system becomes unusable for some reason.

employee monitoring When large employers routinely engage in observing employees' phone calls, e-mails, Web browsing habits, and computer files.

encapsulation In object-oriented programming, the hiding of all internal information of objects from other objects.

encryption The process of converting a message into ciphertext (an encrypted message) by using a key, so that the message appears to be nothing but gibberish. The intended recipient, however, can apply the key to decrypt and read the message. See also public key cryptography and rot-13.

encryption key A formula that is used to make a plaintext message unreadable.

end tag In HTML, the closing component of an element, such as </A>. All elements begin with a start tag; most require an end tag.

enterprise A business organization or any large computer-using organization, which can include universities and government agencies.

enterprise application integration (EAI) A combination of processes, software, standards, and hardware that results in the integration of two or more enterprise systems.

enterprise computing The use of technology, information systems, and computers within an organization or a business.

enterprise resource planning (ERP) Enterprise software that brings together various enterprise functions, such as manufacturing, sales, marketing, and finance, into a single computer system.

enterprise storage system The collection of storage within an organization. The system typically makes use of servers connected to hard disks or massive RAID systems.

enterprise systems Information systems that integrate an organization's information and applications across all of the organization's functional divisions.

entity-relationship diagram (ERD) In the design of information systems, a diagram that shows all the entities (organizations, departments, users, programs, and data) that play roles in the system, as well as the relationships between those entities.

ergonomic Describes a product that matches the best posture and functionality of the human body.

Ethernet A set of standards that defines local area networks (LANs) capable of operating at data transfer rates of 10 Mbps to 1 Gbps. About 80 percent of all LANs use one of several Ethernet standards.

Ethernet card A network interface card (NIC) designed to work with Ethernet local area networks (LANs).

ethical hacker (white hat) Hackers and crackers who have turned pro, offering their services to companies hoping to use hacker expertise to shore up their computer systems' defenses.

ethical principle A principle that defines the justification for considering an act or a rule to be morally right or wrong. Ethical principles can help people find their way through moral dilemmas.

event-driven In programming, a program design method that structures the program around a continuous loop, which cycles until an event occurs (such as the user clicking the mouse).

exception report In a transaction processing system (TPS), a document that alerts someone of unexpected developments, such as high demand for a product.

exclusion operator In database and Internet searching, a symbol or a word that tells the software to exclude records or documents containing a certain word or phrase.

executable file A file containing a script or program that can execute instructions on the computer. Program files usually use the .exe extension in the filename.

execute One of four basic operations carried out by the control unit of a microprocessor. The execute operation involves performing a requested action, such as adding or comparing two numbers.

execution cycle In a machine cycle, a phase consisting of the execute and write-back operations.

executive information system (EIS) A system that supports management's strategic planning function.

executive support system (ESS) A type of decision support system designed to provide high-level executives with information summarizing the overall performance of their organization on the most general level.

Exiting Quitting or closing down an application or program.

expansion board A circuit board that provides additional capabilities for a computer.

expansion bus An electrical pathway that connects the microprocessor to the expansion slots. Also called I/O bus.

expansion card See expansion board.

expansion slot A receptacle connected to the computer's expansion bus that accepts an expansion board.

expert system In artificial intelligence (AI), a program that relies on a database of if-then rules to draw inferences, in much the same way a human expert does.

Extensible Business Reporting Language (XBRL) Similar to XML, a language that uses standardized formatting that allows enterprises to publish and share financial information, including net revenue, annual and quarterly reports, and SEC filings, with each other and industry analysts across all computer platforms and the Internet.

Extensible Markup Language (XML) A set of rules for creating markup languages that enables Web authors to capture specific types of data by creating their own elements. XML can be used in HTML documents.

extension A three-letter suffix added to a DOS filename. The extension is often supplied by the application and indicates the type of application that created the file.

external drive bay In a computer case, a receptacle designed for mounting storage devices that is accessible from the outside of the case.

external modem A modem with its own case, cables, and power supply that plugs into the serial port of a computer.

extranet A corporate intranet that has been opened to external access by selected outside partners, including customers, research labs, and suppliers.

eye-gaze response system A biological feedback device that enables quadriplegics to control computers by moving their eyes around the screen.

F

facsimile transmission (fax) The sending and receiving of printed pages between two locations, using a telephone line and fax devices that digitize the page's image.

fair use An exception to copyright laws made to facilitate education, commentary, analysis, and scholarly research.

Fast Ethernet An Ethernet standard for local area networks (LANs) that enables data transfer rates of 100 Mbps using twisted-pair cable; also called 100baseT.

fault tolerance The ability to continue working even if one or more components fail, such as is found in a redundant array of independent disks.

fax modem A modem that also functions as a fax machine, giving the computer user the capability of sending word processing documents and other files as faxes.

fetch One of four basic operations carried out by the control unit of a microprocessor. The fetch operation retrieves the next program instruction from the computer's memory.

fiber-optic cable A network cable made from tiny strands of glasslike material that transmit light pulses with very high efficiency and can carry massive amounts of data.

field In a database, an area for storing a certain type of information.

field emission display (FED) A flat-panel display technology that uses tiny CRTs to produce each on-screen pixel.

field name Describes the type of data that should be entered into the field.

file A document or other collection of information stored on a disk and identified as a unit by a unique name.

file allocation table (FAT) A hidden on-disk table that keeps vital records concerning exactly where the various components of a given file are stored. The file allocation table is created at the conclusion of the formatting process.

file compression The reduction of a file's size so that the file can be stored without taking up as much storage space and can be transferred more quickly over a computer network.

file compression utility A program to reduce the size of files without harming the data.

file infector A computer virus that attaches to a program file and, when that program is executed, spreads to other program files.

file management program An application that enables users to create customized databases and store in and retrieve data from those databases.

file manager (My Computer in Windows, File Manager in Mac OS X, and various file management utilities in Linux) A utility program that enables you to organize and manage the data stored on your disk.

file menu In a graphical user interface (GUI), a pull-down menu that contains standard file-management commands, such as Save and Save As.

file server In client/server computing, a computer that has been set aside (dedicated) to make program and data files available to client programs on the network.

File Transfer Protocol (FTP) An Internet standard for the exchange of files between two computers connected to the Internet. With an FTP client, you can upload or download files from a computer that is running an FTP server. Normally, you need a user name and password to upload or download files from an FTP server, but some FTP servers provide a service called anonymous FTP, which enables anyone to download the files made available for public use.

filename A unique name given to a stored file.

filter In e-mail, a rule that specifies the destination folder of messages conforming to certain criteria.

filtering software A program that attempts to prevent minors from accessing adult material on the Internet.

firewall A program that permits an organization's internal computer users to access the Internet but places severe limits on the ability of outsiders to access internal data.

FireWire port An input-output port that combines high-speed performance (up to 400 Mbps) with the ability to guarantee data delivery at a specified speed, making the port ideal for use with real-time devices such as digital video cameras. Synonymous with 1394 port. FireWire is Apple Computer's name for 1394 port technology.

flame In Usenet and e-mail, a message that contains abusive, threatening, obscene, or inflammatory language.

flash memory A special type of read-only memory (ROM) that enables users to upgrade information contained in memory chips. Also called flash BIOS.

flash memory card Wafer-thin, highly portable solid state storage system that is capable of storing as much as 1 gigabyte of data. Used with some digital cameras, the card stores digitized photographs without requiring electrical power to maintain the data.

flash memory reader A slot or compartment in digital cameras and other devices into which a flash memory card is inserted.

flat file A type of file generated by a file management program. Flat files can be accessed in many different ways but cannot be linked to data in other files.

flatbed scanner A device that copies an image (text or graphics) from one side of a sheet of paper and translates it into a digital image.

flat-panel display A low-power, lightweight display used with notebook computers (and increasingly with desktop computers).

floating-point notation A method for storing and calculating numbers so that the location of the decimal point isn't fixed but floating. This allows the computer to work with very small and very large numbers.

flooding A type of antisocial behavior found on Internet Relay Chat characterized by sending repeated messages so that no one else can engage in the conversation.

floppy disk A removable and widely used data storage medium that uses a magnetically coated flexible disk of Mylar enclosed in a plastic envelope or case. Although 5.25-inch floppy disks were standard, they became obsolete due to the development of the smaller, more durable 3.5-inch disk.

floppy disk drive A mechanism that enables a computer to read and write information on a removable medium that provides a convenient way to move data from one computer to another.

flowchart In structured programming, a diagram that shows the logic of a program.

FMD-ROM (fluorescent multilayer disc–read-only memory) disc A type of high-capacity storage disc with multiple layers whose fluorescent coating allows for storage of up to a terabyte of data.

folder A graphical representation of a directory. Most major operating systems display directories as though they were file folders.

folder structure An organized set of primary and secondary folders within which to save your files.

footprint The amount of room taken up by the case on the desk.

foreground application In a multitasking operating system, the active application.

Form In the Microsoft Access database management system, the object used to collect data.

form factor A specification for mounting internal components, such as the motherboard.

format 1. A file storage standard used to write a certain type of data to a magnetic disk (also called file format). 2. To prepare a magnetic disk for first use. 3. In word processing, to choose the alignment, emphasis, or other presentation options so that the document will print with an attractive appearance.

format menu In a graphical user interface (GUI), a pull-down menu that allows you to modify such features as font style and paragraph settings.

formatting The process of modifying a document's appearance so that it looks good when printed.

Formatting toolbar In Microsoft Office, a default-loaded toolbar that includes icons for various functions, including choosing document font size and style.

formula In a spreadsheet program, a mathematical expression embedded in a cell that can include cell references. The cell displays the formula's result.

formula bar In a spreadsheet program, an area above the worksheet that displays the contents of the active cell. The formula bar enables the user to work with formulas, which normally do not appear in the cell.

Fortran An early third-generation language that enabled scientists and engineers to write simple programs for solving mathematical equations.

fourth-generation language (4GL) A programming language that does not force the programmer to consider the procedure that must be followed to obtain the desired result.

fragmentation A process in which the various components of a file are separated by normal reading and writing operations so that these components are not stored close together. The result is slower disk operation. A defragmentation utility can improve a disk's performance by placing these file components closer together.

fragmented A disk with portions of files scattered here and there.

frames In a video or animation, the series of still images flashed on-screen at a rapid rate.

frame rate In a video or animation, a measurement of the number of still images shown per second.

freeware Copyrighted software that can be freely copied but not sold.

front panel An area on the front of most computers containing various indicator lights and controls.

full backup The process of copying all files from a secondary storage device (most commonly a hard disk) to a backup medium, such as a tape cartridge.

function In spreadsheet programs such as Microsoft Excel, one of the two basic types of formulas (along with mathematic expressions). In a function, operations can be performed on multiple inputs.

function keys A row of keys positioned along the top of the keyboard, labeled F1 through F12, to which programs can assign various commands.

G

G or GB Abbreviation for gigabyte, approximately one billion (one thousand million) bytes or characters.

Gantt chart A bar chart that summarizes a project's schedule by showing how various activities proceed over time.

Gbps A data transfer rate of approximately one billion bits per second.

General Public License (GPL) A freeware software license, devised by the Open Software Foundation (OSF), stipulating that a given program can be obtained, used, and even modified, as long as the user agrees to not sell the software and to make the source code for any modifications available.

general-purpose application A software program used by many people to accomplish frequently performed tasks such as writing (word processing), working with numbers (spreadsheets), and keeping track of information (databases).

genetic algorithm An automated program development environment in which various alternative approaches to solving a problem are introduced; each is allowed to mutate periodically through the introduction of random changes. The various approaches compete in an effort to solve a specific problem. After a period of time, one approach may prove to be clearly superior to the others.

geosynchronous orbit A circular path around the Earth in which a communications satellite, for example, has a velocity exactly matching the Earth's speed of rotation, allowing the satellite to be permanently positioned with respect to the ground.

GIF (Graphics Interchange Format) A bitmapped color graphics file format capable of storing images with 256 colors. GIF incorporates a compression technique that reduces file size, making it ideal for use on a network. GIF is best used for images that have areas of solid color.

GIF animation A graphics file that contains more than one image stored using the GIF graphics file format. Also stored in the file is a brief script that indicates the sequence of images, and how long to display each image.

gigabit A unit of measurement approximately equal to one billion bits.

Gigabit Ethernet An Ethernet local area network (LAN) that is capable of achieving data transfer rates of 1 Gbps (one billion bits per second) using fiber-optic cable.

gigabit per second (Gbps) A data transfer measurement equivalent to one billion bits per second.

gigabits per second points of presence (gigaPoPs) In Internet II, a high-speed testbed for the development of next-generation Internet protocols, a point of presence (PoP) that provides access to a backbone service capable of data transfer rates in excess of 1 Gbps (one billion bits per second).

gigabyte (G or GB) A unit of measurement commonly used to state the capacity of memory or storage devices; equal to 1,024 megabytes, or approximately one billion bytes or characters.

globalization Conducting business internationally where the transaction of goods and services is transparent to the consumer.

Global Positioning System (GPS) A satellite-based system that enables portable GPS receivers to determine their location with an accuracy of 100 meters or less.

global unique identifier (GUID) A uniquely identifying serial number assigned to Pentium III processor chips that can be used by Web servers to detect which computer is accessing a Web site.

graphical MUD A multiuser dungeon (MUD) that uses graphics instead of text to represent the interaction of characters in a virtual environment.

graphical user interface (GUI) An interface between the operating system and the user. Graphical user interfaces are the most popular of all user interfaces but also require the most system resources.

graphics accelerator A display adapter (video card) that contains its own dedicated processing circuitry and video memory (VRAM), enabling faster display of complex graphics images.

graphics file A file that stores the information needed to display a graphic. Popular graphics file formats include BMP (Windows Bitmap), JPEG, and GIF.

groupware The software that provides computerized support for the information needs of individuals networked into workgroups.

H

hacker Traditionally, a computer user who enjoys pushing his or her computer capabilities to the limit, especially by using clever or novel approaches to solving problems. In the press, the term *hacker* has become synonymous with criminals who attempt unauthorized access to computer systems for criminal purposes, such as sabotage or theft. The computing community considers this usage inaccurate.

hacker ethic A set of moral principles common to the first-generation hacker community (roughly 1965–1982), described by Steven Levy in *Hackers* (1984). According to the hacker ethic, all technical information should, in principle, be freely available to all. Therefore, gaining entry to a system to explore data and increase knowledge is never unethical. Destroying, altering, or moving data in such a way that could cause injury or expense to others, however, is always unethical. In increasingly more states, unauthorized computer access is against the law. See also cracker.

handheld computer See personal digital assistant.

handling input and output One of the five basic functions of an operating system in which your computer interacts with input devices and shows you the results of its work on output devices.

haptics A field of research in developing output devices that stimulate the sense of touch.

hard copy Printed computer output, differing from the data stored on disk or in memory.

hard disk A secondary storage medium that uses several rigid disks (platters) coated with a magnetically sensitive material and housed in a hermetically sealed mechanism. In almost all modern computers, the hard disk is by far the most important storage medium. Also called hard disk drive.

hard disk controller An electronic circuit that provides an interface between a hard disk and the computer's CPU.

hard disk drive See hard disk.

hardware The physical components, such as circuit boards, disk drives, displays, and printers, that make up a computer system.

head actuator Mechanism on a floppy disk drive that moves the read/write head to the area that contains the desired data.

head crash In a hard disk, the collision of a read/write head with the surface of the disk, generally caused by a sharp jolt to the computer's case. Head crashes can damage the read/write head, as well as create bad sectors.

header In e-mail or a Usenet news article, the beginning of a message. The header contains important information about the sender's address, the subject of the message, and other information.

head-mounted display (HMD) See headset.

headset A wearable output device with twin LCD panels for creating the illusion that an individual is experiencing a three-dimensional, simulated environment.

heat sink A heat-dissipating component that drains heat away from semiconductor devices, which can generate enough heat in the course of their operation to destroy themselves. Heat sinks are often used in combination with fans to cool semiconductor components.

help menu In a graphical user interface (GUI), a pull-down menu that provides access to interactive help utilities.

help screen In commercial software, information that appears on-screen that can provide assistance with using a particular program.

help utilities Programs, such as a table of contents of frequently requested items, offered on most graphical user interface (GUI) applications.

hexadecimal number A number that uses a base 16 number system rather than a decimal (or base 10) number system.

hierarchy chart In structured programming, a program planning chart that shows the top-down design of the program and the relationship between program modules. Also called structure chart.

High Definition Television (HDTV) The name given to several standards for digital television displays.

high-level programming language A programming language that eliminates the need for programmers to understand the intimate details of how the computer processes data.

history list In a Web browser, a window that shows all the Web sites that the browser has accessed during a given period, such as the last 30 days.

home and educational programs General-purpose software programs for personal finance, home design and landscaping, encyclopedias and other computerized reference information, and games.

home page 1. In any hypertext system, including the Web, a document intended to serve as an initial point of entry to a web of related documents. Also called a welcome page, a home page contains general introductory information, as well as hyperlinks to related resources. A well-designed home page contains internal navigation buttons that help users find their way among the various documents that the home page makes available. 2. The start page that is automatically displayed when you start a Web browser or click the program's Home button. 3. A personal page listing an individual's contact information, and favorite links, and (generally) some information—ranging from cryptic to voluminous—about the individual's perspective on life.

home phone-line network (HomePNA) A linked personal communications system that works off a home's existing phone wiring, thus being easy to install, inexpensive, and fast. The acronym PNA is derived from the Home Phone Networking Alliance.

home power-line network A linked personal communications system that works by connecting computers to one another through the same electrical power outlet, thus providing the convenience of not having to locate each computer in the home next to a phone jack.

home radio-frequency (RF) network A linked personal communications system that connects computers using wireless radio signals, making computers portable throughout the house.

hot swapping Connecting and disconnecting peripherals while the computer is running.

hub In a local area network (LAN), a device that connects several workstations and enables them to exchange data.

hyperlink In a hypertext system, an underlined or otherwise emphasized word or phrase that, when clicked, displays another document.

hypermedia A hypertext system that uses various multimedia resources, such as sounds, animations, and videos, as a means of navigation as well as decoration.

hypermedia system A hypertext system that uses various multimedia resources, such as sounds, movies, and text, as a means of navigation as well as illustration.

hypertext A method of preparing and publishing text, ideally suited to the computer, in which readers can choose their own paths through the material. To prepare hypertext, you first "chunk" the information into small, manageable units, such as single pages of text. These units are called nodes. You then embed hyperlinks in the text. When the reader clicks a hyperlink, the hypertext software displays a different node. The process of navigating among the nodes linked in this way is called browsing. A collection of nodes interconnected by hyperlinks is called a web. The Web is a hypertext system on a global scale.

Hypertext Markup Language (HTML) A language for marking the portions of a document (called elements) so that, when accessed by a program called a Web browser, each portion appears with a distinctive format. HTML is the markup language behind the appearance of documents on the Web. HTML is standardized by means of a document type definition in the Standard Generalized Markup Language (SGML). HTML includes capabilities that enable authors to insert hyperlinks, which when clicked display another HTML document. The agency responsible for standardizing HTML is the World Wide Web Consortium (W3C).

Hypertext Transfer Protocol (HTTP) The Internet standard that supports the exchange of information on the Web. By defining uniform resource locators (URLs) and how they can be used to retrieve resources anywhere on the Internet, HTTP enables Web authors to embed hyperlinks in Web documents. HTTP defines the process by which a Web client, called a browser, originates a request for information and sends it to a Web server, a program that responds to HTTP requests and provides the desired information.

I

I/O bus See expansion bus.

I/O device Generic term for any input or output device.

icon In a graphical user interface (GUI), a small picture that represents a program, a data file, or some other computer entity or function.

identify theft A form of fraud in which a thief obtains someone's Social Security number and other personal information, and then uses this information to obtain credit cards fraudulently.

image editor A sophisticated paint program for editing and transforming complex bitmapped images, such as photographs.

image processing system A filing system in which incoming documents are scanned and stored digitally.

impact printer A printer that generates output by striking the page with something solid.

inbox In e-mail, a default folder that contains any new mail messages, as well as older messages that have not been moved or deleted.

inclusion operator In database or Web searching, a symbol or keyword that instructs the search software to make sure that any retrieved records or documents contain a certain word or phrase.

incremental backup The process of copying files that have changed since the last full backup to a backup medium, such as a tape cartridge.

information Processed data.

information hiding A modular programming technique in which information inside a module remains hidden with respect to other modules.

information kiosk An automated presentation system used for public information or employee training.

information overload A condition of confusion, stress, and indecision brought about by being inundated with information of variable value.

information processing cycle A complete sequence of operations involving data input, processing, storage, and output.

information system A purposefully designed system that brings data, computers, procedures, and people together to manage information important to an organization's mission.

information systems (IS) department In a complex organization, the division responsible for designing, installing, and maintaining the organization's information systems.

information technology (IT) professionals Businesspeople who work with information technology in all its various forms (hardware, software, networks) and functions (management, development, maintenance).

information technology steering committee Within an organization, the group, which generally includes representatives from senior management, information systems personnel, users, and middle managers, that reviews requests for systems development and decides whether or not to move forward with a project.

information warfare A military strategy that targets an opponent's information systems.

infrared A data transmission medium that uses the same signaling technology used in TV remote controls.

inheritance In object-oriented (OO) programming, the capacity of an object to pass its characteristics to subclasses.

inkjet printer A nonimpact printer that forms an image by spraying ink from a matrix of tiny jets.

input The information entered into a computer for processing.

input device Any device that is capable of accepting data so that it is properly represented for processing within the computer.

input/output (I/O) bus See expansion bus.

insertion point See cursor.

install To set up a program so that it is ready to function on a given computer system. The installation process may involve creating additional directories, making changes to system files, and other technical tasks. For this reason, most programs come with setup programs that handle the installation process automatically.

instant messaging (IM) system Software program that lets you know when a friend or business associate is online. You can then contact this person and exchange messages and attachments.

instruction A unique number assigned to an operation performed by a processor.

instruction cycle In a machine cycle, a phase consisting of the fetch and decode operations.

instruction set A list of specific instructions that a given brand and model of processor can perform.

intangible benefits Gains that have no fixed dollar value, such as access to improved information or increased sales due to improved customer services.

integrated circuit (IC) A semiconductor circuit containing more than one transistor and other electronic components; often referred to as a chip.

integrated program A program that combines three or more productivity software functions, including word processing, database management, and a spreadsheet.

intelligent agent An automatic program that is designed to operate on the user's behalf, performing a specific function in the background. When the agent has achieved its goal, it reports to the user.

Intelligent Transportation System (ITS) A system, partly funded by the U.S. government, to develop smart streets and smart cars. Such a system could warn travelers of congestion and suggest alternative routes.

interactive multimedia A presentation involving two or more media, such as text, graphics, or sound, and providing users with the ability to choose their own path through the information.

interface A means of connecting two dissimilar computer devices. An interface has two components, a physical component and a communications standard, called a protocol. The physical component provides the physical means for making a connection, while the protocol enables designers to design the devices so that they can exchange data with each other. The computer's standard parallel port is an example of an interface that has both a distinctive physical connector and a defining, standard protocol.

internal drive bay In a computer's case, a receptacle for mounting a storage device that is not easily accessible from outside the computer's case. Internal drive bays are typically used to mount nonremovable hard drives.

internal modem A modem that fits into the expansion bus of a personal computer. See also external modem.

internal speaker One of the components inside a computer's system unit, typically for emitting beeps and other low-fidelity sounds.

International Telecommunications Union (ITU) A branch organization of the United Nations that sets international telecommunications standards.

Internet An enormous and rapidly growing system of linked computer networks, worldwide in scope, that facilitates data communication services such as remote logon, file transfer, electronic mail, the World Wide Web, and newsgroups. Relying on TCP/IP, the Internet assigns every connected computer a unique Internet address (called an IP address) so that any two connected computers can locate each other on the network and exchange data.

Internet2 The next-generation Internet, still under development.

Internet address The unique, 32-bit address assigned to a computer that is connected to the Internet, represented in dotted decimal notation (for example, 128.117.38.5). Synonymous with IP address.

Internet appliance A device that provides much of a personal computer's functionality but at a much lower price, connects to a network, such as the Internet, and has limited memory, disk storage, and processing power.

Internet hard drive Storage space on a server that is accessible from the Internet.

Internet programs General-purpose software programs for e-mailing, instant messaging, Web browsing, and videoconferencing.

Internet Protocol (IP) One of the two core Internet standards (the other is the Transmission Control Protocol, TCP). IP defines the standard that describes how an Internet-connected computer should break data down into packets for transmission across the network, and how those packets should be addressed so that they arrive at their destination. IP is the connectionless part of the TCP/IP protocols.

Internet Relay Chat (IRC) A real-time, Internet-based chat service, in which one can find "live" participants from the world over. IRC requires the use of an IRC client program, which displays a list of the current IRC channels. After joining a channel, you can see what other participants are typing on-screen, and you can type your own repartee.

Internet service A set of communication standards (protocols) and software (clients and servers) that defines how to access and exchange a certain type of information on the Internet. Examples of Internet services are e-mail, FTP, Gopher, IRC, and Web.

Internet Service Provider (ISP) A company that provides Internet accounts and connections to individuals and businesses. Most ISPs offer a range of connection options, ranging from dial-up modem connections to high-speed ISDN and ADSL. Also provided is e-mail, Usenet, and Web hosting.

Internet telephony The use of the Internet (or of nonpublic networks based on Internet technology) for the transmission of real-time voice data.

Internet telephony service providers A long-distance voice messaging service that provides telephone service by means of the Internet or private data networks using Internet technology.

InterNIC A consortium of two organizations that provide networking information services to the Internet community, under contract to the National Science Foundation (NSF). Currently, AT&T provides directory and database services, while Network Solutions, Inc., provides registration services for new domain names and IP addresses.

interoperability The ability to work with computers and operating systems of differing type and brand.

interpreter In programming, a translator that converts each instruction into machine-readable code and executes it one line at a time. Interpreters are often used for learning and debugging, due to their slow speed.

interrupt handlers Miniprograms in an operating system that kick in when an interrupt occurs.

interrupt request (IRQ) Lines that handle the communication between input or output devices and the computer's CPU.

interrupts Signals generated by input and output devices that inform the operating system that something has happened, such as a document has finished printing.

intranet A computer network based on Internet technology (TCP/IP) that meets the internal needs of a single organization or company. Not necessarily open to the external Internet and almost certainly not accessible from the outside, an intranet enables organizations to make internal resources available using familiar Internet tools. See also extranet.

IP address A 32-bit binary number that uniquely and precisely identifies the location of a particular computer on the Internet. Every computer that is directly connected to the Internet must have an IP address. Because binary numbers are so hard to read, IP addresses are given in four-part decimal numbers, each part representing 8 bits of the 32-bit address (for example, 128.143.7.226).

IPOS cycle A sequence of four basic types of computer operations that characterize everything computers do. These operations are input, processing, output, and storage.

IrDA port A port housed on the exterior of a computer's case that is capable of sending and receiving computer data by means of infrared signals. The standards that define these signals are maintained by the Infrared Data Association (IrDA). IrDA ports are commonly found on notebook computers and personal digital assistants (PDAs).

IRQ conflict A serious system failure that results if two devices are configured to use the same IRQ but are not designed to share an IRQ line.

ISDN (Integrated Services Digital Network) A worldwide standard for the delivery of digital telephone and data services to homes, schools, and offices using existing twisted-pair wiring.

ISDN adapter An internal or external accessory that enables a computer to connect to remote computer networks or the Internet by means of ISDN. (Inaccurately called an ISDN modem.)

IT industry The industry that consists of organizations focused on the development and implementation of technology and applications.

iteration control structure See repetition control structure.

J

Java A cross-platform programming language created by Sun Microsystems that enables programmers to write a program that will execute on any computer capable of running a Java interpreter (which is built into today's leading Web browsers). Java is an object-oriented programming (OOP) language similar to C++, except that it eliminates some features of C++ that programmers find tedious and time-consuming. Java programs are compiled into applets (small programs executed by a browser) or applications (larger, standalone programs that require a Java interpreter to be present on the user's computer), but the compiled code contains no machine code. Instead, the output of the compiler is bytecode, an intermediary between source code and machine code that can be transmitted by computer networks, including the Internet.

Java Virtual Machine (VM) A Java interpreter and runtime environment for Java applets and Java applications. This environment is called a virtual machine because, no matter what kind of computer it is running on, it creates a simulated computer that provides the correct platform for executing Java programs. In addition, this approach insulates the computer's file system from rogue applications. Java VMs are available for most computers.

Jaz drive A removable drive from Iomega that can store up to 2 GB.

joint application development (JAD) In information systems development, a method of system design that involves users at all stages of system development. See also prototyping.

joystick An input device commonly used for games.

JPEG (Joint Photographic Experts Group) A graphics file format, named after the group that designed it. JPEG graphics can display up to 16.7 million colors and use lossy compression to reduce file size. JPEG is best used for complex graphics such as photographs.

K

K or KB Abbreviation for kilobyte, approximately one thousand bytes or characters.

Kbps A data transfer rate of approximately one thousand bits per second.

kernel The essential, core portion of the operating system that is loaded into random access memory (RAM) when the computer is turned on and stays in RAM for the duration of the operating session. Also called supervisor program.

key escrow The storage of users' encryption keys by an independent agency, which would divulge the keys to law enforcement investigators only on the production of a valid warrant. Key escrow is proposed by law enforcement officials concerned that encryption would prevent surveillance of criminal activities.

key field or primary key This field contains a code, number, name, or some other information that uniquely identifies the record.

key interception The act of stealing an encryption key.

key recovery A method of unlocking the key used to encrypt messages so that the message could be read by law enforcement officials conducting a lawful investigation. Key recovery is proposed by law enforcement officials concerned that encryption would prevent surveillance of criminal activities.

keyboard An input device providing a set of alphabetic, numeric, punctuation, symbolic, and control keys.

keyword In a command-line interface, words that tell the operating system what to do (such as "format" or "copy").

kilobits per second (Kbps) A data transfer rate of approximately one thousand bits of computer data per second.

kilobyte (K or KB) The basic unit of measurement for computer memory and disk capacity, equal to 1,024 bytes or characters.

kiosk A booth that provides a computer service of some type.

know-and-have authentication A type of computer security that requires using tokens, which are handheld electronic devices that generate a logon code.

knowledge base A database of represented knowledge.

knowledge management system An information system that captures knowledge created by employees and makes it available to an organization.

knowledge representation The process of eliciting rules from human experts.

L

land Flat reflective areas on an optical disc.

laptop computer A portable computer larger than a notebook computer but small enough to be transported easily. Few are being made now that notebook computers have become so powerful.

laser printer A popular nonimpact, high-resolution printer that uses a version of the electrostatic reproduction technology of copying machines.

last-mile problem The lack of local network systems for high-bandwidth multimedia communications that can accommodate the Information Superhighway.

last-mile technologies Digital telecommunications services and standards, such as coaxial cable and ISDN, that serve as interim solutions to the limitations associated with the twisted pair analog phone wiring still common in many homes and businesses.

latency In a packet-switching network, a signal delay that is introduced by the time network routers consume as they route packets to their destination.

launch To start an application program.

layer In a computer network, a level of network functionality governed by specific network protocols. For example, the physical layer has protocols concerned with the transmission of signals over a specific type of cable.

LCD monitors The thinner monitors used on notebooks and some desktop computers.

LCD projector An output device that projects a computer's screen display on a screen similar to those used with slide projectors.

leased line A permanently connected and conditioned telephone line that provides wide area network (WAN) connectivity to an organization or a business.

left pane In the My Computer primary file management utility for PCs, one of two main default windows. It displays links to system tasks, such as viewing system information. See also right pane.

legacy system A technically obsolete information system that remains in use, often because it performs its job adequately or is too expensive to replace.

level 2 (L2) cache See secondary cache.

libel A form of defamation that occurs in writing.

life cycle In information systems, the birth, development, use, and eventual abandonment of the system.

light pen An input device that uses a light-sensitive stylus to draw on-screen or on a graphics tablet or to select items from a menu.

link See hyperlink.

Linux A freeware operating system closely resembling UNIX developed for IBM-compatible PCs but also available for other platforms, including Macintosh.

liquid crystal display (LCD) A small, flat-screen monitor that uses electrical current to control tiny crystals and form an image.

listserv An automatic mailing list server developed by Eric Thomas for BITNET in 1986.

load To transfer program instructions from storage to memory.

local area network (LAN) A computer network that connects computers in a limited geographical area (typically less than one mile) so that users can exchange information and share hardware, software, and data resources.

local exchange switch A telephone system device, based on digital technology and capable of handling thousands of calls, located in the local telephone company's central office.

local loop In the public switched telephone network (PSTN), the last segment of service delivery, typically consisting of analog connections from neighborhood distribution points.

LocalTalk A protocol developed by Apple Computer that provides peer-to-peer networking among Apple Macintosh computers and Macintosh-compatible peripherals such as laser printers. LocalTalk is a low-level protocol that works with twisted-pair phone cables.

location (position) awareness A technology that uses GPS-enabled chips to pinpoint the location of a cell phone (and its user).

log in To authenticate yourself as a user with a valid account and usage privileges on a multiuser computer system or a computer network. To log in, you supply your user name and password. Also called log on.

log on See log in.

logic bomb A flaw concealed in an otherwise usable computer program that can be triggered to destroy or corrupt data.

logic error In programming, a mistake made by the programmer in designing the program. Logic errors will not surface by themselves during program execution because they are not errors in the structure of the statements and commands.

logical data type A data type that allows only a yes or no answer.

logical operations One of two groups of operations performed by the arithmetic-logic unit (ALU). The logical operations involve comparing two data items to see which one is larger or smaller.

looping See repetition control structure.

lossless compression In data compression, a method used to reduce the size of a file that enables the file to be restored to its original size without introducing errors. Most lossless compression techniques reduce file size by replacing lengthy but frequently occurring data sequences with short codes; to decompress the file, the compression software reverses this process and restores the lengthy data sequences to their original form.

lossy compression In data compression, a method of reducing the size of multimedia files by eliminating information that is not normally perceived by human beings.

low-level language A language that describes exactly the procedures to be carried out by a computer's central processing unit, such as machine or programming language.

M

M or MB Abbreviation for megabyte, approximately one million bytes or characters of information.

Mac OS Operating system and user interface developed by Apple Computer for Macintosh computers; introduced the first graphical user interface.

machine cycle A four-step process followed by the control unit that involves the fetch, decode, execute, and write-back operations. Also called processing cycle.

machine dependence The dependence of a given computer program or component on a specific brand or type of computer equipment.

machine language The native binary language consisting of 0s and 1s that is recognized and executed by a computer's central processing unit.

machine translation Language translation performed by the computer without human aid.

macro In application software, a user-defined command sequence that can be saved and executed to perform a complex action.

macro virus A computer virus that uses the automatic command execution capabilities of productivity software to spread itself and often to cause harm to computer data.

magnetic storage device In computer storage systems, any storage device that retains data using a magnetically sensitive material, such as the magnetic coating found on floppy disks or backup tapes.

magnetic-ink character recognition (MICR) system A scanning system developed by the banking industry in the 1950s. Check information is encoded onto each check before it is used to reduce processing time when the check comes back to the bank.

mainframe A multiuser computer system that meets the computing needs of a large organization.

maintenance release A minor revision to a software program, indicated by the decimal in the version number, that corrects bugs or adds minor features.

management information system (MIS) A computer-based system that supports the information needs of management.

managing applications One of the five basic functions of an operating system that enables a user to work with two or more applications at the same time.

managing memory One of the five basic functions of an operating system that gives each running program its own portion of memory and attempts to keep the programs from interfering with each other's use of memory.

markup language In text processing, a system of codes for marking the format of a unit of text that indicates only that a particular unit of text is a certain part of the document, such as an abstract, a title, or an author's name and affiliation. The actual formatting of the document part is left to another program, called a viewer, which displays the marked document and gives each document part a distinctive format (fonts, spacing, and so on). HTML is a markup language.

mass storage See storage.

math coprocessor A separate chip that frees the main processor from performing mathematical operations, usually operations involving floating-point notation.

mathematic formula In spreadsheet programs such as Microsoft Excel, one of the two basic types of formulas (along with functions). In a mathematic formula, or expression, the mathematic order of operation is followed.

maximize To enlarge a window so that it fits the entire screen.

mechanical mouse A type of mouse that uses a rotating ball to generate information about the mouse's position.

megabits per second (Mbps) In networking, a data transfer rate of approximately one million bits per second.

megabyte (M or MB) A measurement of storage capacity equal to 1,024 kilobytes, or approximately one million bytes or characters.

megapixel Type of digital camera that has a charge-coupled device with at least one million elements.

memo In databases, a data type used for large units of text.

memory Circuitry that stores information temporarily so that it is readily available to the central processing unit (CPU).

memory address A code number that specifies a specific location in memory.

memory shaving A type of computer crime in which knowledgeable thieves remove some of a computer's RAM chips but leave enough to start the computers.

menu The list of words, such as file, edit, and view, signifying categories of tasks that can be accomplished within an application.

menu bar In a graphical user interface (GUI), a rectangular bar (generally positioned near the top of the application window) that provides access to pull-down menus. On the Macintosh, an active application's menu bar is always positioned at the top of the screen.

menu-driven user interface An interface between the operating system and the user in which text-based menus show options, rather than requiring the user to memorize the commands and type them in.

Metcalfe's Law A prediction formulated by Bob Metcalfe, creator of Ethernet, that the value of a network increases in proportion to the square of the number of people connected to the network.

method In object-oriented programming, a procedure or operation that processes or manipulates data.

microcomputer A computer that uses a microprocessor as its CPU.

microphone An input device that converts sound into electrical signals that can be processed by a computer.

microprocessor See central processing unit (CPU).

Microsoft Windows Generic name for the various operating systems in the Microsoft Windows family, including, but not limited to, Microsoft Windows CE, Microsoft Windows 3.1, Microsoft Windows 95, Microsoft Windows 98, and Microsoft Windows NT.

Microsoft Windows CE An operating system for palmtop and personal digital assistant computers developed by Microsoft Corporation.

Microsoft Windows NT A 32-bit operating system developed by Microsoft Corporation for use in corporate client/server networks. The operating system consists of two components, Microsoft Windows NT Workstation (for users' systems) and Microsoft Windows NT Server (for file servers).

Microsoft Windows XP The first Microsoft operating system family that uses the same, underlying 32-bit code for all three versions (consumer, corporate desktop, and server).

microwave An electromagnetic radio wave with a very short frequency.

middleware In object-oriented programming, standards that define how programs find objects and determine what kind of information they contain.

MIDI (Musical Instrument Digital Interface) A standard that specifies how musical sounds can be described in text files so that a MIDI-compatible synthesizer can reproduce the sounds. MIDI files are small, so they're often used to provide music that starts playing automatically when a Web page is accessed. To hear MIDI sounds, your computer needs a sound card. MIDI sounds best with wavetable synthesis sound cards, which include sound samples from real musical instruments.

minicomputer A multiuser computer that meets the needs of a small organization or a department in a large organization.

minimize To reduce the size of a window so that it appears only as an icon or an item on the taskbar.

minitower case A smaller version of a system unit case designed to sit on the floor next to a desk.

mnemonic In programming, an abbreviation or a word that makes it easier to remember a complex instruction.

mobile telephone switching office (MTSO) In a cellular telephone system, the switching office that connects all of the individual cell towers to the central office and the public switched telephone network.

modeling A method by which spreadsheet programs are able to predict future outcomes.

modem Short for modulator/demodulator, a device that converts the digital signals generated by the serial port to the modulated analog signals required for transmission over a telephone line and, likewise, transforms incoming analog signals to their digital equivalents. The speed at which a modem transmits data is measured in units called bits per second, or bps. (Although bps is not technically the same as baud, the terms are often and erroneously used interchangeably.)

modifier keys Keys that are pressed to modify the meaning of the next key that's pressed.

modular programming A programming style that breaks down program functions into modules, each of which accomplishes one function and contains all the source code and variables needed to accomplish that function.

modulation protocol In modems, the communications standard that governs how the modem translates between the computer's digital signals and the analog tones used to convey computer data over the Internet. Modulation protocols are defined by ITU standards. The V.90 protocol defines communication at 56 Kbps.

module A part of a software program; independently developed modules are combined to compile the final program.

monitor A television-like device that produces an on-screen image.

Moore's Law A prediction by Intel Corp. cofounder Gordon Moore that integrated circuit technology advancements would enable the semiconductor industry to double the number of components on a chip every 18 to 24 months.

motherboard A large circuit board containing the computer's central processing unit, support chips, random access memory, and expansion slots. Also called a main board.

mouse A palm-sized input device, with a ball built into the bottom, that is used to move a pointer on-screen to draw, select options from a menu, modify or move text, and issue commands.

mousepad A clean, flat surface for moving a mouse on.

MPEG (Moving Pictures Experts Group) A set of standards for audio and video file formats and lossless compression, named after the group that created it.

MPEG Audio Layer 3 (MP3) A sound compression standard that can store a single song from an audio CD in a 3M file. MP3 files are easily shared over the Internet and are costing recording companies billions of dollars in lost royalties due to piracy.

MP2 One of several standardized audio formats for representing sounds digitally, developed by the Moving Picture Experts Group (MPEG). See Moving Picture Experts Group (MPEG) and MPEG Audio Layer 3 (MP3).

MS-DOS An operating system for IBM-compatible PCs that uses a command-line user interface.

MSN® TV An Internet service that allows customers to access the Web using a television set as a display.

multifunction devices Machines that combine printing, scanning, faxing, and copying.

multimedia The presentation of information using graphics, video, sound, animation, and text.

multimedia and graphics software General-purpose software programs for professional desktop publishing, image editing, three-dimensional rendering, and video editing.

multiplexing A technique that enables more than one signal to be conveyed on a physical transmission medium.

multitasking In operating systems, the capability to execute more than one application at a time. Multitasking shouldn't be confused with multiple program loading, in which two or more applications are present in random access memory (RAM) but only one executes at a time.

multiuser dungeon (MUD) A text-based environment in which multiple players can assume online personas and interact with each other by means of text chatting.

N

nanorobots Atoms and molecules used to perform certain tasks in nanotechnology.

nanotechnology Manipulating materials on an atomic or molecular scale in order to build microscopic devices.

native application A program that runs on a particular brand and model of processor or in a particular operating system.

natural language A human language, such as English or Japanese.

near-online storage A type of storage that is not directly available, but can be made available by a simple action such as inserting a disk.

nest In structured programming, to embed one control structure inside another.

netiquette Short for network etiquette. A set of rules that reflect long-standing experience about getting along harmoniously in the electronic environment (e-mail and newsgroups).

network A group of two or more computer systems linked together to enable communications by exchanging data and sharing resources.

network access point (NAP) A special communications device that sends and receives data between computers that contain wireless adapters.

network administrator (sometimes called *network engineers*) Computer professionals who install, maintain, and support computer networks, interact with users, handle security, and troubleshoot problems.

network architecture The overall design of a computer network that specifies its functionality at every level by means of protocols.

network attached storage (NAS) devices High-performance devices that provide shared data to clients and other servers on a local area network.

network computer (NC) A computer that provides much of a PC's functionality at a lower price. Network computers don't have disk drives because they get their software from the computer network.

network interface card (NIC) An adapter that enables a user to connect a network cable to a computer.

network layers Separate divisions within a network architecture with specific functions and protocols, allowing engineers to make changes within a layer without having to redesign the entire network.

network operating system (NOS) The software needed to enable data transfer and application usage over a local area network (LAN).

network topology The physical layout of a local area network (LAN), such as a bus, star, or ring topology, that determines what happens when, for example, two workstations try to access the LAN or transmit data simultaneously.

neural network In artificial intelligence, a computer architecture that attempts to mimic the structure of the human brain. Neural nets "learn" by trial and error and are good at recognizing patterns and dealing with complexity.

newsgroup In Usenet, a discussion group devoted to a single topic. Users post messages to the group, and those reading the discussion send reply messages to the author individually or post replies that can be read by the group as a whole.

node In a LAN, a connection point that can create, receive, or repeat a message.

nonprocedural Not tied down to step-by-step procedures. In programming, a nonprocedural programming language does not force the programmer to consider the procedure that must be followed to obtain the desired result.

nonvolatile Not susceptible to loss. If power is lost, the data is preserved.

notebook computer A portable computer that is small enough to fit into an average-size briefcase but includes nearly all peripherals commonly found on desktop computers.

nuking A type of antisocial behavior found on Internet Relay Chat characterized by exploiting bugs that cause computer crashes.

numeric check Ensures that numbers are entered into a field.

O

object 1. In object-oriented programming (OOP), a unit of computer information that contains data and all the procedures or operations that can process or manipulate the data. 2. Nontextual data. Examples of objects include pictures, sounds, or videos.

object code In programming, the machine-readable instructions created by a compiler from source code.

object-oriented database The newest type of database structure, well suited for multimedia applications, in which the result of a retrieval operation is an object of some kind, such as a document. Within this object are miniprograms that enable the object to perform tasks such as displaying graphics. Object-oriented databases can incorporate sound, video, text, and graphics into a single database record.

object-oriented (OO) programming A programming technique that creates generic building blocks of a program (the objects). The user then assembles different sets of objects as needed to solve specific problems. Also called OOP, for object-oriented programming.

Office Clipboard In Microsoft Office, a feature that temporarily stores in memory whatever has been cut or copied from a document, allowing for those items to be used within any Office application.

office suite See software suite.

offshoring The transfer of labor from workers in one country to workers in other countries.

off-the-shelf software See packaged software.

on-board video Video circuitry that comes built into a computer's motherboard.

online Directly connected to the network.

online analytical processing (OLAP) In a decision support system (DSS), a method of providing rich, up-to-the-minute data from transaction databases.

online banking The use of a Web browser to access bank accounts, balance checkbooks, transfer funds, and pay bills.

online processing The processing of data immediately after it has been input by a user, as opposed to waiting until a predetermined time, as in batch processing.

online service A for-profit firm that makes current news, stock quotes, and other information available to its subscribers over standard telephone lines. Popular services include supervised chat rooms for text chatting and forums for topical discussion. Online services also provide Internet access.

online stock trading The purchase or sale of stock through the Internet.

online storage A type of storage that is directly available, such as a hard disk, and requires no special action on the user's part to enable.

online travel reservations A rapidly growing area of e-commerce that allows consumers to use the Internet to research, book, and purchase airline flights, hotel rooms, and rental cars.

open To transfer an existing document from storage to memory.

open source software Software in which the source code is made available to the program's users.

operating system (OS) A program that integrates and controls the computer's internal functions and provides a user interface.

operational decisions Management decisions concerning localized issues (such as an inventory shortage) that need immediate action.

operational feasibility Capable of being accomplished with an organization's available resources.

operational support system (OSS) A suite of programs that supports an enterprise's network operations.

optical character recognition (OCR) Software that automatically decodes imaged text into a text file. Most scanners come with OCR software.

optical mark reader (OMR) A reader that senses magnetized marks made by the magnetic particles in lead from a pencil.

optical storage A storage system in which a storage device retains data using surface patterns that are physically encoded on the surface of plastic discs. The patterns can be detected by a laser beam.

optical storage device A computer storage device that retains data in microscopic patterns, detectable by a laser beam, encoded on the surface of plastic discs.

options Choices within an application that allow users to change defaults and to specify how they want the program to operate.

output The results of processing information, typically shown on a monitor or a printer.

output devices Monitors, printers, and other machines that enable people to see, hear, and even feel the results of processing operations.

outsourcing The transfer of a project to an external contractor.

P

packaged software Ready-to-use software that is sold through mass-market channels and contains features useful to the largest possible user base. Synonymous with off-the-shelf software and shrink-wrapped software.

packet In a packet-switching network, a unit of data of a fixed size—not exceeding the network's maximum transmission unit (MTU) size—that has been prepared for network transmission. Each packet contains a header that indicates its origin and its destination. See also packet switching.

packet sniffer In computer security, a device that examines all traffic on a network and retrieves valuable information such as passwords and credit card numbers.

packet switching One of two fundamental architectures for a wide area network (WAN); the other is a circuit-switching network. In a packet-switching network such as the Internet, no effort is made to establish a single electrical circuit between two computing devices; for this reason, packet-switching networks are often called connectionless. Instead, the sending computer divides a message into packets, each of which contains the address of the destination computer, and dumps them onto the network. They are intercepted by devices called routers, which send the packets in the appropriate direction. The receiving computer assembles the packets, puts them in order, and delivers the received message to the appropriate application. Packet-switching networks are highly reliable and efficient, but they are not suited to the delivery of real-time voice and video.

page In virtual memory, a fixed size of program instructions and data that can be stored on the hard disk to free up random access memory.

page description language (PDL) A programming language capable of precisely describing the appearance of a printed page, including fonts and graphics.

paging An operating system's transference of files from storage to memory and back.

paint program A program that enables the user to paint the screen by specifying the color of the individual pixels that make up the screen display.

parallel conversion In the development of an information system, the operation of both the new and old information systems at the same time to ensure the compatibility and reliability of the new system.

parallel port An interface that uses several side-by-side wires so that one or more bytes of computer data can travel in unison and arrive simultaneously. Parallel ports offer faster performance than serial ports, in which each bit of data must travel in a line, one after the other.

parallel processing The use of more than one processor to run two or more portions of a program simultaneously.

partition A section of a storage device, such as a hard disk, that is prepared so that it can be treated as if it were a completely separate device for data storage and maintenance.

Pascal A high-level programming language that encourages programmers to write well-structured programs, named after seventeenth-century mathematician Blaise Pascal.

passive matrix LCD An inexpensive liquid crystal display (LCD) that sometimes generates image flaws and is too slow for full-motion video. Also called dual scan LCD.

password A unique word that a user types to log on to a system. Passwords should not be obvious and should be changed frequently.

password guessing In computer security, a method of defeating password authentication by guessing common passwords, such as personal names, obscene words, and the word "password."

path The sequence of directories that the computer must follow to locate a file.

pattern recognition In artificial intelligence, the use of a computer system to recognize patterns, such as thumbprints, and associate these patterns with stored data or instructions.

PC 100 SDRAM A type of SDRAM capable of keeping up with motherboards that have bus speeds of 100 MHz.

PC card Synonymous with PCMCIA card. A computer accessory (such as a modem or network interface card) that is designed to fit into a compatible PC card slot mounted on the computer's case. PC cards and slots are commonly used on notebook computers because they offer system expandability while consuming a small fraction of the space required for expansion cards.

peer-to-peer network A computer network design in which all the computers can access the public files located on other computers in a network.

pen computer A computer operated with a stylus, such as a personal digital assistant (PDA).

peripheral A device connected to and controlled by a computer, but external to the computer's central processing unit.

PCI (Peripheral Component Interconnect) bus A type of expansion bus used with Macs and PCs to communicate with input and output devices, containing expansion slots to accommodate plug-in expansion cards.

Personal Communication Service (PCS) A digital cellular phone service that is rapidly replacing analog cellular phones.

personal computer (PC) A computer system that meets the computing needs of an individual. The term PC usually refers to an IBM-compatible personal computer.

Personal Computer Memory Card International Association (PCMCIA) card See PC card.

personal computing Any situation or setup where one person controls and uses a PC for personal or business activities.

personal digital assistant (PDA) A small, handheld computer that accepts input written on-screen with a stylus. Most include built-in software for appointments, scheduling, and e-mail. Also called palmtop.

personal firewall A program or device that is designed to protect home computer users from unauthorized access.

personal information manager (PIM) A program that stores and retrieves a variety of personal information, such as appointments. PIMs have been slow to gain acceptance due to their lack of convenience and portability.

personal productivity program Application software, such as word processing software or a spreadsheet program, that assists individuals in doing their work more effectively and efficiently.

phased conversion In the development of an information system, the implementation of the new system in different time periods, one part at a time.

photo checkout systems Used with POS terminals, a security check that accesses a database of customer photos and displays the customer's picture when a credit card is used.

photo-editing program A program that enables images to be enhanced, edited, cropped, or sized. The same program can be used to print the images on a color printer.

phrase searching In database and Web searching, a search that retrieves only documents that contain the entire phrase.

picture messaging A mobile service that allows you to send full-color pictures, backgrounds, and even picture caller IDs on your cell phone.

pilot conversion In the development of an information system, the institution of the new system in only one part of an organization. When that portion of the organization is satisfied with the system, the rest of the organization then starts using it.

pipelining A design that provides two or more processing pathways that can be used simultaneously.

pit A microscopic indentation in the surface of an optical disc that absorbs the light of the optical drive's laser, corresponding to a 0 in the computer's binary number system.

pixel Short for picture element, the smallest element that a device can display and out of which the displayed image is constructed.

plagiarism The presentation of somebody else's work as if it were one's own.

Plain Old Telephone Service (POTS) A term used to describe the standard analog telephone service.

plaintext A readable message before it is encrypted.

platform A distinct type of computer that uses a certain type of processor and operating system, such as a Macintosh or an Intel-based Windows PC.

platter In a hard drive, a fixed, rapidly rotating disk that is coated with a magnetically sensitive material. High-capacity hard drives typically have two or more platters.

plotter A printer that produces high-quality output by moving ink pens over the surface of the paper.

Plug and Play (PnP) A set of standards jointly developed by Intel Corporation and Microsoft that enables users of Microsoft Windows–based PCs to configure new hardware devices automatically. Operating systems equipped with plug-and-play capabilities can automatically detect new PnP-compatible peripherals that may have been installed while the power was switched off.

point of presence (PoP) A locality in which it is possible to obtain dialup access to the network by means of a local telephone call. Internet service providers (ISPs) provide PoPs in towns and cities, but many rural areas are without local PoPs.

point-and-shoot digital cameras Digital cameras that typically include automatic focus, automatic exposure, built-in automatic electronic flash with red eye reduction, and optical zoom lenses with digital enhancement.

point-of-sale (POS) terminal A computer-based cash register that enables transaction data to be captured at the checkout stand. Such terminals can automatically adjust inventory databases and enable managers to analyze sales patterns.

pointer An on-screen symbol, usually an arrow, that shows the current position of the mouse.

pointing device Any input device that is capable of moving the on-screen pointer in a graphical user interface (GUI), such as a mouse or trackball.

pointing stick A pointing device introduced by IBM that enables users to move the pointer around the screen by manipulating a small, stubby stick that protrudes slightly from the surface of the keyboard.

popup menu A menu that appears at the mouse pointer's position when you click the right mouse button.

port An interface that controls the flow of data between the central processing unit and external devices such as printers and monitors.

portable Able to be easily removed or inserted or transferred to a different type of computer system.

Portable Network Graphics (PNG) A graphics file format closely resembling the GIF format but lacking GIF's proprietary compression technique (which forces publishers of GIF-enabled graphics software to pay a licensing fee).

portal On the Web, a page that attempts to provide an attractive starting point for Web sessions. Typically included are links to breaking news, weather forecasts, stock quotes, free e-mail service, sports scores, and a subject guide to information available on the Web. Leading portals include Netscape's NetCenter (www.netcenter.com), Yahoo! (www.yahoo.com), and Snap! (www.snap.com).

positioning performance A measure of how much time elapses from the initiation of drive activity until the hard disk has positioned the read/write head so that it can begin transferring data.

post-implementation system review In the development of an information system, the ongoing evaluation of the information system to determine whether it has met its goals.

power-on light A light on the front panel of most computers that signals whether the power is on.

power-on self test (POST) The series of system integrity tests that a computer goes through every time it is started (cold boot) or restarted (warm boot). These tests verify that vital system components, such as the memory, are functioning properly.

power outage A sudden loss of electrical power, causing the loss of all unsaved information on a computer.

power supply A device that supplies power to a computer system by converting AC current to DC current and lowering the voltage.

power surge A sudden and sometimes destructive increase in the amount of voltage delivered through a power line.

power switch A switch that turns the computer on and off. Often located in the rear of a computer.

preemptive multitasking In operating systems, a method of running more than one application at a time. Unlike cooperative multitasking, preemptive multitasking allows other applications to continue running if one application crashes.

presentation graphics A software package used to make presentations visually attractive and easy to understand.

primary cache A small unit (8 KB to 32 KB) of ultra-fast memory included with a microprocessor and used to store frequently accessed data and improve overall system performance.

primary folder A main folder such as is created at the root of a drive to hold further subfolders. Also called top-level folder.

primary storage See online storage.

printed circuit board A flat piece of plastic or fiberglass on which complex patterns of copper pathways have been created by means of etching. These paths link integrated circuits and other electrical components.

printer An output device that prints computer-generated text or graphics onto paper or another physical medium.

privacy The right to live your life without undue intrusions into your personal affairs by government agencies or corporate marketers.

private key A decryption key.

problem A state of difficulty that needs to be resolved; the underlying cause of a symptom.

procedural language A programming language that tells the computer what to do and how to do it.

procedure The steps that must be followed to accomplish a specific computer-related task.

processing The execution of arithmetic or comparison operations on data.

processing cycle See machine cycle.

processor See central processing unit (CPU).

professional organizations (associations) IT organizations that can help you keep up with your area of interest as well as provide valuable career contacts.

professional workstation A very powerful computer system for engineers, financial analysts, and other professionals who need exceptionally powerful processing and output capabilities. Professional workstations are very expensive.

profile In a consumer-oriented operating system such as Windows 98, a record of a user's preferences that is associated with a user name and password. If you set up two or more profiles, users see their own preferences. However, profiles do not prevent users from accessing and overwriting each others' files. Compare with account.

program A list of instructions telling the computer what to do.

program development life cycle (PDLC) A step-by-step procedure used to develop software for information systems.

program maintenance In phase 6 of the PDLC, the process in which the programming team fixes program errors discovered by users.

program specification In software development, a technical description of the software needed by the information system. The program specification precisely defines input data, the processing that occurs, the output format, and the user interface.

programmer A person skilled in the use of one or more programming languages. Although most programmers have college degrees in computer science, certification is an increasingly popular way to demonstrate one's programming expertise.

programming language An artificial language composed of a fixed vocabulary and a set of rules used to create instructions for a computer to follow.

project dictionary In the development of information systems, a compilation of all terminology relevant to the project.

project notebook In the development of an information system, a place where information regarding system development is stored.

project plan A specification of the goals, scope, and individual activities that make up a project.

project proposal In phase 1 of the SDLC, a document that introduces the nature of the existing system's problem, explains the proposed solution and its benefits, details the proposed project plan, and concludes with a recommendation.

protocol In data communications and networking, a standard specifying the format of data and the rules to be followed. Networks could not be easily or efficiently designed or maintained without protocols; a protocol specifies how a program should prepare data so that it can be sent to the next stage in the communication process. For example, e-mail programs prepare messages so that they conform to prevailing Internet mail standards, which are recognized by every program involved in the transmission of mail over the network.

protocol stack In a computer network, a means of conceptualizing network architecture in which the various layers of network functionality are viewed as a vertical stack, like the layers of a layer cake, in computers linked to the network. When one computer sends a message to the network, the message goes down the stack and then traverses the network; on the receiving computer, the message goes up the stack.

protocol suite In a computer network, the collection of network protocols that defines the network's functionality.

prototyping In information systems development, the creation of a working system model that is functional enough to draw feedback from users. Also called joint application development (JAD).

providing the user interface One of the five basic functions of an operating system in which the part of the operating system that you see and interact with and by which users and programs communicate with each other is provided.

pseudocode In structured programming, a stylized form of writing used as an alternative to flowcharts to describe the logic of a program.

public domain software Noncopyrighted software that anyone may copy and use without charge and without acknowledging the source.

public key In public key cryptography, the encoding key, which you make public so that others can send you encrypted messages. The message can be encoded with the public key, but it cannot be decoded without the private key, which you alone possess.

public key cryptography In cryptography, a revolutionary new method of encryption that does not require the message's receiver to have received the decoding key in a separate transmission. The need to send the key, required to decode the message, is the chief vulnerability of previous encryption techniques. Public key cryptography has two keys: a public one and a private one. The public key is used for encryption, and the private key is used for decryption.

public key encryption A computer security process in which an encryption (or private) key and a decryption (or public) key are used to safeguard data.

public key infrastructure (PKI) A uniform set of encryption standards that specify how public key encryption, digital signatures, and CA-granted digital certificates should be implemented in computer systems and on the Internet.

public switched telephone network (PSTN) The world telephone system, a massive network used for data communication as well as voice.

pull-down menu In a graphical user interface (GUI), a named item on the menu bar that, when clicked, displays an on-screen menu of commands and options.

pumping and dumping An illegal stock price manipulation tactic that involves purchasing shares of a worthless corporation and then driving the price up by making unsubstantiated claims about the company's value in Internet newsgroups and chat rooms. The perpetrator sells the shares after the stock price goes up but before other investors wise up to the ploy.

Q

query In the Microsoft Access database management system, the object used to ask questions of the database.

query language A retrieval and data-editing language for composing simple or complex requests for data.

quoted size The front surface measured diagonally on a cathode-ray tube monitor, a figure that is greater than the viewable area, since some of the surface is hidden and unavailable for display purposes. See viewable area.

QWERTY keyboard A keyboard that uses the standard keyboard layout in which the first six letters on the left of the top row spell "QWERTY."

R

radio A wireless signaling technology that sends data by means of electromagnetic waves that travel through air and space between separate or combined transmitting and receiving devices.

RAID (redundant array of independent disks) A storage device that groups two or more hard disks containing exactly the same data.

Rambus DRAM Type of RAM that uses a narrow but very fast bus to connect to the microprocessor.

random access An information storage and retrieval technique in which the computer can access information directly, without having to go through a sequence of locations.

random access memory (RAM) Another name for the computer's main working memory, where program instructions and data are stored to be easily accessed by the central processing unit through the processor's high-speed data bus. When a computer is turned off, all data in RAM is lost.

random access storage device A storage device that can begin reading data directly without having to go through a lengthy sequence of data.

range check Verifies that the entered data fall within an acceptable range.

rapid application development (RAD) In object-oriented programming, a method of program development in which programmers work with a library of prebuilt objects, allowing them to build programs more quickly.

raster graphics See bitmapped graphics.

ray tracing A 3-D rendering technique in which color intensity on a graphic object is varied to simulate light falling on the object from multiple directions.

read To retrieve data or program instructions from a storage device such as a hard or floppy disk.

read/write The capability of a primary or secondary storage device to record (write) data and to play back (read) data previously recorded or saved.

read/write head In a hard or floppy disk, the magnetic recording and playback device that travels back and forth across the surface of the disk, storing and retrieving data.

read-only Capable of being displayed or used but not altered or deleted.

read-only memory (ROM) The part of a computer's primary storage that contains essential computer instructions and doesn't lose its contents when the power is turned off. Information in read-only memory cannot be erased by the computer.

record In a database, a group of one or more fields that contains information about something.

reengineering See business process reengineering (BPR).

refresh rate The frequency with which the screen is updated. The refresh rate determines whether the display appears to flicker.

register 1. In a microprocessor, a memory location used to store values and external memory addresses while the microprocessor performs logical and arithmetic operations on them. 2. In commercial software and shareware, to contact the software vendor and submit a form that includes personal information such as the user's name and address. Registering allows the software vendor to inform the user of important information and software updates.

registration fee An amount of money that must be paid to the author of a piece of shareware to continue using it beyond the duration of the evaluation period.

registry 1. A database that contains information about installed peripherals and software. 2. In Microsoft Windows, an important system file that contains configuration settings that Windows requires in order to operate.

relational database management system (RDBMS) A type of database software that uses the contents of a particular field as an index to reference particular records.

removable hard disk A hard disk that uses a removable cartridge instead of a sealed unit with a fixed, nonremovable platter.

repetition control structure In structured programming, a logical construction of commands repeated over and over. Also called looping or iteration control structure.

repetitive strain injury (RSI) See carpal tunnel syndrome.

Report In the Microsoft Access database management system, the object used to present data.

report generator In programming, a programming language for printing database reports. One of four parts of a database management system (DBMS) that helps the user design and generate reports and graphs in hard copy form.

request for proposal (RFP) In the development of information systems, a request to an outside vendor to write a proposal for the design, installation, and configuration of an information system.

request for quotation (RFQ) In the development of information systems, a request to an outside vendor or value-added reseller (VAR) to quote a price for specific information components.

requirements analysis A process in phase 1 of the SDLC that determines the requirements of the system by analyzing how the system will meet the needs of end users.

reset switch A switch on the front panel of most computers that can restart the computer in the event of a failure.

resolution A measurement, usually expressed in linear dots per inch (dpi) both horizontally and vertically, of the sharpness of an image generated by an output device such as a monitor or a printer.

restore To return a window to its size and position before it was maximized.

return on investment (ROI) The overall financial yield of a project at the end of its lifetime. ROI is often used by managers to decide whether a project is a good investment.

right pane In the My Computer primary file management utility for PCs, one of two main default windows. It displays the various files and drives you can choose from. See also left pane.

ring topology The physical layout of a local network in which all nodes are attached in a circle, without a central host computer.

rip and tear A confidence scam that involves convincing people that they have won a large sweepstakes prize but they cannot obtain the needed information unless they pay a fee. The prize never materializes, and the perpetrators disappear.

robot A computer-based device that is programmed to perform useful motions.

robotics A division of computer science that is devoted to improving the performance and capabilities of robots.

rot-13 In Usenet newsgroups, a simple encryption technique that offsets each character by 13 places (so that an e becomes an r, for example).

router In a packet-switching network such as the Internet, one of two basic devices (the other is a host). A router is an electronic device that examines each packet of data it receives and then decides which way to send it toward its destination.

routine (also referred to as a procedure, function, or subroutine) A section of code that executes a specific task in a program.

row In a spreadsheet, a block of cells going across the screen.

S

safe mode An operating mode in which Windows loads a minimal set of drivers that are known to function correctly.

salami shaving A computer crime in which a program is altered so that it transfers a small amount of money from a large number of accounts to make a large profit.

sales force automation (SFA) software Software that automates many of the business processes involved with sales, including processing and tracking orders, managing customers and other contacts, monitoring and controlling inventory, and analyzing sales forecasts.

satellite In data communications, a communications reflector placed in a geosynchronous (stationary) orbit.

satellite radio A type of communications technology that broadcasts radio signals back and forth between satellites orbiting more than 22,000 miles above the Earth and radio receivers on Earth.

save To transfer data from the computer's memory to a storage device for safekeeping.

save as A command that enables the user to store a document with a new name.

saving In an application software program, the process of transferring a document from the computer's temporary memory to a permanent storage device, such as a hard disk, for safekeeping.

scalability A hardware or software system's ability to continue functioning effectively as demands and use increase.

scanner A device that copies the image (text or graphic) on a sheet of paper and translates it into a digital image. Scanners use charge-coupled devices to digitize the image.

script A short program written in a simple programming language, called a scripting language.

scripting language A simple programming language that enables users to create useful programs (scripts) quickly. VBScript is one example of a scripting language.

scroll To bring hidden parts of a document into view within the application workspace.

scroll arrow An arrow appearing within the scroll bar that enables the user to scroll up or down (or, in a horizontal scroll bar, left and right) by small increments.

scroll bar A vertical or horizontal bar that contains scroll arrows and a scroll box. The scroll bar enables the user to bring hidden portions of a document into view within the application workspace.

search engine Any program that locates needed information in a database, but especially an Internet-accessible search service (such as AltaVista or HotBot) that enables you to search for information on the Internet.

search operator In a database or a Web search engine, a word or a symbol that enables you to specify your search with precision.

search utility A utility program which enables you to search an entire hard disk for a file (in Microsoft Windows it is called the Search Companion; in Mac OS it is called Find File).

secondary cache A small unit (256 K to 1 MB) of ultra-fast memory used to store frequently accessed data and improve overall system performance. The secondary cache is usually located on a separate circuit board from the microprocessor, although backside cache memory is located on the processor. Also called level 2 (L2) cache.

secondary folder See subfolder.

secondary storage See near-online storage.

sector A pie-shaped wedge of the concentric tracks encoded on a disk during formatting. Two or more sectors combine to form a cluster.

secure electronic transfer (SET) An online shopping security standard for merchants and customers that uses digital certificates.

secure mode In a Web browser, a mode of operation in which all communication to and from the server is encrypted.

seek time In a secondary storage device, the time it takes for the read/write head to reach the correct location on the disk. Seek times are often used with rotational speed to compare the performance of hard drives.

selection control structure In structured programming, a method of handling a program branch by using an IF-THEN-ELSE structure. This is more efficient than using a GOTO statement. Also called conditional or branch control structure.

sequence control structure In structured programming, a logical construction of programming commands executed in the order in which they appear.

sequential storage device A storage device that cannot begin reading data until the device has moved through a sequence of data in order to locate the desired beginning point.

serial port An input/output (I/O) interface that is designed to convey data in a bit-by-bit stream. Compare with parallel port.

server A computer dedicated to providing information in response to external requests.

setup program A utility program provided by a computer's manufacturer that enables users to specify basic system configuration settings, such as the correct time and date and the type of hard disk that is installed in the system. Setup programs are accessible by pressing a special key (such as Delete) during the computer's power-on self test (POST).

shareware Copyrighted software that may be tried without expense but requires the payment of a registration fee if you decide to use it after a specified trial period.

sheets In Microsoft Excel workbook files, the 255 sets of columns and rows intersecting at cells.

shill In an auction, an accomplice of the seller who drives up prices by bidding for an item that the shill has no intention of buying.

shoulder surfing In computer security, a method of defeating password authentication by peeking over a user's shoulder and watching the keyboard as the user inputs his or her password.

signature capture A computer system that captures a customer's signature digitally, so that the store can prove that a purchase was made.

single-lens reflex (SLR) digital camera Expensive digital camera that offers features such as interchangeable lenses, through-the-lens image previewing, and the ability to override the automatic focus and exposure settings.

single point of failure (SPOF) Any system component, such as hardware or software, that causes the entire system to malfunction when it fails.

single tasking operating system Capable of running only one application at a time.

site license An agreement with a software publisher that allows multiple copies of the software to be made for use within an organization.

slide In a presentation graphics program, an on-screen image sized in proportion to a 35mm slide.

sleep See standby.

Small Computer System Interface (SCSI) A bus standard for connecting peripheral devices to personal computers, including hard disks, CD-ROM discs, and scanners.

small office/home office (SOHO) Small businesses run out of homes or small offices—a rapidly growing market segment.

Smalltalk An early object-oriented programming language that many OO promoters believe is still the only pure OO language.

smart card A card that resembles a credit card but has a microprocessor and memory chip, enabling the card to process as well as store information.

smart tags In Microsoft Office, icons attached to items, allowing various choices for how text is treated when pasted within an application or between applications.

snapshot printer A thermal transfer printer that prints the output of digital cameras at a maximum size of 4 by 6 inches. Snapshot printers are less expensive than other thermal transfer printers.

social engineering A method of defeating password authentication by impersonating a network administrator and asking users for their passwords.

soft copy A temporary form of output, as in a monitor display.

software One of two basic components of a computer system (the other is hardware). Software includes all the instructions that tell the computer what to do.

software engineering A new field that applies the principles of mainstream engineering to software production.

software license An agreement included with most commercial software that stipulates what the user may and may not do with the software.

software piracy Unauthorized duplication of copyrighted software.

software suite A collection of full-featured, standalone programs that usually share a common command structure and have similar interfaces.

software upgrading The process of keeping a version of an application current with the marketplace, whether through patches, service releases, or new versions.

solid state storage device This device consists of nonvolatile memory chips, which retain the data stored in them even if the chips are disconnected from their current source.

sound board See sound card.

sound card An adapter that adds digital sound reproduction capabilities to an IBM-compatible PC. Also called a sound board.

sound file A file containing digitized sound that can be played back if a computer is equipped with multimedia.

sound format A specification of how a sound should be digitally represented. Sound formats usually include some type of data compression to reduce the size of sound files.

source code The typed program instructions that people write. The program is then translated into machine instructions that the computer can execute.

spaghetti code In programming, source code that contains numerous GOTO statements and is, in consequence, difficult to understand and prone to error.

spam Unsolicited e-mail or newsgroup advertising.

speaker A device that plays the computer's audio output.

specialized search engines Web location programs that index particular types of information, such as job advertisements.

speculative execution A technique used by advanced CPUs to prevent a pipeline stall. The processor executes and temporarily stores the next instruction in case it proves useful.

speech recognition The use of a computer system to detect the words spoken by a human being into a microphone, and translate these words into text that appears on-screen. Compare with speech synthesis.

spreadsheet A program that processes information in the form of tables. Table cells can hold values or mathematical formulas.

spreadsheet programs The computer equivalent of an accountant's worksheet.

spyware Internet software that is placed on a computer without the user's awareness, usually during a shareware or freeware download.

SQL Abbreviation for Structured Query Language. SQL is a standardized query language for requesting information from a database.

standalone program An application sold individually.

standard toolbar In Microsoft Office, a default-loaded toolbar that includes icons for various functions, including opening, closing, and printing files.

standby A low-power state that allows an operating system to be restored to full power quickly without going through the lengthy boot process; called sleep in the Mac OS.

star topology The physical layout of a local network in which a host computer manages the network.

start tag In HTML, the first component of an element. The start tag contains the element's name, such as <H1> or <P>.

starting the computer One of the five basic functions of an operating system in which a computer loads the operating system into the computer's RAM.

status bar An area within a typical application's window that is reserved for the program's messages to the user.

storage A general term for computer components that offer nonvolatile retention of computer data and program instructions.

storage area network (SAN) Links high capacity storage devices to all of an organization's servers, which makes any of the storage devices accessible from any of the servers.

storage device A hardware component that is capable of retaining data even when electrical power is switched off. An example of a storage device is a hard disk. Compare with memory.

storage media A collective term used to describe all types of storage devices.

store One of four basic operations carried out by the control unit of a microprocessor that involves writing the results of previous operations to an internal register.

strategic decisions Executive decisions concerning the organization's overall goals and direction.

streaming audio An Internet sound delivery technology that sends audio data as a continuous, compressed stream that is played back on the fly.

streaming video An Internet video delivery technology that sends video data as a continuous, compressed stream that is played back on the fly. Like streaming audio, streaming video begins playing almost immediately. A high-speed modem is required. Quality is marginal; the video appears in a small, on-screen window, and motion is jerky.

strong AI In artificial intelligence, a research focus based on the conviction that computers will achieve the ultimate goal of artificial intelligence, namely, rivaling the intelligence of humans.

structural unemployment Unemployment caused by advancing technology that makes an entire job obsolete.

structure chart See hierarchy chart.

structured programming A set of quality standards that make programs more verbose but more readable, more reliable, and more easily maintained. A program is broken up into manageable components, each of which contributes to the overall goal of the program. Also called top-down program design.

stylus A pen-shaped instrument used to draw on a graphics tablet or to input commands and handwriting to a personal digital assistant (PDA).

subdirectory A directory created in another directory. A subdirectory can contain files and additional subdirectories.

subfolder A folder within a folder, usually created to allow for better file organization. Also known as secondary folder.

subject guide On the World Wide Web, an information discovery service that contains hyperlinks classified by subjects in broad categories and multiple levels of subcategories.

subnotebook A portable computer that omits some components (such as a CD-ROM drive) to cut down on weight and size.

subscriber loop carrier (SLC) A small, waist-high curbside installation of the public switched telephone network that transforms local home and business analog calls into digital signals and routes them through high-capacity cables to the local exchange switch.

summary report In a transaction processing system (TPS), a document that provides a quick overview of an organization's performance.

Super Video Graphics Array (SVGA) An enhancement of the VGA display standard that can display as much as 1,280 pixels by 1,024,768 lines with as many as 16.7 million colors.

supercomputer A sophisticated, expensive computer that executes complex calculations at the maximum speed permitted by state-of-the-art technology. Supercomputers are used mostly by the government and for scientific research.

superscalar architecture A design that lets the microprocessor take a sequential instruction and send several instructions at a time to separate execution units so that the processor can execute multiple instructions per cycle.

superuser status In multiuser operating systems, a classification normally given only to network administrators, enabling them to access and modify virtually any file on the network. If intruders obtain superuser status, they can obtain the passwords of everyone on the network.

surge protector An inexpensive electrical device that prevents high-voltage surges from reaching a computer and damaging its circuitry.

swap file In virtual memory, a file on the hard disk used to store pages of virtual memory information.

swapping In virtual memory, the operation of exchanging program instructions and data between the swap file (located on the hard disk) and random access memory (RAM).

symmetric key encryption Encryption techniques that use the same key for encryption and decryption.

symptom An indication or a sign of something; an unacceptable or undesirable result.

syn flooding See denial of service (DoS) attack.

synchronous DRAM (SDRAM) The fastest available memory chip technology.

Synchronous Optical Network (SONET) A standard for high-performance networks using optical fiber.

syntax The rules governing the structure of commands, statements, or instructions given to a computer.

syntax error In programming, a flaw in the structure of commands, statements, or instructions.

synthesizer An audio component that uses FM (frequency modulation), wavetable, or waveguide technology to create sounds imitative of actual musical instruments.

system A collection of components purposefully organized into a functioning whole to accomplish a goal.

system clock An electronic circuit in the computer that emits pulses at regular intervals, enabling the computer's internal components to operate in synchrony.

system requirements The stated minimum system performance capabilities required to run an application program, including the minimum amount of disk space, memory, and processor capacity.

system software All the software used to operate and maintain a computer system, including the operating system and utility programs.

system unit A boxlike case that houses the computer's main hardware components and provides a sturdy frame for mounting and protecting internal devices, connectors, and drives.

system utilities Programs such as speaker volume control and antivirus software that are loaded by the operating system.

systems analysis A discipline devoted to the rational and organized planning, development, and implementation of artificial systems, including information systems.

systems analyst A computer professional who helps plan, develop, and implement information systems.

systems development life cycle (SDLC) An organized way of planning and building information systems.

systems engineering A field of engineering devoted to the scientific study of artificial systems and the training of systems analysts.

system utilities Programs, such as file management and file finder, that provide a necessary addition to an operating system's basic system-management tools.

T

T1 A high-bandwidth telephone trunk line capable of transferring 1.544 megabits per second (Mbps) of data.

T3 A high-bandwidth fiber-optic line capable of handling 43 megabits per second (Mbps) of computer data.

table In the Microsoft Access database management system, the object used to store data.

tablet PC A type of notebook computer that has an LCD screen that the user can write on using a special-purpose pen or stylus.

tactical decisions Middle management decisions about how to best organize resources to achieve their division's goals.

tactile display A display that stimulates the sense of touch using vibration, pressure, and temperature changes.

tailor-made applications Software designed for specialized fields or the consumer market, such as programs that handle the billing needs of medical offices, manage restaurants, and track occupational injuries.

tangible benefits In a cost-benefit analysis, benefits such as increased sales, faster response time, and decreased complaints that can be easily measured.

task pane In Microsoft Office, a feature that usually appears on the right side of an opened application window and that provides various options, such as for opening or formatting work.

TCP/IP The two most important Internet protocols. See Transmission Control Protocol and Internet Protocol.

technical skills Skills such as knowledge and experience in networking, Microsoft Windows XP, UNIX, C++, and Internet-related technologies.

technical feasibility Able to be accomplished with respect to existing, proven technology.

telecommuting Performing work at home while linked to the office by means of a telecommunications-equipped computer system.

teleconferencing A simple and secure wired voice communications application in which more than two distant people conduct business by conference call.

terabyte (T or TB) A unit of measurement commonly used to state the capacity of memory or storage devices; equal to 1,024 gigabytes, or approximately one trillion bytes or characters.

terminal An input/output device consisting of a keyboard and a video display that is commonly used with mainframe and minicomputer systems.

text messaging A mobile service, similar to using your phone for instant messaging or as a receiver and transmitter for brief e-mail messages.

thermal transfer printer A printer that uses a heat process to transfer colored dyes or inks to the paper's surface. Although thermal transfer printers are the best color printers currently available, they are very expensive.

third-generation language (3GL) A programming language that tells the computer what to do and how to do it but eliminates the need for understanding the intimate details of how the computer works.

thread 1. In multithreading, a single type of task that can be executed simultaneously with other tasks. 2. In Usenet, a series of articles on the same specific subject.

time bomb A destructive program that sits harmlessly until a certain event or set of circumstances makes the program active.

time-limited trial versions Internet-offered commercial programs capable of being used on a trial basis for a period of time, after which the software is unusable.

title bar In a graphical user interface (GUI), the top bar of an application window. The title bar typically contains the name of the application, the name of the document, and window controls.

toggle key A key on a keyboard that functions like a switch. When pressed, the function is turned on, and when pressed again, the function is turned off.

token A handheld device used to gain access to a computer system, such as an automated teller machine (ATM).

toolbar In a graphical user interface (GUI), a bar near the top of the window that contains a row of graphical buttons. These buttons provide quick access to the most frequently used program commands.

tools menu In a graphical user interface (GUI), a menu that provides access to special program features and utilities, such as spell-checking.

top-down program design See structured programming.

top-level domain (TLD) name The last part of an Internet computer address. For computers located in the United States, it indicates the type of organization in which the computer is located, such as commercial businesses (com), educational institutions (edu), and government agencies (gov).

top-level folder See primary folder.

topology See network topology.

touch screen A touch-sensitive display that enables users to input choices by touching a region of the screen.

touchpad An input device for portable computers that moves the pointer. The touchpad is a small pad in front of the keyboard that moves the pointer when the user moves a finger on the pad.

tower case A tall and deep system unit case designed to sit on the floor next to a desk and easily accommodate add-on components.

track One of several concentric circular bands on computer disks where data is recorded, similar to the grooves on a phonographic record. Tracks are created during formatting and are divided into sectors.

trackball An input device, similar to the mouse, that moves the pointer. The trackball looks something like an inverted mouse and does not require the desk space that a mouse does.

trackpad See touchpad.

trackpoint An input device on some notebook computers that resembles a tiny pencil eraser; you move the cursor by pushing the tip of the trackpoint.

tracks The concentric circular bands on a hard disk. Data is recorded in the tracks, which are divided into sectors to help keep track of where specific files are located.

trade show A periodic meeting in which computer product manufacturers, designers, and dealers display their products.

traditional organizational structure In an organization, a method used to distribute the core functions of the organization into divisions such as finance, human resources, and operations.

training seminars Computer-related training sessions, typically presented by the developer of a new hardware or software product or by a company specializing in training IT professionals in a new technology.

transaction processing system (TPS) A system that handles the day-to-day operations of a company; examples include sales, purchases, orders, and returns.

transfer performance A measure of how quickly read/write heads are able to transfer data from a hard disk to memory.

transistor A device invented in 1947 by Bell Laboratories that controls the flow of electricity. Due to their small size, reduced power consumption, and lower heat output, transistors replaced vacuum tubes in the second generation of computers.

Transmission Control Protocol (TCP) One of two basic Internet protocols (the other is Internet Protocol, IP). TCP is the protocol (standard) that permits two Internet-connected computers to establish a reliable connection. TCP ensures reliable data delivery with a method known as Positive Acknowledgment with Re-transmission (PAR). The computer that sends the data continues to do so until it receives a confirmation from the receiving computer that the data has been received intact.

trap door In computer security, a security hole created on purpose that can be exploited at a later time.

Trojan horse An application disguised as a useful program but containing instructions to perform a malicious task.

Turing test A test developed by Alan Turing and used to determine whether a computer could be called intelligent. In a Turing test, judges are asked to determine whether the output they see on computer displays is produced by a computer or a human being. If a computer program succeeds in tricking the judges into believing that only a human could have generated that output, the program is said to have passed the Turing test.

turnover line In an indentation, the second and subsequent lines.

twisted pair An inexpensive copper cable used for telephone and data communications. The term *twisted pair* refers to the braiding of the paired wires, a practice that reduces interference from electrical fields.

two-megapixel Type of digital camera that can produce sharp images at higher enlargements such as 8 by 10 inches.

U

ubiquitous computing A scenario for future computing in which computers are so numerous that they fade into the background, providing intelligence for virtually every aspect of daily life.

uninstall To remove a program from a computer system by using a special utility.

uninterruptible power supply (UPS) A device that provides power to a computer system for a short period of time if electrical power is lost.

universal product code (UPC) A label with a series of bars that can be either keyed in or read by a scanner to identify an item and determine its cost. UPC scanners are often found in point-of-sale (POS) terminals.

universal serial bus (USB) An external bus architecture that connects peripherals such as keyboards, mice, and digital cameras. USB offers many benefits over older serial architectures, such as support for 127 devices on a single port, Plug and Play, and higher transfer rates.

UNIX A 32-bit operating system that features multiuser access, preemptive multitasking, multiprocessing, and other sophisticated features. UNIX is widely used for file servers in client/server networks.

upload To send a file to another computer by means of a computer network.

URL (uniform resource locator) In the World Wide Web, one of two basic kinds of Universal Resource Identifiers (URI), a string of characters that precisely identifies an Internet resource's type and location. For example, the fictitious URL http://www.wolverine.virginia.edu/ ~toros/winerefs/merlot.html identifies a World Wide Web document (http://), indicates the domain name of the computer on which it is stored (www.wolverine.virginia.edu), fully describes the document's location in the directory structure (~toros/winerefs/), and includes the document's name and extension (merlot.html).

Usenet A worldwide computer-based discussion system that uses the Internet and other networks for transmission media. Discussion is channeled into more than 50,000 topically named newsgroups, which contain original contributions called articles, as well as commentaries on these articles called follow-up posts. As follow-up posts continue to appear on a given subject, a thread of discussion emerges; a threaded newsreader collates these articles together so readers can see the flow of the discussion.

user A person who uses a computer and its applications to perform tasks and produce results.

user ID A word or name that uniquely identifies a computer user. Synonymous with user name.

user interface The part of system software that interacts with the user.

user name A unique name that a system administrator assigns to you that you use as initial identification. You must type this name and also your password to gain access to the system.

utilities See system utilities.

V

value-added network (VAN) A public data network that provides value-added services for corporate customers, including end-to-end dedicated lines with guaranteed security. VANs, however, also charge an expensive per-byte fee.

value-added reseller (VAR) An independent company that selects system components and assembles them into a functioning system.

VBScript A scripting language used to write short programs (scripts) that can be embedded in Web pages.

vector graphic An image composed of distinct objects, such as lines or shapes, that may be moved or edited independently. Each object is described by a complex mathematical formula.

vendor A company that sells goods or services.

VGA connector A physical connector that is designed to connect a VGA monitor to a video adapter.

video adapter Video circuitry that fits into an expansion bus and determines the quality of the display and resolution of your monitor. Also called display adapter.

video capture board See video capture card.

video capture card An expansion board that accepts analog or digital video signals, which are then compressed and stored.

video card See video adapter.

video editor A program that enables you to view and edit a digitized video and to select special effects.

Video Graphics Array (VGA) A display standard that can display 16 colors at a maximum resolution of 640 pixels by 480 pixels.

video RAM (VRAM) A random access memory chip that maximizes the performance of video adapters.

videoconferencing A technology enabling two or more people to have a face-to-face meeting even though they're geographically separated.

view menu In a graphical user interface (GUI), a menu that provides access to document viewing options, including normal layout, print layout, and document magnification (zoom) options.

viewable area The front surface on a cathode-ray tube monitor actually available for viewing, which is less than the quoted size. See quoted size.

virtual memory A means of increasing the size of a computer's random access memory (RAM) by using part of the hard disk as an extension of RAM.

virtual private network (VPN) A method of connecting two physically separate local area networks (LANs) by using the Internet. Strong encryption is used to ensure privacy.

virtual reality (VR) A computer-generated illusion of three-dimensional space. On the Web, virtual reality sites enable Web users to explore three-dimensional virtual reality worlds by means of VR plug-in programs. These programs enable you to walk or "fly" through the three-dimensional space that these worlds offer.

Virtual Reality Modeling Language (VRML) A scripting language that enables programmers to specify the characteristics of a three-dimensional world that is accessible on the Internet. VRML worlds can contain sounds, hyperlinks, videos, and animations as well as three-dimensional spaces, which can be explored by using a VRML plug-in.

virus See computer virus.

vision technology See eye-gaze response system.

Visual Basic (VB) A programming language developed by Microsoft based on the BASIC programming language. Visual Basic is one of the world's most widely used program development packages.

Visual Studio .NET A suite of products that contains Visual Basic .NET, which enables programmers to work with complex objects; Visual C++, which is based upon C++; and Visual C# (pronounced "C sharp"), which is a less complex version of C++ that is used for rapid application development of Web programs.

voice recognition See speech recognition.

volatile Susceptible to loss; a way of saying that all the data disappears forever if the power fails.

W

warm boot To restart a computer that is already operating.

waterfall model A method in information systems development that returns the focus of the systems development project to a previous phase if an error is discovered in it.

waveform A type of digitized audio format used to record live sounds or music.

wavetable synthesis A method of generating and reproducing musical sounds in a sound card. Wavetable synthesis uses a prerecorded sample of dozens of orchestral instruments to determine how particular notes should sound. Wavetable synthesis is far superior to FM synthesis.

Web See World Wide Web (WWW).

Web-based training (WBT) Computer-based training implemented via the Internet or an intranet.

Web browser A program that runs on an Internet-connected computer and provides access to information on the World Wide Web (WWW).

Web cam A low-cost video camera used for low-resolution videoconferencing on the Internet.

Web-database integration The latest trend in database software, techniques that make information stored in databases available through Internet connections.

Web-enabled devices Devices that have the ability to connect to the Internet and e-book readers.

Web page A document you create to share with others on the Web. A Web page can include text, graphics, sound, animation, and video.

Web portal (portal) A Web site that provides multiple online services; a jumping off place that provides an organized way to go to other places on the Web.

Web server On the Web, a program that accepts requests for information framed according to the Hypertext Transfer Protocol (HTTP). The server processes these requests and sends the requested document.

Web site A computer that is accessible to the public Internet and is running a server program that makes Web pages available.

Web technology In application software, the capability to save files in a form that contains a Web document's underlying HTML codes, greatly facilitating file conversion.

WebTV See MSN® TV.

wheel mouse A type of mouse that has a dial that can be used to scroll through data on-screen.

whistleblowing Reporting illegal or unethical actions of a company to a regulatory agency or the press.

whiteboard A separate area of a videoconferencing screen enabling participants to create a shared workspace. Participants can write or draw in this space as if they were using a chalkboard in a meeting.

wide area network (WAN) A commercial data network that provides data communications services for businesses and government agencies. Most WANs use the X.25 protocols, which overcome problems related to noisy analog telephone lines.

Wi-fi A collection of wireless transmission standards for wireless networks.

wildcard A symbol that stands for any character or any group of characters.

window border The outer edge of a window on a graphical user interface (GUI); in Microsoft Windows it can be dragged to change the size of the window.

window controls In a graphical user interface (GUI), a group of window management controls that enable the user to minimize, maximize, restore, or close the window.

Windows Bitmap (BMP) A bitmapped graphics format developed for Microsoft Windows.

Windows Update Microsoft operating system update service that keeps your operating system up-to-date with any fixes (service patches) or protections against external environment changes.

wired Connected by a physical medium.

wireless Connected through the air or space.

wireless LANs (WLANs) Local area networks that use a radio signal spread over a seemingly random series of frequencies for greater security.

wizard In a graphical user interface (GUI), a series of dialog boxes that guide the user through a complex process, such as importing data into an application.

word processing program An office application that enables the user to create, edit, format, and print textual documents.

word size The number of bits a computer can work with at one time.

word wrapping A word processing feature that automatically moves words down to the beginning of the next line if they extend beyond the right margin.

workbook In a spreadsheet program, a file that can contain two or more spreadsheets, each of which has its own page in the workbook.

workflow automation An information system in which documents are automatically sent to the people who need to see them.

workgroup A collection of individuals working together on a task.

workgroup computing Any situation in which all of the members of a workgroup have specific hardware, software, and networking equipment that enables them to connect, communicate, and collaborate.

workstation A powerful desktop computer that meets the computing needs of engineers, architects, and other professionals who require detailed graphic displays. In a LAN, a workstation runs application programs and serves as an access point to the network.

World Wide Web (WWW) A global hypertext system that uses the Internet as its transport mechanism. In a hypertext system, you navigate by clicking hyperlinks, which display another document (which also contains hyperlinks). Most Web documents are created using HTML, a markup language that is easy to learn and that will soon be supplanted by automated tools. Incorporating hypermedia (graphics, sounds, animations, and video), the Web has become the ideal medium for publishing information on the Internet. See also Web browser.

World Wide Web Consortium (W3C) An independent standards body made up of university researchers and industry practitioners devoted to setting effective standards to promote the orderly growth of the World Wide Web. Housed at the Massachusetts Institute of Technology (MIT), W3C sets standards for HTML and many other aspects of Web usage.

worm A program resembling a computer virus that can spread over networks.

WWW See World Wide Web (WWW).

X

X.25 A packet-switching network protocol optimized for use on noisy analog telephone lines.

xDSL See DSL (Digital Subscriber Line).

XML (eXtensible Markup Language) A set of rules for creating markup languages that enables programmers to capture specific types of data by creating their own elements.

Z

Zero configuration (Zeroconf) A method for networking devices via an Ethernet cable that does not require configuration and administration.

Zip disk A removable storage medium that combines the convenience of a floppy disk with the storage capacity of a small hard disk (100 to 200 MB).

Zip disk drive A popular removable storage medium, created by Iomega Corporation, that provides 100 to 200 MB of storage on relatively inexpensive ($10 each) portable disks.

zombie A computer commandeered by a hacker to do what the hacker's program tells it to do.

Index

Ability to share, 98
AC. *See* Alternating current
Access time, 82
Account (for money), 224
Accounting, 224
Accounting Department, 224, 245
Active use mode, 141, 144
Active window, 123
Actors, 248
Actual, 235
Ad hoc (reports), 231
Adobe Acrobat®, 13
Adobe Dreamweaver, 196
Adobe Flash, 195
Adobe Macromedia, 104
Adobe Photoshop, 107
Advanced Research Project Agency Network. *See* ARPANET
Advances in technology, 82
Adware, 182, 211
Agility, 180
Allen, Paul, 60
Alt and Ctl, 40
AltaVista, 176
Alternate, 40
Alternating current (AC), 30
AMD®, 142
American Standard Code for Information Interchange (ASCII), 30, 77
Analysis & Predictive Reporting, 233
Anonymous, 215
Antivirus software, 212
Apple, 143
Apple iWork, 107
Application, 6, 264
Application sharing, 229
Application software, 92, 117
Applications architects, 243–244
Archiving, 83
ARPANET, 169
Arrow, 40
Arrow keys, 40
ASCII. *See* American Standard Code for Information Interchange
Ask, 217
Asynchronous, 110
Attachments, 107, 182
Attitude, 5, 12
Authenticates, 119

B2B. *See* Business-to-business
B2C. *See* Business-to-consumer
Backup, 81, 83, 127, 213

Backup storage plan, 84
Banner advertisements, 201
Barcode, 43
Barcode readers, 43
Basic input/output system (BIOS), 118
BCC. *See* Blind carbon copy
Best practice, 6, 268
Binary system, 30
BIOS, 118. *See also* Basic input/output system
Bits, 30, 76
Blind carbon copy (BCC), 183
Blog, 197
Blogger, 197
Blu-Ray disc (BD), 80
Bookmarks, 175. *See also* Favorites
Booting, 118
Box, 9, 25
Broadband. *See* Broadband Internet access
Broadband Internet access, 176
Brochure websites, 196
Browser, 170, 172. *See also* Web browser
Browser application software, 172
Browser hijacking, 181
Budget reports, 234
Bus lines, 29
Bus topology, 158
Bus width, 29
Business, 224
Business awareness, 268
Business collaboration, 228
Business computer hardware, 8
Business database, advantages of, 260
Business database scenario and implications (case study), 261
Business failures, 268
Business functional behaviors, 224
Business intelligence analysts, 244
Business plan, 179
Business process, 262
Business strategies, 65
Business system reporting, 231. *See also* Reporting
Business-to-business (B2B), 178
Business-to-consumer (B2C), 178
Business, understanding, 245–246
Byte, 30, 76

C2C. *See* Consumer-to-consumer
Cache, 10, 54–55, 193
Caching, 175
Campus Area Network (CAN), 160
CAN. *See* Campus Area Network

Capacity, 79, 82
Caps lock, 40
Carbon Copy (Cc), 183
Carbon footprint, 145
Carbon reproduction, 137
Case, 28. *See also* Chassis
Case scenarios in UML, 248
Categories (of websites), 196
Cathode Ray Tube (CRT), 43
Cc. *See* Carbon copy
CD, 80
CD-R, 80
CD-RW, 80
Cell, 94
Center for European Nuclear Research. *See* CERN
Central processing unit (CPU), 28, 37
CEO. *See* Chief Executive Officer (CEO)
CERN, 169
Change order, 249
Chassis, 28. *See also* Case
Check, 217
Chief Information Officers (CIOs), 136, 243
CIOs. *See* Chief Information Officers
Circuit board, 28. *See also* Printed circuit board
Classic websites, 196
Clearing price, 63
Click fraud, 213
Client/Server model, 170
Clients, 152, 170
Clipboard, 98
Clock rate, 29
Close, 112
Cluster, 79
CMOS chip, 32. *See also* Complimentary metal-oxide semiconductor
Cold boot, 118–119
Collaboration, 110, 224, 229
Commerce website, 198
Commercial website, 197
Communication, 182
Compact disc (CD), 80
Competency, 5
Competent computer user, 268
Competitive advantage, 7
Complete backup, 128
Complimentary metal-oxide semiconductor. *See also* CMOS
Computer competency, 5
Computer display screen, 43
Computer keyboard, 40
Computer network, 17, 151–154

295

Computer security, 207
Computer virus, 181, 209
Computers, 9
Concept development phase of SDLC, 248
Connectivity, 176
Consumer-to-consumer (C2C), 179
Content, 105, 172
Content managers, 172
Content website, 197
Conversational interaction, 110
Cookies, 175
Copy, 12, 98
Core competency, 5
Cornerstone, 93
Corporate memory, 96
Corporate performance, 138
Corporate website, 197
Cost, 83, 114
Cost per thousand impressions (CPM), 201
Cox Communications, 176
CPU. *See* Central processing unit
CPU Cache, 55
Critical thinking, 5, 268
Critical thoughtfulness, 135
CRT. *See* Cathode Ray Tube
Cut and paste, 12, 98

Data, 16
Data integrity, 247, 260
Data mining, 109, 216
Data redundancy, avoiding, 260
Data security, 84
Data validation, 260
Data warehousing, 96
Database administrators (DBAs), 244
Database designers, 259
Database management systems (DBMS), 13, 15, 95, 255
Database schema, 257
Database software, 13, 15, 95
Database structure, 256–259
Databases, 12, 255, 260
DBAs. *See* Database administrators (DBAs)
DBMS. *See* Database management systems (DBMS)
DC. *See* Direct current
Defrag, 127. *See also* Disk defragmentation and Defragmentation
Defragmentation, 56, 127
Dell, 143
Demand (reports), 231
Denial-of-service attack (DoS attack), 211
Design (website), 172
Design for end of life, 138
Design layout, 105
Design phase of SDLC, 248
Desktop, 9, 123
Destination, 12, 98
Destination file, 12, 98
Development phase of SDLC, 249
Device drivers, 58, 121

Diffusion, 57, 65, 136
Digital cameras, 42
Direct current (DC), 30
Directories, 10
Directory searches, 177
Directory website, 198
Disaster recovery, 85
Discussion board, 229
Disk defragmentation, 127. *See also* Defrag
Disk management, 11
Disk storage, 11, 55
.doc, 192
Documentation, 249
Doing business, 179
Domain name, 171
DoS attack. *See* Denial-of-service attack
Dots per inch (dpi), 44
dpi. *See* Dots per inch
Drivers, 121. *See also* Device drivers
Dumpster diving, 217
DVD, 80
Dynamic (website styles), 196, 200

Ease of use, 124
EBCDIC. *See* Extended Binary Coded Decimal Interchange Code
E-commerce, 181. *See also* Electronic commerce
Economic considerations, 145
Economics, 153
80 Plus, 143
Electronic commerce, 178. *See also* E-commerce
Electronic computing tools, 229
Electronic Product Environmental Assessment Tool (EPEAT), 138–139, 144, 146
Elements, 194
E-mail, 12, 80, 161, 182
E-mail/Instant Messaging. *See* E-mail; Instant messaging; Texting
Embedded computing, 59
Embedded operating systems, 59
Employment website, 198
End of life management, 138
End-user, 92
Energy conservation, 139
Energy costs, 137
Energy Star®, 138, 142, 144, 146
Enterprise resource planning (ERP), 109, 246
Entity relationship diagrams (ERM), 257
Environmental Protection Agency (EPA), 138, 142
Environmentally sensitive materials, 138
EPA. *See* Environmental Protection Agency
EPEAT. *See* Electronic Product Environmental Assessment Tool
ERM. *See* Entity relationship diagrams (ERM)
ERP. *See* Enterprise resource planning

Escape, 40
Executive reporting, 236
Expansion cards, 33
Expansion slots, 33
Extended Binary Coded Decimal Interchange Code (EBCDIC), 77
External hard disks, 79
External hard drive, 33

FAT, 11, 56–57, 79. *See also* File allocation table
Fat client, 199
Favorites, 175. *See also* Bookmarks
Fields (columns), 259, 263
File allocation table, 11, 56, 79. *See also* FAT
File management, 10
File manager, 10, 57
File name, 125
File size, 126
File type, 125
Firewall, 162, 184, 207–208
FireWire, 34–35
Firmware, 117. *See also* ROM chips; System software
Flash memory, 79
Flash memory/USB Flash Thumb Drive, 79
Flat panel monitors, 43
Flatbed scanners, 42
Floppy disk, 79
Folders, 10, 124
Followers, 7, 86
Forecast, 235
Forecast reports, 234
Form, 16, 256
Formulas, 94
Four basic elements of a computer network, 157
Fragmented, 127
Function, 40
Function keys, 40
Functions, 94

GAAP. *See* Generally accepted accounting principles
Gaming website, 198
Gantt chart, 229
Gates, Bill, 60
GEC. *See* Green Electronics Council
Generally accepted accounting principles (GAAP), 224
GIF. *See* Graphic files
Gigahertz, 29
Google, 176
Google Docs & Spreadsheets, 110, 230
Governmental website, 197
Graphic files (GIF, JPEG), 175
Graphical (reporting), 233
Graphical User Interface (GUI), 10, 57, 59, 92, 121
Green, 135

INDEX **297**

Green computing (PCs), 136, 142, 146
Green Computing Business Plans, 143–144, 146
Green Electronics Council (GEC), 138
Greenhouse effect, 135
GUI, 121. *See also* Graphical User Interface

Hacker, 207
Handheld, 9
Hard copy, 42
Hard disk, 79
Hard disk drive, 79
Hardware, 9–10
HD-DVD (High Definition DVD), 80
Head applications developers, 243
Head elements, 194
Header, 182
Hewlett-Packard (HP), 143
Hierarchy, 57. *See also* Tree
High definition DVD. *See* HD-DVD
History files, 217
Holographic storage, 82
Homepage, 170
Host, 170. *See also* Server
How often, 84
HP. *See* Hewlett-Packard
HTML, 169, 192–193
HTTP, 169, 171
Hub, 156
Human error, 83
Human resource departments, 224–225
Humility, 5
Hyperlink, 172
Hypertext, 193
Hypertext Markup Language. *See* HTML
Hypertext Transfer Protocol. *See* HTTP

Icon, 59
Identity fraud, 217. *See also* Identity theft
Identity theft, 213, 217. *See also* Identity fraud
Identity Theft and Assumption Deterrence Act, 218
iDrive, 81. *See also* Internet Drive
Image editing software, 103
Image elements, 195
Image scanners, 42
Imagination, 5, 74
Incremental backup, 128
Information, 16
Information technology, 4
Information technology auditors, 244
Information technology (IT) competencies, 180
Information technology jobs, 243–245
Information technology staff consultants, 245
Ingenuity, 5
Initiation phase of SDLC, 248
Ink-jet printers, 45
Input, 37
Input device, 37

Instant messaging, 161, 229. *See also* Texting
Intel®, 142
Intellectual property, 63, 74
Intention, 104
Interactivity, 172
Internal hard disks, 79
Internet, 154, 160
Internet address, 171
Internet Drive, 81. *See also* iDrive
Internet fraud, 213
Internet hosting service, 176
Internet Protocol address (IP), 171
Internet service provider (ISP), 176
Intranet, 105, 183, 197, 207, 229
IP. *See* Internet Protocol address
ISP. *See* Internet service provider
IT. *See* Information technology

Java enabled, 195
JavaScript, 175, 195
Jobs, Steve, 60
JPEG. *See* Graphic files

Keyboard, 37, 40
Keypad, 40
Keyword search engines, 177
Keywords, 176
KM. *See* Knowledge management systems
"Know the business", 245–246
Knowledge management systems (KM), 230
Knowledge transfer, 230

LAN. *See* Local Area Network
Laptop, 9
Laser printer, 45
Leaders, 7, 86
Left click, 40
Legacy systems, 243
Lenovo, 143
Link. *See* Hyperlink
Link elements, 195
Linux, 10 , 52, 63
Local Area Network (LAN), 160, 246
Location, 83
Logic boards, 28. *See also* Motherboard
Login, 119

MAC address, 155
Mac OS, 10, 52, 60
Machine code, 37
Machine language, 37
Magnetic tape, 80
"Mail Merge" function, 263
Mainframe computers, 9
Maintain, 217
Maintenance of data in DBMS, 260
Malware, 181, 210
MAN. *See* Metropolitan Area Network
Management Level Reporting, 235
Management reporting, 236

Management tools, 229
Market research, 180
Market segment, 104
Marketing, 226
Marketing department, 226
Markup language, 194
Mass storage, 81
Materials selection, 138
Maximize, 123–124
Mechanical mouse, 40
Media, 19, 79
Memory management, 10
Menus, 92, 124
Message, 107, 182
Metasearch engines, 177
Metropolitan Area Network (MAN), 160
Microcomputers, 7
Microphone, 42
Microprocessor, 28
Microsoft Access, 246, 259, 264
Microsoft Excel 2007®, 245, 259–260, 263
Microsoft Excel 2010®, 14
Microsoft Expression Web 2008 for Mac, 104
Microsoft Expression Web 2010, 104
Microsoft FrontPage, 196
Microsoft Groove, 110
Microsoft Lotus Notes, 110
Microsoft Office 2008® for Mac, 92–93
Microsoft Office 2010® for Windows, 92–93
Microsoft Project, 229
Microsoft Windows, 10, 52
Microsoft Word 2010®, 13
Middleware, 243–244
Midrange computers, 9
Minimize, 112, 114
Modification date, 125
Molecular storage, 83
Moore, Gordon, 27. *See also* Moore's Law
Moore's Law, 7, 27
Motherboard, 28. *See also* System board
Mouse, 40
Multicore chips, 29
Multimedia application software, 107
Multitasking, 10, 54, 92, 120

Named range, 95
NASA. *See* National Aeronautics and Space Administration
National Aeronautics and Space Administration (NASA), 135
National Center for Atmospheric Research, 135
Natural disasters, 83
Network administrator, 157, 244
Network cables, 156
Network Interface Card, 154
Network Interface Controller (NIC), 155
Network protocol, 156
Network security, 160
Networking operating systems, 12, 58, 157

New Technology File System (NTFS), 79
News website, 198
NIC. *See* Network Interface Controller
Node, 152
Non-proprietary, 63
Non-volatile, 31, 55
NOS. *See* Network Operating Systems
NTFS. *See* New Technology File System
Num lock, 40
Numeric cell, 94
Numeric keypad, 40

Object embedding, 12, 98
Object linking, 12, 98
Object Linking and Embedding, 12, 98
Object oriented analysis (OOA), 248
Object oriented design (OOD), 248
Object oriented programming languages, 248
OCR. *See* Optical character recognition
Off/Standby mode, 143
Office, 92
Old software and hardware, disposing of, 137
OLE. *See* Object linking and embedding
Online advertising, 200
Online application software, 230
Online chat, 229
OOA. *See* Object oriented analysis (OOA)
OOD. *See* Object oriented design (OOD)
Open source software, 63
Operating system, 10, 52, 65, 92
Optical character recognition (OCR), 42
Optical mouse, 41
OS. *See* Operating system
Output, 37, 43
Output device, 37

P2P. *See* Peer to Peer Network
Packaging, 139
Packets, 58
Pages, 120
Paper consumption, 144
Passwords, 161, 213
Paste, 12, 98
Patches, 129
PDF, 107. *See also* Portable document files
Peer to Peer Network (P2P), 158
People, 4, 7, 19, 224
PeopleSoft, 109
Periodic (reports), 231
Peripheral devices, 37. *See also* Input device; Output device
Permissions, 162
Personal information manager (PIM), 107
Personal website, 196
Phishing, 183, 215
Physical storage media, 76
PIM. *See* Personal information manager
Pixels, 44
Placement, 226
Planning phase of SDLC, 248

Platform, 10, 52, 65
Platform neutral, 107, 192
Plotters, 45
Plug and play, 35, 58. *See also* FireWire; Universal Serial Bus
Pointing devices, 40
Popup Blockers, 175
Port, 33
Portable document files (PDF), 13
Power consumption and waste, regulations on, 137
Power supply, 30
Power supply unit (PSU), 30
Presentation application programs, 96
Presentation softwares, 12, 16
Presentational elements, 195
Previous, 235
Pricing, 226
Primary storage, 31, 74
Printed circuit board (PCB), 28. *See also* Circuit board
Printers, 44
Privacy, 184, 207, 215
Process, 10, 44, 54
Product longevity/life cycle extension, 138
Production departments, 227
Productivity suite, 12–13. *See also* Software suite
Products, 226
Profile, 119
Project management software, 12, 229
Promotion, 226
Proprietary, 63
Protocol, 155
Proxy server, 208
PSU. *See* Power supply unit
Purchase scams, 215

Queried, 16
Query, 256
QWERTY, 40
Qwest, 176

RAD. *See* Rapid application development (RAD)
R&D. *See* Research and development
Radio frequency identification (RFID), 43 *See also* RFID
RAID, 80
RAM, 10, 55, 74. *See also* Random access memory
RAM chipsets, 32
Random Access Memory, 10, 55, 74
Rapid application development (RAD), 249
Raster graphics, 103
Read, 76
Read/write head, 78
Reconciled (TPS), 232
Reconciliation errors, reducing, 260
Records (rows) in Excel spreadsheet, 263
Reduced Instruction Set Computer. *See* RISC

Redundant Array of Inexpensive Disks. *See* RAID
Registers, 10, 55
Registry, 118
Relational, 16
Reporting, 231. *See also* Business system reporting
Reporting Summarization Levels, 231
Reports, 256
Requirement phase of SDLC, 248
Research, 226
Research and development (R&D), 226
Resolution, 44
Responsible recycling, 144
Restore, 112, 114
Return, 40
Reverse Phishing/Keylogging, 211
RFID, 43. *See also* Radio frequency identification
Ribbon, 92, 124
Right click, 40
Ring topology, 159
RISC (Reduced Instruction Set Computer), 29
Risk management, 207, 209
ROM chips, 32
Rules of business, 179

Safety, 124
SAP AG, 109
Sarbanes-Oxley Act of 2002, 224
SAS Systems, 109
SCAM (Stingy, Check, Ask, Maintain), 217
Schema, 256, 264
School website, 198
SDLC. *See* System development life cycle
Search Engine Optimization (SEO), 105
Search engine results, 201
Search engine website, 198
Search engines, 176
Secondary storage, 32, 74–75
Sectors, 79, 127
Security, 85, 175, 260
Senior IT auditors, 244
Senior web developers, 244
SEO. *See* Search Engine Optimization
Sequence diagrams in UML, 248
Server, 152, 170. *See also* Host
Server-side processing, 200
Service, 242
Set of rules for database systems, 256
Shift, 40
Shoulder surfing, 217
Signatures (of viruses), 128
Singular table, 260
Sleep mode, 143–144
Snow Leopard, 60
Social networking advertising, 201
Software, 9, 12, 154

Software prototyping, 249
Software suite, 12. *See also* Productivity suite
Source data, 12, 98
Source file, 98
Spam, 183, 217
Spam filters, 183
Spamming, 211
Speakers, 45
Speech recognition software, 42
Spreadsheets, 12–13, 94, 245–246, 263–264
Spyware, 181, 210
SQL. *See* Structured query language (SQL)
Stand-alone, 58
Standard, 192
Standardization, 124
Star topology, 159
Static websites, 196
Status indicators, 40
Stingy, 217
Storage, 74
Storage characteristics, 79
Strategic decisions, 231, 244
Streamlined business process, 180
Strong passwords, 161, 213
Structural (block) elements, 195
Structured query language (SQL), 261
Stylus, 41
Subject, 182
Subject line, 107
Supervisory reporting, 236
Supply, 63
Swap files, 120–121
Symbiotic relationship of information technology, 243
Synchronous, 110
System board, 28. *See also* Motherboard
System development life cycle (SDLC), 229, 243, 248
System patches, 212
System software, 7, 9–10, 12, 91, 117. *See also* Firmware
System unit, 27, 29
System update, 129
System utilities, 119
Systems, methodologies for developing, 248

Tab, 40
Tables, 256
Tactical decisions, 231
Tangible property, 74, 76
TCP/IP, 58, 156. *See also* Transmission Control Protocol/Internet Protocol
Technology followers, 65
Technology leaders, 65
Telecommuting, 146
Telephony, 183
Terms of Service Agreement (TOS), 183
Testing and integration phase of SDLC, 249
Text cell, 94
Texting, 229. *See also* Instant messaging
Thin client, 200
Thoughtfulness, 19
Thread, 229
Time, 185
Time available, 84
Toolbars, 124
Topology, 157
Torvalds, Linus, 63
TOS. *See* Terms of Service Agreement
Touch pad, 41
TPS. *See* Transaction processing system
Track, 79, 125, 127
Tracking cookie, 216
Transaction processing system (TPS), 232
Translated, 37, 42
Transmission Control Protocol/Internet Protocol (TCP/IP), 58, 156
Tree, 57. *See also* Hierarchy
Trojan horse, 181, 210
Trojan horse virus, 208
Type of data, 83

UDP, 156. *See also* User Diagram Protocol
UML. *See* Unified Modeling Language
Unicode, 77
Unified Modeling Language (UML), 229, 243, 247–248
Uniform Research Locators (URL), 171
Universal Serial Bus (USB), 35, 58
UNIX, 10, 52, 62
Unsecure computer, 207
URL. *See* Uniform Research Locators
Usability, 175

USB. *See* Universal Serial Bus
U.S. Department of Energy, 138, 142
User Diagram Protocol (UDP), 156
User interface, 121, 124

Vaporware, 249
Variance, 235
Variance reports, 234
Vector graphics, 103
Video and data conferencing, 229
Video cameras, 42
Video sharing website, 198
Viewers, 104
Virtual memory, 10–11, 55, 120
Virtual storefronts, 178
Viruses, 83, 181, 213
Voice over Internet Protocol (VoIP), 183
VoIP. *See* Voice over Internet Protocol
Volatile memory, 55

WAN. *See* Wide Area Network
Warm boot, 118–119
Web authoring, 104
Web browser, 17
Web browsing, 161
Web camera, 43. *See also* Webcams
Web designers, 244
Web developers, 172. *See also* Web masters
Web hosting, 176
Web masters, 172. *See also* Web developers
Web server, 192
Webcams, 43. *See also* Web camera
Webinar, 228
Website, 192
"What-if" analysis, 15, 95
Wheel button, 40
Wide Area Network (WAN), 160
Windows, 7, 60, 92, 123
Windows (software), 60
Word processors, 12–13
World Wide Web, 169. *See also* WWW
Worms, 181, 210
Wozniak, Steve, 60
Write, 76
WWW, 169, 171. *See also* World Wide Web
WYSIWYG interface, 104

Yahoo!, 176